Russian Literature and Cognitive Science

Crosscurrents: Russia's Literature in Context

Series Editor: Bradley Gorski, Georgetown University

Embodying what is specific to a single culture as well as what is common to all humankind, literature has always been a privileged mode of discourse in Russia. *Crosscurrents* takes cognizance of Russian literature's simultaneous particularity and universality by exploring the aesthetic, cultural, political, temporal, and geographical contexts in which it has been written. Monographs and edited collections in the series focus on literature written across cultural periods, geographical divides, and intellectual disciplines. We welcome proposals and manuscripts focused on the intersections between literature and law, religion, philosophy, science, film, the arts, and other disciplines as well as on Russian émigré literature, literature written in Russian by non-Russians, and comparisons of different cultural periods.

Titles in the Series

Russian Literature and Cognitive Science, edited by Tom Dolack
Nijinsky's Feeling Mind: The Dancer Writes, The Writer Dances, by Nicole Svobodny
Napoleon in the Russian Imaginary: The Idea of the Great Man in the Works of Pushkin, Tolstoy, Dostoevsky, Merezhkovsky, and Evgenii Tarle, by Gary Rosenshield
Literary Biographies in The Lives of Remarkable People Series in Russia: Biography for the Masses, Volume 1, edited by Carol Ueland & Ludmilla A. Trigos
Dostoevsky as Suicidologist: Self-Destruction and the Creative Process, by Amy D. Ronner
Wingless Desire in Modernist Russia: Envy and Authorship in the 1920s, by Yelena Zotova
Babel in Russian and Other Literatures and Topographies: The Tower, the State, and the Chaos of Language, by Martin Meisel
Russian Symbolism in Search of Transcendental Liquescence: Iconizing Emotion by Blending Time, Media, and the Senses, by Anastasia Kostetskaya
Chekhov's Letters: Biography, Context, Poetics, edited by Carol Apollonio and Radislav Lapushin
Physical Pain and Justice: Greek Tragedy and the Russian Novel, by Gary Rosenshield

Russian Literature and Cognitive Science

Edited by Tom Dolack

LEXINGTON BOOKS
Lanham • Boulder • New York • London

Published by Lexington Books
An imprint of The Rowman & Littlefield Publishing Group, Inc.
4501 Forbes Boulevard, Suite 200, Lanham, Maryland 20706
www.rowman.com

86-90 Paul Street, London EC2A 4NE

Chapter one originally published in "The Pushkin Project"
(Academic StudiesPress, 2023).

British Library Cataloguing in Publication Information Available

Library of Congress Cataloging-in-Publication Data

Names: Dolack, Tom, editor.
Title: Russian literature and cognitive science / edited by Tom Dolack.
Description: Lanham : Lexington Books, 2025. | Series: Crosscurrents : Russia's literature in context | Includes bibliographical references and index.
Identifiers: LCCN 2024037500 (print) | LCCN 2024037501 (ebook) | ISBN 9781666941692 (cloth) | ISBN 9781666941708 (ebook)
Subjects: LCSH: Russian literature—History and criticism. | Psychology and literature. | LCGFT: Literary criticism. | Essays.
Classification: LCC PG2944 .R87 2025 (print) | LCC PG2944 (ebook) | DDC 891.709—dc23/eng/20240827
LC record available at https://lccn.loc.gov/2024037500
LC ebook record available at https://lccn.loc.gov/2024037501

∞™ The paper used in this publication meets the minimum requirements of American National Standard for Information Sciences—Permanence of Paper for Printed Library Materials, ANSI/NISO Z39.48-1992.

Contents

Preface

The impetus for the present book arose when, after more than a decade of panels at various national conferences in the United States, we realized that the ranks of those interested in the intersection of cognitive science (broadly defined) and Slavic culture had swelled into the dozens. It was then that the decision was made that it was time to gather at least some of this research into a single place.

Some of this work has been going on for decades—long enough that the underlying cognitive science has seen major shifts, and so it should not be surprising that the application of cognitive science to the study of literature would also have undergone major shifts. The earliest roots of the field go back to psychoanalysis. Here the field owes much to the work of Daniel Rancour-Laferriere. The scholar who has bridged all stages of the field, and who has been the most prolific in producing psychologically informed readings of Russian literature, is Brett Cooke, who is quite rightly included in this book. It was Brett's initial idea to assemble this collection, and I am grateful to him for entrusting the idea to me.

There is no single way of approaching anything with cognitive science. It is too multiform. There are as many approaches as there are scholars in the field. It should thus be no surprise that each chapter of this book has a different approach, draws from different fields and subfields of psychology, and employs a different methodology. What is lost in cohesion is more than gained in breadth and richness. For those searching, there are plenty of approaches here to choose from. Indeed, there are so many that there was no obvious way of grouping the chapters together, nor even a clear order to place the chapters in. I have elected to begin with the chapters with the broadest methodologies—beginning with those grounded in evolutionary approaches to culture—moving through work with more of a social-psychology bent, and progressing to approaches increasingly focused on the individual. There is no objective way to quantify this, so there is of necessity a subjective element to my exact ordering.

The book begins with David Bethea's work, which uses an evolutionary approach to female mate selection to show how it is Dunya's choices that drive the plot in Pushkin's "The Stationmaster." David Danaher applies Mihaly Csikszentmihalyi's theory of flow to the mowing scene in *Anna Karenina*, moving from Levin's self-discovery to the achievement of a common cause. He ends by examining ways of making Tolstoy's insights relevant to students in the classroom. Keeping with Tolstoy, in the next chapter, Sarah Mohler argues that his use of visual imagery in *War and Peace* invites readers to co-experience that imagery in a way that can develop their own ethical prowess. My own contribution attempts to show, using the example of Pushkin's *Eugene Onegin*, how cognitive approaches can operate on multiple levels ranging from personal history up through social and historical context, and these levels can be brought together to make a more complete and nuanced cognitive approach to literature.

Staying on Pushkin, Ekaterina Chelpanova uses the lens of cognitive narratology to examine the stories "The Queen of Spades" and "The Coffin-Maker." With a focus on the concept of honor, she shows how narrative can construct the worldview the author wishes to express. Chapter 6 by Katherina Kokinova builds on Wolfgang Iser's concept of gaps and on cognitive psychology's notion of context to construct a cognitive theory of reader reception using Nabokov's "The Vane Sisters" as a locus.

Moving from narratology to social psychology, Kelly Knickmeier Cummings looks at Sologub's *The Petty Demon*. She uses social cognition and a medical-humanities approach to examine how the reader's relation with the hero changes as the protagonist's psychological state deteriorates. Brett Cooke studies a different form of deterioration in the self-destructive hero of Nabokov's *The Defense*. He argues that Nabokov challenges our metamental capacities by forcing his readers to take on the perspective of a hero with autism, and in so doing contributes to the evolution of narrative technique.

Next up, Michał Mrugalski brings to bear enactive inference to show how Bely uses Modernist technique to express a form of Terrorist Realism. Irina Meier's focus is a more modern form of violence: mass shooters. She demonstrates how Dostoevsky prefigured the psychology of school shooters in his Underground Men. In their joint chapter, Anna Novikova and Julia Lerner also focus on contemporary events by developing a new methodology for studying new electronic media. They use cognitive rhetoric to analyze the online media sphere in the months following the full-scale invasion of Ukraine in 2022.

Anna Lazareva, in her chapter drawing on fieldwork in Ukraine, also uses cognitive rhetoric but applies it to dream analysis. She discusses the question of where plot structures of dreams come from: dream mentation itself or the narrative forms that people impose on their dreams by telling and interpreting dream images. The thirteenth chapter by Angelina Rubina combines Lacanian psychoanalysis and Michael Tomasello's approach to the evolution of norm psychology to study the relationship between language, society, and individual identity in Baranskaya's *A Week Like Any Other*.

In our last chapter, Denis Akhapkin, another scholar who has been thinking of cognitive poetics for some time, gives us our only chapter devoted to lyric poetry. He focuses on the rhetorical device of *deixis am phantasma*, or pointing to something that isn't present, but focusing specifically on the context of literary allusion. His work draws on experimental studies he has helped carry out and so represents one of the growing trends within the broader field: the empirical study of literary response.

Should anyone prefer to read the chapters in chronological order of their subject matter, I would suggest the following order: 4, 1, 5, 3, 2, 7, 9, 8, 6, 14, 13, 10, 12, 11.

Transliteration is a fraught business. A strictly academic system looks odd to anyone outside the field. Yet some system is needed for unfamiliar names. Any choice can at best satisfice. Here, contributors are using commonly used transliterations (Tolstoy, not Tolstoi) and the transliterations used in cited translations. All other instances, as well as Russian sources in the bibliography, use the Library of Congress system.

Thank you to everyone who has taken part in our panels over the years, either as presenters, discussants, or audience members. A full list would extend into the dozens. A special thanks to Jasper Mislak at Lexington Books for his guidance and expertise in ushering this to publication.

Finally, a welcome to those new either to Russian literature or to cognitive approaches to culture. My sincerest wish for this book is that, no matter where you are coming from, you learn some new things and gain new perspectives.

Introduction

Tom Dolack

A MATTER OF DEFINITION AND APPLICATION

To begin, we should get a handle on what "cognitive" means in "cognitive science." There is no simple answer. Broadly, we can define cognitive as the brain's processing of information. This can take the form of learning, remembering, planning, dreaming, problem-solving, or just what we call thinking. We could say that a cognitive approach to literature is one that takes into consideration the operation of the nervous system. Saying "the brain" would not be correct because cognition involves the entire body (the "brain in a jar" trope of science fiction is exactly that—fiction).

This is a broad definition, but that is a good thing. It allows for the inclusion of insights from a range of fields and can act as a hedge against dogmatism. But it can also lead to overuse and mission creep. There is nothing that we ever do that does not involve our brain; therefore, if you cock your head, virtually any approach can be a cognitive approach. Thus, some guidelines are useful.

Cognitive approaches can do different things on different levels. From a psychological point of view, they can examine what goes on in the mind and body of a person reading a text. Strictly speaking, this is the psychology of reading. That information in turn can be used to inform how a text should be read, or how it is statistically likely to be read by an average reader. This would align it with reader reception (Holland 2002). The same line of thought can be applied to the author and the act of writing. The approach can also be applied more broadly to historical trends or national literatures, since history is the sum of the choices made by individual people, and individual choices are influenced by psychology. This would count as literary cultural evolution (Martindale 1990). Most broadly, you could study the deep history of narrative in an anthropological sense: how and why did narrative evolve to begin with? Why does such a thing even exist? (Boyd 2009). While not cognitive per se, a related and productive approach that falls under the same umbrella is cognitive historicism, which examines the influence of theories of cognition contemporary to the author, regardless of whether there is any connection with reality (Crane 1998; Domínguez 2016).

Finally, what most literary critics care about—although it shouldn't be the only thing—is the generation of novel readings of texts. To this end, cognitive science can be used to different ends. I have argued previously that the sciences can be used as a slalom gate to weed out assumptions about human behavior that do not match current understandings (2012). If an approach assumes something about human bonding, for instance, that we know not to be true, that approach may not be useful unless the author consciously made that same assumption. In order for an approach to be generally applicable, it must be grounded in reality. Beyond this, I would argue that cognitive science can be used like other sources of literary criticism. From this perspective, anything that supplies a productive lens on a literary text is fair game. This form of bricolage allows us to get past one stumbling block of a cognitive approach to narrative: literary characters don't have minds. We attribute fully human minds to them because our theory of mind compels us to do so (Zunshine 2006). It should not matter that we can't put an imaginary character into an MRI machine so long as an approach allows us to see things we couldn't before.

WHY LITERARY SCHOLARS SHOULD CARE

Why should a literary critic care about cognitive science or any of its related fields (evolutionary biology, developmental psychology, physical anthropology, etc . . .)? My response is that over the last few decades, the sciences have been steadily encroaching on territory that was formerly considered the purview of the humanities, and while I do not think that the sciences should or even can replace the humanities, their findings are directly relevant to humanist inquiry, and humanists should not ignore this work.

Just a few examples. Arguments that have been raging in epistemology since the eighteenth century are steadily (although perhaps asymptotically) being resolved. Hume seems to be beating Locke as we learn not just that, but how our senses modulate what we know about the outside world. In fact, we are only just now beginning to appreciate how limited a slice of reality we have access to due to the restrictions of our senses. The cognitive neuroscientist Anil Seth even takes this to the point that he describes our conscious awareness as being a "controlled hallucination," not because what is in our heads is false, but because our minds need to recreate and anticipate what is happening on the "outside" (Seth 2021).

Another philosophical argument is taken up with the study of innate concepts. Kant believed that we had a priori concepts that made it possible to understand what an object is. In order to understand the nature of an object, concepts like quantity and time would need to come preprogrammed in our minds. Modern psychology tends to think in more concrete terms. We know that specific categories of words, such as colors or tools, can be knocked out due to a brain lesion. We appear to have innate ontological categories that guide our expectations about the world. These categories make sense in an evolutionary context (it saves precious time to not have to learn whether a tree can attack every time you see one). But they also influence our cultural representations as they make certain concepts either easier to process or more inherently interesting (Atran 2002).

Emotions are another area that would seem too subjective to be amenable to neuroscience. Feelings are so personal. What could be more intrinsic to the reading experience than the subjective feeling it gives you? And yet those subjective feelings are produced by a finite set of hormones and neurotransmitters on a nervous system tuned by evolution to respond to certain stimuli in a certain way. The study of the biology of emotion is in many respects indicative of the overall field. It began with the assumption of cultural universals, which turned into self-fulfilling prophecies (Darwin [1872] 1965; Ekman 1982). As research continued, arguments arose about exactly how many emotions are, in fact, universal (4? 7? lots?), and then whether any of them actually are (Barrett 2017). The picture that is emerging matches what we find in other areas of psychology: there is a foundation of evolutionary consistency underlying a layer of cultural specificity that in turn can respond to individual context. Literary production is much better suited to describing this sort of multivalent complexity than an average lab study where very specific details are isolated one at a time (Hogan 2011), and where the part can be mistaken for the whole.

Indeed, even the most subjective of experiences has proved at least partially amenable to the scientific process. The neurobiological study of consciousness has been nothing short of a boom industry over the last two decades.[1] There is a fundamental distinction made in the field between the "hard" and the "soft" problem of consciousness. The first attempts to explain qualia, or specific conscious experiences like the blueness of blue. The easy problem, which is far from easy, is to explain the neurobiology of conscious experience. The results of this work are still quite incomplete, but they paint a picture that fits with what we know from other fields.

Consciousness is, at least on one of its many levels, about intercommunication in the brain. Information processing in humans is much more of a feedback loop, which helps make us special (Edelman 2004).

Perhaps not coincidentally, it is just such interconnectedness that may also underline creativity itself. In this view, new ideas aren't new in and of themselves, but are new combinations of old ideas. This makes a good example of how seemingly far-flung aspects of neuroscience can, in fact, be relevant to the study of the arts. The study of consciousness can be viewed as a model for the production of art and, at the same time, help account for the experience of the art that consciousness produces.

THE DIFFERENT LEVELS OF EXAMINATION FROM A COGNITIVE PERSPECTIVE

Typically, an introduction such as this would present an overview of the field covering the major trends and scholars. However, as there are already multiple such introductory works that do an admirable job surveying the territory—better than I can do (Richardson 2004; Zunshine 2010b, 2015a; Troscianko and Burke 2017)—I see no need to reinvent the wheel.

Instead, I would like to present the field from a different direction, one that highlights how cognitive approaches can place literary study within the full context of the study of cultural production, ranging from our deep evolutionary heritage to neural circuits in our brains. If we conceive of the products of human imagination as being located in the middle of a spectrum, occupying the human-level scale, what is gained by looking off to the incredibly large scale of our deep history, or the very small scale of the neuron? The short answer is that not only are our creations located between those two abysses, but so are we as human beings who are the product of the choices and chances of our ancestors over the past millions of years, the societies and families we grew up in, and the second-to-second firings of the galaxy of neurons in our skulls. Cognitive approaches can work on many different levels; they are not just about stuff that happens between our ears. This is not to say that one cognitive approach or another is necessarily relevant at all times, just to say that cognitive approaches are one of many relevant approaches that are necessary for understanding the full range of the human experience.

Let's begin with the telescope and work our way to the microscope. It is difficult to draw conclusions about cultural activity from the distant past, even when concrete objects such as handaxes, arrowheads, or butchered bones are preserved by the archaeological record. But it is far harder to draw conclusions about behaviors or capacities that leave behind no physical artifacts. When did fully human consciousness arise? When did symbolic thought begin? Who told the first stories or worshiped the first spirits? We can but guess; fortunately, we don't need to guess blindly. We can speculate based on how we know brains and societies work today that certain capacities must predate others. For instance, the ability to absorb norms is required for living in groups of any real size (Tomasello 2015), so we can conclude that norm psychology came online earlier than large group size. There has been especially productive work on the origins of religious behavior which combines lab studies, anthropological study of extant hunter-gatherer societies (not an automatic stand-in for our distant ancestors since all human societies change over time, but the closest we can get in flesh and blood), and examination of the archaeological record including cave paintings and the very oldest artifacts we've found. The picture that is emerging is that religious behavior was instrumental to our ability to form large groups, work together, and even to preserve useful information about the environment. These discoveries, among others, are of direct relevance to the anthropology of narrative and the other arts. If the earliest religious narratives about the origins of the world and the proper order of things helped to unite groups that would go on to expand throughout Africa and then beyond, they helped as narrative at least as much as religion. Much of what we have surmised about the origins of our earliest behaviors is relevant to the origins of artistic behavior and therefore can help to answer why those behaviors exist at all and what purpose they serve today.

Coming from another direction, there have been productive attempts to apply the evolutionary study of behavior to literature. As just a thumbnail sketch, evolutionary psychology assumes that the mind isn't a single "organ," but is composed of many smaller mental organs that are each the result of evolutionary pressures.[2] As such, they were formed to respond to the primary demands of survival and reproduction, especially such as they were tens to hundreds of thousands of years ago. These include obtaining accurate information about the physical environment; understanding animal behavior sufficiently to track and hunt prey and avoid being prey; navigating the social demands of small-band life, including understanding social ranks, dealing with threats, repaying social debts, and helping to punish scofflaws; maintaining the relationships necessary for finding mates; and raising children. "Literary Darwinists" point out that much of fiction (although hardly all of it) is focused specifically on these exact issues (Carroll et al. 2012). Another line of thought in the field looks at "literary universals," or features that appear in unrelated literary traditions—that is, that seem to arise independently—and therefore are possibly the result of innate psychology and not imitation (Hogan 2003).[3] Such universals, when confirmed, can supply insight into the psychology of narrative as, if one of the fundamental assumptions of the field is correct, they must exist for a reason.

This "deep history" gives us insight into the earliest beginnings of narrative culture and so can give provisional answers to questions we often don't even think to ask, such as "Why do we waste time with things that never happened, and never could?" even if the answers are less useful in dissecting the details of specific texts. But as we draw back on the magnification of the telescope, objects closer to us come into focus. The next step from deep history would be simply history. This presents new challenges. How can history, which is often centered on individuals, be amenable to a psychological approach, which tends to focus on generalities of human cognition? The answer is that history can be viewed as just another type of environment. And the great trend in evolutionary psychology in recent years has been to tease out how environment-dependent many of our evolved psychological mechanisms are (Boyer 2020). For instance, we seem to unconsciously evaluate our environment in terms of stability and safety. Based on that evaluation, we can be more or less inclined to make decisions based on short-term or long-term benefits. It makes little sense to plan for twenty years ahead if you think you could die next week. Unstable environments lead to increased risk-taking. This should be true of the social as well as the cultural sphere. There is a chicken-and-egg problem here, but it is no coincidence that the periods of the most intense cultural ferment in Russian culture followed the 1812 Napoleonic invasion, the early twentieth-century revolutions, and the decade following the fall of the Soviet Union. Historical events can also affect other common aspects of cultural production, such as openness to foreign influences or acceptance of violence. None of this is to deny the very real, direct influences of history. Things like censorship, arrests, and murder have plagued Russian letters for its entire existence. But this approach adds an additional level of explanation to complex cultural trends.

If history can leave its mark, then obviously so can society. Cultural psychologists have long known that social norms leave an imprint on how people think and process the world around them. Richard Nisbett's work, for instance, has shown substantive differences in how Asians and Westerners *tend* to approach the world, with Asians being "holistic" and Westerners being "analytic." "Holistic" implies attention to the big picture, context, and relationships. "Analytic" involves a focus on isolated attributes and categories, as well as rules. The differences appear to be wholly cultural since second-generation immigrants tend to think the way those around them think, not how their parents do (Mesoudi, Magid, and Hussain 2016).

A major trend in cultural psychology recently has been to think of cultures along a spectrum of WEIRDness (western, educated, industrial, rich, democratic; Henrich, Heine, and Norenzayan 2010). This approach appears to be more flexible as it can look at behaviors independently (a culture may be WEIRD in one metric, but not WEIRD in another). Interestingly, studies often show that the most "Western" of countries are actually the Scandinavian countries; seemingly non-WEIRD countries like China can show high variability across measures; and Russia, either because of or despite the centuries of arguments between the Westernizers and the Slavophiles, often comes out in the middle of such rankings. Such broad cultural differences should be visible at the level of individual texts if we look at enough of them. Expectations about individualism vs. group allegiance should steer readers' expectations and thus influence the production of narrative.[4]

As the circle tightens and we get closer to the work itself, contemporary psychology offers us new ways of looking at long-standing issues. These new approaches don't necessarily overturn common sense, but they have clarified some issues that have been argued about for literally ages. Child development and the role of parents and genes can now be studied in a much more quantitative fashion (which has still not erased all of the mystery). What has long been the purview of psychoanalysis and therapy is now also amenable to gene array analysis. We have a better understanding of the full range of effects of mental disorders such as schizophrenia and bipolar disorder, as well as the comparative influence of upbringing and environment. For instance, the trend of late is, despite the often-automatic association of the two, to downplay the connection between manic episodes and artistic productivity. Treatment for mania, in fact, is likely better for artistic production than the risks of remaining untreated (Andreasen 2008; Miller, Perich, and Meade 2019). Geneticists are finding that there is virtually nothing that isn't genetically influenced, but also that everything more complicated than the simplest phenotypes is controlled not just by multiple genes, but by hundreds or thousands of separate genes, each exerting a small amount of influence. Furthermore, while the genetic component of different behaviors and qualities varies, it frequently falls between 40 and 60 percent, still leaving a large role for the environment, no matter how genetic a trait is.[5] There is no such thing as genetic determinism. Family dynamics have also gotten some new light, casting doubt on the importance of birth order, and showing that peers are at least as vital for child development as parents (Harris 1998). Child temperament may even be just as important in eliciting parenting style as parenting style is in child behavior. All of this enables a more complex way of looking at the interplay between a writer's biography, social and historical background, and the work itself.

OVERVIEW OF COGNITIVE APPROACHES IN OTHER FIELDS

It is my general contention that for literary scholars interested in the cognitive sciences and evolutionary theory, it is more productive in the short term to look at what fields closer to our own have been doing with a cognitive approach. fMRI scans and discussions of dopamine receptors will only be of direct use to a small percentage of us. Of more use will be to see how other fields in the humanities and social sciences have adapted the tools of cognitive psychology to study human behavior and cultural artifacts. I will try to show here that there is much that literary studies can take from sister and cousin fields, ranging from a priori assumptions to concrete methodology. There is no reason to reinvent the wheel when there are decades of work elsewhere that have made mistakes for us.

Philosophy

In some respects, a connection between philosophy and cognitive science should be no surprise given the importance of logic to the study of computation and the importance of morality in contemporary evolutionary thinking. Arguably, the greatest recent contributions to Darwinian thinking have come from a philosopher, Daniel Dennett (Dennett 1995, inter alia). In reading on the subject, it seems obligatory to begin discussions of the evolution or neuroscience of morality with Hume and Locke before getting to Darwin or Panksepp.

The directional arrow goes most often from philosophy to cognitive science, and so the field can more accurately be described as the philosophy of neuroscience. In this capacity, the questions that are addressed include things like "what constitutes an explanation in neuroscience?" or "should psychological processes be studied based on internal brain structures, or on their external manifestations such as behavior?"

When the arrow goes in the other direction, it is often in an attempt to base philosophical arguments on known or well-studied aspects of our evolutionary heritage or mental processing. Does it make sense to argue for a social or moral system that cuts against millions of years of primate evolution? To take one concrete example from the field of moral philosophy, we can look at trolleyology (Greene 2013), familiar to viewers of *The Good Place*, which probes our innate reactions to concrete moral dilemmas (hitting a switch to sacrifice someone is ok; pushing someone in front of a trolley to sacrifice someone is not ok). This points to innate (cognitive) biases toward certain moral behaviors, which have implications for the behavior of literary characters.

History

Interdisciplinary approaches to history have led to what is often called "deep history," which looks at history not just since the advent of writing, but further back to the beginnings of agriculture, to the dispersal of modern hominins, or even to our evolutionary separation from other hominids. The attempt to separate a discipline traditionally rooted in the written word from actual texts can potentially show literary scholars how to do the same thing—at least if they wish to gain some knowledge of the anthropological roots of narrative that surely go far beyond the oldest tablets or papyri. While such narratives obviously leave no trace, this underwater part of the storytelling iceberg can be indirectly probed using other means. This is already being done with folktales (Graça da Silva and Tehrani 2016).

Another approach to history tries to develop rules about its development in the way that we have rules for individual development. Cliodynamics attempts to amass data about societies and peoples in order to elicit patterns (Turchin 2008). The project has expanded to a set of databases (https://seshatdatabank.info/) devoted to specific topics such as the growth of social complexity and the rise of punishing gods. The goal is to see the correlations and tendencies in history that get overlooked if you look only at the fine-grain stuff.

Economics

The field of behavioral economics has been another growth industry in recent years, if not decades. The basic assumption is that consumers cannot be abstracted down to mindless automatons who respond with complete rationality. Instead, people are concrete human beings with complex (but not so complex that they can't be generalized) behavioral reactions that are context-dependent. A primary tool for measuring such behavior has been games, for instance, the Dictator Game, where one person can dictate how a sum of money is split, but if the other person turns the offer down, nobody gets anything. Standard economics says that people should accept anything above 0 because something is better than nothing; therefore, offers should be uneven. Reality, however, shows that people are willing to turn down offers they see as unfair, and the dictators, understanding that, tend to offer 50/50 splits, or close to it, at least in Western societies (Henrich et al. 2005). The conclusion is that understanding human psychology is important to understanding human economic interactions. Behavior can't be assumed based on a priori assumptions about maximizing anything. This, in turn, has implications for our moral psychology.

The lesson can be applied to other behaviors as well, not just economic ones. The choice of what to read, what to view or listen to, what to write or produce, all of these are behaviors and do not happen in a vacuum. They occur not only in social, historical, and cultural settings but also in human brains shaped by eons of evolution. Such behavior is flexible but not infinitely so. It can be generalized, if not concretely predicted. It is reasonable to assume that conclusions about decision-making in one area will prove fruitful when applied to another area, assuming the proper translation.

Anthropology

Anthropology has seen perhaps the most productive use of cognitive approaches of any of the social sciences or humanities. To understand what our ancestors did not 2,000, but 200,000 years ago, anthropologists must think about what the brains of those individuals were capable of. But how can you tell what a brain could do without seeing what it did do? This is a complex question, and it involves a methodology I think can be useful for humanists as well—they use different lines of inquiry and triangulate. The human lineage split off from what would become chimpanzees and bonobos between 6 and 10 million years ago. We can speculate about what traits that last common ancestor possessed based on similarities between the three species (social hierarchies, food sharing, or basic tool use, for instance). We can also extrapolate about cognitive function based on artifacts. For example, the half-man, half-lion *Löwenmensch* figure that dates back 35,000–40,000 years ago indicates a mind capable of creating imaginary blends, a possible precursor of religion.

We have a similar problem with cognitive approaches to literature—not because literature is hundreds of thousands of years old (although narrative could be), but because the behavior is so complicated. There is no technology that allows us to track all of the neural circuits involved in the act of reading, and even if one did exist, we don't know enough about the brain to do that much with such information. This is why a cognitive approach should best be viewed from as multidisciplinary a perspective as possible.

Religious Studies

Perhaps no other field outside of literary study can provide as much guidance for cognitive approaches to literature as cognitive approaches to religion. Religious studies has the same problem as physical anthropologists (lack of archaeological record), but also frequently study the same thing as literature scholars: texts. Despite the fact that the earliest religious behaviors have left zero unambiguously religious artifacts (there are some ambiguous ones such as cave paintings or the *Löwenmensch*), the field has pieced together a set of mental functions that, arguably, are necessary for the existence of religion, and possibly for the success of our species.

The primary one of these has been the concept of "minimally counterintuitive imagery." The minimal part need not concern us, but counterintuitive imagery is imagery that violates our expectations of natural categories. We have innate (a term that requires separate unpacking) understandings of categories such as things, tools, animals, and other humans (Atran 1990). Rocks don't move on their own, but ducks do. Humans talk and think, but trees don't. Entities that violate these expectations are inherently more interesting, and hence the proliferation of talking trees, bodiless spirits, flying stones, and so on . . . in religion, both modern and traditional (Atran 2002; Boyer 2001). But this kind of imagery is not exclusive to religion; it also populates folklore, film, and literature of all sorts. Counterintuitive imagery is a calling card of narrative, not just of religion, and so cognitive approaches to narrative can learn quite a bit from cognitive approaches to religion.

Other approaches more grounded in evolutionary theory emphasize the role religions theoretically played in our social development: religion helped us to follow group-beneficial rules, work together to overcome obstacles including other groups, or harness fear of supernatural punishment (Wilson 2002; Norenzayan 2013; Johnson 2016). Here, too, it is possible for scholars of (deep) literary history to learn a thing or two. If religious narratives evolved to play a role in human societies, then other kinds of narrative likely performed a similar function (among others, of course).

Music

All of the arts have their own separate cognitive approach. Cognitive approaches to music tend to focus on inherent qualities of our appreciation of music, possible universals, and theoretical origins. The approach has several things to lend to literary studies. The first is that it does not shy away from thinking in terms of deep history or of searching for details that unite music cross-culturally. Musical cognitivists tend to be lumpers rather than splitters. This is perhaps due to the fact that, minus lyrics, music of any time or place is accessible to anyone else. The second is that the approach is inherently embodied. Cognitivists in music never forget that rhythm is tied to physical motion and that sound waves are a physical property and are received by a specific set of organs. While literary theorists don't always deny this element, it is much more complicated with literature as the reactions it triggers are physically much more dispersed throughout the body. We understand the neurology of sound much better than the neurology of the emotions.

And there are similarities that musicology has studied better. Without the inherent distraction of words, music history has paid more attention to the evolution of forms. Cognitive approaches to music, thus, talk about the formation of mental schemata. Daniel Levitin also lays out a basic element of cognitive science that should be better appreciated by literary scholars, especially those of poetry: "[t]he setting up and then manipulating of expectations is the heart of music, and it is accomplished in countless ways" (2006, 110).

Visual Arts

Cognitive approaches to visual art throw one of the primary problems in the field into sharp relief. There is no part of human cognition that is better understood than our visual system. We can trace what happens from a photon landing on the retina to the production of a mental image. We know the different kinds of receptors. We can trace how the information is processed across the usefully named VI through V5 areas. We know how depth is processed from the two-dimensional image projected on the lens. We know how color perception is affected by lighting (the cause of the famous black/blue vs. white/gold dress incident of 2015). We know that shape, direction, speed, and outline are all processed separately. And so on.

With this understanding, cognitive approaches to painting can give minutely detailed descriptions of how a painting produces its visual effects. This can be fascinating, as great painters often play off of the subtlest tricks of our brains (Zeki 1999; Kandel 2016).

GETTING STARTED WITH COGNITIVE APPROACHES TO BEHAVIOR

There is so much work in the field that keeping up on it in real time is difficult; getting a handle on it from scratch is vastly harder. Throw on top of this the, in my opinion, necessity of getting a grounding in the underlying science, and things truly become daunting. What I offer here is a very personal and idiosyncratic guide to gaining a foothold in both the science and the humanities devoted to cognition.

It is not necessary for the majority of cognitive poetics to know your central sulcus from your dorsolateral prefrontal cortex, but some knowledge of basic brain functioning can be useful. Fortunately, there are many, many popular books that lay out the general to specific functioning of the brain. For a more detailed introduction, the best place is likely a textbook, but I will focus on the popular-science introductions, many of which are written by experts in the field. A good place to start for the functioning of individual neurons, the most basic level of brain function, is Joseph LeDoux's *The Synaptic Self* (2003). LeDoux walks through what makes a neuron fire or stop firing. He shows how a unit that is completely binary (a neuron fires or it doesn't) can combine with other similar units in incredibly complex ways. Steven Pinker's overtitled *How the Mind Works* (1997) demonstrates how neurons can connect to form circuits that perform complex calculations in the way that a computer can.

Once you have a grounding in how the brain functions within a skull, you can start to understand how it operates with the rest of the body in a given environment, and in relation to other people. Here's where approaches especially begin to fracture as each subfield of psychology often has its own way of looking at each behavior, and each approach usually has its own validity. This is why it is important as outsiders to the field to read as widely as possible in order to put the pieces together. You don't want to describe the elephant based solely on examining its tail. Take the study of imitation as just one example. Developmental psychology points out that imitation comes online either at birth, or shortly thereafter, and can play a role in multiple aspects of learning as well as self-formation (Meltzoff and Decety 2003). Other psychologists could demonstrate that imitation is actually not innate but is a "cognitive gadget" (Heyes 2016). A moral psychologist could point to the way that imitation allows us to develop moral comprehension (Prinz 2005). Coming from a more evolutionary or anthropological perspective can show how central imitation is to the evolution (cultural and otherwise) of the various human species (Mesoudi 2011). Other anthropologists demonstrate that there are different kinds of imitation that focus on the object itself, on the actions of a specific person, or what everyone around us seems to be doing, and that these three types of imitation arise under different social and environmental conditions (Richerson and Boyd 2005). And these are only some of the approaches to a topic that has been of direct relevance to literary theory since Plato. My point is that in investigating an aspect of psychology or cognitive science that is relevant to literary study—and there are many—it is important to examine it from different perspectives, and there is virtually never a single "psychological" perspective, but rather a bunch of them that don't always align.

As we move from neurons firing to living beings operating in a constantly changing environment, it will become increasingly more important for the literary scholar to operate by analogy. By this, I mean that since there is so little work done on narrative, song, and poetry, the decorative and depictive arts, and so on in cognitive science and evolutionary anthropology, it is necessary to steal from work that comes at our interests from another direction. This is often nobody's fault: again, stories and music don't leave behind physical traces. We can't examine fossils to find out when the first song was composed. At best, we have the remains of flutes (which can be hard to distinguish from bones with bite marks or holes drilled to extract marrow), cave paintings, or unearthed figures, or supposed remains of jewelry or makeup. All of these lead to discussions of the earliest symbolic behavior—which would mean other forms of symbolic behavior were also around at that time. Humanists can be of use here as the term symbolism seems to get used loosely in these contexts. For instance, is jewelry or bodily decoration inherently a sign of symbolism? Tantalizing details, perhaps, but little to go by, and assuredly not the first that ever existed. Cognitive scientists, for their part, need to isolate the narrowest, simplest aspects of behavior in order to examine them without interference. Because of this, what they examine, even when nominally related to the study of literature, is often so simple as to seem unhelpful to us.

Instead, it can be more useful to read up on tangentially related fields. One such example is Michael Gazzaniga's work on split-brain patients. These are people who have had the corpus callosum—the band of nerves that connect the two hemispheres of the brain—severed, often to stop debilitating seizures. Such patients function remarkably well but do show peculiar deficiencies. Take the phenomenon where an image is presented to only one half of the visual field of such patients, and thus only the opposite brain hemisphere has access to that information. If an image is presented on the left side, the language centers of the brain (located in the left hemisphere) don't have access to that information, and the patient responds that there is no image. Yet, the left hand of the patient (controlled by the same right hemisphere that sees the image) can click a button to register the presence of the image. The real fun begins when different images are presented to each hemisphere. The most famous example is a patient who was shown a chicken foot on the right (left hemisphere) and a snowy landscape on the left (right hemisphere). The patient then picked pictures that matched what they saw. He picked a chicken head and a shovel. The language center, however, did not "see" the snow, and so Gazzaniga did not expect them to be able to formulate why they picked a shovel. And yet, when asked, he calmly explained that the shovel was needed to clean out the chicken shed. The patient's left hemisphere clearly invented a narrative to make post-hoc sense out of a choice made due to information it had no access to. What better proof is there that narratives—even fictitious ones—are central to our processing of the world and that we create them effortlessly and constantly? It's not difficult to see how this automatic need to fill in informational gaps with narrative plays a role in our reading of literature, where the reader must often play an active role in supplementing missing information. Indeed, this fits well with Karin Kukkonen's use of predictive processing (2020).

FUTURE RESEARCH

There are many open doors for those who wish to work in cognitive approaches to Russian literature. Reading around in the work that has been done in cognitive approaches in other disciplines shows just how many different possibilities there are. Only some such approaches are included in this volume. For those wishing to make their mark, what follows are a few pointers for alleys to explore. Since the application of cognitive approaches to Russian literature is such a new endeavor, while being much less new in other fields, there is much to borrow from. Those interested in pursuing these approaches could do much worse than simply reading some of the work, especially the other collections of essays on the topic (Richardson and Spolsky 2004; Zunshine 2010a, 2015b; Jaén and Simon 2013, 2016; Burke and Troscianko 2017), cited in this book and picking the approaches that jibe with their particular interests. There is work done that at least touches on the full range of theoretic concerns in literary study, from formal aspects of poetry and prose genres (Tsur 2008) to postcolonial theory (Hogan 2004; Keen 2015) and queer theory (Vincent 2015); the study of literature and affect (Jacobs 2015; Papp-Zipernovszky et al. 2022); the digital humanities allow for the testing of hypotheses across a much broader swath of texts than ever before. Instead of the dozens to hundreds of texts a human can read, thousands or even millions can be studied; on the other extreme there are studies that are beginning to link together an individual's personal history with how they experience fictive worlds (Gerrig and Mumper 2017). If an aspect of human behavior has been studied cognitively and is relevant to the production of literature, it is a potential source of methodology.

It is also not sufficiently appreciated just how influential Russian and Soviet science was on the formation of cognitive science. There is definitely room for work that builds on the research of Ivan Pavlov, Lev Vygotsky, Alexander Luria, Andrei Markov, and others. Another branch of the field can view these approaches as a form of "neo-Formalism" that can put some of the foundational work in our field, such as alienation, on an empirical footing, or can see some of those insights with new eyes. Formalism always fancied itself a scientific undertaking. The science may have finally caught up to the aspirations.

The present volume is intended merely as a starting point, the beginning of a conversation I hope everyone will feel welcome to participate in.

NOTES

1. As just a partial list, see: Crick (1994), Dehaene (2014), Graziano (2019), Damasio (2018), and Seth (2021).

2. For an overview of and argument for "modularity" see Mercier and Sperber (2017, 68-75).

3. See also the Literary Universals Project: https://literary-universals.uconn.edu/.

4. Along these lines, see Larsen's work on Medieval Norse romance (2022).

5. The tension between these two facts is captured by two books, both with the title *Blueprint*, by Richard Plomin and Nicholas Christakis (2018; 2019).

BIBLIOGRAPHY

Andreasen, Nancy C. 2008. "The Relationship between Creativity and Mood Disorders." *Dialogues in Clinical Neuroscience* 10 (2): 251–55. https://doi.org/10.31887/DCNS.2008.10.2/ncandreasen.

Atran, Scott. 1990. *Cognitive Foundations of Natural History: Towards an Anthropology of Science*. Cambridge: Cambridge University Press.

Atran, Scott. 2002. *In Gods We Trust: The Evolutionary Landscape of Religion*. Oxford: Oxford University Press.

Barrett, Lisa Feldman. 2017. *How Emotions are Made: The Secret Life of the Brain*. Boston: Houghton Mifflin Harcourt.

Boyd, Brian. 2009. *On the Origin of Stories: Evolution, Cognition, and Fiction*. Cambridge, MA: Harvard University Press.

Boyer, Pascal. 2001. *Religion Explained: The Evolutionary Origins of Religious Thought*. New York: Basic Books.

Boyer, Pascal. 2020. *Minds Make Societies: How Cognition Explains the World Humans Create*. New Haven: Yale University Press.

Burke, Michael, and Emily Troscianko. 2017. *Cognitive Literary Science: Dialogues between Literature and Cognition*. New York: Oxford University Press.

Carroll, Joseph, Jonathan Gottschall, John A. Johnson, and Daniel J. Kruger. 2012. *Graphing Jane Austen: The Evolutionary Basis of Literary Meaning*. New York: Palgrave Macmillan.

Christakis, Nicholas A. 2019. *Blueprint: The Evolutionary Origins of a Good Society*. New York: Little, Brown Spark.

Crane, Mary Thomas. 1998. "Male Pregnancy and Cognitive Permeability in Measure for Measure." *Shakespeare Quarterly* 49 (3): 269–92. https://doi.org/10.2307/2902259.

Crick, Francis. 1994. *The Astonishing Hypothesis: The Scientific Search for the Soul*. New York: Scribner.

Damasio, Antonio. 2018. *The Strange Order of Things: Life, Feeling, and the Making of Cultures*. New York: Pantheon Books.

Darwin, Charles. [1872] 1965. *The Expression of the Emotions in Man and Animals*. Chicago: The University of Chicago Press.

Dehaene, Stanislas. 2014. *Consciousness and the Brain: Deciphering How the Brain Codes Our Thoughts*. New York: Viking.

Dennett, Daniel. 1995. *Darwin's Dangerous Idea: Evolution and the Meanings of Life*. New York: Simon & Schuster.

Dolack, Tom. 2012. "Homo Oneginensis: Pushkin and Evo-Cognitive Approaches to Literature." *STYLE* 46 (3_4): 338–54.

Domínguez, Julia. 2016. "The Janus Hypothesis in Don Quixote: Memory and Imagination in Cervantes." In *Cognitive Approaches to Early Modern Spanish Literature*, edited by Isabel Jaen and Julien Jacques Simon, 54–74. New York: Oxford University Press.

Edelman, Gerald. 2004. *Wider Than the Sky: The Phenomenal Gift of Consciousness*. New Haven: Yale University Press.

Ekman, Paul. 1982. *Emotion in the Human Face*. 2nd ed. Studies in Emotion and Social Interaction. Cambridge: Cambridge University Press.

Gerrig, Richard J., and Micah L. Mumper. 2017. "How Readers' Lives Affect Narrative Experiences." In *Cognitive Literary Science: Dialogues between Literature and Cognition*, edited by Michael Burke, and Emily Troscianko, 239–57. New York: Oxford University Press

Graça da Silva, Sara, and Jamshid J. Tehrani. 2016. "Comparative Phylogenetic Analyses Uncover the Ancient Roots of Indo-European Folktales." *Royal Society Open Science* 3 (1): 150645. https://doi.org/10.1098/rsos.150645.

Graziano, Michael. 2019. *Rethinking Consciousness: A Scientific Theory of Subjective Experience*. New York: W.W. Norton.

Greene, Joshua. 2013. *Moral Tribes: Emotion, Reason, and the Gap between Us and Them*. New York: The Penguin Press.

Harris, Judith Rich. 1998. *The Nurture Assumption: Why Children Turn out the Way They Do*. New York: Free Press.

Henrich, Joseph, Robert Boyd, Samuel Bowles, Colin Camerer, Ernst Fehr, Herbert Gintis, Richard McElreath, et al. 2005. "'Economic Man' in Cross-Cultural Perspective: Behavioral Experiments in 15 Small-Scale Societies." *Behavioral and Brain Sciences* 28 (6): 795–815. https://doi.org/10.1017/S0140525X05000142.

Henrich, Joseph, Steven J. Heine, and Ara Norenzayan. 2010. "The Weirdest People in the World?" *Behavioral and Brain Sciences* 33 (2–3): 61–83. https://doi.org/10.1017/S0140525X0999152X.

Heyes, Cecilia. 2016. "Homo Imitans? Seven Reasons Why Imitation Couldn't Possibly be Associative." *Philosophical Transactions of the Royal Society B: Biological Sciences* 371 (1686): 20150069. https://doi.org/10.1098/rstb.2015.0069.

Hogan, Patrick Colm. 2003. *The Mind and Its Stories: Narrative Universals and Human Emotion*. Cambridge: Cambridge University Press.

Hogan, Patrick Colm. 2004. *Empire and Poetic Voice: Cognitive and Cultural Studies of Literary Tradition and Colonialism*. Albany: State University of New York Press.

Hogan, Patrick Colm. 2011. *What Literature Teaches Us about Emotion*. New York: Cambridge University Press.

Holland, Norman N. 2002. "Where is a Text? A Neurological View." *New Literary History* 33 (1): 21–38.

Jacobs, Arthur M. 2015. "Neurocognitive Poetics: Methods and Models for Investigating the Neuronal and Cognitive-Affective Bases of Literature Reception." *Frontiers in Human Neuroscience* 9: 186.

Jaén, Isabel, and Julien Jacques Simon, eds. 2013. *Cognitive Literary Studies: Current Themes and New Directions*. Austin: University of Texas Press.

Jaén, Isabel, and Julien Jacques Simon, eds. *Cognitive Approaches to Early Modern Spanish Literature*. New York: Oxford University Press.

Johnson, Dominic. 2016. *God is Watching You: How the Fear of God Makes Us Human*. New York: Oxford University Press.

Kandel, Eric. 2016. *Reductionism in Art and Brain Science: Bridging the Two Cultures*. New York: Columbia University Press.

Keen, Suzanne. 2015. "Human Rights Discourse and Universals of Cognition and Emotion: Postcolonial Fiction." In *The Oxford Handbook of Cognitive Literary Studies*, edited by Lisa Zunshine, 347–366. New York: Oxford University Press.□□□□□□

Kukkonen, Karin. 2020. *Probability Designs: Literature and Predictive Processing*. New York: Oxford University Press.

Larsen, Mads. 2022. "Courtliness as Morality of Modernity in Norse Romance." *Evolutionary Studies in Imaginative Culture* 6 (2): 43–56. https://doi.org/10.26613/esic.6.2.298.

LeDoux, Joseph E. 2003. *Synaptic Self: How Our Brains Become Who We Are*. New York: Penguin Books.

Levitin, Daniel J. 2006. *This Is Your Brain on Music: The Science of a Human Obsession*. New York, N.Y: Dutton.

Martindale, Colin. 1990. *The Clockwork Muse: The Predictability of Artistic Change*. New York: BasicBooks.

Meltzoff, Andrew N., and Jean Decety. 2003. "What Imitation Tells Us about Social Cognition: A Rapprochement between Developmental Psychology and Cognitive Neuroscience." *Philosophical Transactions: Biological Sciences* 358 (1431): 491–500.

Mercier, Hugo, and Dan Sperber. 2017. *The Enigma of Reason*. Cambridge, MA: Harvard University Press.

Mesoudi, Alex. 2011. *Cultural Evolution: How Darwinian Theory Can Explain Human Culture and Synthesize the Social Sciences*. Chicago: University of Chicago Press.

Mesoudi, Alex, Kesson Magid, and Delwar Hussain. 2016. "How Do People Become W.E.I.R.D.? Migration Reveals the Cultural Transmission Mechanisms Underlying Variation in Psychological Processes." *PLOS ONE* 11 (1): e0147162. https://doi.org/10.1371/journal.pone.0147162.

Miller, Natalie, Tania Perich, and Tanya Meade. 2019. "Depression, Mania and Self-Reported Creativity in Bipolar Disorder." *Psychiatry Research* 276 (June): 129–33. https://doi.org/10.1016/j.psychres.2019.05.006.

Norenzayan, Ara. 2013. *Big Gods: How Religion Transformed Cooperation and Conflict*. Princeton: Princeton University Press.

Papp-Zipernovszky, Orsolya, Anne Mangen, Arthur Jacobs, and Jana Lüdtke. 2022. "Shakespeare Sonnet Reading: An Empirical Study of Emotional Responses." *Language and Literature* 31 (3): 296–324. https://doi.org/10.1177/09639470211054647.

Pinker, Steven. 1997. *How the Mind Works*. New York: Norton.

Plomin, Robert. 2018. *Blueprint: How DNA Makes Us Who We Are*. Cambridge, MA: MIT Press.

Prinz, Jesse J. 2005. "Imitation and Moral Development." In *Perspectives on Imitation: From Neuroscience to Social Science: Vol. 2: Imitation, Human Development, and Culture*, edited by Susan Hurley and Nick Chater, 267–82. Cambridge, MA: MIT Press.

Richardson, Alan. 2004. "Studies in Literature and Cognition: A Field Map." In *The Work of Fiction: Cognition, Culture, and Complexity*, edited by Alan Richardson and Ellen Spolsk, 1–29. London: Routledge.

Richardson, Alan, and Ellen Spolsky, eds. 2004. *The Work of Fiction: Cognition, Culture, and Complexity*. London: Routledge.

Richerson, Peter J., and Robert Boyd. 2005. *Not by Genes Alone: How Culture Transformed Human Evolution*. Chicago: University of Chicago Press.

Seth, Anil. 2021. *Being You: A New Science of Consciousness*. New York: Dutton.

Tomasello, Michael. 2015. *A Natural History of Human Morality*. Cambridge, MA: Harvard University Press.

Troscianko, Emily T., and Michael Burke. 2017. "Introduction: A Window on to the Landscape of Cognitive Literary Science." In *Cognitive Literary Science: Dialogues between Literature and Cognition*, edited by Michael Burke and Emily T. Troscianko, 1–14. New York: Oxford University Press. https://doi.org/10.1093/acprof:oso/9780190496869.003.0001.

Tsur, Reuven. 2008. *Toward a Theory of Cognitive Poetics*. 2nd, expanded and updated ed. Portland, OR: Sussex Acad. Press.

Turchin, Peter. 2008. "Arise 'Cliodynamics'." *Nature* 454 (7200): 34–35. https://doi.org/10.1038/454034a.

Vincent, J. Keith. 2015. "Sex on the Mind: Queer Theory Meets Cognitive Theory." In *The Oxford Handbook of Cognitive Literary Studies*, edited by Lisa Zunshine, 199–221. New York: Oxford University Press.

Wilson, David Sloan. 2002. *Darwin's Cathedral: Evolution, Religion, and the Nature of Society*. Chicago: University of Chicago Press.

Zeki, Semir. 1999. *Inner Vision: An Exploration of Art and the Brain*. New York: Oxford University Press.

Zunshine, Lisa. 2006. *Why We Read Fiction: Theory of Mind and the Novel*. Columbus: Ohio State University Press.

Zunshine, Lisa, ed. 2010a. *Introduction to Cognitive Cultural Studies*. Baltimore: Johns Hopkins University Press.

Zunshine, Lisa. 2010b. "What Is Cognitive Cultural Studies?" In *Introduction to Cognitive Cultural Studies*, edited by Lisa Zunshine, 1–33. Baltimore: Johns Hopkins University Press.

Zunshine, Lisa. 2015a. "Introduction to Cognitive Literary Studies." In *The Oxford Handbook of Cognitive Literary Studies*, edited by Lisa Zunshine, 1–10. New York: Oxford University Press. https://doi.org/10.1093/oxfordhb/9780199978069.013.0001.

Zunshine, Lisa, ed. 2015b. *The Oxford Handbook of Cognitive Literary Studies*. New York: Oxford University Press.

1

Pushkin's "The Stationmaster"

Morality Meets Sexual Selection

David Bethea

Two deep-seated idea clusters universally embedded in human beings' personal stories are those relating to morality and romantic choice (the latter being known in evolutionary terms as sexual selection).[1] In this chapter I will look at Pushkin's short tale "The Stationmaster," in which these issues play a prominent role but are handled, as we might expect with Pushkin, in an unorthodox way—a way that flips on its head a universally revered biblical parable, with the result that the reader is forced to consider the existential (as in "how best to survive") dividing line between familial duty, on the one hand, and romantic desire, on the other. Likewise, as we might expect with Pushkin, the Russian language plays a key role in bringing aspects of the decision-making process to the surface.

As a jumping-off point into a discussion of Pushkin's tale, let us remind the reader of the proto-cognitive basis of all organic life, including the cellular life going on in our bodies. Why start here? Because there is something about the cell as a bounded, autonomous living unit that is reminiscent of how a tightly structured literary text models life. In the words of biochemist and "natural genetic engineering" theorist James Shapiro:

> Cells do not act blindly. We know from physiology and biochemistry and molecular biology that cells are full of receptors. They monitor what goes on outside. They monitor what goes on inside. And they are continually taking in that information and using it to adjust their actions, their biochemistry, their metabolism, the cell cycle, etc., so that things come out right. That's why I use the word cognitive to apply to cells, meaning they do things based on

> knowledge of what's happening around them and inside of them. Without that knowledge and the systems to use that knowledge they couldn't proliferate and survive as efficiently as they do. (Mazur 2015, 14–15)

This idea of a "knowing" ("they [cells] do things based on knowledge") that is always already immanent in organic life at the cellular level has implications throughout the biosphere. As philosopher Thomas Nagel might say, it is an aspect of "mind" in nature that the materialist neo-Darwinian branch of modern evolutionary biology has not yet sufficiently accounted for (2012).[2] Hence it may also not be too much of a stretch to speak of a Pushkin tale in analogous terms: monitoring "what goes on outside" (the context) and "what goes on inside" (the text) and making adjustments accordingly, its language seems organically "aware."

THE PLOT: A "MORAL TONE" AND THE PARABLE OF THE PRODIGAL SON

"The Stationmaster" is one of the stories in Pushkin's collection *The Belkin Tales* (Povesti Belkina 1830), the poet's debut in prose. The stories in the collection play off each other (and the tongue-in-cheek "From the Editor" preface) thematically and structurally, all of which contributes to their "organic," as in parts-to-whole and whole-to-parts, character. The story opens with the exceedingly "philanthropic" voice of Titular Councilor AGN, a narrator highly susceptible to events happening around him. A titular councilor is someone in the middle to lower range (level nine of fourteen) of the Table of Ranks established by Peter the Great in 1722. From the outset, our narrator operates in a voice zone designed to whip up feelings of compassion for the plight of stationmasters—those poor souls on the bottom rungs of the bureaucratic ladder who run the post houses where teams of horses are changed for the next leg of a journey. Usually, these individuals are retired soldiers one generation removed from the peasantry/serfdom. Their lives are difficult because the status of a new arrival, say that of a nobleman or high-ranking officer, can trump that of a traveler who has been waiting in line for hours for the next available horses, with the result that the stationmaster is blamed for the delay.

> Who has not cursed stationmasters?—Who has not quarreled with them frequently? Who has not demanded the fateful book from them in moments of anger, in order to enter in it a useless complaint against their highhandedness, rudeness, and negligence? [. . .] Let us be fair, however, and try to imagine ourselves in their position: then, perhaps, we shall judge them with more lenience. What is a stationmaster? A veritable martyr of the fourteenth class, whose rank is enough to shield him only from physical abuse, and at

> times not even from that. [. . .] Day or night, he does not have a moment's quiet. The traveler takes out on him all the irritation accumulated during a tedious ride. (Pushkin [1830] 1983, 93)

The narrator's tone prepares the reader to perceive a segment of the Russian population differently. The pathos permeating this initial exposition suggests that a charitable gap needs to be filled: stationmasters have tended to be viewed as bothersome background only ("Who has not cursed stationmasters?") and not as individual human beings performing a set of difficult and demeaning duties. However, Pushkin never displays sentimentality for its own sake. As we proceed further into the plot of "The Stationmaster," we will need to be on guard against our own humanitarian biases.

After lamenting the plight of stationmasters in general, the narrator proceeds to tell us a story about a specific stationmaster, Samson Vyrin. The tale begins in 1816, which by now seems well in the past, and takes place somewhere in a backwater described merely as "X" province. The younger version of Titular Councilor AGN, who occupies an even lower rank as the action commences, has had his fill of stationmasters and their now rude, now fawning, but consistently bumbling ways. Moreover, he is appearing at this station after a downpour and is grumpy and in need of a change of clothes. Two things immediately attract his attention upon entering the building: the first is the beauty of the stationmaster's daughter, and the second is the set of pictures adorning the stationhouse wall. As the understated Pushkin always selects details with care, we need to proceed here carefully.

First, the daughter is introduced:

> "Hey, Dunia!" called out the stationmaster. "Light the samovar and go get some cream." As these words were pronounced, a young girl aged about fourteen appeared from behind the partition and ran out on the porch. I was struck by her beauty.
>
> "Is that your daughter?" I asked the stationmaster.
>
> "Aye, truly she is," answered he, with an air of satisfaction and pride, "and what a sensible, clever girl, just like her late mother." (Pushkin [1830] 1983, 94–95)

Immediately following this comes the description of the pictures:

> He started copying out my order for fresh horses, and I passed the time by looking at the pictures that adorned his humble but neat dwelling. They illustrated the parable of the Prodigal Son. In the first one, a venerable old man, in nightcap and dressing gown, was bidding farewell to a restless youth who was hastily accepting his blessing and a bag of money. The sec-

> ond one depicted the young man's lewd behavior in vivid colors: he was seated at a table, surrounded by false friends and shameless women. Farther on, the ruined youth, in rags and with a three-cornered hat on his head, was tending swine and sharing their meal; deep sorrow and repentance were reflected in his features. The last picture showed his return to his father: the warmhearted old man, in the same nightcap and dressing gown, was running forward to meet him; the Prodigal Son was on his knees; in the background the cook was killing the fatted calf, and the elder brother was asking the servants about the cause of all the rejoicings. Under each picture I read appropriate verses in German. All this has remained in my memory to this day, together with the pots of balsam, the bed with the colorful curtain, and other objects. I can still see the master of the house himself as if he were right before me: a man about fifty years of age, still fresh and agile, in a long green coat with three medals on faded ribbons. (Pushkin [1830] 1983, 95)

These passages introduce plot elements that, when combined, produce different potential storylines, the roads taken and not taken, in the tale to come. One suggests one set of possibilities for the Dunia-Vyrin relationship, the other another set. We don't know yet which way these details will lead, but we can be sure Pushkin will push them in a direction that challenges our expectations, which—the taking on of the challenge—is the first step toward survival in the evolutionary process. Experiment and learn. Again, recall Shapiro's micro-level formulation:

> [c]ells do not act blindly. [. . .] They monitor what goes on outside. They monitor what goes on inside. And they are continually taking in that information and using it to adjust their actions [. . .] so that things come out right. (Mazur 2015, 14–15)

Here the "inside" is what happens *in* the story, with regard to the characters' actions, while the "outside" is what happens *beyond its frame*, in the minds of the readers. From this point forward, Dunia's beauty will be key, as will Vyrin's self-satisfaction and pride in his daughter; the moral of the Prodigal Son parable will also loom large in the arc of all future actions. Even the fact that the pictures are accompanied by "appropriate" (*prilichnye*, as in "respectable") German verses will play a role.

What follows after this sets the ball rolling. Dunia prepares the tea and notices that the young narrator can't take his eyes off her. Her reaction is not shyness; she has spent time in her father's uncivil world (it is she who is quickly able to calm down an angry traveler with her charm), and she answers his questions without hesitation. He calls her playfully a "little coquette" (*malen'kaia koketka*). This, too, is not an irrelevant detail. Next, the narrator plies Vyrin with "punch" (alcoholic, another leitmotif) to loosen his tongue and get him to share his stories. The three seem to become fast friends and the stereotype of the difficult stationmaster and the depressing station fades away. The last thing that happens before our young traveler leaves the station is that, significantly, he asks Dunia for a kiss. This moment requires discussion because in our world it is normally seen as highly improper and potentially abusive for an adult to "hit on" a fourteen-year-old girl for favors. But this, Russia in 1816, is a different context and the kiss is meant to imply an as yet undetermined balance of power. This "transaction" is also about survival instinct. We sense Dunia's vulnerability, but we also sense her resiliency and playfulness. Notice that Dunia *takes the initiative* to see the young man off:

> At last I said good-bye to them; the father wished me a pleasant journey, and the daughter came to see me to the cart. On the porch I stopped and asked her to let me kiss her; she consented . . . I have accumulated many recollections of kisses [. . .] but none has made such a lasting and delightful impression on me as the one I received from Dunia. (Pushkin [1830] 1983, 95)

The plot thereafter unfolds in stages, with each new stage introduced by a subsequent visit to the station by the narrator. Several years later, the narrator is in the area again and recalls the pleasant, vital stationmaster and his comely daughter. He decides to drop by to see how the two are doing. Possibly by now Dunia is married. He finds Vyrin much changed—palpably older, withdrawn, and sullen. He also notices that the station house has fallen into disrepair; there are no flowers in the window, and most importantly, there is no Dunia. Sensing that something is wrong and that he won't be able to get the story by simply asking Vyrin about it, he changes tactics and offers the old man some rum-laced punch: perhaps this will get him to talk. The ruse works.

Vyrin now tells the story of what happened to his beloved daughter. Everything at home rested on her. She cooked, she cleaned, she greeted the visitors, she kept everyone happy. Ladies gave her handkerchiefs and earrings; gentlemen asked to stay for supper just to get a longer look at her. "[W]ho'd dare say I didn't love my Dunia, didn't cherish my child? Who had a good life if she didn't?" exclaims Vyrin. "But no, you cannot drive off evil by curses: you cannot escape your fate" (Pushkin [1830] 1983, 97). Three years ago, a handsome young hussar named Minskii was traveling through and demanded horses. His first reaction upon learning that no horses were available was to raise his voice and his whip, but as soon as he saw Dunia, he calmed down and found an excuse to linger at the station. He ordered something to eat. When Vyrin went out to see to the exchange of horses, he returned to find Minskii seriously ill. The guest had to stay the night, and the next day, with him worse, a doctor was summoned from the nearest city. When the doctor arrived, he examined the patient and prescribed several days of bed rest, all the while communicating with the sick man exclusively in German. Strangely, he also joined Minskii for a hearty meal and a bottle of wine. During Minskii's "recovery" Dunia tended to him constantly, wrapping his head with a cool cloth and bringing him lemonade to drink. When it was finally time for the hussar to leave, he offered to take Dunia to mass at the other end of the village. Dunia hesitated, but at her father's urging, agreed to go with Minskii. She did not return.

Almost as soon as Dunia left, the stationmaster suspected that something was amiss. As he traced her steps, he learned that she did not take mass that day and that, indeed, she continued on of her own free will with Minskii but was crying the entire way. She was clearly torn between her devotion to her father and her attraction toward a potential young lover. Now it was Vyrin who took ill in earnest and, being looked after by the same doctor, found out that Minskii's illness had been a cruel charade. Taking leave from his post and tracking down the hussar's domicile to fashionable St. Petersburg, Vyrin decided to go and "bring [my] lost sheep home" (Pushkin [1830] 1983, 99). He located Minskii at a high-class hotel, and when he confronted the young man, Minskii reacted in a manner consistent with his wealth and aristocratic station: he recognized Vyrin, acknowledged (though breezily) his guilt, explained that what had happened couldn't be undone, told him he couldn't part with Dunia, stuffed some banknotes into his sleeve, and quickly ushered him out the door. In other words, in this world dominated by class and power, Minskii took what he wanted without compunction. The only response Vyrin could offer was a moralistic cliché: please, sir, return Dunia because "what is done cannot be undone" (Pushkin [1830] 1983, 99), which in Russian is more suggestive—"what has fallen from the cart is ruined [and thus can't be put back]."

Wanting to see his "poor Dunia" one last time, Vyrin contrived that same evening to bluff his way into the apartment house where Minskii was keeping Dunia and, after barging in, observed the couple together:

> In the room, which was elegantly furnished, he saw Minskii seated, deep in thought. Dunia, dressed in all the finery of the latest fashion, sat on the arm of his easy chair like a lady rider on an English saddle. She was looking at Minskii with tenderness, winding his dark locks around her fingers, which glittered with rings. Poor stationmaster! Never had his daughter appeared so beautiful to him; he could not help admiring her. (Pushkin [1830] 1983, 101)

When Dunia looked up and saw her father, she fell to the floor in a faint. On this occasion, Minskii was not nearly so apologetic to his pursuer. He grabbed the old man by the collar and threw him out onto the stairwell. In the end, Vyrin was forced to accept this state of affairs—the injustice of the class structure that allowed someone to first deceive him and then steal his daughter in this manner. But this stage of the story was still not quite ended. The stationmaster wrapped up his loss of Dunia in the following way:

> "It's almost three years now," he concluded, "that I've been living without Dunia, having no news of her whatsoever. Whether she is alive or dead, God only knows. Anything can happen. She is not the first, nor will she be the last, to be seduced by some rake passing through, to be kept for a while and then discarded. There are many of them in Petersburg, of these foolish young ones: today attired in satin and velvet, but tomorrow, verily I say, sweeping the streets with the riffraff of the alehouse. Sometimes, when you think that Dunia may be perishing right there with them, you cannot help sinning in your heart and wishing her in the grave." (Pushkin [1830] 1983, 101)

The final stage of the story involves a third visit by the narrator. Now some more time has passed, and when the titular councilor returns to the site where he first met Vyrin and first kissed Dunia, everything has changed. It's been a year since Vyrin has died and his station house is now occupied by a brewer. The brewer's wife tells the narrator that Vyrin died from drink. The narrator laments his wasted trip and the seven rubles it cost him to hire the horses to bring him here. It is autumn, the most dismal time in a dismal part of the country. Before leaving, however, the narrator asks the brewer's wife where Vyrin is buried and whether someone can show him the way; she offers her ragamuffin son Vanka as a guide. The little cemetery on the outskirts of town where the stationmaster's grave is located turns out to be, in the narrator's telling, one of the saddest sites he has ever seen. As a place, it is a fitting setting for the tears, the *slëzy*, that are the trademark of Vyrin's story. But in pointing out the grave, the boy provides significant new information: the stationmaster's resting place has not been totally forgotten; in fact, it was visited by a magnificent lady sometime after Vyrin died.

> "There was a lady, though, traveled through these parts in the summer: she did ask after the old stationmaster and went a-visiting his grave."
>
> "What sort of a lady?" I asked with curiosity.
>
> "A wonderful lady," replied the urchin; "she was traveling in a coach-and-six with three little masters, a nurse, and a black pug; when they told her the old stationmaster'd died, she started weeping and said to the children, 'You behave yourselves while I go to the graveyard.' I offered to take her, I did, but the lady said, 'I know the way myself.' And she gave me a silver five-kopeck piece—such a nice lady!" (Pushkin [1830] 1983, 102–103)

After lying prone for a long time on the stationmaster's grave, the lady rises, goes into the village, makes a donation to the priest, gives the boy a silver five-kopeck piece, and departs. This information causes Titular

Councilor AGN to change his mind about the futility of his final visit. He too gives the boy a five-kopeck piece and no longer regrets either the trip or the seven-ruble expense.

In presenting the plot of "The Stationmaster," I have gone into more detail than is normally the case because the "facts" of the plot do not work their magic unless they are interpreted both figuratively and literally, ironically, and "on the level." The force field spreading out between the literal meaning of Vyrin's and Dunia's story and its blurred, semantically shaded opposite is precisely where the learning and conceptual experimentation take place that are essential "survival skills" for the reader. By parsing Vyrin's and Dunia's actions, as well as the narrator's responses to those actions, we can test ourselves on where they come down on the issue of what are the limits, if any, to parental love, filial devotion, and exogamous (marrying/mating outside one's social group) desire.

The irony in the storyline becomes immediately discernible if the parable of the Prodigal Son is kept in mind as we analyze Dunia's choices in the role of seemingly wayward child and Vyrin's reactions in the role of doting parent. First, Dunia is not a son but a daughter, and her options, given her social class and sex, are even fewer than those open to Vyrin. Here we notice that the father's feelings for his offspring are perhaps forgivable, but they also tend to reflect back on himself (he brags about her "*s vidom dovol'nogo samoliubiia,*" literally "with an appearance of self-satisfied pride/vanity") and do nothing to promote the girl's personal growth and independence. Her role in the station house is to perform the same chores as her mother. Second, Dunia is given no patrimony, no "bag of money," that she then squanders among "false friends" and "shameless" lovers. Indeed, despite the ambiguity of her relations with Minskii, she is never presented as displaying anything approaching the "lewd behavior" in the parable's second picture. When Vyrin does find her, she is not dressed in rags sharing provender with swine, but attired and bejeweled in the latest fashion. Third, Vyrin does not act as the kind father waiting at home in the parable; instead, he flips roles and he goes out looking for his "lost sheep" (from another parable!) in the story. And fourth, when this "prodigal daughter" finally does return home she is not greeted by the forgiving father but by his silent, "judging" grave.

Let us consider once again Vyrin's social class and where the moral precepts in the story are coming from. Vyrin is not educated, and the pictures depicting the Prodigal Son's pathway from greedy adolescent to contrite young man are accompanied by "decorous German verses," which the stationmaster cannot read. Here we also remember that it was German that Minskii and the doctor spoke in order to trick the stationmaster about his guest's fake illness. In other words, neither the parable as pictured on the wall nor its linguistic glosses help Vyrin in his search for his daughter.

He ignores what the parable is instructing the "good" father to do, that is, wait at home for the son to return and forgive him if he does so, and, moreover, in his ignorance, he is taken advantage of by others who use their superior knowledge (the German of the "decorous verses") against him. This is, of course, completely unfair and is the basis of the tears shed by the stationmaster later in his telling and the sympathy that the narrator feels for him as he listens.

But there are various conflicting emotions taking place in this word-picture of Vyrin and his plight, and that is where Pushkin's irony and the need for conceptual experimentation on the reader's part come in. Just as James Shapiro argues for a "cognitive" basis to the smallest unit of life, a basis that is immanent and inseparable from the cell's functional needs, so do evolutionary biologists and primatologists like Frans de Waal see *morality as growing out of the animal world* and not being superimposed on it from outside or above:

> This brings me back to my bottom-up view of morality. The moral law is not imposed from above or derived from well-reasoned principles; rather, it arises from ingrained values that have been there since the beginning of time. The most fundamental one derives from *the survival value of group life* [my emphasis—DB]. The desire to belong, to get along, to love and be loved, prompt us to do everything in our power to stay on good terms with those on whom we depend. Other social primates share this value and rely on the same filter between emotion and action to reach a mutually agreeable modus vivendi. We see this filter at work when chimpanzee males suppress a brawl over a female, or when baboon males act as if they failed to notice a peanut. It all comes down to inhibitions. (2013, 228)

If we think about Vyrin's actions in the story and apply de Waal's lens to them, other considerations emerge. To begin with, the "well-reasoned principles" of the church, however revered and practiced over generations, may not work in certain situations. Experimentation may be needed if survival is at stake. The hallmarks of morality—empathy, fair play, reciprocity, compassion, altruism, sacrifice for the group—may not be enough if the self is in danger of disappearing entirely. That is Dunia's quandary, which her father, who loves her dearly but blindly, cannot see. She is everything to her father, but she has no life of her own, which Pushkin characteristically leaves unsaid. Perhaps we need to bring out a more "Dunia-centric" view of the plot? The most linguistically telling moment in "The Stationmaster" is when the narrator explains the stationmaster's mistake in letting Dunia go in the following way: "[l]ater the poor stationmaster could not understand how he could have permitted Dunia to go off with the hussar; what had blinded him?" (Pushkin [1830] 1983, 98). In Russian, the "what had blinded him" is rendered literally as "how the blindness had come upon him." It's an impersonal construction. The word for stationmaster in Russian is *smotritel'*, or "he who looks after"—that is, a kind of "watchman." Vyrin believes he has not looked properly after his daughter and that by mistake he has let her get away, but that is not what the morality of the tale is really about. The father is smitten by the daughter's beauty and cleverness, but in his pride, he can see her only in her role as housekeeper, station ornament, and charmer of disgruntled travelers. Through the narrator, Pushkin presents Vyrin's case in a sympathetic light. Many, if not most readers are on the side of Vyrin when they begin to think about what has happened. But then we consider Dunia and her life choices, and the range of morally acceptable positions expands. Morality and fair play exist *in the balance* between the individual and the group.[3] The point is that this is all there already, in what linguistically is the equivalent of a "cellular level," in Pushkin's puns and plot construction: initially, our sympathy for the abandoned father leads us in one direction, which is reinforced by the narrator's rhetorical embellishments ("the poor stationmaster"), but then the play with words, including the "blindness" that obstructs the "watching" man's vision, leads us in another direction.

SEXUAL SELECTION

The other "bottom-up" shaper of emotional and cognitive responses to the story is sexual selection, a term Pushkin would not have used, but which he implicitly understood. At this point, it behooves readers, in particular female readers, to try to imagine themselves as Dunia. What are Dunia's realistic options given her station in life? Lest we forget, Pushkin has given Dunia a peasant name; she is not called Natalia or Olga; thus, everywhere she goes in life, those who pay attention to social hierarchies will know her first by what her name suggests. This would not be much different from a young female today with a name like Juana or Jayla as opposed to Jane or Joan. Dunia is the underdog. In the story, she makes a miraculous transformation from *devochka*, generic "girl," to *barynia*, "married lady of rank," although, again, there is no evidence in the text that she and Minskii have married. This transformation is highly improbable, but Pushkin brings it to life against the odds, and in the constant shadow of the Prodigal Son parable. Why? First, because the poet's creativity is always on the side of young life emerging and of the experiments and risks taken that end up bearing fruit. Finding the right rhyme word in a poem, the one that brings together in an *Aha!* moment both the sound and sense of things in a new way, is just another version of this same instinctive move. But here, the poetic texture of life arriving on the scene is transposed to a prose plot and the story of a lower-class girl with limited prospects. This is where our current understanding of sexual selection comes in. Minskii has the wealth and social status, but it is *ultimately Dunia who chooses him*. She is the one taking the risks. Her moment of decision, captured in her hesitation to leave with Minskii when he offers to drive her to the church, is a crucial inflection point in the tale. Dunia is clearly depicted as an attractive person *and* a good person. When she leaves her father and the church-related moral code his world represents (the pictures on the wall) and chooses to go off with Minskii and the sexual attraction/mate choice he represents, she does not cease to be good. This is the lesson readers will have to internalize. But more is needed before they can understand.

Choosing a mate with whom one will have children is the most awesome decision one can make in life, with the burden for that awesomeness falling disproportionately on the woman. Matters are further complicated by the fact that sexual intercourse itself is an event so suffused with primal feeling that it is seemingly without mind. As the comic stereotype goes, this is especially true of the male side. Still, even with this implicit asymmetry, or power imbalance, it can be argued that evolution has been able to do its work. Just as morality has grown slowly but surely out of the animal world (de Waal 2013), so too has our hominid sexual behavior, with its patterns of courting/withholding, displaying/concealing, importuning/retreating, been adapted over time into something resembling a teetering balance. Likewise, over the millennia, the idea of the sex act—not necessarily how it was performed, but how it was imagined—evolved into more than the "beast with two backs" (*Othello*) and the female's role into more than that of an unwilling body upon whom sex is performed. Recent forays into evolutionary biology tell us, for example, that the female's capacity for arousal is more varied than thought previously.[4] Here, biology and culture are in a kind of tug-of-war, with the male who needs to guarantee paternity, in order for his genetic material to make it to the next generation, restricting female access to other donors *through culture*, including the taboos and prohibitions that insist on monogamy. Sex is of course still sex, and sex-related dehumanization and violence still happen in the world, and too often. But two things can be true at the same time.

As with so much else having to do with the discovery of the immanence of our animal nature, it all goes back to Darwin. And perhaps the most important shift in Darwin's thinking as he progressed from *On the Origin of Species* (1859) to *Descent of Man* (1871) was his honing in on the role of sexual selection, as opposed to natural selection, in the evolutionary process.

> Sexual selection depends on the success of certain individuals over others of the same sex in relation to the propagation of the species; whilst natural selection depends on the success of both sexes, at all ages, in relation to the general conditions of life ([1871] 2010, 445).

Using birds as his most vivid examples, Darwin showed that in certain animals with sufficiently developed nervous systems and cerebral capacity, what tended to happen with regard to the propagation of the species was that choices were made that were "aesthetically motivated," having to do with physical ornamentation and allure, or song or dance, rather than strictly pragmatic, or having to do with protection (the strength or combative ability of the male) or health (no obvious disease, or what later generation scientists would describe as the choice of "good" genes). This distinction is all the more important because subsequent history has, with few exceptions, given Darwin's own thoroughly thought-through judgments and observations about what was at work in sexual selection short shrift. Beginning with Victorians like St. George Mivart and Alfred Russel Wallace, Darwin's co-discoverer of natural selection, and continuing up through present-day (largely gene-centered) neo-Darwinians (Prum 2017, 28–53),[5] it has been broadly assumed that sexual selection is really a subset of natural selection, which is to say, all mating choices made by animals, including humans, are determined primarily by the practical benefits brought by the impregnating male to the receptive female. According to the Wallace/neo-Darwinian line of thought, the adaptations that happen randomly and then are selected for preserving in subsequent generations because they provide a survival benefit are what count in the natural world, hence the idea of *natural* selection. Genetic mutations ("allele frequencies") affecting trait distribution that help a species to survive (when they work) or cause them to die out (when they don't)—think of the famous example of different finches' beaks in the Galapagos—should be considered the transactional items of record in the evolutionary process. Sexual selection, to the extent that it exists, and the neo-Darwinians by now admit that it does, is still only natural selection by another name.

But Darwin's description of the astonishing displays of the male Argus pheasant and the equally astonishing responses of the female Argus pheasant to those displays makes the hard-science (micro-level-upward) attempts to treat this interaction as purely practical, only about "honest" advertising of health and security, and not about an ever more extravagant beauty, seem stubbornly wrong-headed and purblind:

> I know of no fact in natural history more wonderful than that the female Argus pheasant should be able to appreciate the exquisite shading of the ball-and-socket ornaments and the elegant patterns on the wing-feathers of the male. He who thinks that the male was created as he now exists must

> admit that the great plumes, which prevent the wings from being used for flight, and which, as well as the primary feathers, are displayed in a manner quite peculiar to this one species during the act of courtship, and at no other time, were given to him as an ornament: If so, he must likewise admit that the female was created and endowed with the capacity of appreciating such ornaments. I differ only in the conviction that the male Argus pheasant acquired his beauty gradually, through the females having preferred during many generations the more highly ornamented males; the aesthetic capacity of the females having been advanced through exercise or habit in the same manner as our own taste is gradually improved. (Darwin [1871] 2010, 447.)

The economy of mating sequence that Darwin observed so brilliantly here, which we could render in shorthand as "increase in male ornamental beauty leads to increase in female interest/receptivity," shifted the focus to the female for the first time. No longer was it simply the "aggressive" male mounting the "passive" female because it was time to mate and the urge was there, which would be how natural selection explained it in the Victorian era; now it becomes a function of female choice precisely because this is what the female *desires*. Moreover, the change over time in the male Argus pheasant's appearance, the plumes that have become more and more magnificently patterned, have done so *in response to* the female choosing the more extravagant over the less extravagant because that is what arouses her, which also means that the males with "lesser" plumes are rejected and fall away as suitors when their heritable material is not passed on. The male's beautiful wings and the female's discriminating glance are engaged in a coevolutionary dance that, in big-picture terms, changes everything. It didn't matter whether sexual selection had emerged out of natural selection during evolution's broad sweep. What mattered was that sexual selection was pushing species development in another direction, one that was qualitatively different. Darwin could already see in his time that large swaths of human culture, including the fashion industry and the arbitrary, non-utilitarian nature of "style" (compare: "in the same manner as our own taste is gradually improved"), come down to female choice and an arousal that has its origins in sexual selection.

Yale ornithologist Richard Prum builds in fascinating ways on Darwin's original formulations and pushes them further still. Through extensive fieldwork and laboratory study, he makes the case for a science more attuned to how animals, in this case birds, experience the aesthetic in nature. Whether describing in the minutest detail aspects of avian anatomy or analyzing birds' social behavior across a bewildering array of species, Prum probes the moment when the animal world begins to discern the "attractive" or the "aesthetic," when biological morphology and female mate choice come together to reveal the first glimmerings of "mind" in nature.[6] For example, the male bowerbird constructs an elaborate bower for the female made of brightly colored objects and twigs that is tantamount to a miniature throne room. The interested female then comes through the "back door" and tries out the throne to see if it appeals to her. If it doesn't, she exits out the front of the bower structure; if it does, she remains in place to mate.

> Essentially, the evolutionary function of the bower is to provide a setting for aesthetic evaluation that also protects the female from "date rape." [. . .] Because bowers function as both *objects* of choice and *enhancements* of the freedom of choice, they create a new kind of ever-escalating, aesthetic evolutionary feedback. (Prum 2017, 203)

Prum's and others' research indicates, moreover, that this exercise of choice is deliberate and based on a careful winnowing process. In short, the "ladies" are "shopping for" a male that pleases them:

> Most females visited a number of males over a series of days and then returned to revisit a smaller number before finally selecting one of those for their mate. Their choices were strongly skewed toward those males with better-constructed and more highly decorated bowers. These revolutionary data are a strong indication that female bowerbirds make their aesthetic mate choices based on a pool of interactive, experiential data, rather than in response to a simple, hardwired cognitive stimulus threshold. (Prum 2017, 194)

But perhaps Prum's most spectacular example of how biology prepares the way for culture's appreciation of art and beauty involves the anatomy of waterfowl and certain duck species' practice of rough sex. As with Argus pheasants and bowerbirds, female ducks choose their mates based on a coevolved calculus of dances, calls, and feather displays. It turns out that non-territorial, non-monogamous (hence sexually indiscriminate) male ducks—for example, Muscovy ducks, pintails, ruddy ducks, and mallards—often surround females in greater numbers and force themselves on them in coercive acts of copulation that in human culture would be called rape. It also happens, as one of Prum's colleagues, Patricia Brennan, discovered in her research, that the male drake's penis (ninety-seven percent of birds do not have penises) is extremely long in comparison to the actual size of the duck and, when extended during copulation, is flexible (not hard), corkscrew-shaped, and designed to enter into the female in a counterclockwise motion as it seeks out the ovum. But, at the same time, the female's anatomy, which is constructed equally fantastically in an intricate clockwise fashion, makes it challenging for the male's sperm to find its way to the egg, especially if the "intromission" is unwanted:

> How is it, then, that the mate the female chooses can manage to overcome the twists and whorls of her defensive anatomy? How does voluntary sex differ from forced? [. . .] [Brennan's] duck-farm observations revealed that when female Muskovys were actively soliciting copulations, they assumed the conspicuously horizontal precopulatory display posture, dilated the cloacal muscles, and released copious amounts of lubricating mucus. It seems clear that females can make the reproductive tract a fully functioning and welcoming place when they want to. [. . .]
>
> What are the ridiculously long penises of these ducks *doing* inside the female's body? The answer turns out to be, "It depends." If the copulation is solicited, then clearly the female is in for the full ride. [. . .] However, by being overwhelmingly successful at bottling up the penis during forced intromission, and preventing the vast majority of attempts at forced fertilizations, female ducks have managed to maintain the advantage in the sexual arms race. (Prum 2017, 175)

Once again, in shorthand, females *who have chosen males they want* are also able to thwart attempts to impregnate by males they don't want. Discrimination or aesthetic judgment based on beauty/attractiveness trumps physical force, although violence can still certainly be there in the behavior of the frantic males competing with each other to pass on their genetic material.

DUNIA'S CHOICE

These two value force fields—morality and sexual selection—are at the heart of "The Stationmaster" and Dunia's difficult choice. Pushkin captures this agonizing decision-making process through the eyes of the father as well as through the eyes of the sympathetic narrator. When Vyrin sees Dunia caressing Minskii—it is she who is physically playing with his dark curls—we are witness to all the power and beauty of this mate choice in a minimum of words (Pushkin's signature) that only brings out the pain of the father and the sexual attraction, even obsessiveness, of the young couple more forcefully. Once again, the crucial scene:

> Dunia, dressed in all the finery of the latest fashion, sat on the arm of his easy chair like a lady rider on an English saddle. She was looking at Minskii with tenderness, winding his dark locks around her fingers, which glittered with rings. Poor stationmaster! Never had his daughter appeared so beautiful to him; he could not help admiring her. (Pushkin [1830] 1983, 101)

Why would Dunia be looking at Minskii tenderly and touching him in this way except that *she loves him*? Sex has been portrayed for long portions of cultural history as the man being "in the saddle," the king who is "reigning" and "reining" the female body politic. But here it is Dunia who is in control; she sits on the arm of the chair like a "lady rider on an English saddle." Minskii is situated not above her, the mount, but below her, as though he is the one being ridden. Her beauty is culturally mediated, cloaked in the "latest finery" and ornamented with glittering rings—signs of social status that make her more desirable. But she understands (and Pushkin understands) that, for young life to emerge, her beauty needs to be joined with Minskii's dashing vitality and social capital, while the father, who has the strong moral claim, can only look on in misery.[7]

In the human realm, it is not the drab female who chooses the fantastically accoutered male. Roles have largely reversed, while gender, a wholly subjective category that is not the same as biological sex, enters the picture.[8] Over millions of years, evolution has built out an entire ecosystem between the human mind's imaginings and the sex act itself: skin can serve as ornamentation (tattoos) just as the add-ons of dress and jewelry can; what one doesn't show can create as much of a come-on as what one does show. This is the basis of Freud's argument that art exists as diversion, foreplay ("sublimation"): words in their way work like the presence or absence of clothing to arouse and make us curious. But that is only part of the story. The Dunia of "The Stationmaster" not only survives, she survives, one might say, *beautifully*. She survives as a woman making tough choices, a woman who may be aware of her own beauty (the "little coquette" of the first scene) but who is not sentimental about that beauty. Natural selection moves forward passively, stumbling onto ways to survive without thinking about it, but sexual selection, because it chooses based on what it wants, *makes itself aware of itself as it decides.* It also is linked to the birth of artistic representation because the latter, when done well, gives us the sense of life emerging, which involves sex, to be sure, but is also more than sex.

Human life emerging is mind and body acting in concert and moving about in the world in ways that balance morality and sexual selection against each other, for the sake of the group or population. The reason the narrator was pleased by the ending to the tale provided by Vanka was because it reinserted a moral counterweight to the earlier scenes of Dunia choosing her own desires over her father's. The story needs the lad's vivid description of the lovely lady who comes to visit the stationmaster's grave. Pushkin, in his playful seriousness, tells a modern parable of the Prodigal Son that is turned upside down in every way: son is daughter, daughter is not prodigal, father turns to drink and becomes "prodigal" himself, daughter returns home to father too late, father doesn't forgive the child ("you cannot help sinning in your heart and wishing her in the grave"), and so on. The church's prescriptions don't help when applied narrowly. But the essence of a moral worldview is retained. Dunia does feel guilty that she abandoned her father, and she knows that her happiness—the well-heeled *barchata* ("little masters/nobles"), the nursemaid, the lapdog, the impressive carriage—has been purchased at a cost. She shows this by tipping Vanka and making an offering at the church. "'What sort of lady?' I asked with curiosity. 'A nice [*slavnaia*] lady,' replied the urchin" (Pushkin [1830] 1983, 102). We never find out whether Minskii and Dunia have wed, as Pushkin refuses to close this moralistic loop. Common-law marriages between noblemen and women outside their social class did happen; in any event, it is beside the point. Pushkin, who had difficult relations with his own parents, wrote this story on the eve of his marriage to one of the most beautiful young women in Russia, Natalia Goncharova. He too was trying to find a balance between a past littered with mistakes of prodigality and the prospect of married life and a new family. And he was writing these efforts into "The Stationmaster" by giving his heroine *agency*—something he would do increasingly with the female characters of his mature period.[9]

NOTES

1. This essay is a reworking and adaptation of a chapter in my *The Pushkin Project: Russia's Favorite Writer, Modern Evolutionary Thought, and Teaching Inner-City Youth* (2023).
2. "My guiding conviction is that mind is not just an afterthought or an accident or an add-on, but a basic aspect of nature" (2012, 16).
3. See, for example, the first chapter of Michael Tomasello's *A Natural History of Human Morality* (2016).
4. The scientific literature here is vast. A classic text on the subject is David M. Buss (2016), especially the chapter "What Women Want" (31–77). See also Daniel Bergner (2013).
5. "Neo-Darwinians" are such scholar-scientists as, for example, W. D. Hamilton, John Maynard Smith, George Williams, Richard Dawkins, Daniel Dennett.
6. It can be argued that Prum is being highly speculative here. Couldn't the choices about prey or the ability to negotiate hierarchies of dominance also be signs of "mind"? Yes. But I still believe Prum's research is a necessary corrective to the exclusively utilitarian approach to mate choice of the neo-Darwinians, just as I think the female's response (her calculated *choice*) to what can only be called aesthetic criteria is a crucial dividing line in this case. My thanks to Tom Dolack for this observation.
7. See Buss (2016, 35).
8. Other primates also show sex-typical behavior by watching others. Frans de Waal compares these behaviors in humans, chimpanzees, and bonobos in his most recent book *Different: Gender Through the Eyes of a Primatologist* (2022).
9. Compare Tatiana (*Eugene Onegin*), Liza ("The Queen of Spades"), Masha Mironova (*The Captain's Daughter*).

BIBLIOGRAPHY

Bergner, Daniel. 2013. *What Do Women Want? Adventures in the Science of Female Desire*. New York: Ecco.

Bethea, David M. 2023. *The Pushkin Project: Russia's Favorite Writer, Modern Evolutionary Thought, and Teaching Inner-City Youth*. Boston: Academic Studies Press.

Buss, David M. [1994] 2016. *The Evolution of Desire: Strategies of Human Mating*. Rev. ed. New York: Basic.

Darwin, Charles. [1871] 2010. *The Descent of Man*. Mineola: Dover.

De Waal, Frans. 2013. *The Bonobo and the Atheist: In Search of Humanism among the Primates*. New York: Norton.

De Waal, Frans. 2022. *Different: Gender Through the Eyes of a Primatologist*. New York: Norton.

Mazur, Susan. 2015. *The Paradigm Shifters: Overthrowing "The Hegemony of the Culture of Darwin."* New York: Caswell Books, 2015.

Nagel, Thomas. 2012. *Mind and Cosmos: Why the Materialist Neo-Darwinian Conception of Nature is Almost Certainly False*. New York: Oxford University Press.

Prum, Richard O. *The Evolution of Beauty: How Darwin's Forgotten Theory of Mate Choice Shapes the Animal World—and Us*. New York: Doubleday.

Pushkin, Alexander. [1830] 1983. *The Complete Prose Fiction*. Translated by Paul Debreczeny. Stanford: Stanford University Press.

Tomasello, Michael. 2016. *A Natural History of Human Morality*. Cambridge, MA: Harvard University Press.

2

Flow and Selfhood in Leo Tolstoy's *Anna Karenina*

A Case Study of the Mowing Scene

David S. Danaher

The cognitive psychologist Keith Oatley has argued that stories are narrative simulations "that run not on computers but on minds" (2011, 17). In reading, we create "our own version of the piece of fiction, our own dream, our own enactment" (Oatley 2011, 18), and the mental model of the narrative we construct connects "to aspects of our own selves, to our own memories, to our own concerns" (Oatley 2011, 19). The cognitive literary analyst Lisa Zunshine has developed a framework compatible with Oatley's, calling the novel a "cognitive experiment" (2006, 22) in which readers are expected to "try on" characters' mental states for psychological size (2006, 17). In this study, I will explore the import of Oatley's and Zunshine's approach to fiction as cognitive simulation for a reading of the famous mowing scene in Tolstoy's *Anna Karenina* (1878).

More concretely, I will read Levin's mowing experience through the lens of the experimental psychologist Mihaly Csikszentmihalyi's concept of flow (1990)[1] with help from the psychologist Jerome Bruner's work on narrativity and selfhood (1990). At the same time, however, we who seek to read literary works through the lens of cognitive science should be careful to ask ourselves what specifically a cognitive reading can tell us about a given work that has not already been said, if in different terms, by literary critics.[2] As Zunshine has rightly cautioned, we should be "suspicious of any cognitive reading so truly 'original' that it can find no support in any of the existing literary critical paradigms" (2006, 5). In this spirit, I aim for a dialogue with scholars who have written generally on Tolstoy as both thinker and literary stylist and in particular on the mowing scene.

The fruits of this dialogue between experimental psychologists and literary scholars will result in a cognitively refreshed reading of the mowing scene, which means that I will present a renewed reading of this much-analyzed scene through the lens of cognitive psychology. More concretely speaking, this reading will add to our understanding of Tolstoy as a psychological realist and careful stylist who seems to have anticipated research from late twentieth-century cognitive science. Reading the mowing scene through a cognitive lens will also help us appreciate more clearly Tolstoy's intent: what, in other words, was he trying to model for readers at the time and how can we, as contemporary readers who know little to nothing about mowing with a scythe, make sense of—if not personally relate to—Levin's experience? This approach to the mowing scene also has direct implications for how we might teach the novel, and I will explore aspects of this below.

Much cognitive literary analysis proceeds, generally speaking, in one direction only: we apply ideas taken from the realm of cognitive psychology to help us better understand literary texts. Given, however, that an authentic dialogue is a two-way conversation, I will conclude this study by suggesting how Tolstoy's fictional account of mowing in *Anna Karenina* may also help us better understand Csikszentmihalyi's concept of flow.

LEVIN'S MOWING-AS-FLOW

Csikszentmihalyi's 1990 book summarizes decades of research "on the positive aspects of human experience—joy, creativity, the process of total involvement with life [he] call[s] *flow*" (1990, xi). Briefly defined, flow is a state of mind in which a person becomes completely immersed in an activity; it is how people describe their state of mind when consciousness is harmoniously ordered and they want to do what they are doing for its own sake (Csikszentmihalyi 1990, 6). Csikszentmihalyi conducted interviews with thousands of people from different walks of life (ages, genders, classes, occupations) in an effort to map out the parameters of flow, and the research clearly indicated that different kinds of optimal experiences "were described in the same way" (1990, 4).

It is remarkable to note that the parameters of a flow experience, as Csikszentmihalyi describes them, map directly onto Tolstoy's description of Levin's experience of mowing. In *Anna Karenina*, then, Tolstoy seemingly anticipates research in experimental cognitive psychology that would be articulated more than a century later. The details here are telling, and I will focus on five central aspects of a flow experience that emerge from Csikszentmihalyi's research and are explicitly reproduced in Tolstoy's mowing scene.[3]

1. Flow occurs when we confront a task that we have a chance of completing, and that task usually has clear goals and is bounded by clear rules. This allows for immediate feedback on what we are doing, and, in turn, facilitates the development of a definite degree of control over the task.

This is precisely what Levin experiences while mowing. Indeed, the Tolstoy scholar Richard Gustafson has analyzed the development of Levin's mowing experience, arguing that the mowing scene can be divided into three parts that "represent the three stages of Levin's learning his task" (1982, 101). In the first stage of engaging in the task, he mows with an older peasant named Titus, who serves as a tutor. Levin has mowed before but not, as the text informs us, in a long while, and in this first stage his strokes of the scythe are irregular, and, as a result, he "mowed poorly for the first few minutes" (iv) while still managing not to fall behind the other mowers. After a collective pause for breakfast, Levin returns to mowing in a position between an older experienced peasant and a younger one mowing for the first time, and here Levin "is neither master nor novice, just in-between, entering the intermediate stage of his learning" (Gustafson 1982, 102). In this second stage, Levin begins to experience mowing more and more as flow along the parameters outlined below. By Gustafson's third and culminating stage, Levin has achieved a definite degree of control over the task, and he mows joyfully in full flow.

2. As we experience flow, our sense of time is altered: hours pass by in minutes, and minutes may seem to stretch out for hours. Tolstoy profiles this sensation twice during Levin's mowing. Early on, while still struggling to mow proficiently, "Levin lost all awareness of time and had no idea whether it was late or early" (iv). Later, when Levin has entered flow and become absorbed in the task of mowing, this detail is repeated: "Levin did not notice how the time passed. If he had been asked how long he had been mowing, he would have said half an hour—yet it was nearly dinner-time" (v).

3. In experiencing flow, "the person's attention is completely absorbed by the activity" to the point that "the activity becomes spontaneous, almost automatic" (Csikszentmihalyi 1990, 53). In flow, we stop being aware of ourselves as distinct from the task we are performing (Csikszentmihalyi 1990, 53), and performing the task comes to seem effortless.

Details in Tolstoy's unfolding of the mowing scene again map onto this aspect of the flow experience. Levin clearly becomes absorbed in the activity: "He thought of nothing, desired nothing, except not to lag behind and to do the best job he could" (iv). It begins to rain, and Levin "suddenly felt a pleasant sensation of coolness on his hot, sweaty shoulders" (iv), but he is so absorbed in the task that he is initially unable to understand the source of the coolness. After this, a change "now began to take place in his work which gave him enormous pleasure" (iv), and he starts to experience moments "when he forgot what he was doing and began to feel light, and in those moments his swath came out as even and good as Titus's" (iv). When Levin's absorption is interrupted by actively thinking about the task, "he at once felt how hard the work was and the swath came out badly" (iv). Gradually, however, as Levin gives himself over to the task, mowing ceases to "seem so hard to him" (v). He experiences "more and more often those moments of unconsciousness [. . .] when it was possible for him not to think of what he was doing" when, seemingly, the "scythe cut by itself" (v).

Csikszentmihalyi notes that flow experiences are often far from being actually effortless in that they may require intense physical exertion, as in rock climbing, or highly disciplined mental focus, as in creative writing (1990, 54). Tolstoy makes this element of Levin's experience also explicit, emphasizing that Levin's awareness of the physical demands of mowing diminishes as he becomes more proficient—and more absorbed—in the task.

4. While in flow, our deep but seemingly effortless involvement in the task removes us from awareness of the worries and frustrations of everyday life. In the mowing scene, this aspect of flow follows in part from point 2: Levin's absorption in the task leaves no room for conscious thought devoted to everyday concerns. Indeed, the longer he mows,

> the more often he felt those moments of oblivion during which it was no longer his arms that swung the scythe, but the scythe itself that lent motion to his whole body, full of life and conscious of itself, and, as if by magic, without a thought of it, the work got rightly and neatly done on its own. (v)

These "blissful moments" (v) of oblivion distance Levin from his everyday worries.

This aspect of mowing-as-flow also takes shape also from Tolstoy's deliberate juxtaposition of the mowing scene with the preceding chapters (ii and iii) that set the stage for mowing, in which everyday worries and frustrations, prompted in part by Koznyshev's visit to Levin's country estate, are given center stage. Gustafson's analysis frames this juxtaposition in terms of the novel as a whole, noting that part III of the novel deals with various "crises of vocation," and that this provides the immediate context for the mowing scene (1982, 97). Indeed, Gustafson highlights Levin's frustrating conversation with Koznyshev in chapter iii over the tension between the "personal" and "common" interest (*lichnoe* vs *obshchee delo*) as it relates to Levin's quest for a vocation, noting that the opening of chapter iv introduces mowing as the "personal matter [*lichnoe delo*] that had occupied Levin during his conversation with his brother" (iv). There are other thematic and linguistic echoes of Levin's conversation with Koznyshev from chapter iii in the two mowing chapters that Gustafson does not mention in his analysis, and these reinforce the point that mowing distances Levin from the vexation (*razdrazhenie*) that he experiences during the argumentative conversation. Following on Gustafson's point, chapter iii's conversation also frames Levin's mowing revelation in philosophical terms: what Levin learns in mowing becomes understood as a general (or, again, "common") philosophical truth (*obshchaia istina*, which echoes the phrase *obshchee delo*) about the relationship between the personal/individual and the common/general. In mowing, Levin arrives at a philosophical truth not through verbal argument grounded in logical reasoning (*rassuzhdenie*) but instead wordlessly and—via flow—with his whole being. In the post-mowing chapter vi, Koznyshev implicitly acknowledges this by conceding certain points made by Levin during the pre-mowing conversation in chapter iii—and also by being infected with Levin's rapturous state of mind after the mowing has been completed (more on this point below).

Numerous linguistic details also connect chapters ii and iii with the mowing chapters. There is, for example, a repetition of the verb *razobrat'*, which has a variety of contextual meanings that include "to disassemble, dismantle," "to sort out," and "to discern" something through perception. In chapter ii, Koznyshev at one point "sorts" his fishing rods ("His brother sat down under the bush, sorting [*razobrav*] his fishing rods"). In chapter iii, Levin is distracted from his brother's conversational argument as he peers into the distance to try to discern (*razobrat'*) whether what he sees is a horse or a mounted steward, and a vexing response to a point made by his brother is followed by Levin's having finally perceived (*razobrav*) "that what he saw was the plowing"—and this act of perception both foreshadows Levin's eagerness to take part in mowing and suggests that what happens on the land (plowing, mowing) is somehow associated with the conversation between the two brothers. The *razobrat'* localized motif is, then, about sorting out the relationship between parts and wholes, and this word is used to denote both disassembling something into constituent parts (the fishing rods, which serve as an emblem for disassembling through rational analysis[4]) as well as reassembling parts into a perceived whole (Levin's discernment of the distant plowing). In this way, given that individual people are constituent parts of the larger social whole, this micro-motif echoes the overarching thematic tension that Gustafson highlights between personal interest (*lichnoe delo*) and the common cause (*obshchee delo*).

Other linguistic echoes that frame the mowing experience in terms of the preceding argument include: "shrugging of shoulders," which Koznyshev does dismissively in response to a point made by Levin in iii and which in iv the mowers, including Levin, then do "joyfully under the pleasant freshness" of the rain; Levin's rhetorically negative invocation of the "birches [*berezki*] we stick up on the day of the Trinity" (iii) juxtaposed with the "boletus mushrooms [that is, *berezovye* or birch mushrooms in the original Russian]" that the older, experienced peasant seemingly effortlessly bends down to pick up while mowing to save as a "treat" for his old woman (iv); and the phrase "from all sides [*so vsekh storon*]" that conveys Levin's dismay during the argument in iii ("He felt himself roundly beaten [*On chuvstvoval, chto on razbit so vsekh storon*]"), but then his joy in iv at being surrounded by others absorbed in the common task of mowing ("Crowding on all sides in the short swaths, [. . .] the mowers urged each other on" [*Tesnivshiesia po korotkim riadam kostsy so vsekh storon (. . .) podgoniali drug druga*].[5] In each of these instances, the selected phrase has a negative connotation in the context of the argument in iii that is then transformed into a positive meaning in iv in the context of Levin's mowing experience, which implies that Levin's mowing acts somehow as a corrective to the argument with Koznyshev that precedes it.

Indeed, we can draw inspiration once again from Csikszentmihalyi's work to concretize one aspect of the way that the mowing scene acts as a corrective to the vexing conversation that precedes it. Csikszentmihalyi draws an essential and fruitful distinction between "pleasure" on the one hand and "enjoyment" on the other (1990, 46ff). Pleasure, Csikszentmihalyi notes, is important for our quality of life, but we can feel it without much effort, and it does not ultimately lead to psychological growth: "Pleasure helps to maintain order, but by itself cannot create new order in consciousness" (1990, 46). Enjoyment, however, is characterized by "forward movement: by a sense of novelty, of accomplishment," so that playing a sport stretches one's abilities and is, in this way, not merely pleasurable, but enjoyable (Csikszentmihalyi 1990, 46). Pleasure is evanescent, and "the self does not grow as a consequence of pleasurable experiences" (Csikszentmihalyi 1990, 47); enjoyment, however, transforms the self: "After an enjoyable event we know that we have changed, that our self has grown: in some respect, we have become more complex as a result of it" (Csikszentmihalyi 1990, 46). Bringing this distinction to bear on the text, we can say that Koznyshev takes a shallow and clichéd kind of pleasure being in the countryside while, in contrast, mowing is clearly an enjoyable experience that transforms Levin's sense of self—and the contradictory nature of their views on nature and the countryside is an explicit theme in the chapter that immediately precedes the actual mowing.

We could also mention here, following Gustafson, that, as the mowing scene develops, the narration shifts from a strong focus on Levin's personal consciousness of the activity—his personal challenges of engaging in mowing as a flow experience—to a collectively joyful representation of the task along with lyrical descriptions of the natural beauty of the mown spaces. Levin does not merely forget the spiritual vexation he experiences in iii during the argument with his brother, but that vexation is transformed, via the language of the text, into a kind of spiritual revelation as a result of his mowing. This is both consistent with Csikszentmihalyi's assertion that a flow experience "excludes the interference of disorder in consciousness" (1990, 58) and is simultaneously indicative of the way that Tolstoy's depiction of mowing-as-flow puts Levin on the path toward spiritual transformation (more on this immediately below).

5. In flow, concern for the self disappears, yet paradoxically a stronger sense of self emerges from the experience; flow is not about pleasure, but rather about complexifying enjoyment. Csikszentmihalyi argues that, in a normal life, we spend a lot of time thinking about ourselves, but in flow this preoccupation with self disappears because "there is no room for self-scrutiny" (1990, 63). This loss of self-consciousness does not, however, result in a loss of self and "certainly not a loss of consciousness, but rather, only a loss a consciousness *of* the self" (Csikszentmihalyi 1990, 64). When we are free from self-preoccupation in this way, "we actually have a chance to expand the concept of who we are," which means that the flow-induced loss of self-consciousness may "lead to self-transcendence, to a feeling that boundaries of our being have been pushed forward" (Csikszentmihalyi 1990, 64). It is seemingly paradoxical that losing our sense of self in a flow experience may complexify our sense of self—that sense emerges stronger after the experience is over—but the post-flow self that a person reflects upon "is not the same self that existed before the flow experience: it is now enriched by new skills and fresh achievements" (Csikszentmihalyi 1990, 66). In this respect, it almost seems that "occasionally giving up self-consciousness is necessary for building a strong self-concept" (Csikszentmihalyi 1990, 64).

This aspect of a flow experience is not merely reproduced in Levin's mowing—it lies at the heart of Tolstoy's project "to transform the nature of realism" (Gustafson 1986, 203) as we see that project play out in the mowing scene. Gustafson argues that Tolstoyan realism is deeply emblematic because "he sees that the world is the embodiment and revelation of spiritual truth," which means "his representation of that world must embody and reveal that truth" (1986, 203). For Tolstoy, nature is a privileged place for emblematic revelation, and Levin's mowing illustrates this well: "The privileged moment in Tolstoy's fiction is the characters' encounter with the expanse of nature" in which moments of movement outward and toward this expanse become "emblematic of the characters' discovery of the Divine" (Gustafson 1986, 213). In these privileged moments, characters are removed from both a preoccupation with the self and the kind of human interaction depicted in Levin's argument with Koznyshev, and they "feel the sudden joy of life" (Gustafson 1986, 213). In emblematic realism, then, a character's—and, since Tolstoy uses narrative focalization to prompt reader simulation, a reader's—experience of nature often represents "a moment of grace": an encounter with nature in Tolstoy's writing often results, as it does here with Levin, in the birth of a character's inner spiritual life (Gustafson 1986, 213).[6]

Indeed, mowing for Levin is not mere pleasure, like fishing in the countryside is for Koznyshev, but a kind of deep enjoyment that complexifies him as an individual and helps him understand better his life's vocation: the experience changes the way Levin sees himself and his relationship to the world. His mowing experience can be read, then, as a catalyst for spiritual transformation, and this is a reading that Gustafson highlights in his analysis. What Levin learns in mowing, and what other Tolstoyan characters either know intuitively or discover through other experiences, often mediated by an encounter with nature, is a "knowledge of God which comes with the loss of self," and by means of this knowledge certain essential questions of identity and vocation are at least partly resolved (Gustafson 1986, 455). The loss of self-consciousness that comes with flow is key here for Gustafson: "For Tolstoy the recollection of self as personality blocks the awareness of the Divine" (Gustafson 1986, 338). Tolstoy is less concerned with individual personalities than with an individual's participation in the world as a whole, and as a result of mowing, Levin's "part rejoins the whole and, dispersed throughout, the 'I' finally reaches the 'non-I' and lives in everything, in a loving seizure of the All" (Gustafson 1986, 455). In losing his sense of self, Levin takes a step on the path by which one "achieves salvation through deification" (Gustafson 1986, 455).[7]

This reading suggests a twist on the tension between the personal and the common/general that is such a sore point in the pre-mowing argument with his brother. For Levin, mowing-as-flow is not so much an individual experience, like Koznyshev's fishing, as much as it is the spiritually revelatory experience of an individual whose consciousness of his personal self has been muted as he works with others in a common effort: his mowing is not understood as a personal achievement but rather as a transformative experience of who he is and of his place in the world. We might see this as one significant way in which Tolstoy differs from Csizkszentmihaly: the latter focuses exclusively on individual experiences of flow.

In Tolstoy's framing, moreover, the strong spiritual dimension of this revelatory experience impacts not only Levin himself: it changes the way others view the world, at least in a certain circumscribed sense, given that his post-flow rapturous state of mind leads to an irrepressible cheerfulness with which he infects his brother. In vi, the narrator twice repeats that Koznyshev does not want to part from his brother (*rasstavat'sia s bratom*), and the awkwardness of the conversation that preceded, but is closely linked to, Levin's mowing is more or less forgotten. This chapter also brings a letter from Stiva, who writes that Dolly is in the country near Levin's estate, and he urges Levin to go visit. This news and the subsequent visit will set the stage for reconciliation between Levin and Kitty. Mowing-as-flow thus has implications in the novel that ripple outward—toward other characters as well as toward Levin's future self.

It should go without saying that mowing-as-flow is not the endpoint of Levin's struggle to understand himself, but it is a key moment in that struggle.[8] Gustafson has argued that the mowing scene is emblematic of a life moment in which discord and division are replaced by love and harmony and that, for Tolstoy, "this fundamental action is the sole vocation of human life" (1982, 106). In mowing, Levin experiences this action as a "process of learning," and this is represented neither as a disembodied mystical experience (like other characters in the novel have) nor as a process of abstract mentation (as illustrated by Koznyshev's intellectual practice), but as something that "must happen right here in ordinary life" (Gustafson 1982, 106). Levin does not master this "fundamental action" while mowing, "but he does practice it, and in this sense the mowing scene is an emblem of the practice of love" (Gustafson 1982, 107).

NARRATIVITY AND SELFHOOD

To unpack even more what is cognitively and aesthetically at stake in the mowing scene, we can turn briefly to another late twentieth-century experimental psychologist, Jerome Bruner, and specifically to his work on narrativity and selfhood. Bruner argues that the self is a largely discursive construction; that is, we *narrate* selfhood to ourselves and to others (1990, 114). We develop and revise our self-narratives as we have new experiences, which means that selfhood is "not a static thing or substance, but a configuring of personal events into an historical unity which includes not only what one has been but also anticipations of what one will be" (Bruner 1990, 116). Bruner echoes Tolstoy, then, in envisioning the self as a *practice* in that it is distributed in the experiences and interactions that we have, the activities we engage in and then talk about with others (Bruner 1990, 117). Given this, it is easy to agree that Tolstoy represents

Levin's experience of mowing—indeed, across Levin's character arc—in a way that conforms to Bruner's conception.

At the same time, however, Bruner makes clear that selfhood is also necessarily mediated through a culture-specific folk psychology: the self "must be treated as a construction that, so to speak, proceeds from the outside in as well as from the inside out, from culture to mind as well as from mind to culture" (1990, 108). All cultures have

> as one of their most powerful cognitive instruments [. . .] a set of more or less connected, more or less normative descriptions about how human beings 'tick,' what our own and other minds are like, what one can expect situated action to be like, what are possible modes of life, how one commits oneself to them, and so on. (Bruner 1990, 35)

Moreover, we learn our culture's folk psychology at an early age, and we "learn it as we learn to use the very language we acquire and to conduct the interpersonal transactions required in communal life" (Bruner 1990, 35). A given culture's folk psychology therefore has canonical status in that it "summarizes not simply how things are but (often implicitly) how they should be"—and when things are as they should be, "the narratives of folk psychology are unnecessary" (Bruner 1990, 39–40). We might say that Bruner emphasizes the common (*obshchee*) symbolic systems that people in a given culture use to construct meaning: these systems constitute "a very special kind of communal tool kit that make the user a reflection of the community" (1990, 11).

As Bruner further argues, however, stories often prove meaningful to the extent that they serve to explicate deviations from these entrenched symbolic systems in a form that is understandable to others: "it is only when constituent beliefs in a folk psychology are violated that narratives are constructed" (1990, 47). What gives many stories verisimilitude is that their function "is to find an intentional state that mitigates or at least makes comprehensible a deviation from a canonical pattern" (Bruner 1990, 49–50). Moreover, another critical feature of storytelling for Bruner is that it "specializes in the forging of links between the exceptional and the ordinary" (Bruner 1990, 47). It should be easy to see how Levin's experience of mowing also models this aspect of Bruner's narrative framework.

Concretely speaking, Levin's quest for selfhood is marked by the tension he experiences between self-authenticity and the cultural expectations deriving from the aristocratic milieu that he inhabits. Put succinctly, Levin is always swimming against the folk psychology entrenched in that milieu. Koznyshev's persona and the argumentative discussion that precedes the mowing illustrate this tension, but Levin's character in this regard is already well established by the time the reader gets to the mowing scene. We could say that one aspect of it is Levin's disdain for fellow nobles who live primarily for pleasure: Koznyshev fits into this given his attitude toward vacationing in the countryside, but it is really Oblonsky who embodies this attitude most prominently. Other characters, like Karenin, seem to accept their roles in the aristocracy and see it as their vocation to make the best possible career within the system as it exists. Levin, however, finds himself uncomfortable with pursuing either of these life paths: he struggles to find his own way, and he violates the norms of his milieu in just about every situation. As the text makes clear, it is already a considerable violation of canonical social norms for an estate-owning aristocrat to mow alongside the peasants.

In Bruner's framework, Levin's dilemma is that the self is not located in "the fastness of immediate private consciousness but in a cultural-historical situation as well" (1990, 107). Tolstoy narrates Levin's mowing as an experience that becomes a concrete, physical catalyst for reshaping the much broader folk psychology of self that is imposed by the cultural-historical situation of his milieu. His mowing liberates him, at least provisionally, as a kind of practice that violates expected folk-psychological norms, from the artificiality and inauthenticity of the pleasure- and career-seeking nobles that populate the pages of the novel. In this way, it is also an ordinary activity that comes to have, in Tolstoy's larger narrative, an exceptional impact. Tolstoy's aim here is to defamiliarize the existing communal toolkit by narrating an alternative symbolic representation.

The revelatory experience of mowing for Levin is, at the same time, carefully crafted by Tolstoy so that readers of the novel may themselves try it on for psychological size. This means that Levin's experience serves as a model also for readers, which is a point implicit in Bruner's approach to narrativity and selfhood. Indeed, Gustafson, among others, has clarified that the highest aim of Tolstoy's narrative technique "is to create in the reader a sense of at-onement with the represented character or event" so that the reader's knowledge "tends toward an internalization of the represented experience" (1986, 264). The world as Tolstoy takes pains to represent it "enters the reader's consciousness, not as knowledge about something alien, but as something the reader himself is experiencing," and readers come to know the other as they know themselves (Gustafson 1986, 264). Gustafson points out that moments of moral decision in Tolstoy's fiction tend to be represented not as moments of active decision-making "but as moments of tiny, tiny alterations of consciousness" that Tolstoy brings into focus by showing them "in process and slow motion" (1986, 303). These moments of altered consciousness—of mowing that becomes a symbolic act of transgression against entrenched cultural expectations—are represented "as journeys of self-discovery" for both the characters in the novel and readers of it (Gustafson 1986, 303).

In this connection and to shift from Bruner back to Csikszentmihalyi (1996), we might also ask to what extent we consider Levin to be a creative person. Csikszentmihalyi's work on creativity emerged concurrently with his work on flow, and in it he draws a distinction between someone who is "personally creative" and someone whose creative production has impacted a society's culture as a whole in some important respect (1996, 25). Levin is certainly depicted by Tolstoy as *personally* creative, and we might also see him on a path toward possibly becoming creative in Csikszentmihalyi's broader sense, that is, as someone "whose thoughts or actions change a domain, or establish a new domain" (1996, 28). Tolstoy shows readers this possibility in process, especially since readers already know of Levin's (never-realized) intention to write a book on agriculture that will attempt to change the way that domain is viewed. At the same time, we must also acknowledge that Levin's character in the novel is an emblematic force for Tolstoy's own high-impact creativity in the specific society in which he lived as well as in the greater world at the time—and, at least to some degree, since that time. If high-impact creativity is a "systemic rather than an individual phenomenon" (Csikszentmihalyi 1996, 23), then we must see Levin's mowing as one specific moment in Tolstoy's larger creative career, a moment that narrates—and simultaneously invites the reader to simulate—one character's flow-mediated epiphany and the impact that this experience has on that character's quest for self-understanding.[9]

TEACHING THE MOWING SCENE

One challenge of teaching *Anna Karenina* to twenty-first-century students is to somehow bridge the temporal and cultural gap between the society that Tolstoy describes and our own in order to facilitate a reading of the novel as a cognitive simulation that we ourselves may try on for psychological size. Few contemporary readers, for example, know anything at all about mowing with a scythe. For Russian readers at the time, however, the setting of the novel and the specific activities depicted were not exotic. How, then, can we mediate between these two differing perspectives and do so in a way that creates what L. Dee Fink has called a "significant learning experience" (2003) for student-readers of the novel?

Fink notes that a significant learning experience requires students to be actively engaged in their own learning with a view toward an experience that "results in significant changes in the students, changes that continue after the course is over and even after the students have graduated" (2003, 7). Significant learning may take different forms, and Fink develops a useful taxonomy for us to consider and which I will briefly summarize here

(2003, 30–60). *Foundational knowledge* provides content-based understanding, and in our case, this would mean knowledge of Tolstoy as a writer, of *Anna Karenina* as a particular novel in his oeuvre, and of the situatedness of the mowing scene within that novel. Another dimension in the taxonomy is the *application* of foundational knowledge for critical, creative, or practical thinking and action, and this could take many forms depending on didactic intent. *Integration* is another dimension, one that profiles the development of connections between ideas, people, and realms of life. The *human dimension* of learning is yet another: it explores "the personal and social implications" of the learning, which may then result in a new self-image for students or "a new vision of what they want to become" (Fink 2003, 31); closely related to this is also a *caring* dimension that allows students to develop new feelings, interests, and values. Finally, we have a dimension in which students *learn how to learn*, which might mean that they develop tools for critical reading that extend beyond the specific text under consideration. In his methodological work on designing significant learning experiences, Fink emphasizes above all that we as teachers need to move beyond a focus on foundational knowledge to other dimensions in the learning taxonomy: in other words, we need to go beyond mere "content mastery" (2003, 33).

One way to do so with regard to teaching the mowing scene that simultaneously helps bridge the cultural/temporal gap is to frame Levin's mowing, as this study does, in terms of cognitive psychology—to mediate our reading of the mowing scene through Csikszentmihalyi's concept of flow and Bruner's ideas on narrativity and selfhood. If primed with the parameters of a flow experience and with a description of Bruner's framework, students could themselves conduct a close reading of the mowing scene, much like the one presented in this study, to map out the similarities (and also differences) between Tolstoy's depiction and the frameworks developed by Csikszentmihalyi and Bruner. In addition to this, students could be asked to provide examples of flow experiences from their own lives, if not also examples of the power of narrative framing for self-understanding. Could they, in other words, read the impact of Levin's mowing through a similar and familiar cognitive experience that has provided them with not just pleasure, but complexifying enjoyment, and that may, even in some strategic way, have significantly impacted the development of their own self-images?

One goal here would be to move beyond a primary focus on the novel's content (that is, foundational knowledge) to engage holistically with other dimensions of Fink's learning taxonomy, and a pedagogical approach to the mowing scene such as the one outlined above would open space for doing so. It would be not too far-fetched to claim that Levin himself, while mowing, has a "significant learning experience"—indeed, this is the main thrust of this scene in the novel as a whole. Levin does not merely cut grass, which would be the foundational goal of mowing. His flow experience also develops his abilities for critical and creative thinking, it facilitates a deeper sense of integration of self to others and to the world around him, it results in a new self-conception, and it cultivates a profound sense of caring—and all these correlate directly with dimensions of significant learning in Fink's taxonomy. Levin arguably also learns better how to learn: his experience mowing teaches him something about the All that provides him with a lens through which to view, or rather reevaluate, his life as a whole. This last point is key for Tolstoy, but it seems to be equally key in Fink's taxonomy. What Levin essentially learns is the need to integrate the "personal" (*lichnoe*) and the "common" (*obschee*), and Fink's analysis strongly implies that this is also valid, in a domain-specific way, for any learning experience that could be authentically termed "significant."

A related goal in mediating a reading of the mowing scene through ideas in modern cognitive psychology would be to underline that Levin's experience is not anomalous, even if the act of mowing itself for contemporary readers is decidedly so. The provisional lessons Levin learns are not merely idiosyncratic to this fictional mowing experience in this particular novel. They are, in fact, general human lessons, and we see this most clearly when we frame the mowing scene in terms of flow and the psychological process of self-understanding. For students, then, Levin's mowing experience, like so many moments throughout *Anna Karenina*, may become an emblem for understanding their own selves and lives.[10]

CONCLUSION

As I suggested at the start of this study, fictional narratives may be understood as cognitive simulations, and I would add here that we see this play out in exemplary fashion in Tolstoy's fiction. If, moreover, we could select only one novel that we might want to read as a kind of "cognitive experiment" (Zunshine 2006, 22), then we would be hard-pressed to find a better one than *Anna Karenina*.

It should not, then, be surprising that a key scene from that novel would lend itself so well to a critical treatment that relies on ideas from late-twentieth-century research in cognitive psychology. Zooming out, we could also say that an explicitly cognitive approach to the mowing scene also helps us understand why Tolstoy famously claimed that he could not synopsize the meaning of *Anna Karenina*—because to do so would have required him to rewrite the novel all over again. As this critical dissection of Levin's mowing makes clear, the meaning of the novel is a function of how it affects us as readers as we respond to the simulational prompts of Tolstoy's prose. The true meaning of the novel "lies in the experience, in all its cognitive richness, of reading it" (Danaher 2017, 351) by trying the various characters' experiences on for psychological size.

At the same time, I have also tried to model here how we might apply notions from cognitive science to literary analysis in a way that promotes an authentic *dialogue* between cognitive psychologists and literary critics. One key element of my argument has been that cognitive science deepens our appreciation of Tolstoy as a psychological realist. More specifically, we might say that reading the mowing scene through the lens of cognitive psychology has allowed us to recast in more general terms—as well as detail a concrete psychological mechanism for—the literary-critical analysis that Gustafson and others have offered. In other words, Tolstoy's "emblematic" realism in the mowing scene can be understood not so much as the stylistic choice of one particular author but rather as a narrativized instance of much more general cognitive processes that have been amply documented. In this sense, then, we have a productive framework for reading the mowing scene in order to construct a mental model of the narrative that connects to, and here I again cite Oatley, "aspects of our own selves, our own memories, to our own concerns" (2011, 19): in reading Tolstoy, we are able to create "our own dream, our own enactment" (2011, 18).

Since, however, a dialogue is a two-way conversation, I would like to conclude also by asking: how might reading Tolstoy impact our understanding of cognitive psychology? While there are undoubtedly multiple ways of responding to this question, I will focus here on what our analysis of Levin's mowing might add to how we understand Csikszentmihalyi's concept of flow. Having returned to the literature on flow several decades after first reading it in order to prepare this study, I was struck immediately by Csikszentmihalyi's narrow focus on flow as one individual's experience. As Csikszentmihalyi frames it, research on flow provides individuals with the tools they need to control their own inner experience—to maximize individual happiness by exerting control over one's inner life (1990, 6). After listing obstacles to achieving flow that abound in modern society, he writes that there is "no way out of this predicament except for an individual to take things in hand personally"; since values and institutions no longer provide as supportive a framework as they once did, each of us must "use whatever tools are available to carve out a meaningful, enjoyable life" (Csikszentmihalyi 1990, 16). The goal of his book that summarizes decades of his research on flow is to "present general *principles*, along with concrete examples of how some people have used these principles, to transform boring and meaningless lives into ones full of enjoyment" (Csikszentmihalyi 1990, xi). To perhaps overstate the point, Csikszentmihalyi seems to dismissively shrug his shoulders in asking "what else can we possibly do but take care of our personal psychic lives?" In doing so, he implicitly severs the connection between individuals and the larger contexts—social, economic, political, ecological—they inhabit.[11]

In this regard, we must emphasize that Tolstoy's project differs fundamentally from Csikszentmihalyi's. As we have seen, Tolstoy's purpose is to interrogate the limitations of a life focused on the personal (*lichnoe*) at the expense of the common (*obshchee*)—and more to the point, to provoke in the reader a reconceptualization (a spiritualization) of the relationship between those two concepts. While Csikszentmihalyi sees flow as leading to micro-targeted inner control of experience, Levin's mowing-as-flow blossoms outward.

As critical readers of *Anna Karenina*, we do not have to agree with the Tolstoyan particulars of Levin's trajectory from mowing-as-flow to an implied spiritual rebirth in which personal consciousness merges with the All. At the same time, however, we should recognize that Tolstoyan flow necessarily involves a communal—indeed, a philosophically communal—dimension that is frustrated in Csikszentmihalyi's understanding. Put another way, we might say that Tolstoyan flow necessarily ripples outward along channels that are evocative of the dimensions of significant learning in Fink's taxonomy. With this, we return to the implications of not just reading but also teaching Levin's mowing as a flow experience. The key point of difference between Csikszentmihalyi's and Tolstoy's projects could be offered for the students' consideration. How might a flow experience that is initially situated in one person's consciousness stream outward? More generally speaking, might the spiritual transcendence that individuals experience in flow be harnessed into something that has the power to transform the world?

NOTES

1. I will be limiting my discussion of the concept of flow to Csikszentmihalyis original studies.

2. See Danaher 2007 for both an interrogation of how cognitive readings may add to our appreciation of a text's literariness, as well as an exploration of Tolstoy's use of metaphorical analogy in *Anna Karenina* that is designed to model this standard.

3. The parameters of flow are discussed in Csikszentmihalyi 1990, 49–70. I have simplified the original discussion here by merging certain related parameters. I will cite specific page numbers only when quoting Csikszentmihalyi directly. The mowing scene occurs in part III of the novel in chapters iv and v, while chapters ii and iii set the stage for Levin's experience and chapter vi describes his

infectious post-mowing bliss. Given the variety of published versions of the novel in both the original Russian and in translation, I will cite the scene by reference to chapter (ii, iii, iv, or v). Specific contexts are drawn from Tolstoy 1934 (in Russian) and Tolstoy 2000 (in English).

4. Analysis, etymologically speaking, means "un-loosening": it concerns dismantling something into its constituent parts, and this is the opposite of what Levin learns by mowing.

5. Note that the latter two-word motifs are obscured in English translation.

6. This is also consistent with Gary Saul Morson's analysis of Tolstoy's writing in terms of what he calls prosaics, which suggests "that the most important events in history, culture, and the psyche may be the most ordinary and prosaic ones, which we do not notice just because they are so ordinary" (Morson 1988, 2). Morson has further claimed that *Anna Karenina* is the most important work of prosaics ever written and the finest novel.

7. Gustafson also highlights a contrast here between Levin and his thematic counterpart, the novel's eponymous heroine, noting that while Anna may see the world transformed on her final journey to suicide, she always remains conscious of herself, which blocks awareness of the Divine: "No matter how hard she tries, Anna cannot forget herself. Everything she sees, and even how she sees, is very much of this world" (Gustafson 1986, 366).

8. We might add that Levin's struggle never reaches a definitive endpoint. The novel depicts only steps in that direction, that is, various learning experiences, like mowing, that are represented as practice toward that elusive goal.

9. Gustafson, in fact, analyzes Levin's mowing against the background of Tolstoy's larger philosophical-aesthetic project, asserting that the "primary rule for reading Tolstoy [. . .] is that the later clarifies the earlier," especially given that Tolstoy's life "was one continuous process of self-articulation" (1982, 96).

10. It falls outside the scope of this study to offer a detailed lesson plan for teaching the mowing scene, and the comments here are intended merely as suggestions for developing such a plan; much will depend, of course, on the overall context of the course in which the novel figures. Those interested in reimagining ways of teaching canonical texts from the Slavic regions—which may serve as models for how to refresh the teaching of any cultural text—should consult the forthcoming volume *Cultural Texts and Significant Learning Experiences* (edited by Danaher and Okłot) that is part of the Academic Studies Press series Issues in the Teaching of East European and Eurasian Languages and Cultures.

11. To be fair to Csikszentmihalyi, I should mention that he does acknowledge obstacles to achieving personal happiness that are beyond an individual's control—"slavery, oppression, exploitation" (1990, 85)—and he does claim that the flow framework has potentially significant sociopolitical implications (1990, 191ff), but the overarching target of his research is individual consciousness.

BIBLIOGRAPHY

Bruner, Jerome. 1990. *Acts of Meaning*. Cambridge: Harvard University Press.

Csikszentmihalyi, Mihaly. 1990. *Flow: The Psychology of Optimal Experience*. New York: HarperPerennial.

Csikszentmihalyi, Mihaly. 1996. *Creativity, Flow, and the Psychology of Discovery and Invention*. New York: HarperCollins.

Danaher, David S. 2007. "Cognitive Poetics and Literariness: Metaphorical Analogy in *Anna Karenina*." In *Perspectives on Slavic Literature*, edited by Kris van Heuckelom and David S. Danaher, 183–207. Amsterdam: Pegasus.

Danaher, David S. 2017. "Fiction as Cognitive Simulation: The Motif of Doubling in Leo Tolstoy's *Anna Karenina*." In *Each Venture a New Beginning: Studies in Honor of Laura A. Janda*, edited by Anastasia Makarova, Stephen M. Dickey, and Dagmar S. Divjak, 341–52. Bloomington: Slavica Publishers.

Danaher, David S., and Michał Okłot, eds. Forthcoming 2025. *Cultural Texts and Significant Learning Experiences (Issues in the Teaching of East European and Eurasian Languages and Cultures)*. Brookline, MA: Academic Studies Press.

Fink, L. Dee. 2003. *Creating Significant Learning Experiences: An Integrated Approach to Designing College Courses*. San Francisco: Jossey-Bass.

Gustafson, Richard. 1982. "Levin's Mowing and the Task of Life." *Ulbandus Review* 2 (2): 96–111.

Gustafson, Richard. 1986. *Leo Tolstoy, Resident and Stranger: A Study in Fiction and Theology*. Princeton: Princeton University Press.

Morson, Gary Saul. 1988. "Prosaics and Anna Karenina." *Tolstoy Studies Journal* 1: 1–12.

Oatley, Keith. 2011. *Such Stuff as Dreams: The Psychology of Fiction*. Oxford: Wiley-Blackwell.

Tolstoy, Lev. 1934. *Polnoe sobranie sochinenii, tom 18, Anna Karenina*. Moscow-Leningrad: Khudozhestvennaia literatura.

Tolstoy, Leo. 2000. *Anna Karenina*. Translated by Richard Pevear and Larissa Volokhonsky. New York: Penguin Classics.

Zunshine, Lisa. 2006. *Why We Read Fiction: Theory of the Mind and the Novel*. Columbus: Ohio State University Press.

3

Facial Imagery, Reader Visualization, and the Visual Ethics of *War and Peace*

Sarah B. Mohler

Leo Tolstoy's reputation as a visual author derives from his intuitive understanding of how reader visualization draws on the same processes the mind uses to process visual stimuli to conceptualize the world. In my close analysis of *War and Peace* (1869), I will integrate current research on mental simulation to show how Tolstoy's protagonists use mental imagery, especially of faces, to conceptualize knowledge, orient themselves ethically in the world, and learn the truth about themselves and others. We will see the impact their ability or inability to visualize the faces of people closest to them has on the ethical decisions they make. I will argue that by revealing the content and formulation of his protagonists' mental imagery, Tolstoy encourages readers to co-experience and simulate the visualization process of his protagonists. By doing so, he teaches us not only how to utilize mental imagery to enhance the vivacity and verisimilitude of our mental construction of his novel but also how to use mental imagery within the rich ethical context of our own lives.

In *The Cambridge Introduction to Russian Literature* (2008), Caryl Emerson delineates three ideas that make Russian culture and its literature unique from any other: the conceptualization of space as vast but also stifling, the agency attributed to the written or spoken word, and the power of the human face (22). She links both the agency of the word and the power of the human face to Russian Orthodox worship. While the word contained the very essence of God, icons transcended their portrayal of physical nature and provided a way to access the divine (24). The face, Emerson states, was understood to be "a responsive mirror, the soul made flesh"

(31). Emerson defines the Russian word *lik* as not only designating the face but "a responsive face that contains eyes that gaze out on other faces, ears that receive others' words. Eyes on such a face transmit divine light" (30). She goes on to explore the many facets of words derived from *lik*, such as *lichnost'*, used in Russian spiritual philosophy to convey "personality" imbued with "moral and interpersonal responsibility"; *lichnoe*, that which is personal or unique to the individual, which she translates literally as "belonging to the face," and *lichina*, the "mask" created by a human face whose unresponsiveness and impassivity make it "lifeless," "rigid," and ultimately "demonic" (30). Emerson credits Tolstoy as being a consummate master of using the word to vividly evoke the *lik* of his characters in *War and Peace*, most notably Natasha's joyous, receptive face with its mobile and expressive features, Hélène's statuesque, impervious "marble beauty" that becomes a *lichina* or mask, and Princess Mar'ia's inner spiritual icon-like beauty that shines through her plain features (30–31).[1] In essence, with the artistry of his words, Tolstoy creates not just characters but verbal icons, whose moral and spiritual power is activated by the reader's visualization of them. Tolstoy's characters not only feel real to readers; readers feel transported to the fictional world, co-present and responsive to them.

Ivan Turgenev turned a more skeptical eye to this much-vaunted visual and life-like aspect of Tolstoy's writing. In a letter to Pavel Annenkov in 1868, he remarked:

> Tolstoy amazes the reader with the toe of Alexander's boot and Speransky's laugh, forcing one to think that he knows *everything* because he has gone into even these details—but it is only these details that he knows. A trick and no more, but the public has fallen for it.

He went on to complain: "how wearisome are those deliberate and insistent repetitions of one and the same trait—the down on Princess Bolkonsky's upper lip, and so on" (Knowles 1978, 181).

For much of literary history, the visual imagery readers reported experiencing was perceived as ancillary to the analysis of the words themselves. Likewise, many psychologists and neuroscientists regarded mental imagery as "epiphenomenal" rather than integral to information processing of the brain. In 1995, neuroscientist Stephen Kosslyn published *Image and Brain: The Resolution of the Imagery Debate.* This title was optimistic since the debate about how the brain creates, sustains, and utilizes mental imagery continues (Issajeva 2019). Nevertheless, Kosslyn articulated a rich and fully developed theory of how the brain processes mental imagery and the important role mental imagery plays in human cognition, including memory, problem-solving, and creativity. According to Kosslyn's theory, the brain accesses information stored in associative memory in the posterior superior temporal and dorsolateral prefrontal cortices; it processes attributes such as motion and spatial relationships separately in the occipital-temporal cortex and posterior parietal lobe; and it uses the posterior parietal lobe to maintain, inspect, and manipulate imagery. Area V1 of the occipital lobe plays a particular importance in visualization because it is here that mental images are generated through particular patterns of neurons firing. These neurons are mapped to correspond to how neurons fire in the retina (Kosslyn 1995, 380–383) demonstrating how closely the activation of mental imagery mimics the processing of visual stimuli. Kosslyn's research was conducted by means of measuring blood flow and electrical activity in the brain (45–46) and recording response times to specific mental imagery tasks (402–403). He demonstrated that many of the same neural pathways and areas of the brain used to process visual stimuli and retrieve and inspect images stored in associative memory were used in the generation of mental imagery (289–301). He was also able to gather extensive data and analyze the results of other neuroscientists' research to show which areas of the brain are activated when we scan, zoom in/out, rotate, or change the size or color of mental images; compare visual stimuli to mental images stored in associative memory; compare mental images with other mental images; and generate imagery based on verbal commands (309–310).

Kosslyn's theories of mental imagery not only provided a rich explanation of how the brain forms and manipulates visual imagery but it also opened up scientific investigation into readers' ability to form visual images. Current research now seeks to measure vividness, assess content, and measure the impact of visual imagery on readers' understanding, immersion, emotional response, and recall of texts. A breakthrough in the understanding of the mental simulation of texts occurred in 2009, when Nicole K. Speer et al published the results of an experiment in which twenty-eight participants had their brain activity tracked by an fMRI machine while reading texts of 1,500 words or less describing a boy's day. They found that readers created situational models of the text similar to ones they would use to navigate the real world. The results of the fMRI showed that the areas of the brain involving "processing goal-directed human activity, navigating spatial environments, and manually manipulating objects" (Speer et al. 2009, 995–996) were activated by corresponding descriptions in the narrative. Speer and the other researchers paid particular attention to analyzing brain activity at points of change in the narrative where readers would have to update their working situation model of the story. They found that situation changes in the narrative activated regions of the brain "associated with the act of projecting one's self into a remembered, anticipated, or imagined situation" (997). These results demonstrated how closely readers' simulations of narratives correlated with real-world experiences, sensory processing, and mental and physical engagement.

Current mental simulation research is now using eye movement tracking along with participants' self-reports to discover how mental simulation relates to the visual processing of a text. In 2018, Mak and Willems published research that measured the length of time readers fixated on words in a text as a marker for active processing of the text. They found that readers whose gaze fixated longer on parts of the text that required perceptual simulation also fixated longer on parts of the text that required "mentalizing," the simulation of thoughts, emotions, and intentions (19). They also found a strong correlation between gaze duration involving aspects of the story related to perception and mentalizing with greater self-reports of absorption or "transportation" into the fictional world, stronger emotional responses to the texts, a greater liking of the text, and the ability to take on the visual perspectives of characters within the text (15–16). These results support other findings that correlate vivid visual imagery with story world absorption (Kuijpers et al. 2014) and to changes in readers' beliefs (Fitzgerald and Green 2017). Fitzgerald and Green theorize that readers link story beliefs to images generated while reading narratives. These linkages persist in readers' memories even when the reading experience is finished, reactivating the beliefs whenever images from the text are recalled (54). A few studies have even indicated that reader transportation leads to heightened empathy and prosocial behavior in a real-world context (see Bal and Veltkamp 2013; and Johnson 2012). Thus, research suggests that readers are not only cognitively primed to process texts as they would real-world experiences, but that their visualization of the settings, events, characters, and characters' mental processes and visual perspectives heightens their absorption and moral engagement with the texts, which may also heighten their ability to apply insights gained from the narrative to their own lives and the ethical situations they encounter.

This research provides an exciting context for our discussion of Tolstoy's evocation of visual mental imagery, which I will refer to as "reader visualization." There is no doubt that Tolstoy believed in the moral purpose of art and hoped that his work would ethically engage his readers[2] However, before he could persuade us, Tolstoy had to first immerse us into the fictional world of the novel and help us create vivid heroes and heroines, whose emotions we co-experience and whose perceptions we adopt.

As Turgenev noted, Tolstoy's physical descriptions of characters fixate on certain distinctive traits—Hélène's white shoulders, the little princess' downy upper lip, Andrei's smile, and Princess Mar'ia's radiant gaze.

Tolstoy returns to these again and again until the images formed in the reader's mind achieve an extraordinary vividness. Turgenev disparaged this repetition, but without constantly retraining our focus onto these traits, the neurons creating these images in the V1 area of the brain would stop firing and the impression would gradually fade. Thus, it is this repetition of significant traits in combination with the slow accretion of other details about a character's personality, habits, thoughts, and emotions, that explains why so many readers feel their images of Tolstoy's characters grow in substance and solidity even though his descriptions remain concise.

It is no accident that the facial features Tolstoy most often chooses as distinctive features for his heroes and heroines are eyes and lips. Not only does this correlate with the spiritual and ethical importance of the emotionally responsive *lik* in Russian culture, as noted by Emerson, research on eye movement has shown that the eyes, nose, and upper lip attracted far more attention than any other part of the face in experiments where participants were asked to gauge a person's emotions (Schurgin et al. 2014, 13).

When describing characters, especially when first introduced, Tolstoy focuses on a holistic portrayal of the face, describing facial shape and noting the general physical qualities as well as the moral or emotional impressions they evoke in the viewer. For example, when Princess Mar'ia is introduced to the reader, Tolstoy describes her as going "back to her room with the sad, anxious look that rarely left her, making her sickly, plain face even plainer"[3] (Tolstoi [1869] 1979, Book X, Part X, Chapter X). Tolstoy's subsequent descriptions of characters often note movement or changes in facial expressions or coloring. These are exactly the "experiential" methods for creating vivid mental images of faces that Elspeth Jajdelska et al delineate in "Crying, Moving, and Keeping It Whole: What Makes Literary Description Vivid?" (2010, 447). Jajdelska demonstrates that the experiential method of facial description that strengthens visualization of faces correlates with the results of psychological studies that track the facial aspects individuals encode upon first meeting a person (444) and those which are shown to assist in facial recall (452–453). By using these facial description techniques, Tolstoy is ensuring that when we read descriptions of his characters, we focus exactly on the qualities we would focus on and remember if we met them in real life.

Elaine Scarry remarks in her landmark work of introspection on the reader visualization process, *Dreaming by the Book* (1999), that authors seldom allow their heroes and heroines to be successful visualizers because this requires the authors to reveal too many of their own techniques for promoting mental imagery (28). I believe Tolstoy is an exception to this rule. The heroes and heroines of *War and Peace*, Natasha, Pierre, Nikolai,

Mar'ia, and Andrei, are all adept at visualization. Tolstoy's vivid descriptions of their mental imagery, which often focus on the faces of loved ones, allow us as readers not only to co-visualize but also to co-experience the feelings associated with this mental imagery, as well as witness how this mental imagery impacts their self-knowledge, understanding of relationships, and ethical responses.

The attention Tolstoy devotes to the visualization of faces is significant. In their key study, "Why Never Forgetting a Face Matters: Visual Imagery and Social Memory" (1982), William B. Swann Jr. and Lynn Carol Miller found that individuals who habitually formed vivid visual images of others had more accurate memories of social situations and remembered more key details about the attitudes, activities, and life histories of others. Swann and Miller theorized that linking information important to social cognition to an image of someone aided in the organization and recall of that information and that the effort of encoding a vivid visual image might correspond with a more thorough and complete study of the individual (476).

After Prince Andrei leaves to join the army, his sister Mar'ia is able to visualize him by picturing the haughty yet tender look in his eyes when he bid her farewell and the gently ironic way he gazed at her when she gave him an icon in parting. This suggests that sometimes only a thin line divides visualization from the visually encoded memories activated during recall. In this instance, imagining the icon that Mar'ia held and then gave to Andrei to hold activates motor simulation that reinforces Mar'ia's visual imagery (Kuzmičová 2013, 117–118). Mar'ia's visualization of Andrei is made all the more vivid for the readers who have read multiple descriptions of Andrei and others handling the icon since Mar'ia gave it to him.

Nikolai and Natasha, another brother and sister who are skillful visualizers, have retained vividly poetic recollections from childhood. While discussing their first encounter as children with a black man, Nikolai remarks that, even now, he is not sure whether it really happened, whether they dreamed about it, or if they had simply been told about it (Tolstoi [1869] 1979, Book 2, Part 4, Ch. 10), suggesting how readily dream, memory, and imaginationare blended in the poetic natures of Nikolai and Natasha. In contrast, their cousin, Sonia, is embarrassed by the fact that she is unable to recall this and other experiences with the same sense of vitality. It is precisely this inability to visualize a face or recognize a song from its initial notes that Natasha comes to perceive as emblematic of something vital lacking in her cousin (Tolstoi, [1869] 1979, Book 2, Part 4, Ch. 9), who otherwise possesses so many admirable and lovable qualities. Sonia's embarrassment causes her to play along when Nikolai and Natasha engage in their memory games and to state later while fortune-telling that she can divine something in the mirror when Natasha cannot (Tolstoi [1869] 1979, Book 2, Part 4, Ch. 12).

Individuals who cannot vividly relive past experiences, recall clear visual memories, or use visualization may have a form of aphantasia or an inability to experience conscious mental imagery (Pearson 2019, 630–631). Current research has shown that the differences in individuals' ability to form mental imagery may be due to brain formation. Scientists have found that individuals who form vivid mental images have larger frontal lobes and considerably smaller visual cortices in the V1 area of the brain as well as "quieter" visual cortices whose background processing does not interfere with the processing of visual information (627–628). It may seem counterintuitive that vivid visualizers have a smaller V1, but research has shown that although the processing of visual stimuli and the creation of mental imagery occur in the same areas of the brain and use the same neural pathways, the processing of mental imagery, which involves retrieval and binding of information, flows from the frontal regions to the posterior regions, whereas the processing of visual perception starts in the posterior and flows to the frontal regions for lookup and identification (Canales-Johnson et al 2021, 2). Pearson theorizes that strong visualizers might prefer processing information visually, while weak visualizers favor other information processing strategies (Pearson 2019, 629–630).

Sonia has at least one memory that suggests she is a weak visualizer rather than someone with aphantasia: she vividly remembers an incident on the day she came to live with the Rostovs as their ward. For some reason, it is the braid on Nikolai's school uniform that she fixates upon as a child, and the memory is engraved in her mind by the nurse's threat to sew *her* up in the braid (Tolstoi [1869] 1979, Book 2, Part 4, Ch. 10). It makes sense that this is the memory Sonya vividly retains since it occurs on a day with great emotional resonance. In addition, the memory features Nikolai, whom Sonya has long been in love with. However, when Natasha asks Sonya if she can *truly* remember Nikolai in every detail when he is away at war, Sonia, since she is not a strong visualizer, talks about the depth of her feelings for him instead. For Sonia, visualization is no indication of the strength of her feelings, but for Natasha, it most certainly is, and she contrasts her visualization of her brother with Boris, the boy she is no longer infatuated with:

> "Do you remember him?" Natasha suddenly asked after a moment's silence.
>
> Sonia smiled. "Remember Nicolas?"
>
> "No, Sonia, do you remember him really well, so that you remember everything about him?" Natasha asked, with an insistent gesture,

clearly wishing to give her words the most serious meaning. "I remember Nikolenka, I do," she said, "but I can't remember Boris. Not at all."
"What? You don't remember Boris?" asked Sonia in surprise.
"It's not that I don't remember—I know what he's like, but I don't remember him like I do Nikolenka. Him I just shut my eyes and remember, but Boris—no." (She shut her eyes.) "No—nothing at all."
"Oh, Natasha!" said Sonia rapturously in a grave tone, looking away from her friend as if she considered her unworthy of hearing what she was about to say and were speaking to someone different with whom one couldn't joke. "I've fallen in love with your brother, and no matter what happens to him or to me, I'll never stop loving him—for the rest of my life." (Tolstoi [1869] 1979, Book 1, Part 3, Ch. 6)

For Natasha, it is not sufficient simply to construct an accurate mental image of the way a person looks. For her, visualizing someone's face leads to imagining them in the fullness of their particular personality so that their mental representation activates your knowledge, understanding, and emotional response to that person. It is a creative act with enormous ethical implications for further interactions with that individual. This explains why Natasha attaches so much importance to visualization. It also explains why she can visualize Nikolai completely but not Boris. While her attachment to her brother remains strong, her infatuation with Boris has faded, causing his image to fade as well, perhaps because she less and less often calls his face to mind.

Natasha, who of all the Rostovs is described as "the most gifted with the ability to perceive the nuances in an intonation, a glance, or facial expression" (Tolstoi [1869] 1979, Book 1, Part 3, Ch. 6), is the one to whom visualization comes the most naturally. Later, when Boris has returned and she is again able to visualize him, she exhibits a singularly artistic ability to imagine both him and Pierre in terms of particular geometric shapes and gradients of color. She describes Boris as "narrow [uzkii]" and "pale gray [seryi, svetlyi]," whereas Pierre appears to her as "blue, dark blue with some red, and he's square-ish [sinii, temno-sinii s krasnym, i on chetverougol'nyi]" (Tolstoi [1869] 1979, Book 2, Part 3, Ch. 13). Clearly, of the two, Pierre's vivid, complex colorization strikes her more favorably. Her mother uses this as an opportunity to scold Natasha for flirting with both men. Nonetheless, Natasha's visualization uncovers the essential qualities of Boris' colorless personality and narrow view of the world, and Pierre's solidity and depth.

But what of Sonia? We have already discussed that she is not a strong visualizer, which explains at least partially why she cannot recall Nikolai in the way Natasha expects despite her feelings for him. We also know that Sonia lacks something vital that prevents her from experiencing life as deeply as she might or from communicating the depth of her feelings to others. The only exception is when Countess Rostova pressures her to write to Nikolai and release him from their engagement so that he can marry Princess Mar'ia. Faced with the threat of losing him, Sonia's love for Nikolai becomes truly passionate. She agrees to write Nikolai, but only because she knows that Russian Orthodoxy forbids Nikolai from marrying Mar'ia if Natasha marries Andrei, Mar'ia's brother. Tolstoy connects Sonia's fit of passion to visualization in this passage by having the sight of Andrei lying wounded in the next room prompt Sonia to remember the image she had pretended to see while fortune-telling. Just as she convinced herself that she really did see something in the mirror, Sonia now convinces herself that all the details of the scene before her were in her vision and embellishes it: "At the time she'd seen nothing at all but had described the first thing that came into her head; but what she thought up now seemed to her as real as any other memory" (Tolstoi [1869] 1979, Book 4, Part 1, Ch. 8). Previously, Sonia lied about visualizing things she did not see out of embarrassment. Here she does so in order to persuade herself and others that Andrei and Natasha are destined to be together so that she and Nikolai can marry. The vividness of her visualization corresponds with her desperation to believe there is still hope she and Nikolai can be together.

Tolstoy's Prince Andrei is a passionate man who represses his feelings. Like Natasha, he, too, is adept at mental simulation, not only visual but auditory, as well. In his most profound moments of connection with the divine, he personifies nature and gives a voice to the blue sky of Austerlitz, the ripples on the water during his conversation with Pierre at the ferry, and the old oak tree that becomes a symbol of renewal and rebirth. However, after the death of his wife, the Little Princess, and his own near death at Austerlitz, he is numb, guilt-ridden, and grieving. A chance encounter with Natasha when he goes to the Rostov estate on business ignites a longing for vitality and awakens in him a desire for a new way of perceiving:

> The girl was shouting something, but realizing he was a stranger, without looking at him, ran away laughing.
>
> Prince Andrei for some reason suddenly felt an ache. The day was so lovely, the sun so bright, and everything surrounding him so cheerful; yet that slender, pretty girl didn't know or care to know of his existence and was content and happy in her own separate—no doubt foolish—carefree, merry life. "What is she so joyful about? What is she thinking of? Not of military regulations, not the system of quitrent for the Ryazan serfs. What is she thinking of? What was she so happy for?" Prince Andrei couldn't help asking himself. (Tolstoi [1869] 1979, Book 2, Part 3, Ch. 2)

This chance encounter with Natasha initiates a series of inner transformations that eventually leads Prince Andrei out of his depressed state. Throughout his visit that day, Prince Andrei steals glances at Natasha, continually wondering about her thoughts and the source of her happiness. Later that evening, he is presented with a singular opportunity to find out. Unable to sleep, he opens his bedroom window to discover that both Natasha and Sonia are awake in the room above his. Afraid to move, lest he betray his unintentional presence, Prince Andrei listens to their conversation and is captivated by the poeticism of Natasha's nature.

Tolstoy deftly embeds certain verbal cues into the passage to facilitate both Andrei's and the reader's visualization of Natasha. From below, Prince Andrei listens to Natasha describe step by step how she would like to sit on her heels, wrap her arms around herself, and then spread them out "Like this [*Vot tak*]!" (Tolstoi [1869] 1979, Book 2, Part 3, Ch. 2) in order to fly away. He hears the girls scuffle as Sonia tries to draw Natasha away from the ledge. When Sonia's attempt fails, and Natasha remains there to enjoy the moonlight, her presence on the ledge is conveyed to him by the rustling of her dress. Although he would like to catch a glimpse of Natasha, he cannot do so without alerting her to the fact that he has been eavesdropping, making the situation awkward for them both. Rather than objectify Natasha, this episode more firmly establishes Prince Andrei's recognition of his own otherness in relation to her subjectivity: "'No notion of my existence!' thought Prince Andrei as he listened to her talk, for some reason hoping yet fearing she would say something about him" (Tolstoi [1869] 1979, Book 2, Part 3, Ch. 2).

This scene suggests that the Tolstoyan equation of seeing and knowing may be reversible: by gaining insight into other people's inner lives, we learn to *see* them better, thus gaining the ability to visualize them in the context of their own surroundings and in the fullness of their particular personalities. In turn, by endeavoring to capture nuances in character, mood, gesture, and expression in order to refine our visualization, we are drawn into further interaction with the object of our interest.

Prince Andrei's response to what he has learned impels him to become more closely acquainted with Natasha when he meets her again at a ball in Petersburg. In their very first conversation, he reminds her of their encounter as he was driving up the road to Otradnoe and tells her about inadvertently overhearing her conversation with Sonia on the window ledge. Natasha is pleased the encounters have left a favorable impression on him. After the ball, Prince Andrei pays the Rostovs a call and is further captivated by Natasha. That night he is unable to sleep due to the new thoughts and feelings that have welled up within him: "It never entered his head that he was in love with the Rostov girl; he was not thinking of her; he was only picturing her to himself, and consequently, his entire life revealed itself to him in a new light" (Tolstoi [1869] 1979, Book 2, Part 3, Ch. 19). The nature of Prince Andrei's visualization is seen in its effect: it alters his customary mode of thinking so that life appears in an entirely fresh way. He has not yet realized he is in love with Natasha because he is not conscious of the cascade of internal transformations that were initiated by his first encounter with her. Thus, in this passage, Tolstoy demonstrates that experiential and sensory knowledge—visual, tactile, and auditory—too complex for Prince Andrei to consciously process, much less verbalize, is activated when he visualizes Natasha. The more he visualizes her, the more strongly these thoughts, feelings, and impressions are tied to the image of her he conjures, making it even easier to visualize her in the future.

By learning to visualize Natasha, Andrei also learns to apply visualization to other areas of life. Visualization becomes the tool Andrei uses when he wishes to think about the needs and life circumstances of others and to ascertain how his actions will affect them. Though he once idolized one of Tsar Alexander I's closest advisors, Michael Speransky, for his push for governmental reforms, Andrei begins to doubt not only Speransky's but also his own motivations for engaging in reform and searches out new perspectives from which to judge the success or failure of their work:

> He remembered his legal reform work, and how he had painstakingly translated the articles of the Roman and French codes into Russian, and he was ashamed. Then he vividly pictured Bogucharovo, his activities in the country, his trip to Ryazan, remembered the peasants, and Dron, the village elder, and, mentally applying to them the Personal Rights he had divided into paragraphs, he was amazed he could spend so much time on such pointless work. (Tolstoi [1869] 1979, Book 2, Part 3, Ch. 18)

Visualization, thus, can be credited with the ability to radically change an individual's perspective on love, work, and life itself. In this case, Andrei sees the futility of formulating legislation and legal codes in the abstract without keeping the needs, desires, and circumstances of particular individuals in mind. As we saw with Natasha, when Andrei visualizes Dron, Andrei's knowledge of Dron's manner, preferences, beliefs, and life circumstances are activated, and it becomes easier for Andrei to simulate Dron's beliefs and feelings about the reform and perceive that the reforms will not be welcomed or have the beneficial effect he hopes.

Prince Andrei and Natasha become engaged, but he soon leaves to go to war. Early on in their engagement, Natasha can easily picture him and simulate his thoughts and beliefs. When Nikolai makes a joke about a fiancé already being "chosen" for his sister, Natasha attempts to analyze

Nikolai's attitude toward her proposed marriage to Andrei and imagine Andrei's reaction to the evening they have spent in the country:

> "What did Nikolai's smile mean when he said 'someone's already been chosen'? Is he glad or not? He somehow thinks my Bolkonsky wouldn't approve of or understand our gaiety. But he would understand everything. Where is he now?" wondered Natasha, and her face suddenly grew serious. However, this lasted only a second. "Don't think about it, don't you dare think about it," she told her herself. (Tolstoi [1869] 1979, Book 2, Part 4, Ch. 7)

Natasha is shown suppressing her natural propensity for visualization in this passage. Because of her impatience and passionate nature, she cannot bear to picture Andrei, knowing that she will have to wait an entire year before she is reunited with him. It simply hurts too much. However, by refusing to use her talent for visualizing him, she increasingly cuts herself off from the one means that would have fostered her sense of connection to him during the long wait. Because she does not allow herself to recall Andrei's face, imagine his experiences while away at war, or simulate what his beliefs or attitudes might be to the events occurring in her life, her emotional connection to him weakens.

Nikolai senses Natasha's repression and does indeed have doubts about the depth of her feelings for Prince Andrei. Just as Natasha tries to deduce his attitude toward her engagement by analyzing his smile, Nikolai tries to analyze whether Natasha is truly in love by observing her behavior:

> Her brother often wondered while looking at her. She did not seem at all like a girl in love and parted from her fiancé. She was calm, serene, and as lighthearted as ever. This surprised Nikolai and even made him regard Bolkonsky's courtship a bit dubiously. He didn't believe that her fate was decided, especially since he had never seen her with Prince Andrei. It always struck him that there was something off about this proposed marriage. (Tolstoi [1869] 1979, Book 2, Part 4, Ch. 1)

Nikolai places particular importance on not having seen Natasha with Prince Andrei. Had he been able to observe them, he would have been able to tell from their gestures, facial expressions, and their attitude toward each other whether his doubts were well-founded or not. In addition, Nikolai's only encounters with Andrei have occurred within a military context. For Nikolai, Andrei is symbolic of "war," while Natasha is symbolic of "peace," further interfering with his ability to visualize them together.

As Natasha's separation from Andrei lengthens, she continues to suppress her visualization of him to protect herself from being consumed by longing. She takes no joy in his letters, nor does she use them to create new mental pictures of him, because it pains her that he is seeing new places and new people without her. She also finds it increasingly hard to write to him because she "cannot conceive of the possibility of authentically expressing in a letter even a thousandth part of what she was in the habit of conveying with her voice, her smile, and her glance" (Tolstoi [1869] 1979, Book 2, Part 4, Ch. 13). On the night of her fateful trip to the opera, Natasha imagines Andrei's "searching, curious" eyes and "manly yet childlike smile," exclaiming, "Oh, how I see those eyes!" then breaks off in frustration because she cannot be with him: "No, better not to think of him, not to think, forget, forget completely for the present. I can't bear this waiting!" (Tolstoi [1869] 1979, Book 2, Part 5, Ch. 8). At the opera, when confronted by Anatol Kuragin's intimately suggestive gaze, she is confused by the feelings it arouses in her. She watches Hélène and her father for some sign as to whether Anatol's actions are honorable but receives no help from them. Sadly, she does not attempt to do the one thing that would have allowed her to recognize Anatol as a scoundrel until it is too late: to simulate seeing him through Prince Andrei's eyes—a process that came so naturally to her when she was not suppressing her power to visualize his face. On this night, it has terrible consequences. She is seduced by Anatol's charms, which results in a scandalous near-elopement and the subsequent breaking off of her engagement to Andrei.

Nikolai, a soldier and a hunter, on the other hand, relies so much on his powers of visualization to help him successfully navigate challenges and foresee danger (Imbriano et al 2020, 1495–1496) that he does not stop to analyze the circumstances that limit his powers of visualization. We see this threaten his future happiness in regards to his love of Princess Mar'ia:

> He tried to picture what it would be like if he were free. How would he have proposed to her? Would she have become his wife? But, no, he could not imagine it. He felt rattled, and no clear picture appeared in his mind. He'd long ago formed a picture of his future with Sonia, and it was all simple and clear just because it had all been thought through and he knew all there was to know about Sonia; but it was impossible to visualize a future with Princess Mar'ia because he did not understand her but simply loved her. (Tolstoi [1869] 1979, Book 4, Part 1, Ch. 7)

Habitually visualizing people or situations one way can prevent us from visualizing alternatives or considering them from new perspectives. This is the case with Nikolai's visualization of a future with Sonia. He has known Sonia since childhood. He is familiar with her every gesture, mood, habit, and preference and can visualize them in great detail. Because their engagement is a long-standing one, he has often imagined what marriage to Sonia would be like. However, he does not yet know

Princess Mar'ia well enough to visualize a future with her. Because he relies so much on his powers of visualization to guide his actions, this shakes him profoundly. It makes him doubt that such a future is possible when, in reality, all he must do is get to know Princess Mar'ia better in order to visualize the happiness that could be theirs. He and Maria's further acquaintance makes this possible, and their eventual marriage, based on Tolstoy's parents' marriage, is a very happy one.

Just as Tolstoy teaches us the benefits of visualization and to understand its limits, he warns us that visualization sometimes provides a glimpse into our own darkest needs and fears. After Natasha's betrayal, Prince Andrei joins the army, hoping to bury his sorrow in sacrifice for his country. His visualizations grow darker as he grows increasingly more cynical. When he observes the men in his regiment bathing in a pond near Bald Hills, he cannot help but imagine the young, healthy bodies of the soldiers as cannon fodder. Likewise, Pierre reacts with a mixture of confusion and horror when he suddenly is able to visualize Hélène's body naked (Tolstoi [1869] 1979, Book 1, Part 3, Ch. 1). He cannot erase the image of Hélène's unclothed body from his mind once it is there. From that moment on, Pierre feels that his fate is sealed and that Hélène must be his wife, so that he can make an honest man of himself. In a similar fashion, Mar'ia's daydreams of having children, a husband, and a home lead her to visualize "earthly" love, which she considers wicked, not just for its sexuality but because it would require her to put her own needs and desires above caring for her elderly father (Tolstoi [1869] 1979, Book 1, Part 3, Ch. 3). Her conflicted feelings become evident during Anatol's courting of her when she imagines a diabolical figure with Anatol's features lurking in the corner of her bedroom. Her visualization frightens her so much that she asks one of the maids to sleep in her bedroom. Considering Anatol is a cad, these visions also warn her that he is not who he seems, something she senses but does not yet consciously know (Tolstoi [1869] 1979, Book 1, Part 3, Ch. 5).

War and Peace is famed for its length. It tells the intertwined stories of the Rostovs, Bolkonskys, and Pierre Bezukhov against the backdrop of the Napoleonic wars as Tolstoy pursues his critique of history and great men over 800 pages—enough pages for several novels. But what if this length was precisely the number of pages needed to teach readers how to visualize the responsive faces [*liki*] of the characters and imagine the ethical situations the novel portrays in vivid and nuanced detail so they have the most cognitive impact? Tolstoy asks us repeatedly to visualize Mar'ia's luminous eyes, the nuances in Andrei's smile, and Natasha's darting glance because these are the facial features that focus our attention, convey the most emotion, and draw us into a relationship with others in real life. Every repetition of these descriptions encodes them more deeply into our minds and makes them easier to recall. It is this repetition of significant physical traits, in combination with the slow accretion of other details about a character's personality, habits, thoughts, and emotions, that explains why so many readers feel their images of Tolstoy's characters grow in substance and solidity over the course of the novel, even when Tolstoy's descriptions remain concise. Not only do we have Tolstoy's descriptions of his characters, but we have his characters' visualization of each other to draw on to enhance the vividness of our own imaginings. When Natasha visualizes Andrei's smile, we do, too. This shared focus and co-experiencing with Natasha of the thoughts, beliefs, and emotions evoked by Andrei's smile aligns us more strongly with her, elicits our empathy, and helps us to simulate her inner experience with more nuance.

Studying the techniques Tolstoy uses in *War and Peace* to enhance the mental imagery of readers is a worthy scholarly endeavor[4] because of the role mental imagery plays in enhancing readers' transportation into the fictional world, which we now know, based on the research I have discussed, increases readers' enjoyment, emotional engagement, identification with characters, and ability to adopt characters' mental states and perspectives. However, it is even more important to analyze because of the way Tolstoy thematizes visualization as a way to conceptualize knowledge, orient ourselves ethically in the world, and learn about ourselves and others. When we as readers actively visualize characters, take on their points of view, and enact their visualizations of others, we participate in their ethical dilemmas, understand the cognitive errors they make, and rehearse our own responses to moral quandaries.[5]

What, then, are the lessons Tolstoy would have us learn from *War and Peace*? From Natasha, we learn that frequently recalling and visualizing the faces of others helps us remain close to them emotionally and makes it easier for us to simulate their thoughts, responses, beliefs, and emotions. She also warns us of the detrimental effect on relationships if we do not keep loved ones "in mind." From Andrei, we learn that visualizing individual people's responses helps us incorporate the particular needs, desires, and circumstances of others into our planning, whether we are creating a business plan, legislation, or advocating for reform. From Nikolai, we learn that our ability to visualize a person or situation develops over time and depends on deepening knowledge and familiarity. He cautions us that we often find it easier to visualize "safe" options we are familiar with, which may deter us from exploring options we do not yet know enough about to visualize clearly. From Mar'ia and Pierre, we learn that what we visualize can be the key to acknowledging the desires and fears we may be hiding from ourselves.

NOTES

1. Emerson is not alone. Both Richard Gustafson in *Leo Tolstoy: Resident and Stranger* (1986) and Amy Mandelker in *Framing Anna Karenina* (1993) have written extensively on the impact that Russian Orthodoxy had on Tolstoy's visuality and how Tolstoy's narratives function as "verbal" icons. Other scholars have pointed to additional influences, such as Tolstoy's admiration and study of Goethe's *zarte Empirie* or "delicate empiricism" (Bortoft 1996, 90). Orwin contends in *Tolstoy's Art and Thought 1847–1880* (1993) that both Goethe and Tolstoy sought wisdom through an ever-deepening investigation of the world, in which the act of observation led to mutual engagement, closer observation, and a refining of previous theories (28–29). In his article, "Gazing on Life's Page: Perspectival Vision in Tolstoy" (1998), Thomas Seifrid argues that Western optical inventions, such as the *camera obscura* (441) and the magic lantern (443), had just as significant an impact on Tolstoy's conceptualization of *War and Peace*. Both Robert Louis Jackson in "The Ethics of Vision II: The Tolstoyan Synthesis" (1993) and Gary Saul Morson in "Reader as Voyeur" (1991) demonstrate how central moral/immoral visual interaction is to Tolstoy's ethics.

2. For Tolstoy, art was the transference of thought and feeling from the artist to the audience. He believed good art was art that elevated the audience's thoughts, helped them understand their shared humanity, and strengthened their connection to others and to God. He would articulate this philosophy best in *What is Art?* (1898).

3. This and all other translations from *War and Peace* are my own.

4. Tolstoy masterfully employs all of the visualization-enhancing cognitive techniques Elaine Scarry delineates in *Dreaming by the Book*. For a close analysis of Tolstoy's use of these techniques, see my dissertation, "The Prosaics of the Mind's Eye: Reader Visualization, Perspectival Engagement, and the Visual Ethics of Tolstoy's *War and Peace*." For a close analysis of how these techniques have inspired illustrations, plays, and film adaptations of *War and Peace*, see my "War and Peace Visualized: From Page to Stage and Screen" (2013).

5. It has long been the case that readers and critics have gravitated toward either Tolstoy or Dostoevsky and valorized one at the expense of the other. No one was guiltier of this than Mikhail Bakhtin, who praised Dostoevsky's dialogism and denigrated Tolstoy for his monologism (Bakhtin 1981, 72). But could it be that this much-vaunted dichotomy points to different ways readers have of simulating the fictional worlds of each author? Perhaps visualizers experience the fictional world of *War and Peace* as more open, more free, and "verbalizers," more closed. How might our critical endeavors benefit from acknowledging a visual equivalent to Bakhtin's concept of dialogism—one that affirms that both the exchange of gazes and the visual simulation of others and their perspectives require the same mutual engagement, ethical responsibility, and dynamic creation of meaning as dialogic speech acts?

BIBLIOGRAPHY

Bakhtin, M. M. 1981. *The Dialogic Imagination: Four Essays by M. M. Bakhtin*, edited by Michael Holquist, translated by Caryl Emerson and Michael Holquist. Austin: University of Texas Press.

Bal, P. Matthijs and Martjin Veltkamp. 2013. "How Does Fiction Reading Influence Empathy? An Experimental Investigation on the Role of Emotional Transportation." *PLOS ONE* 8, no. 1, e55341. https://journals.plos.org/plosone/article?id=10.1371/journal.pone.0055341.

Bortoft, Henri. 1996. *The Wholeness of Nature: Goethe's Way toward a Science of Conscious Participation in Nature*. Barrington: Lindisfarne Books.

Canales-Johnson, Andrés, Renzo C. Lanfranco, Juan Pablo Morales, David Martínez-Pernia, Joaquín Valdés, Alejandro Ezquerro-Nassar, Álvaro Rívera-Rei, et al. 2021. "In Your Phase: Neural Phase Synchronization Underlies Visual Imagery of Faces." *Nature* 11, 2401. https://doi.org/10.1038/s41598-021-81336-y.

Emerson, Caryl. 2008. *The Cambridge Introduction to Russian Literature*. Cambridge: Cambridge University Press.

Fitzgerald, Kaitlin and Melanie C. Green. 2017. "Narrative Persuasion: Effects of Transporting Stories on Attitudes, Beliefs, and Behaviors." In *Narrative Absorption*, edited by Frank Hakemulder, Moniek M. Kuijpers, Ed. S. Tan and Katalin Bálint, 49–67. Amsterdam: John Benjamins Publishing Company.

Gustafson, Richard. 1986. *Leo Tolstoy: Resident and Stranger*. Princeton: Princeton University Press.

Imbriano, Gabriella, Tamara J. Sussman, Jingwen Jin, and Aprajita Mohanty. 2020. "The Role of Imagery in Threat-Related Perceptual Decision Making." *Emotion* 20, no. 18, 1495–1501. http://dx.doi.org/10.1037/emo0000610.

Issajeva, Jelena. 2020. "Can Theories of Mental Representation Adequately Explain Mental Imagery?" *Foundations of Science* 25, 341–355. https://doi.org/10.1007/s10699-019-09613-8.

Jackson, Robert Louis. 1993. *Dialogues with Dostoevsky: The Overwhelming Questions*. Stanford: Stanford University Press.

Jajdelska, Elspeth, Christopher Butler, Steve Kelly, Allan McNeill, and Katie Overy. 2010. "Crying, Moving, and Keeping It Whole: What Makes Literary Description Vivid?" *Poetics Today* 31, no. 3, 433–463. https://doi.org/10.1215/03335372-2010-002.

Johnson, Dan R. 2012. "Transportation into a Story Increases Empathy, Pro-Social Behaviour, and Perceptual Bias Toward Fearful Expressions." *Personality and Individual Differences* 52, no. 2, 150–155. https://doi.org/10.1016/j.paid.2011.10.005.

Kosslyn, Stephen. 1995. *Image and Brain: The Resolution of the Imagery Debate*. Cambridge: MIT Press.

Kuijpers, M. M., F. Hakemulder, E. S. Tan, and M. M. Doicaru. 2014. "Exploring Absorbing Reading Experiences: Developing and Validating a Self-Report Scale to Measure Story World Absorption." *Scientific Study of Literature* 4, no. 1, 89–122. https://doi.org/10.1075/ssol.4.1.05kui.

Kuzmičová, Anežka. 2013. "The Words and Worlds of Literary Narrative: The Trade-off between Verbal Presence and Direct Presence in the Activity of Reading." In *Stories and Minds: Cognitive Approaches to Literature*, edited by Lars Bernaerts, Dirk de Geest, Luc Herman, and Bart Vervaeck, 107–127. Lincoln: University of Nebraska.

Mak, M. and R. M. Willems. 2019. "Mental Simulation During Literary Reading: Individual Differences Revealed with Eye-tracking." *Language, Cognition and Neuroscience* 34, no. 4, 511–535. https://doi.org/10.1080/23273798.2018.1552007.

Mandelker, Amy. 1993. *Framing Anna Karenina*. Columbus: Ohio State University Press.

Mohler, Sarah. 2006. "The Prosaics of the Mind's Eye: Reader Visualization, Perspectival Engagement, and the Visual Ethics of Tolstoy's *War and Peace*." PhD diss., Princeton University.

Mohler, Sarah. 2013. "*War and Peace* Visualized: From Page to Stage and Screen." *Ulbandus* 15, 109–132.

Morson, Gary Saul. 1991. "The Reader as Voyeur." In *Tolstoy's Short Fiction*, edited by Michael R. Katz. 2nd ed., 379–396. New York: W. W. Norton & Co.

Orwin, Donna. *1993. Tolstoy's Art and Thought*. Princeton: Princeton University Press.

Pearson, Joel. 2019. "The Human Imagination: The Cognitive Neuroscience of Visual Mental Imagery." *Nature* 20, 624–634. https://doi.org/10.1038/s41583-019-0202-9.

Scarry, Elaine. 1999. *Dreaming by the Book*. New York: Farrar, Straus, Giroux.

Schurgin, M. W., J. Nelson, S. Iida, H. Ohira, J. Y. Chiao, and S. L. Franconeri. 2014. "Eye Movements During Emotion Recognition in Faces." *Journal of Vision* 14, no. 14, 1–16.

Seifrid, Thomas. 1998. "Gazing on Life's Page: Perspectival Vision in Tolstoy." *PMLA* 113, 436–448.

Speer, Nicole K., Jeremy R. Reynolds, Khena M. Swallow, and Jeffrey M. Zacks. 2009. "Reading Stories Activates Neural Representations of Visual and Motor Experiences." *Psychological Science* 20, no. 8, 989–999.

Swann, Jr., William B. and Lynn Carol Miller. 1982. "Why Never Forgetting a Face Matters: Visual Imagery and Social Memory." *Journal of Personality and Social Psychology* 43, no. 3, 475–480.

Tolstoi, Lev Nikolaevich. 1979. *Sobranie sochinenii v dvadtsati dvukh tomakh*. 22 vols. Moscow: Khudozhestvennaia Literatura.

Turgenev, Ivan Sergeyevich. 1978. "Letter to P. V. Annenkov. 14 Feb. 1868." In *Tolstoy: The Critical Heritage*, edited by A. V. Knowles, 181. London: Routledge & Kegan Paul.

4

A Multi-Level Cognitive Approach to Pushkin

Tom Dolack

One could argue against a cognitive approach to literary texts by saying either that we cannot know what is in the mind of an author or reader, or that even if we could know, it would not matter for the sake of what literary scholars usually care about, the interpretation of specific texts. The first objection is partly true, but that is not a major obstacle since we deal with such epistemological shortcomings all the time. The second objection has more merit, as cognitive readings of texts frequently focus on levels other than textual explication.

I have argued previously (2012) that the level of the methodological approach should correspond to the level examined. I want to argue here that cognitive approaches to culture are important beyond this. I argue this for one simple reason: The brain is the single place where all influences—internal and external—come together at a single place at a single time. All of the internal inputs of an individual, such as emotions, or bodily states, all eventually impinge on the nervous system and are carried to the brain for processing. Less intuitively, all external stimuli also ultimately lead to the brain. All external influences—speech, sensory input, the actions of other people, our environment, cultural traditions—all eventually wind up in the mind. There is nothing that affects us that does not eventually make its way to the brain. This is not reductive (not at least in the pejorative sense of that term) because that organ is the most complex object in the known universe, with somewhere around 90 billion neurons and hundreds of *trillions* of connections between those neurons. There are about as many neurons in a human brain as there are stars in our galaxy.

Nothing about the brain is simple. Or reductive.

To take seriously this view that a cognitive approach to literature can combine different subfields of cognitive science centered on different levels to form a more complete picture, I would like to look at Alexander Pushkin's masterpiece *Eugene Onegin* (1825–1832) with just such a multi-tiered methodology. First off, what can a cognitive approach tell us about Pushkin himself? How did social and historical context affect him individually? Is there a connection between his personality and his genius? What effect did his education have on his writing? None of these questions is inherently cognitive, but cognitive psychology gives us insight into the facts as we know them. Then comes *Eugene Onegin* the work. How was it composed? Why does such an important work appear so early in the Russian tradition? There is a level of textual analysis and interpretation where the psychology does not help, but an understanding of the neuroscience of creativity can certainly shed light on the creation of Pushkin's great work. Next, can we learn anything about Eugene Onegin the character if we pretend that he was a real person? He is not, but the key point is that readers treat literary characters as if they were. These are not new questions, and they are more than can be covered in a single chapter, but new tools give us new insights, or at least can supply concrete proof of things we had just assumed a priori before.

One key element of my argument as a specifically cognitive approach is that it is a mistake to view "cognitive" as referring only to the firing of individual neurons or the bright splotches of fMRI scans. Rather, all behavior has a cognitive aspect. This is not to say that that is always the appropriate level on which to examine behavior, it clearly is not, but the work of an army of researchers over the last decades has shown that not only is there a cognitive component to all human actions, but that it is an important level of explanation. With this in mind, I plan to look at three different levels of behavior that have led to the phenomenon of *Eugene Onegin*. First is Pushkin the person. The second is the behavior of Eugene Onegin the character. Finally, there is the work itself, which does not behave in any way, yet a cognitive approach can contribute to a discussion of its form and importance in the context of early-nineteenth-century Russian culture.

PUSHKIN THE AUTHOR

We can begin with Pushkin himself. Pushkin and his times are one of the most studied aspects of Russian culture. There are shelves of biographies of him and his friends, and bookcases of histories covering virtually all aspects of the period. So much, in fact, that it could become easy to cherry-pick the scholarship for what one wished to find. But there are trends that emerge, and a reasonably coherent picture emerges both of the man and his environment. In focusing on Pushkin the author, we can focus on several different levels that map onto different critical approaches. We can study Pushkin the individual and the influence of his *biography*, his *place in the tradition*, his *personality* and his *personal relationships*. We can examine Pushkin's place in a *social*, *historical*, and *cultural* context. And we can look from the most distant perspective of *evolutionary* proclivities and how they manifest themselves within the previous contexts.[1] Each of these has a distinct cognitive substrate and can interact in so many possible combinations that each individual person represents a unique, never-before-seen iteration of these levels.

Pushkin's Biography

Pushkin was not well-loved by his family. His mother was not fond of his looks and his father, not without reason, thought him not serious and did not pay him much respect until he got married. It was really only when he entered the Lycée at the age of twelve that he began to come into his own. His formative experiences appear to be either with his peasant nanny or with his fellow students. His father's main contribution to his *Bildung* appears to have been granting the young Pushkin unfettered access to his rather large and wide-ranging library of French books. The knowledge he gleaned from certain of them made him popular with his young adolescent peers in school (Feinstein 1999, 17). The looks he inherited from his great-grandfather, Abram Petrovich Gannibal—born near Lake Chad, he was captured and sold into slavery in Constantinople and eventually found himself under the protection of Peter I and given freedom, education, rank, and a wife; although Pushkin's knowledge of some of these details was off (Teletova 2006)—singled Pushkinout both in negative ways (he had the reputation of being ugly) and positive (the Romantic era had a penchant for the "exotic"). He achieved literary fame before he had even graduated, receiving the imprimatur of Russia's then-greatest poet, Gavrila Derzhavin. Pushkin was loosely associated with revolutionary elements (it's possible they did not fully trust the young poet and kept him at a distance (Lotman 2015, 55)). After the failed Decembrist Uprising, his poems were found in the possession of the would-be revolutionaries and he was exiled to what is now Romania and Ukraine, followed by one of the Pushkin estates. He was allowed to return to Petersburg after the death of Alexander I and he got married in 1831. Money problems would follow him until his death and would keep him in the capital even as he would have done well to leave it. His wife was pursued by George d'Anthès, adopted son and rumored lover of the Dutch minister plenipotentiary (Binyon 2003, 499–501). Natal'ia Pushkin was perhaps incautious, but faithful, yet Pushkin felt the need to issue a challenge, possibly because he felt the Tsar, another of Natal'ia's admirers, would support his family financially after his death, which he did (Tyrkova-Vil'iams 1929–1948, 2:457).

Pushkin's Place in the Literary Tradition

Literarily, Pushkin is recognized as the founder of Russian literature and its greatest writer. His career spans the early years of Russian literature when it was just figuring out what exactly Russian literature was. It was emerging from a period of strong imitation of Western models, figuring out what the dominant style and genres were, and was just establishing Russian, as opposed to Church Slavonic, as the literary language. His work bridges the period of Romanticism and poetry with Realism and long novels. His greatest work, *Eugene Onegin*, is a novel in verse that combines all of these trends.

He wrote at a time when professional networks were small—all the leading cultural actors knew each other and frequently visited one another, although there were two separate coteries, one in Petersburg, one in Moscow—and it was quite possible to have read everything of note written in Russian, while also keeping abreast of the main trends in multiple European traditions. The idea of a "professional writer" was just emerging. Before this, writers wrote either as a hobby in addition to serving in the government or being an estate owner, or they wrote with the specific support of the government.[2] It made for a cultural milieu where there was little distinction between social, political, professional, and cultural relationships.

He also wrote at a time when there was little formal education in Russia. Men were usually educated by a tutor until, if they could and wanted to, they went abroad to attend a university in the West. Mikhail Lomonosov, working his way up from a fishing village to the pinnacle of Russian academia, was a rare exception. Russia's first university was begun in 1724, and there were only nine universities in Russia at the end of the nineteenth century (Ol'denburg 2013). Pushkin was part of the first accepted class to the Imperial Lyceum. He would get no university education. Throughout the nineteenth century, only a small fraction of a percent of the eligible students were enrolled in an institute of higher learning (Kassow 1989, 16). Such a system restricted education and training in the arts to a very small percentage of the population as a whole, and consequently to a small percentage of the available talent pool. This had one advantage for the burgeoning field of Russian letters: it forced the Russian intelligentsia to see how things were done elsewhere, after which they brought back those ideas to Russia. It had the disadvantage of leading, at least at first, to poorly-digested copies of Western works.

A combination of the size of the Russian beau monde and Pushkin's personality brought him into contact with many different parts of Russian society. He knew the greatest cultural figures of his day, the highest-ranking officials up to the tsar himself, but he also caroused with drinkers and cardsharps. He had some familiarity with the peasantry through his time on his estates and his relationship with his nanny Arina Rodionovna. His exile brought him into contact with the populations of Bessarabia (parts of modern-day Ukraine and Romania). His exile and a later cholera epidemic gave him forced isolation. His financial straits required him to publish (the other unthinkable choice would have been to serve as a court flunky).

On a broader level, Pushkin grew up and published during uncertain times. He was born in 1799. The Napoleonic invasion and burning of Moscow happened in 1812. There was the Decembrist Uprising of 1825 following political instability in the wake of Alexander I's death. This led to a period of political repression coupled with revolutionary ferment that would ebb and flow until 1917.

Pushkin's Creativity

All of these elements of Pushkin's environment have a cognitive component to them that can be viewed as one piece among many that account for his role in Russian letters. Let's start with the most abstract idea of all, Pushkin's creativity.[3] Decades of work have shown a light—or rather a few different lights—on creativity as a cognitive process. The finding I consider the most useful for thinking about literary evolution is that the prerequisite for creativity is for two or more different mental concepts to be present in working memory at the same time. That is what is required for new connections to be made: recombination (Vandervert, Schimpf, and Liu 2007; Sandkühler and Bhattacharya 2008; Fink et al. 2012). And it does not matter if the creativity in question is a new style of painting or choosing a new password. From this point of view, creativity is nothing more and nothing less than bringing two or more previously unlinked ideas together.

As simple as this idea is, it is not so simple in reality. The extant ideas in a culture can get recombined rather quickly, so finding a new combination can be difficult. The easiest way to find new ideas is to steal them from other cultures. Not all novel ideas will fit the target culture well and therefore many will die out. And so, creativity will be helped by an environment where there is ready access to outside ideas, and yet not so ready that the target culture is already flooded with them. Population is also an important aspect. The more people there are to absorb a new innovation, to adapt it, and pass it on to others, the higher a chance there is for any adaptation to be successful (Henrich 2004; Deffner, Kandler, and Fogarty 2022). Consequently, there is a minimum population under which there will be very little cultural evolution—not because the individuals in that population lack the intelligence to innovate, but because the demographic factors aren't conducive to the preservation and propagation of innovations. Note that in this regard the effective population for Russia would have been a fraction of its total population given its literacy rate at the time,[4] and possibly only the smaller segment of that which was engaged actively in the literary life of the country. It can also help when that population is mildly fractured with separate groups that can innovate on their own and then export to and import among themselves (Derex, Perreault, and Boyd 2018).

This, as it so happens, is not a bad description of Pushkin's Russia. Russia of the first-third of the nineteenth century, had enough familiarity with European culture through direct experience and the imitations of Russian Classicism. It had the beginnings of a distinctly Russian tradition with the works of writers like Derzhavin, Nikolai Karamzin, and Denis Fonvizin. The effective population for literary evolution (the Russian reading public) had been steadily growing[5] while there were two somewhat isolated, even antagonistic, populations in Petersburg and Moscow. Pushkin knew French from the cradle, and he was exposed to French and Russian letters through his father and uncle from an early age. Pushkin studied some other European languages and was introduced to other authors, including significantly Byron by the Raevskii family.

Pushkin's Personality

On a personal level, Pushkin was intelligent but cared little for authority or rules. He often put his own needs or desires before any long-term considerations (he kept a list of the men whose wives he had slept with). He was productive, but only under his own terms. He had a wide array of friends but also made a lot of enemies (he fought twenty-six attested duels in his lifetime). He was not great with money, his debts being large factors in some of his most life-altering decisions, even up to his final decision to go through with his duel with d'Anthès.

It would not be possible to do so in a scientific manner, but we can attempt to map what we know of Pushkin's biography onto modern typologies of personality. The main system used today for categorizing personality is known as "the big 5" (McCrae and Costa 2003), composed of openness, conscientiousness, extroversion, agreeableness, and neuroticism. Each of these comprises a spectrum with its opposite. My rating of Pushkin is necessarily subjective. He is high on openness to new experiences. He was frequently low on conscientiousness, as his performance in school most clearly attests (the greatest genius of Russian letters only performed outstandingly in handwriting, drawing, and French (Simmons 1971, 45)), but his gambling debts, social reputation, and relations with the government are also evidence. It is notable that his most productive periods were when he was trapped on his estate due to exile or plague. Rating him high on extroversion seems obvious. The fact that he made no sustained effort to play nice with the government functionaries that frequently controlled his fate points to low agreeableness. The issue of Pushkin's emotional stability (neuroticism) is probably the trickiest. He did not appear to experience extreme depression, but his biography does exhibit unevenness in temperament, especially as his worries increasingly pressed on him at the end of his life, and his works betray an occupation, if not a preoccupation, with "spleen" and melancholia. I would call him slightly neurotic.

How does this match with thinking on creativity and the big five? One study that seems to match the general conclusions finds that

> openness to experience and extroversion were significantly positively correlated with creative ability. Openness also correlated positively with creative accomplishments. Although agreeableness was unrelated to creative ability it was negatively correlated with creative accomplishments. (King, Walker, and Broyles 1996, 194–95)

Pushkin fits this quite well, being positive where he needs to be, and also negative where it counts. Of the five, openness seems to be the primary correlate of creativity (McCrae 1987; McCrae and Greenberg 2014). Note that creative ability and creative achievement are separate things, and require different skill sets. Conscientiousness in particular is required for achievement (you need to actually complete projects and navigate a professional system), and yet conscientiousness may be negatively associated with openness. Even Pushkin's penchant for disagreeableness in official contexts was likely an asset. Contrary to popular belief, neuroticism doesn't appear to have any connection with creativity (King, Walker, and Broyles 1996, 195).

Can this give us any additional clues as to why Pushkin was Pushkin? Perhaps some. It cannot tell us why Pushkin specifically became Pushkin; after all he was hardly the only author to match this personality profile in his day. Indeed, some of his friends were even more open and disagreeable (his friend Wilhelm Küchelbecker tried to assassinate the tsar's brother). But it can help us figure out why someone *like* Pushkin became Pushkin.

HISTORICAL AND SOCIAL INFLUENCES

The historical period, of course, also left its mark on Pushkin's formation as a writer. One of the fastest-moving advancements in the cognitive sciences lately has been the investigation of how the environment affects our psychology. This is true on small time scales, for instance, when an image of eyes (triggering the sense of being watched) increases voluntary contributions to pay for communally-available tea and coffee (Bateson, Nettle, and Roberts 2006). It can influence more general behaviors, such as how the means of subsistence in an environment, which is directly tied to local ecology, can affect the psychology of food sharing (Kaplan and Gurven 2005). A stressful or unpredictable environment can lead to early reproduction since doing otherwise could result in not having any children (Hill and Kaplan 1999; Ellis et al. 2009; Boyer 2020, 144–45). "Unpredictable environment" can be triggered by personal experience, such as inadequate caloric intake or a violent home (Belsky, Steinberg, and Draper 1991), or it can be linked to broader events, such as rates of death or natural disaster (Ellis et al. 2009).

While the Pushkins were not quite abusive to their son, they were also not supportive. Pushkin established a closer bond with his peasant nanny. He was glad to be shipped off to the new Lycée (Tyrkova-Williams 1929–1948, 1:42). It also cannot be forgotten that before Pushkin turned twenty-six, he had lived through the assassination of a tsar, a war, the invasion of his country by a foreign army and the burning of the old capital, the flooding of Petersburg, the death of another tsar followed by political turmoil, and a failed revolt followed by a violent crackdown. It is not determinism to point out that a man who inherited the predispositions of his mother and father could have been nudged in the direction of greater risk-taking, personal and professional, as a result of the times he lived in.

And again, it is worth pointing out that increased risk-taking would only be worthwhile in certain cultural settings. Pushkin found out the hard way that political liberality could get him into trouble, but if one had the right connections, cultural and poetic liberality were acceptable. Of course, it did not hurt that Pushkin's politics on certain issues (the Polish question, the Caucasus) were not so liberal. This allowed him to continue publishing and to have the widespread influence that he continues to have. The cultural scene of 1820s and 1830s Russia was a minefield, but one that could be navigated.

Interpersonal Connections

Through a combination of Pushkin's family connections, his education, his innate gregariousness, and the limited number of publishing Russian authors during the first decades of the nineteenth century, Pushkin had personal connections with virtually all cultural actors of note. These connections would serve as a form of cross-pollination that is an important part of creativity.

He wrote at a time of rapid stylistic change. His career began during the reign of Neoclassicism. He came of age during Romanticism, and he helped to usher in the age of Realism. While this fecundity is often viewed as a result of his genius, it can also be viewed as a cause of it. The need to work in so many different genres and styles would have forced him to make connections he otherwise might not have if he had the luxury of sticking to Romantic poetry for his whole career.

Cultural and Demographic Context

If we begin with the assumption that certain cultural environments are more conducive to innovations the same way that some natural environments are, what sort of cultural milieu would be more likely to elicit a single figure that would come to dominate the literary landscape? The scientific study of creativity combined with the growing field of cultural evolution gives us some rough guidelines for what to look for, although they should be recognized as rough.

One surprising insight into the evolution of traditions is that the real key to the emergence and maintenance of a strong tradition isn't quality, but quantity. Avoiding what Oliver Morin calls "the flop problem"—a behavior occurring once and never being copied—requires numbers.

> The Flop Problems can be solved in two ways: a tradition can possess some intrinsic appeal, or it can travel in a population where demography, institutions, and storage techniques make it easier for individuals to have cultural contacts with one another. Traditions can live without one of these conditions, not without both. (2016, 217–18)

Morin is not speaking of "high culture" when he speaks of traditions, and talk of "intrinsic appeal" is tricky with art. It can be argued that some artistic works are more intrinsically interesting, but this runs into the issue that we simply grow tired of styles, we habituate to them, and seek novelty (Tynianov [1927] 2019a; Martindale 1990; Dolack 2010). And so, we're left with the quantity of "cultural contacts." For Morin, the way to do that is to "grow the public domain," and to "communicate abundantly and exchange a lot of information" (2016, 233, 251). That's a numbers game, and it was not until Pushkin's time—independent of Pushkin himself—that there were enough literate Russians, writers writing in Russian, and venues for publishing and reading that work that a stable "Russian tradition" could form. If Pushkin didn't come forward, a different Pushkin would have. It may have taken a bit longer, but there would have been one eventually.

Furthermore, once a writer of Pushkin's stature arose, it greatly decreased the chances of a second one emerging. All cultural products are produced in relation to some combination of models (nobody reinvents the idea of writing anymore), and once a model of sufficient weight comes about, future work will be written in relation to that model (called model-based imitation (Richerson and Boyd 2005, 124)). No matter how good future artists are, they will appear secondary simply by virtue of coming later.

While both the reading public and venues for publication were growing quickly, Russia was also at a crossroads culturally. Russian high culture up to the nineteenth century was highly inflected with Western models. Educated Russians often spoke French better than Russian. After the Napoleonic invasion, there was a sharp, but not complete, break with French culture that ushered in a revival of more homegrown influences as well as concerted efforts to develop a specifically Russian culture where it had not existed before. Indeed, Pushkin's works often thematize this very issue. This led to a mixing of different sources that was also conducive to creativity.

This cognitive approach points us to the elements that can play a role in fostering creativity and in the emergence of a linguistic tradition. These include as large a population of writers and readers as possible, productive interactions with other artists and thinkers, and exposure to a diversity of traditions. It helps to expose all of these environmental factors to an individual who has the talent, inclination, personal qualities, education, time, and means to make use of them. None of this is to say that Pushkin was some sort of miracle that just happened to appear at just the right historical moment. Cultural development, like biological development, is more robust than that. The combination may have been unlikely, but not necessarily unique. Pushkin altered the literary terrain for all who followed him, but in an unaltered landscape, someone eventually would have made use of the same conducive setting to assume a similar, if not the exact same, position in the Russian pantheon.

ONEGIN THE CHARACTER

Eugene Onegin himself is, of course, not real and therefore has no mind. Is there any sense, then, in examining a figment of Pushkin's, and subsequently our, imagination from a cognitive perspective? I would answer that to the extent that we treat literary characters as if they were real, the answer is yes, but that "as if" is an important asterisk. Fictional creations are under no requirement to conform to our own mental biases. And yet they frequently do. So what insights can we gain on this character if we view him as a real person? Do any of his eccentricities make more sense from a psychological perspective? Let me focus on perhaps the strangest thing he does: the murder of Lenskii.

Violence, war, altruism, and peace have been some of the most studied topics in psychology over the last few decades (de Waal 2007; Boehm 2012; Tomasello et al. 2012; Pinker 2012). Explaining violence itself is not that difficult as violence is readily observable in the animal kingdom, including all other primates. Violence is usually selfish, and so makes sense evolutionarily. What stymied scientists for a long time was altruism, specifically being nice to non-kin (Harman 2010). I'm nice to those related to me because they share my genes. Helping them helps me to the extent that they share pieces of me. Helping those who can help me is also no huge mystery. Assuming I can keep track of individuals in my group, I just need to keep track of who has helped me in the past (Wilkinson 1986). But helping, or even simply not cheating, people I've never met and won't meet again requires an explanation.

And the explanation is cultural norms. The same adaptation that allows us to tell if a hemline is in fashion also allows us to treat people with trust even before they have had a chance to earn it. From an early age, we assimilate the norms of our culture to the extent that we often don't even realize that they are byproducts of our specific culture. We assume the local to be universal. So long as we are raised in a culture that establishes rules for handling anonymous interactions, peaceful relations can be established. It is this capacity that underlies the growth of human society beyond small bands (Tomasello 2015); the formation of external organizations to enforce these rules is a later invention.

This is why Onegin's murder of Lenskii is so shocking. While there is certainly variety in the level of trust and acceptance of violence in different societies, nineteenth-century Russian aristocratic society did not accept wanton murder. Duels were seemingly common in the first decades of the century, despite being officially illegal, but there were rules governing how they should be handled, and there were ways to avoid bloodshed or killing built into the system (Lotman 2018, 45). Indeed, it is a great insult when Eugene fails to abide by these rules in his duel, and Lenskii could have considered the duel aborted when Onegin shows up two hours late (Lotman 2014, 366–67). But the duel itself violates basic social assumptions: Onegin and Lenskii are nominally friends, the duel is fought over the flimsiest of reasons (Eugene flirts with Lenskii's fiancée as revenge for being dragged to a party), which turns out to be a misunderstanding (Olga never returned Eugene's feigned interest), and the rules are never really observed.

What can a cognitive approach, then, contribute to our understanding of such a nonsensical act? Again, it helps to approach this from a multilevel perspective. Robert Sapolsky's *Behave* presents a useful rubric for approaching this issue. He sets out to show the different influences at different time scales ranging from the second before an action to our evolutionary heritage going back millennia. Taking a similar approach, let's start with the immediate cause of Onegin's wrath: the party. The text points to what could be considered a disgust reaction or a violation of honor. Despite the fact that the plot has already established Onegin's goodwill toward Tatiana when he lets her down easy following her admission of love, he takes umbrage at her behavior at the party. She is beside herself upon seeing the man she was so recently embarrassed before: "слезы из очей/Хотят уж капать; уж готова/Бедняжка в обморок упасть [tears from her eyes/Are about to flow; the poor thing/is about to faint" (Pushkin [1830] 1950, 113).[6] Such signs

Давно терпеть не мог Евгений:
Довольно их он перенес [. . .]
Надулся он и, негодуя,
Поклялся Ленского взбесить
И уж порядком отомстить. (Pushkin [1830] 1950, 113)
Eugene had long grown sick of those:
He had suffered enough [. . .]
He sulked and, getting indignant,
Swore to enrage Lenskii
And avenge himself like he should.

It is clear that the proximate cause of the indignation is the sign of Tatiana's "girlish [*devich'i*]" reactions, although he is already angry when he arrives.

The scene shows a mix of the personal and the social, the cultural and the individual. Tatiana's emotional reaction is right out of the novels she reads, especially the threat of fainting, and both of them play to gender stereotypes. Eugene's overdone reaction is partly a result of his own personal history (he appears to have encountered this frequently in the past), but he needs to avenge himself on Lenskii "*poriadkom*," which can either be read as "severely" or "as should be/as is socially expected." Since it is Lenskii who later escalates to outright violence, the latter interpretation fits better. The "severe" part comes after. But what sort of reaction does Onegin show? Looking at the text, it appears to be a disgust reaction.

This might seem odd at first, as disgust is not usually associated with teenage sulkiness—not to mention that Onegin does not appear to be at all disgusted with Tatiana—but disgust can, in fact, be the result of norm violation. Rozin et al. note that "sociomoral disgust is triggered by a variety of situations in which people behave without dignity or in which people strip others of their dignity" (1999, 575). Given Onegin's proclivities, it can be easy to see that, from his perspective, Tatiana was lacking dignity at that moment. Onegin's choice of punishment—light flirting with Lenskii's fiancée—also fits this schema. In fact, it is not punishment, per se. Dubreuil notes that such disgust or indignation can elicit "behaviors of mockery, exclusion, and ostracism" (2010). These are all low-cost behaviors. This is the perfect reaction to the situation: it punishes both of the people who have annoyed him at the same time by making them jealous. It is not a coincidence that Olga is both Lenskii's fiancée and Tatiana's sister. It also stands little chance of escalating the situation. Little, but not zero.

Or rather it would be perfect in another environment, but Onegin is no longer in Petersburg where such behavior is commonplace, even expected. Instead, he's among countryfolk. This points to another important insight of psychology: there is no such thing as innately ideal behavior; all behavior is context-dependent and can be either good or bad depending on the environment. We absorb our norms of behavior as children (as Pechorin was keenly aware), but if we move to a new locale with new norms, we must check our priors. And so Onegin miscalculates.

Lenskii does not see the flirtation as a light jibe. It instead elicits what is clearly an honor reaction. It is easy to view Lenskii's summons to be a literary affectation gotten from Romantic books, and it quite clearly is, but it can also have a psychological explanation. Lenskii may seem like the sensitive poet, but his actions have every hallmark of a culture of honor where men (primarily) are quick to violence in response to perceived threats. Cultures of honor arise in societies where resources are scarce or easy to steal, and so deterrence is an important survival strategy. "[T]o maintain credible power of deterrence, the individual must project a stance of willingness to commit mayhem and to risk wounds or death for himself" (Nisbett and Cohen 1996, xv). Cultures of honor are often found in pastoralist societies, although more recent work has shown that they can also survive in societies where institutions are weak and authorities are ineffective (Nowak et al. 2016). This is perhaps the underlying logic behind Nancy Kollmann's argument for the role of honor in sixteenth- and seventeenth-century Russia (1999). Lenskii's quick leap to pistols at dawn may seem bizarre, but it has its own logic. Sapolsky's comment, while not about Russia, seems apt: "[d]ueling was commonplace, the point being not that you were willing to kill but that you were willing to die for your honor" (2017, 285).

Onegin's failure to find a way out of the duel, combined with his lethal shot, also looks different in this light. Just like Lenskii, he too is better off with possible death than definite dishonor. What this shows is that the Petersburg dandy was just a thin veneer over the underlying honorable pastoralist. A few generations of cultural tradition can only do so much in the face of thousands of years of evolution. This approach points to a reality where recent cultural norms are the most visible outside layer, which may be all people ever see, but certain circumstances can draw out behavior from much deeper, ancient sources. This dichotomy pops up elsewhere and shows that Pushkin's characters may not be quite the "creatures of culture" that Todd makes them out to be (1986, 113), but rather that culture and nature are at odds; it's just that nature is not like Rousseau or Herder envisioned it.

That is just one example from a novel whose heroes behave bizarrely on multiple occasions, but the model can be applied elsewhere. Tatiana's rashness in writing to Eugene can be seen as a worthwhile gamble for a girl lacking mating options that are on her level. Her rejection of him later is not just admirable loyalty to her husband but is also a tacit acknowledgment that Eugene is now beneath her socially, a fact that surely changes his tone toward her. The characters all struggle with the proper cultural role to play in the given situations they find themselves in, but at the same time, those cultural roles don't fit with underlying psychological proclivities (violence to protect honor, disgust at a social gaffe, risking ostracism for the sake of a high-risk mating strategy). Custom may be "a despot among people" (Pushkin [1830] 1950, 20), but there are other forces that cannot be ignored.

ONEGIN THE TEXT

Finally, I would like to consider the formal qualities of *Eugene Onegin* the text. Specifically, I will look at the rhyme scheme. This level of inquiry is likely the most conducive for examining how Pushkin exemplifies what we know of the creative process on a cognitive level, and the rhyme scheme of the novel makes a fine example of the creative process I previously described. Since creativity is founded on the combining of disparate elements, on the recombination of old sources, creativity is never a solo endeavor. Everything is created as part of a chain, of which any single work of art is merely the most recent link forged.[7] *Eugene Onegin* is a perfect example of this.

We can start with the genre: as a novel in verse, it is, on the broadest level, a hybrid of lyric verse and the novel. Pushkin chose the most storied form of modern European poetry, the sonnet. But he adapted it for his own purposes, creating the Onegin sonnet with a distinct rhyme scheme: aBaBccDDeFFeGG. Note how the pattern of the quatrains changes, how the middle quatrain can also be viewed as two couplets, and how the last six lines can be read as a quatrain and a couplet, or two tercets. The lines can scan differently based on how the syntax overlaps with the line breaks. Here we can see an example of how Pushkin takes a form that European poetry had grown tired of and makes something flexible that he can bend to his needs. This flexibility, we can conjecture, is central to the form's ability to carry an entire novel.

We can delve deeper here. Borrowing from Gestalt psychology, Reuven Tsur discusses "requiredness" (2008, 115). Texts, especially poetry, set up patterns that demand to be completed. The stronger the pattern, the higher the requiredness. The opening quatrain of the opening stanza sets up an expectation of alternating rhyme. That expectation is not fulfilled when the second stanza consists of two couplets. Any updated expectation is further thwarted when the next four lines feature enclosed rhyme. Even if, after sufficient stanzas, one does get used to this constantly shifting structure, each individual stanza can shift how we interpret the schema. If we look at the second stanza, which can be viewed as a quatrain or two couplets, syntax will influence our reading. It would be natural to read 1.XII as two couplets as there is a sentence break marked by an exclamation mark after the second line: "Как он язвительно злословил!/Какие сети им готовил!/Но вы, блаженные мужья,/С ним оставались вы друзья [How scathingly he cursed!/What nets he prepared for them!/But you, blessed husbands,/You remained friends with him" (Pushkin [1830] 1950, 14). Compare with 5.XI, where there is a complete enjambment between lines six and seven: "В сугробах снежных перед нею/Шумит, клубит волной своею/Кипучий, темный и седой/Поток, не скованный зимой; [Before her among the snowbanks/Hum and rise in waves/A roiling, dark and grey/Wave, unfettered by winter;" (Pushkin [1830] 1950, 104). The first example has a natural and emotive pause, while the second forces the reader to plow through the line break to get to the subject of the verb.

Another cognitive process noted by Tsur (2008, 33–36) also seems at play here. In response to slight ambiguity in visual stimuli, people tend to either level the ambiguity so that it no longer exists, or they sharpen the ambiguity so that it is no longer slight. This can be done in isolation, but Pushkin appears to go out of his way to stop us from getting into a rut and growing bored with what would otherwise become the same thing page after page for around 400 stanzas.

The fact that such variability is possible within a strictly delineated form is key to Pushkin's creativity. He constantly found ways of making the old seem new and of making the new seem familiar. Space permitting, I could make a similar argument for Pushkin's use of language, style, metaphor, and intertextuality. But as special as Pushkin was, he wasn't special in a special way since this is simply how creativity works. As I have tried to show, he did something that nobody before him had done, but he also represented a constellation of forces that nobody before him had gathered in one place. A cognitive approach to creativity can walk a line between focusing on the peculiar individuality of geniuses and having those individual points disappear in a sea of influences. Taking the mind seriously as a central focus for the study of literature allows for the external and internal to meet in one place. It can remove the untouchability of the great cultural figures while supplying a way to approach them. Such a view won't replace any of the existing ways of reading Pushkin or any other artist, but it can supply an organizing principle for bringing together different approaches that have seemed mutually exclusive.

NOTES

1. For a recent and productive evolutionary approach to Pushkin, see Bethea (2023).
2. See Gukovskii (1972) on why the eighteenth century wasn't all panegyric odes.
3. For another psychological approach to Pushkin's creativity, see Cooke (1998).
4. Thirteen percent in those over nine years of age in 1847, according to Mironov (1991, 245).
5. See Brooks (1985) for a broader discussion of these trends.
6. Translations from Pushkin are my own.
7. Tynianov takes a more extreme version of this stance ([1922] 2019b).

BIBLIOGRAPHY

Bateson, Melissa, Daniel Nettle, and Gilbert Roberts. 2006. "Cues of Being Watched Enhance Cooperation in a Real-World Setting." *Biology Letters* 2 (3): 412–14. https://doi.org/10.1098/rsbl.2006.0509.

Belsky, Jay, Laurence Steinberg, and Patricia Draper. 1991. "Childhood Experience, Interpersonal Development, and Reproductive Strategy: An Evolutionary Theory of Socialization." *Child Development* 62 (4): 647–70. https://doi.org/10.1111/j.1467-8624.1991.tb01558.x.

Bethea, David M. 2023. *The Pushkin Project: Russia's Favorite Writer, Modern Evolutionary Thought, and Teaching Inner-City Youth*. Boston: Academic Studies Press.

Binyon, T. J. 2003. *Pushkin: A Biography*. New York: Alfred A. Knopf.

Boehm, Christopher. 2012. *Moral Origins: The Evolution of Virtue, Altruism, and Shame*. New York: Basic Books.

Boyer, Pascal. 2020. *Minds Make Societies: How Cognition Explains the World Humans Create*. New Haven: Yale University Press.

Brooks, Jeffrey. 1985. *When Russia Learned to Read: Literacy and Popular Literature, 1861-1917*. Princeton: Princeton University Press.

Cooke, Brett. 1998. *Pushkin and the Creative Process*. Gainesville: University Press of Florida.

De Waal, Frans B. M. 2007. "Putting the Altruism Back into Altruism: The Evolution of Empathy." *Annual Review of Psychology* 59 (1): 279–300. https://doi.org/10.1146/annurev.psych.59.103006.093625.

Deffner, Dominik, Anne Kandler, and Laurel Fogarty. 2022. "Effective Population Size for Culturally Evolving Traits." *PLOS Computational Biology* 18 (4): e1009430. https://doi.org/10.1371/journal.pcbi.1009430.

Derex, Maxime, Charles Perreault, and Robert Boyd. 2018. "Divide and Conquer: Intermediate Levels of Population Fragmentation Maximize Cultural Accumulation." *Philosophical Transactions of the Royal Society B: Biological Sciences* 373 (1743): 20170062. https://doi.org/10.1098/rstb.2017.0062.

Dolack, Tom. 2010. "Imitation and Literary Evolution." *Politics and Culture* 1. https://www.academia.edu/713618/Imitation_and_Literary_Evolution.

Dolack, Tom. 2012. "Homo Oneginensis: Pushkin and Evo-Cognitive Approaches to Literature." *STYLE* 46 (3_4): 338–54.

Dubreuil, Benoît. 2010. "Punitive Emotions and Norm Violations." *Philosophical Explorations* 13 (1): 35–50. https://doi.org/10.1080/13869790903486776.

Ellis, Bruce J., Aurelio José Figueredo, Barbara H. Brumbach, and Gabriel L. Schlomer. 2009. "Fundamental Dimensions of Environmental Risk: The Impact of Harsh versus Unpredictable Environments on the Evolution and Development of Life History Strategies." *Human Nature* 20 (2): 204–68. https://doi.org/10.1007/s12110-009-9063-7.

Feinstein, Elaine. 1999. *Pushkin: A Biography*. Hopewell, NJ: Ecco Press.

Fink, Andreas, Karl Koschutnig, Mathias Benedek, Gernot Reishofer, Anja Ischebeck, Elisabeth M. Weiss, and Franz Ebner. 2012. "Stimulating Creativity via the Exposure to Other People's Ideas." *Human Brain Mapping* 33 (11): 2603–10. https://doi.org/10.1002/hbm.21387.

Gukovskii, G. A. 1972. *Russkaia poeziia XVIII veka*. Munich: W. Fink Verlag.

Harman, Oren Solomon. 2010. *The Price of Altruism: George Price and the Search for the Origins of Kindness*. New York: Norton.

Henrich, Joseph. 2004. "Demography and Cultural Evolution: How Adaptive Cultural Processes Can Produce Maladaptive Losses: The Tasmanian Case." *American Antiquity* 69 (2): 197–214. https://doi.org/10.2307/4128416.

Hill, Kim, and Hillard Kaplan. 1999. "Life History Traits in Humans: Theory and Empirical Studies." *Annual Review of Anthropology* 28 (1): 397–430. https://doi.org/10.1146/annurev.anthro.28.1.397.

Kaplan, Hillard, and Michael Gurven. 2005. "The Natural History of Human Food Sharing and Cooperation: A Review and a New Multi-Individual Approach to the Negotiation of Norms." In *Moral Sentiments and Material Interests: The Foundations of Cooperation in Economic Life*, edited by Herbert Gintis, Samuel Bowles, Robert Boyd and Ernst Feh, 75–113. Cambridge, MA: MIT Press.

Kassow, Samuel D. 1989. *Students, Professors, and the State in Tsarist Russia*. Berkeley: University of California Press.

King, Laura A., Lori McKee Walker, and Sheri J. Broyles. 1996. "Creativity and the Five-Factor Model." *Journal of Research in Personality* 30 (2): 189–203. https://doi.org/10.1006/jrpe.1996.0013.

Kollmann, Nancy Shields. 1999. *By Honor Bound: State and Society in Early Modern Russia*. Ithaca, NY: Cornell University Press.

Lotman, Yurii. 2014. *Roman A.S. Pushkina "Evgenii Onegin": kommentarii*. Saint-Petersburg: Azbuka.

Lotman, Yurii. 2015. *Aleksandr Sergeevich Pushkin: biografiia pisatelia*. Saint-Petersburg: Azbuka.

Lotman, Yuri. 2018. "The Duel." Translated by Laura E. Christians. *Pushkin Review / Pushkinskii Vestnik* 20: 41–54.

Martindale, Colin. 1990. *The Clockwork Muse: The Predictability of Artistic Change*. New York: BasicBooks.

McCrae, Robert R. 1987. "Creativity, Divergent Thinking, and Openness to Experience." *Journal of Personality and Social Psychology* 52: 1258–65. https://doi.org/10.1037/0022-3514.52.6.1258.

McCrae, Robert R., and Paul T. Costa. 2003. *Personality in Adulthood: A Five-Factor Theory Perspective*. New York: Guilford Press.

McCrae, Robert R., and David M. Greenberg. 2014. "Openness to Experience." In *The Wiley Handbook of Genius*, edited by Dean Keith Simonton, 222–43. Hoboken, NJ: Wiley-Blackwell.

Mironov, Boris N. 1991. "The Development of Literacy in Russia and the USSR from the Tenth to the Twentieth Centuries." *History of Education Quarterly* 31 (2): 229–52. https://doi.org/10.2307/368437.

Morin, Olivier. 2016. *How Traditions Live and Die*. Oxford: Oxford University Press.

Nisbett, Richard E., and Dov Cohen. 1996. *Culture of Honor: The Psychology of Violence in the South*. New York: Westview Press.

Nowak, Andrzej, Michele J. Gelfand, Wojciech Borkowski, Dov Cohen, and Ivan Hernandez. 2016. "The Evolutionary Basis of Honor Cultures." *Psychological Science* 27 (1): 12–24.

Oldenburg, Sergei. 2013. *Tsarstvovanie Imperatora Nikolaia II*. Vol. 1. Nizhnii Novgorod: Chernaia sotnia.

Pinker, Steven. 2012. *The Better Angels of Our Nature: A History of Violence and Humanity*. London: Penguin.

Pushkin, Aleksandr. 1950. *Polnoe sobranie sochinenii v desiati tomakh*. Moskow: Izd-vo Akademii nauk SSSR.

Richerson, Peter J., and Robert Boyd. 2005. *Not by Genes Alone: How Culture Transformed Human Evolution*. Chicago: University of Chicago Press.

Rozin, Paul, Laura Lowery, Sumio Imada, and Jonathan Haidt. 1999. "The CAD Triad Hypothesis: A Mapping between Three Moral Emotions (Contempt, Anger, Disgust) and Three Moral Codes (Community, Autonomy, Divinity)." *Journal of Personality and Social Psychology* 76 (4): 574–86. https://doi.org/10.1037/0022-3514.76.4.574.

Sandkühler, Simone, and Joydeep Bhattacharya. 2008. "Deconstructing Insight: EEG Correlates of Insightful Problem Solving." *PLoS ONE* 3 (1): e1459. https://doi.org/10.1371/journal.pone.0001459.

Sapolsky, Robert M. 2017. *Behave: The Biology of Humans at Our Best and Worst*. New York: Penguin Press.

Simmons, Ernest J. 1971. *Pushkin*. Gloucester, MA: P. Smith.

Teletova, N. K. 2006. "A. P. Gannibal: On the Occasion of the Three Hundredth Anniversary of the Birth of Alexander Pushkin's Great-Grandfather." In *Under the Sky of My Africa: Alexander Pushkin and Blackness*, 46–78. Northwestern University Press.

Todd, William Mills. 1986. *Fiction and Society in the Age of Pushkin: Ideology, Institutions, and Narrative*. Cambridge, MA: Harvard University Press.

Tomasello, Michael. 2015. *A Natural History of Human Morality*. Cambridge, MA: Harvard University Press.

Tomasello, Michael, Alicia P. Melis, Claudio Tennie, Emily Wyman, and Esther Herrmann. 2012. "Two Key Steps in the Evolution of Human Cooperation: The Interdependence Hypothesis." *Current Anthropology* 53 (6): 673–92. https://doi.org/10.1086/668207.

Tsur, Reuven. 2008. *Toward a Theory of Cognitive Poetics*, 2nd expanded and updated ed. Brighton: Sussex Academic Press.

Tynianov, Yuri. [1927] 2019a. "On Literary Evolution." In *Permanent Evolution: Selected Essays on Literature, Theory and Film*, edited and translated by Ainsley Morse and Philip Redko, 267–82. Boston: Academic Studies Press.

Tynianov, Yuri. [1922] 2019b. "The Ode as an Oratorical Genre." In *Permanent Evolution: Selected Essays on Literature, Theory and Film*, edited and translated by Ainsley Morse and Philip Redko, 77–113. Boston: Academic Studies Press.

Tyrkova-Vil'iams, Ariadna. 1929–1948. *Zhizn' Pushkina*. 2 Vols. Paris: YMCA-Press.

Vandervert, Larry R., Paul H. Schimpf, and Hesheng Liu. 2007. "How Working Memory and the Cerebellum Collaborate to Produce Creativity and Innovation." *Creativity Research Journal* 19 (1): 1–18. https://doi.org/10.1080/10400410709336873.

Wilkinson, Gerald S. 1986. "Social Grooming in the Common Vampire Bat, *Desmodus Rotundus*." *Animal Behaviour* 34 (6): 1880–89. https://doi.org/10.1016/S0003-3472(86)80274-3.

5

Staying Imperturbable in the Face of Fate

Alexander Pushkin's Gothic Stories Conveying the Code of Honor in the Face of the Supernatural

Ekaterina Chelpanova

The narrator-reader relationship in Alexander Pushkin's oeuvre is notoriously difficult to determine, and it has been intriguing readers and literary scholars for a long time. When addressing the problem of the reader-narrator relationship in Pushkin's works, scholars have predominantly focused on *Eugene Onegin* (Semenko 1995, 234; Lešić-Thomas 2008). While a considerable volume of scholarship has been dedicated to narrative strategies in Pushkin's other literary works, notably "The Queen of Spades," those publications interpret Pushkin's well-known shifts in narrative mode as a consequence of mixing two aesthetic paradigms, Romanticism and Realism (Grenier 2001, 19), or as an element of a gothic-fantastic genre (Whitehead 2006).

In this chapter, I explore Pushkin's narrative strategies in two gothic stories, "The Queen of Spades" (1834) and "The Coffin-Maker" (1831), through the lens of a more integrative approach, namely, postclassical narratology that draws on Monika Fludernik's and David Herman's theories of narrative. David Herman suggests that the reader projects themselves into the narrative and interprets it "in response to the exigencies of their everyday lives" (2002, 23). This approach provides scaffolding for a more reader-centered analysis of literary texts. Monika Fludernik replaced "the definition of narrativity as event sequence (traditionally based on the plot) with a conception of narrative that relies on representation *of*, and *by means of*, consciousness" and redefined narrative "as rendering not necessarily a plot but a character's or narrator's experiential reality" (2003, 120; italics in original). According to this approach, narratives do not "merely convey semantic content" but "encode in their very structure the way of experiencing the world" (Herman 2010, 156). The ultimate goal of narrating a story, as seen from this angle, is such that the reader, through connecting to the character's or the narrator's "experiential reality" (Fludernik 2003, 120), constructs new "scaffolding for conscious experience" (Herman 2002, 156) or, in other words, redefines their broader values and the way they interact with the world. When Fludernik differentiates between the character's and the narrator's experiential reality, it does not mean that the narrator and the characters possess their own consciousness. Both the narrator and the characters are fictional, yet, the way the split between the characters' and the narrator's experiences is constructed reflects the worldview that the author is trying to convey to the reader.

I concur with those postclassical narratologists who suggest that the reader's response is not necessarily an emotion but rather a certain "mood," and this mood is not necessarily represented in the space of the story itself but rather, as I will show in my chapter, is "evoked" by the story (Caracciolo 2018, 18). Marco Caracciolo defines mood as a bodily feeling, "a shift in the audience's embodied orientation towards the world" (2018, 18). In this article, I will show that the mood that Pushkin's stories evoke is determined by the author's values. These values are not represented or embodied by any of the characters and/or their utterances. To a certain extent, as I will show, they are represented by the narrator's voice, but for the most part they are of non-representational nature but they are evoked through the stories' narrative techniques.

In my reconstruction of the reader's phenomenological experience evoked by the stories' narrative techniques, I rely on Alina Israeli's study of Russian reflexives and passive constructions and Mikhail Bakhtin's theory of the grotesque. I will show how Pushkin's choices of grammatical forms create the experience of a clash between the point of view of the narrator and the space of the story, which eventually creates a particular mood in the reader. Throughout the article, I will provide the Russian original of Pushkin's texts when the Russian grammatical forms and word choices modify the reader's experience as compared to the English version. If the translation does not modify the reader's experience, I will use the English translation.

My decision to unite "The Queen of Spades" and "The Coffin-Maker" is premised on the reader's experience or the mood that these stories evoke. Both stories concern the protagonists' relationship with the supernatural and their attitude toward things that lie outside of human control, such as fate, luck, and death. While many of Pushkin's literary works employ "the agency of a capricious fate" to "make a statement about individual characters" (Bethea and Davydov 1981, 14), my choice of "The Queen of Spades" and "The Coffin-Maker" is based on their direct, non-metaphorical portrayal of the intrusion of the supernatural into human life. In "The Queen of Spades," the main character Hermann tries to manipulate the supernatural through forcing the Old Countess (who, as her portrayal suggests, possesses some supernatural or occult knowledge) to reveal to him the secret of the three cards that will grant him endless luck. The Countess reveals the secret in a dream after her physical death, yet demands that Hermann in return marries her maidservant. He does not fulfill the treaty and as a result gets severely punished by a hostile supernatural force. The maidservant, who was deceived by Hermann, is, on the other hand, favored by fate.

In "The Coffin-Maker," the main character's occupation is making coffins. As a result of his obsession with money, he accidentally gets absorbed by the supernatural when his clients, the dead people, decide to visit him. At the very last moment, he escapes the supernatural visitation and wakes up to his mundane routine.

In many other Pushkin stories, particularly in *The Tales of Belkin,* there are references to the interventions of the supernatural in human life, but in most cases, the supernatural forces are referred to metaphorically. For instance, in "The Stationmaster," the invasion of the supernatural is referred to as a sudden "blindness," while in "The Blizzard," the presence of the supernatural is suggested by the phrase "[a]s if someone was guiding him" (Bethea and Davydov 1981, 12).

Most importantly, in both of Pushkin's stories that are the focus of this chapter, the narrator's attitude toward the characters and the action is constructed as emotionally distant and dispassionate. A detached and restricted—although at times ironic—narrative voice helps sustain "a pervasive sense of the occult" throughout the stories (Davydov 1999, 311). As I suggest, such a narrative voice mimics a dispassionate voice of fate or the supernatural, which does not get involved with problems of the mundane, and the effect of distance between the characters and the narrator is meant to communicate a particular code of honor in regard to the supernatural and things outside of human control, such as luck or death. When applied to Pushkin's gothic stories, the category of honor or keeping the face transcends the social dimension and encompasses the relationship with metaphysical fate (Kollman 1990, 27).

One of the important values conveyed by Pushkin's gothic stories is refraining from emotional involvement in the face of things that lie outside a person's control, such as fate, luck, or misfortune. Presumably, honor, understood as total inner freedom from fear and emotional obsessions, was imagined by Pushkin as an important marker of belonging to the nobility. In his notes "On the Noble Class [*O dvorianstve*]", Pushkin indicated that the key personal qualities that a nobleman should possess are independence and bravery (in the Russian original: *nezavisimost'*, *khrabrost'*) (n.d.). These qualities are not necessarily given by nature but should be trained. The gothic stories shed light on how Pushkin understood "independence." His narrative strategies construct the "mood" of inner independence as total freedom from fears and obsessions, not only in the face of mundane authorities but also metaphysical fate.

Some scholars have denied supernatural readings of "The Queen of Spades" and *The Tales of Belkin*, instead proposing to treat them as moral parables (Rosen 2002; Gregg 2000). This approach is dualistic because it is premised on the idea that the plot of the story and the narratives serve as a package for some deeper ideas. Yet, in Fludernik's and Herman's approach, a story constitutes a wholeness, "a world" within which one cannot juxtapose a plot, an author, a narrator, and some hidden "deeper meaning." This "deeper meaning" eventually is the reader's embodied experience, not an "idea" of some sort.

The first analysis of "The Queen of Spades" through the lens of the reader's experience can be discovered in the work of an early-twentieth-century critic, Dmitrii Darskii. Darskii suggested that the narrator-reader relationship in Pushkin's gothic stories functions as a model of asserting control over anxieties produced by uncontrollable fate. He used the descriptors "dry manner of narration" (*sukhoi slog*) and "despotic laconism" to define Pushkin's narrative mode. In "The Queen of Spades," Darskii wrote:

> In "The Queen of Spades" everything is striking: the style, the epigraphs, the composition, and the idea. First, the style: dry, concentrated, energetic, with a cold hatred towards *belles lettres* and even more so, towards beautiful feelings—the style of a dandy. Dandyism is evident in the barely perceptible pose, in the icy intonation, in the arrogant irony, in the aristocratic tact, a prescriptive mode that privileges maintaining self-control in moments of extreme anxiety; finally, it is evident in the impetuous speed with which the story unfolds. It unfolds with despotic laconism. (2022)

In her book on *The Little Tragedies*, Svetlana Evdokimova also suggests that Pushkin's literary device of "extreme compression of the form" leading to "intense ambiguity at the level of plot, ideas, images and words" communicates a particular code of honor, "bravery" in regard to the uncertainty and unpredictability of life and fate (2004, 15). In his notes on literature, Pushkin himself once compared the narrator's voice to fate, stating that a good narrator should aspire to the same degree of impartiality ("*dramaticheskii poet, bespristrastnyi, kak sud'ba* [a dramatic poet, as dispassionate as fate]"; 2010, 129). Elaborating on this idea, Pushkin also claimed that a good narrator should refrain from expressing their point of view and remain as laconic as possible ("He should not cheat and take any side while sacrificing the other. Neither he, nor his political thoughts, nor his secret and open passions should manifest themselves in the tragedy [. . .]" (2010, 129)).

In Pushkin's two gothic stories, the narrator's objective, coldly dispassionate voice reveals him to be an external, almost "third-person omniscient" observer who possesses the power to manipulate the narrative, while at the same time feigning indifference, avoiding association with any other characters, and breaking off the characters' "line of sight" with their own perspective. The effect of this emotional distance between the narrator is commonly encountered in Renaissance grotesque. While there are many definitions of the grotesque, Mikhail Bakhtin's theory is the closest to postclassical narratology because it relies on the premise that the reader or the spectator that interacts with the grotesque mode of representation projects the experience of this interaction on their broader values and life experiences. According to Bakhtin, through representing the objects of existential fear, such as death, luck, and eternal punishment, in an unfamiliar light, the grotesque mode of representation is aimed at resolving the spectator's or the reader's deeply rooted anxieties about these things. Echoing the contemporary postclassical narratologists, Bakhtin does not mean that grotesque art is supposed to frighten the audience and then provide a resolution of the fear. Both the fear of the supernatural and the resolution of this fear are of non-representational nature and therefore are not contained within the grotesque but are evoked through the interaction with the grotesque.

Similarly, the reader's experience constructed by Pushkin's two gothic stories is of a non-representational nature and is not contained within the stories' plots. This experience or "mood" that the stories evoke can be best defined with Bakhtin's term "fearlessness" (1984, 39), by which Bakhtin understands a liberation from the anxiety about death, luck, and other things that lie outside of human control.

In Pushkin's stories, the narrator's focus of vision does not coincide with any of the characters' perspectives but rises above them, assuming a God-like perspective, and his attitude toward the characters' misfortunes can be best denoted as "extreme objectivity" (Friedman 1975, 136), that is, emphatic emotional coldness. While the main characters of Pushkin's gothic stories, Adrian and Hermann, fall victim to an "alien inhuman force, which rules over men by turning them into marionettes" (Bakhtin 1984, 38), the narrator, observing from a distance, completely lacks the characters' superstitious fear of fate and of those phenomena—death, luck, or misfortune. The narrative strategies employed by Pushkin, on the one hand, strengthen the perception of the characters as marionettes of fate, while, on the other hand, they construct the narrator as being elevated above its laws. From the narrator's perspective, the boundaries between the living and the dead are permeable, and the irreversibility of death is overridden by the image of the ever-living body. Below I will elaborate on the phenomenological unfolding of the narrator's perspective as nonhuman or elevated above the stories' spaces.

SHIFTING THE NARRATOR'S PERSPECTIVE IN "THE QUEEN OF SPADES"

In "The Queen of Spades," the effect of emotional distance between the narrator and the space of the story is a function of the narrator's dynamic perspective, that is, sudden shifts in focalization that complicate the presentation of events and make it difficult to identify exactly whose point of view or focus of vision is being conveyed (Whitehead 2006, 85). The story's opening paragraph is composed primarily of impersonal constructions, with particular use of reflexive verbs. Next, I use the Russian original, since the English translation fails to capture the effect created by the Russian syntax:

> Однажды играли в карты у конногвардейца Нарумова. Долгая зимняя ночь прошла незаметно; сели ужинать в пятом часу утра. Те, которые остались в выигрыше, ели с большим аппетитом, прочие, в рассеянности, сидели перед пустыми своими приборами. Но шампанское явилось, разговор оживился, и все приняли в нем участие. ([1834] 1976, 25)

> One evening, Narumov of the Horse Guards played host to a card party. The long winter night passed unnoticed, and it was after four in the morning when they all sat down to supper. Those who had ended up ahead of the game ate heartily; the rest sat moodily before their empty plates. But champagne was produced, conversation revived, and everybody joined in. ([1831] 1997, 71)

In the Russian text, when a narrative is opened with the subjects "*te* [those]" and "*vse* [everyone, all]," it confuses the reader because these words normally operate as a reference to someone who was introduced earlier. In Pushkin's story opening, it is not clear who is referred to by these words.

Besides this confusion, the paragraph above reveals a dense concentration of reflexives, such as *iavilos', ozhivilsia, ostalis'*. Reflexives are a big group of Russian verbs that end with -sia. My analysis of the use of reflexives in Pushkin's stories focuses only on the verbs with "a truly reflexive meaning" that Alina Israeli defines as expressing the action that is directed toward the subject (Israeli: "object = subject") (1997, 48). Reflexive constructions that are used in the opening of Pushkin's story, according to Israeli's categorization, belong to the type of reflexives that "produce the effect of the action taking place as if by itself" and create "the implication (or at least the illusion) that no one bears responsibility for the action" (1997, 190).

Through judicious use of reflexive constructions and impersonal sentences, the narrator creates the illusion of his own absence. The impression of absent narratorial guidance leads to uncertainty about the expressed point of view. It is challenging for the reader to identify the focalizer. In the beginning, the reader is likely to infer that Tomskii plays this role because he delivers the longest speech. Tomskii is not introduced, and we know nothing about him apart from his name. However, as Whitehead observes, just as the reader becomes accustomed to the idea that they are "seeing" things from Tomskii's perspective, the narrator suddenly reasserts his presence (2006, 85). Abruptly, the narrator interjects, "*V samom dele, uzh rassvetalo* [And indeed, day was already dawning]" ([1834] 1976, 29, 1997, 75).

After the impersonal opening paragraph, the reader is exposed to a cacophony of utterances. The speakers, again, are not introduced. They articulate their remarks one after another. The characters' manner of speaking is unnatural. Hermann delivers just one remark, but this remark is an enigma ("I'm very taken with the game [. . . .] but I'm not in a position to sacrifice the necessary in the hope of acquiring the superfluous") ([1831] 1997, 71). The reader would struggle to parse Hermann's remark; at this stage of the story, the text has not provided sufficient information about his character to contextualize such a seemingly non sequitur. In order to grasp the full implications of Hermann's remark, one must return to this sentence after learning more about this character later in the narrative. According to Gérard Genette, limited scaffolding for the reader, when the narrative resembles "a quick and distant summary," places the reader in a distanced position relative to the characters' perspective, while "a detailed narrative, in 'scene' tempo," "gives the reader a greater impression of presence" and increases empathy for the characters (1988, 46).

The opening of "The Queen of Spades" likewise destabilizes perception through the uncertainty of its temporal and spatial setting. Only the characters' typically Slavic names betray its Russian context. Yet one of the characters bears a German name—indeed, in the English translation it becomes a direct designation of nationality—and the character who utters the longest speech, Tomskii, constantly refers to other countries, distant historical periods, and rumors ("You've heard of the Count

Saint-Germain, the subject of so many weird and wonderful tales"; "People used to ridicule him as a charlatan"; "Casanova says in his memoirs that he was a spy") ([1831] 1997, 73). The lack of guidance in the story's opening, where pronouns precede nouns and names, where the characters are not introduced, and both spatial and temporal markers are deliberately disorienting, impedes identification with the characters and prevents the reader from taking on their perspectives. I suggest that the reader instead identifies with the emotionally distant and dispassionate narrator, whose neutrality and laconicism emphasize his externalized position vis-à-vis the action. By connecting to the position of the narrator, who, as Darskii suggests, "is free and stands high above his work and his characters," the reader also assumes an externalized position relative to the narrative space (2022).

Descriptions of the characters in "The Queen of Spades" are sparse and focus entirely on the characters' appearances, movements, and interactions with various objects:

> The old Countess was sitting in her boudoir in front of the mirror. Three maids surrounded her. One was holding a jar of rouge, the second a box of pins, and the third a tall bonnet with flame-coloured ribbons. The Countess had not the least pretension to beauty, by now long-faded, but had retained all the habits of her youth; she clung rigidly to the fashions of the 70s and was as meticulously long over her toilette as she had been sixty years before. A young lady, her ward, sat by the window at her embroidery. ([1831] 1997, 75)

The brevity of the characters' descriptions emphasizes the narrator's emotionally distant and coldly objective attitude toward them.

In a formal echo of the story's first section, the opening paragraph of the second part is directly followed by an extended dialogue. The narrator's voice, as well as the narrator's comments or judgments, is omitted. The narrative situation in the first part of the story, as well as in the second part, evokes Genette's definition of "nonfocalisation" or "zero focalisation," when "a point is so indefinite, or so remote, with so panoramic a field (the well-known 'view-point of God,' or of Sirius, about which people periodically wonder whether it is a point of view) that it cannot coincide with any character" (1988, 73). Similarly, Norman Friedman defines this situation as a narrative with an "increasingly objectified narrator" who emphasizes his "psychical distance" toward the narrative (1975, 136).

The narrator does make occasional remarks about the characters' personal characteristics later, yet the distance between the narrator and the characters is preserved. For instance, when commenting on the Old Countess's personality, the narrator emphasizes her banal and unoriginal nature. In a moment of metatextual reflection, he observes that she is one of many such "old countesses," a stock character in high society as well as literature, and conducts herself accordingly: "The Countess, of course, was not malicious by nature, but she was willful, like any lady spoilt by society; she was miserly and sunk in a cold selfishness, like all old people who have drunk their fill of love when young and are alienated from the present day" ([1831] 1997, 78).

In his characterization of the Countess as a typical representative of her class and age group, the narrator conveys his externalized perspective. Through his occasional dispassionate (and often skeptical) remarks about human nature in general, the narrator reveals a callous apathy for the characters as individuals. His brief acknowledgment of Lizaveta Ivanovna's unhappiness—"a most forlorn creature"—has been interpreted as a revelation of compassion for her (Grenier 2001, 27). However, the next sentence's reference to Dante communicates the narrator's externalized position and emphasizes that Lizaveta is also just one of many: "[t]he bread of a stranger is bitter, says Dante, and painful the steps of a stranger's stair [. . .]" ([1831] 1997, 78).

OTHER TOOLS OF ALIENATION: REFLEXIVES, PASSIVE CONSTRUCTIONS, AND ANAPHORA

In "The Coffin-Maker," the effect of the clash of perspectives between the narrator and characters is achieved differently. In the opening of "The Coffin-Maker," the narrator foregrounds the fictional nature of the characters and the narrative, stressing their subordinate position relative to his own. By pretending to disclose the secrets of his literary craft to the reader, the narrator delegates some of his power and his capacity for control:

> The cultivated reader is aware that both Shakespeare and Walter Scott portrayed their grave-diggers as cheery, facetious individuals, so that our imagination might be the more affected by antithesis. Out of respect for the truth, we are unable to follow their example and are compelled to admit that the demeanour of our undertaker was wholly appropriate to his gloomy profession. ([1831] 1997, 32)

References to other literary texts highlight the narrator's ability to manipulate the story, casting the distance between his vision and the narrative space into sharp relief. In the following quote, the narrator pretends that he is inviting the reader to observe the creative process of putting a story together:

> Deviating in this instance from the custom of modern-day novelists, I will refrain from describing Adrian Prokhorov's caftan, or the European attire of

> Akulina and Darya. I consider it relevant, however, to point out that both girls had put on yellow hats and red shoes, which they only did on festive occasions. ([1831] 1997, 33)

Another tool for creating the impression of the narrator's indifferent objectivity in regard to the space of the story in "The Coffin-Maker" is the abundant use of passive constructions. I use the Russian original to provide some examples:

> Сии размышления были прерваны [. . .]
> Пожитки [. . .] были взвалены.
> Приглашение было благосклонно принято.
> Тесная квартирка сапожника была наполнена гостями [. . .]
> [. . .] Все было заведено самым строгим порядком.
> Это предложение, как и все, было принято радостно и единодушно.
> Адриан [...] был погружен в печальные размышления.
> Комната полна была мертвецами. ([1831] 1964, 45–56)
>
> These musings were abruptly curtailed [. . .]
> The last belongings [. . .] were loaded up.
> The invitation was graciously accepted.
> The shoemaker's cramped quarters were crowded with guests [. . .]
> [. . .] Everything had been strictly ordered.
> This suggestion, like all the others, was accepted with joyous unanimity.
> Adrian was [. . .] absorbed in cheerless reflection.
> The room was crowded with corpses. ([1831] 1997, 31–37)

In Russian, the passive voice creates emotional distance, as well as an impression of dispassionate objectivity. This is why passive constructions are common in Russian official documents. The use of passives emphasizes that the story is narrated from an impersonal, dispassionate, and objective point of view, the point of view of the law. Israeli mentions that the concentration of passive constructions may be typical of a narrative where "the Agent is an authority figure or authorities in general" (1997, 187).

In Pushkin's text, passive constructions give the impression of self-evident empiricism, uninformed by opinion. They serve to emphasize the narrator's position as external to the narrative, further underscoring his emotional distance. As with the ambiguous *te* [those] and *eti* [these] pronouns discussed above, these constructions syntactically omit the characters as grammatical subjects, in some cases omitting them from the sentence entirely ("the invitation was graciously accepted"; by whom?). According to Israeli, this disproportionate use of passive constructions may represent "the ambiance of distancing from the action" (1997, 187), that is, an attempt to lead the reader to the perception of the narrator as an authorial figure, emotionally neutral and external to the narrative space. Pushkin's remark from his diaries that a good narrator should be "as dispassionate as fate" suggests that in the gothic stories, a neutral and objective narrator's voice communicates the point of view of fate itself.

Like "The Queen of Spades," "The Coffin-Maker" also contains an unusually high concentration of reflexives:

> Вскоре порядок установился; кивот с образами, шкап с посудою, стол, диван и кровать заняли им определенные углы в задней комнате; в кухне и гостиной поместились изделия хозяина
> [. . .] Дом продается и отдается внаймы.
> Дверь отворилась [. . .]
> Над воротами возвысилась вывеска [...]
> [. . .] Беседа продолжалась [. . .]
> [. . .] здесь продаются и обиваются гробы простые и крашеные, также отдаются на прокат и починяются старые.
> Многие мантии от того сузились, многие шляпы покоробились.
> Пиво лилось.
> Полушампанское запенилось.
> Пожар двенадцатого года, уничтожив первопрестольную столицу, истребил и его желтую будку. Но тотчас, по изгнании врага, на ее месте явилась новая [. . .]
> [. . .] дочери его чинились; разговор на немецком языке час от часу делался шумнее [. . .]
> Трюхина, бригадир и сержант Курилкин смутно представились его вооб ражению. ([1831] 1964, 45–56)

> Soon order had been established; the icon-case, the crockery-cupboard, the table, the sofa, and the bed occupied their allotted positions in the back room; the kitchen and the living-room were filled with the master's stock in trade [. . .]
> [. . .] the place was for sale or rent.
> The door opened [. . .]
> The sign was hung up outside the gate [. . .]
> So the talk proceeded [. . .]
> Coffins plain and painted sold and upholstered here, also for rent and old ones repaired.
> Many a cape had shrunk, many a hat gone out of shape.
> The beer flowed.
> The near-champagne foamed.

> The fire of 1812, which had razed Russia's ancient capital, had also destroyed his yellow sentry-box. But as soon as the enemy had been driven out, a new one appeared [. . .]
>
> [. . .] His daughters held back; the German conversation grew noisier as time went by.
>
> Tryukhina, the brigadier, and Sergeant Kurilikin came nebulously to mind. ([1831] 1997, 31–37)

These reflexives emphasize the narrator's externalized, dispassionate point of view. Such neutrality and objectivity on the narrator's part can be read as imitating a nonhuman focus of vision, that is, the position of fate or the supernatural.

The reader's perception of the narrator as an authorial figure, who is emotionally withdrawn from the characters' obsessions, misfortunes, and fortunes, is strengthened by the narrator's derogatory remarks about characters, a technique which applies to both "The Queen of Spades" and "The Coffin-Maker." Adrian Prokhorov is described as a person possessed of nothing but base instincts. Hermann, though almost a caricature of Teutonic fastidiousness and punctuality, is described as equally subordinate to his urges, gradually giving in to an all-consuming compulsion. Descriptions of the Countess focus on her physicality, using the language of decrepitude and decay. For the reader, the narrator's derisive comments about the other characters unconsciously contribute to the perception of him as a controlling agent, a demiurge-like figure standing above the fictional world that he creates. By identifying with the narrator's position, the reader experiences the fictional world of the story not from inside, but from a superior vantage point.

Another device that constructs the narrator's position as external to the space of the stories and the characters' focus of vision is the use of anaphora (repetition). When Hermann begs the Countess to reveal the secret of the three cards, his speech is made rhythmic through the use of anaphora: "If your heart has ever known the emotion of love, if you can remember its raptures, if you smiled just once at the cry of a new-born son, if anything human ever throbbed within your breast [. . .]" ([1831] 1997, 87).

When the characters in "The Coffin-Maker" speak, their dialogue is also punctuated with anaphoras, lending it a percussive rhythm. The following is an example from the housemaid's speech: "What do you mean, master? [. . .] What sort of talk is that?" ([1831] 1997, 34).

Another example can be found in the speech of the German craftsman: "Forgive me, dear neighbor [. . .] Forgive the interruption." ([1831] 1997, 32).

The transition to the space of magic in "The Coffin-Maker" is preceded by the use of anaphora that is omitted in the English translation:

> Тут начали здоровья следовать одно за другим: пили здоровье каждого гостя особливо, пили здоровье Москвы и целой дюжины германских городков, пили здоровье всех цехов вообще и каждого в особенности, пили здоровье мастеров и подмастерьев. [Then the toasts began to follow one after another: every guest's health was drunk separately; they toasted Moscow and a good dozen German towns; they toasted all guilds in general and each in particular; they drank the health of masters and apprentices.]. ([1831] 1964, 36, 1997, 36)

The employment of anaphora exposes the reader to the performative, conventional nature of the literary narrative and contributes to the perception of narrative as being "rehearsed and rhetorically presented" (Bakker 1997, 132). The anaphora also brings "authorial control" over the narrative into the reader's focus (Li 2018, 186). To elucidate how Pushkin employs anaphora to strengthen the impression of distance between the space of the story and the characters, on the one hand, and the narrator, on the other, I provide below an example from a different story, "The Stationmaster" from *The Tales of Belkin,* because anaphora is employed already in the opening paragraph of this story. I use the Russian original because the English translation softens the effect of the rhetorical device:

> Кто не проклинал станционных смотрителей, кто с ними не бранивался? Кто, в минуту гнева, не требовал от них роковой книги, дабы вписать в оную свою бесполезную жалобу на притеснение, грубость и неисправность? Кто не почитает их извергами человеческого рода, равными покойным подьячим или, по крайней мере, муромским разбойникам? Будем однако справедливы, пос тараемся войти в их положение и, может быть, станем судить о них гораздо снисходительнее. ([1831] 1964, 57)

> Is there anyone who has not cursed all stationmasters, or never had occasion to wrangle with them? Anyone who, in a moment of anger, has not demanded the fateful book, in order to inscribe his useless complaint at high-handed treatment, rudeness, and inefficiency? Who does not regard them as outcasts from the human race, the equivalent of the pettifogging quill-drivers of yore, or Murom brigands at the very least? Let us be fair, however, let us try and put ourselves in their shoes and then, it may be, we will judge them much less severely. ([1831] 1997, 38)

This paragraph establishes the emotional distance between the narrator and the reader on the one hand, and the characters on the other, through the employment of imperfective verbs. According to contemporary cognitive linguistics, the imperfective aspect[1] in the opening paragraph of a story in the narrator's voice creates the effect of transcending the characters' space and time and emphasizing the narrator's emotional distance from the characters, his objective, authorial vision that again may be compared to the point of view of fate that observes everyone and everything neutrally and dispassionately. Being exposed to the narrator's focus of vision, the reader is also subconsciously exposed to the view of fate, a view which does not coincide with the characters' perspectives. The narrator's privileged position relative to the narrative space of the two gothic stories and their characters facilitates a sense of exception, that one is suspended above the laws of fate that govern the characters' lives. Below, I elaborate on how the two stories eventually resolve anxieties about phenomena that lie outside of one's control, such as luck, misfortune, and death.

ALTERNATIVE VISION: BLURRING THE BOUNDARIES BETWEEN SPACE, TIME, AND LIFE STAGES

In *Rabelais and His World*, Mikhail Bakhtin suggests that the grotesque serves to resolve anxiety induced by the fear of death, misfortune, or eternal punishment by creating a world of alternative laws, which subvert established conventions about the human body, morality, and mortality. These alternative laws annul the finality of death by rendering the boundaries between life and death permeable. The idea of death as a necessity of nature is replaced by the idea of death as "a renewal, a combination of death and birth" (Rabelais 1984, 51). Reimagining death as a renewal, in Bakhtin's view, creates a joyous atmosphere out of gloomy and macabre material and infects the spectator (or the reader) with an experience of liberation. Pushkin's gothic stories establish such an alternative joyous world by making permeable the boundaries between different epochs, countries, and, most importantly, the living and the dead.

The first tool for exposing the reader to the space of subverted laws of necessity involves blurring the spatial and temporal boundaries of the story, which results in an uncertain chronotope. This applies to both "The Queen of Spades" and "The Coffin-maker." In the opening of "The Queen of Spades," Tomskii's story begins abruptly and abounds with references to foreign countries and distant historical periods: "I should tell you that about sixty years ago my grandmother went to Paris and became all the rage. People flocked after her for a glimpse of la Venus muscovite; Richelieu laid siege to her [. . .]" ([1831] 1997, 72).

In his description of his grandmother's personality, Tomskii refrains from any mention of the present and instead recounts her past, imbuing the story with Western European imagery.

Almost every character in "The Queen of Spades" either blends several national identities together or lacks a defined national identity completely. From a formal standpoint, the Countess lives in Russia, but from Tomskii's story, it becomes obvious that her background, and especially the roots of her magical gifts, are almost entirely French. According to Tomskii's account, she was initiated into magic by a Frenchman, the Count de Saint-Germain.

The vestibule and the bedroom in the Countess's house, the most magical sites in the story, are places where cultures and time periods blend and intertwine. In the Countess's house, one may discover an "antique armchair," "Chinese-papered walls," "two portraits painted in Paris by Madame Lebrun," and "table-clocks by the celebrated Leroy" ([1831] 1997, 85). Mieke Bal suggests that references to the past in the story can be "subjective": although the narrator might not have moved the action to a distant past, by virtue of the narrative mode, the action can be subjectively experienced by the reader as separated by spatial and temporal distance (2009, 88).

"The Coffin-Maker" also employs subjective references to distant historical periods and other countries. While the setting of the story is Russian, by evoking other coffin-makers in world literature, the narrator blurs the temporal boundaries of the story within the reader's experience.

Besides the uncertainty of the chronotope, both stories subvert the laws of necessity by blurring the boundaries between the living and the dead and the stages of bodily life. The Countess's subjective time is unstable; she struggles to distinguish between the distant past and the present, as well as between the living and the dead. She occupies a liminal space between these two human conditions. Her body is weakened, yet she possesses the most magical power compared to the other characters, and this power only strengthens after she dies. She is "long-faded," but nevertheless she has "retained all the habits of her youth" ([1831] 1997, 75). While the Countess is still alive, her face is referred to as "dead," yet this "dead" face can "change unutterably" and "become animated" ([1831] 1997, 86). While she is referred to as "dull" and "lapsing into apathy," her body, defying its description, is always in some sort of motion. In the supernatural reading of the story, after the Countess dies, she still retains the magical powers that she had, and exerts an influence on both on Hermann's and Lizaveta's lives from beyond the grave. In "The Coffin-Maker," those characters who inhabit the macabre world of magic also hover between life and death. For instance, the corpse of Triukhina is "yellow and wax," yet "undefiled by decay" ([1831] 1997, 38).

For Bakhtin, narratives about the body transitioning between life and death subvert the conventions of death's irreversibility and human entrapment by the law of necessity. In a sense, according to Bakhtin, the body freely transitioning between life and death is already an immortal, ever-living body, which, as he argues, is a part of the universe, an everlasting life (1984, 318).

Through the narrator's focus of vision, the reader is exposed to a festive, alternative universe devoid of the imperatives posed by linear time and irreversible death, as well as the necessity of belonging to a particular nation.

POSSIBLE SOURCES OF PUSHKIN'S CODE OF HONOR TOWARD THE SUPERNATURAL

As an avid reader, Pushkin undoubtedly encountered texts that employed the device of the "extremely objective" and dispassionate narrator. Larisa Vol'pert points out that certain features of Pushkin's narrative persona, including laconism, exaggerated emotional neutrality, and derogatory remarks about the characters, resemble narrative models in Jean de La Bruyère's prose (1998, 25). While certain of Pushkin's stylistic devices could have been inspired by seventeenth-century French literature, Pushkin's gothic stories, while viewed through the lens of the reader's experience, are more reminiscent of Boccaccio's narrative techniques in *The Decameron*. In his comments on Boccaccio's *Decameron*, Wayne Booth points out characteristics of Boccaccio's narrator, such as a shifting and uncertain point of view combined with the reader's impression of the narrator's indifference toward the characters, who are portrayed as "two-dimensional, with no revealed depth of any kind" (1983, 9).

Like Pushkin's stories, *The Decameron* models an implacable attitude toward phenomena beyond human control, such as luck, fate, eternal punishment, and the unpredictability of death. According to Millicent Marcus, in Boccaccio's *The Decameron*, the narrator's reluctance to guide the reader through various moral dilemmas and his intentional withholding of judgment endows the reader with an emotionally neutral position toward any anxiety induced by the idea of eternal punishment or the unpredictability of fate (2012, 44). In *The Decameron*, the narrator's emotional neutrality coexists with a lack of narratorial guidance through the moral dilemmas faced by the characters. As Boccaccio's narrator positions himself above Christian morality and the anxiety of eternal punishment, the reader, by identifying with the narrator, assumes a similarly elevated position. Pushkin's narrative techniques in the gothic stories are aimed at achieving a similar reader experience, that is, they convey a code of honor regarding the supernatural that relieves anxiety and normalizes an unflappable attitude in the face of either malicious or favorable fate.

The category of honor in these two Pushkin stories expands its definition as a model of behavior to encompass the ability to successfully manage one's emotions. Through the narrator's cold and dispassionate mode of narration, Pushkin's stories model the skill of maintaining rational control over extreme emotions. William Todd argues that in most of Pushkin's famous texts, the capacity for control over emotions—not only outer control but inner control as well—is celebrated as a sign of true, innate nobility. Todd suggests that in the epilogue to *Onegin*, Tatiana Larina is rewarded for her ability to take powerful emotions under control and perfectly perform her social role while retaining awareness of her inner world (1986, 130). On the other hand, according to Pushkin's hierarchy of psychological skills, obsession leads to misfortune. Hermann and Adrian Prokhorov are defeated by the supernatural as a direct result of their obsession with wealth.

Arguably, the explanation behind this hierarchy of psychological skills and veneration of the ability to maintain emotional distance, as well as the idea of self-control signifying inner nobility, can be traced to the values and lifestyle of the nineteenth-century Russian aristocracy. As Lotman posits, after the epoch of Peter the Great, "the area which is normally left to the unconscious, 'natural' behavior became something to be learnt" and, as a result, "manuals appeared dealing with the norms of everyday conduct" (Lotman and Uspenskii 1984, 232). Lotman concludes that performativity or theatricality became the everyday norm, and noble behavior, as well as noble psychology, became associated with play, superficiality, and adherence to the imposed norm. Perhaps the most distinct example of a prescriptive performative behavior for a nobleman is the duel ritual, which "assigned definite roles to all participants [. . .] and dictated their conduct" (Reyfman 1999, 25).

Nataliia Mazur points out that in Pushkin's case, the appreciation of emotional control drew on the spiritual traditions of his time, popular among the Russian nobility. For Pushkin, who was inspired by classical antiquity, the philosophy of Stoicism was appealing because it claimed that mastering self-control over overwhelming emotions leads to liberation from the power of natural law (2006, 350). Quite possibly, Pushkin became fascinated with the Stoic belief that a person could avoid becoming a marionette in the hands of supernatural forces. The writer could also have been inspired by Renaissance works that employ the device of an emotionally distant, dispassionate, and wittily ironic narrator to communicate staying imperturbable when confronted with forces beyond one's control, such as death or eternal punishment.

CONCLUSION

While these two Pushkin stories portray the individual's absorption by a hostile supernatural force as a consequence of their obsession with gaining fate's favor, the narrator's dispassionate, neutrally objective, or wittily ironic tone models an attitude to fate that can be described as staying imperturbable. The experience of "fearlessness" or subversion of human anxieties about luck and fate is not contained within the stories' spaces but is created through the clash of the characters' and the narrator's perspectives. Following the postclassical narratologists, it is possible to conclude that this experience is of a non-representational nature. Through it, the reader connects to the author's code of honor that is not directly represented in the stories' space, but is conveyed to the reader subconsciously. Within this code of honor, the skill of controlling anxieties is associated with a greater chance of becoming the master of one's own fate. Emotional compulsiveness, on the other hand, is associated with a loss of control over one's fate. Those characters who cannot control their obsessions, such as Hermann, end up being punished, while the characters who have a good handle on their emotions, such as Lizaveta Ivanovna, are generously rewarded, not only by their mortal peers, but more importantly, by supernatural forces. They live long lives and find themselves in positions that allow them to express their talents and achieve their goals. Such a hierarchy of psychological skills draws on different spiritual traditions with which Pushkin engaged, such as Stoicism and the nineteenth-century nobleman's code of honor, according to which keeping face is understood not only as successfully navigating complicated social situations but also as complete refraining from anxieties about phenomena outside the person's control, such as luck, misfortune, or death.

NOTE

1. Aspect is an important category of verbs in Slavic languages. Stephen Dickey defines the semantic meaning of aspect as "the contour of a situation in time" (2000, 2). The imperfective aspect in the opening of Pushkin's story, in the narrator's speech, conveys the "temporal indefiniteness" (Dickey 2000, 5) of the narrator's focus of vision, which means that, from the narrator's point of view, the story he narrates is just one of many, not special.

BIBLIOGRAPHY

Bakhtin, Mikhail. 1984. *Rabelais and his World*. Translated by Hélène Iswolsky. Bloomington: Indiana University Press.

Bakker, Egbert. 1997. *Poetry in Speech: Orality and Homeric Discourse*. Ithaca, NY: Cornell University Press.

Bal, Mieke. 2009. *Narratology: Introduction to the Theory of Narrative*. Translated by Christine Van Boheemen. 3rd ed. Toronto: University of Toronto Press.

Bethea, David, and Sergei Davydov. 1981. "Pushkin's Saturnine Cupid: The Poetics of Parody in *The Tales of Belkin*." *PMLA* 96, no. 1: 8–21.

Booth, Wayne. 1983. *The Rhetoric of Fiction*. Chicago: University of Chicago Press.

Caracciolo, Marco. 2018. "Perspectives on Narrative and Mood." In *How to Do Things with Narrative: Cognitive and Diachronic Perspectives*, edited by Jan Alber and Greta Olson, 15–28. Boston: De Gruyter.

Darskii, Dmitrii. 1995. "*Pikovaia dama*." Fundamental'naia elektronnaia biblioteka, Russkaia literatura i fol'klor. Accessed October 14, 2022. http://feb-web.ru/feb/pushkin/serial/isf/isf-308-.htm.

Davydov, Sergei. 1999. "The Ace in 'The Queen of Spades'." *Slavic Review* 58, no. 2: 309–28.

Dickey, Stephen. 2000. *Parameters of Slavic Aspect: A Cognitive Approach. CSLI Publications*. Stanford: Center for the Study of Language and Information.

Evdokimova, Svetlana. 2004. *Alexander Pushkin's Little Tragedies: The Poetics of Brevity*. Madison: University of Wisconsin Press.

Fludernik, Monika. 2003. "Chronology, Time, Tense and Experientiality in Narrative." *Language and Literature* 12, no. 2: 117–34.

Friedman, Norman. 1975. *Form and Meaning in Fiction*. Athens, GA: University of Georgia Press.

Genette, Gérard. 1988. *Narrative Discourse Revisited*. Translated by Jane Lewi. Ithaca, NY: Cornell University Press.

Gregg, Richard. 2000. "Germann the Confessor and the Stony, Seated Countess: The Moral Subtext of Pushkin's 'The Queen of Spades'." *SEER* 78, no. 4: 613–24.

Grenier, Svetlana. 2001. *Representing the Marginal Woman in Nineteenth-Century Russian Literature: Personalism, Feminism, and Polyphony*. Westport, CT: Greenwood Press.

Herman, David. 2002. *Story Logic. Problems and Possibilities of Narrative*. Lincoln: University of Nebraska Press.

Herman, David. 2010. "Directions in Cognitive Narratology: Triangulating Stories, Media, and the Mind." In *Postclassical Narratology, Approaches and Analyses*, edited by Jan Alber and Monika Fludernik, 137–62. Columbus: Ohio State University Press.

Israeli, Alina. 1997. *Semantics and Pragmatics of the "Reflexive" Verbs in Russian*. Munich: Verlag Otto Sagner.

Kim, Sang Hyun. 2006. "An Intelligent Game by Pushkin: Plot Structure and the Thematic Unity of *The Tales of Belkin*." *Russian Literature* 60, no. 2: 185–225.

Kollmann, Nancy. 1999. *By Honor Bound: State and Society in Early Modern Russia*. Ithaca, NY: Cornell University Press.

Lešić-Thomas, Andrea. 2008. "Focalisation in Pushkin's 'Eugene Onegin' and Lermontov's 'A Hero of Our Time': Loving the Semantic Void and Dizziness of Interpretation." *Modern Language Review* 103, no. 4: 1067–85.

Li, Wanlin. 2018. "Ambiguity as Aesthetic Strategy: Edgar Allan Poe's Ambitions." *Journal of Narrative Theory* 48, no. 2: 164–93.

Lotman, Yurii, and Boris Uspenskii. 1984. "The Poetics of Everyday Behavior in Russian Eighteenth Century Culture." In *Semiotics of Russian Culture* edited by

Ann Shukman, 231–56. Ann Arbor: Dept. of Slavic Languages and Literatures, University of Michigan.

Mazur, Nataliia. 2006. "'Brozhu li ia vdol' ulits shumnykh' i stoicheskaia filosofiia smerti." In *Stikh, iazyk, poeziia. Pamiati Mikhaila Leonovicha Gasparova*, 343–72. Moscow: Rossiisskii gosudarstvennyi gumanitarnyi universitet.

Millicent, Marcus. 2012. "The Seriousness of Play in Boccaccio's 'Decameron'." *Italian Issue Supplement. Tra Amici: Essays in Honor of Giuseppe Mazzotta. MLN* 127, no. 1: 42–46.

Pushkin, Aleksandr Sergeevich. [1831] 1964. *Povesti pokoinogo Ivana Petrovicha Belkina*. Edited by Boris Ottokar Unbegaun. Oxford: Basil Blackwell.

Pushkin, Aleksandr Sergeevich. [1834] 1976. *Pikovaia dama*. Letchworth: Bradda Books.

Pushkin, Alexander. [1831] 1997. *Tales of the Late Ivan Petrovich Belkin. The Queen of Spades. The Captain's Daughter. Peter the Great's Blackamoor*. Translated by Alan Myers and Andrew Kahn. Oxford: Oxford University Press.

Pushkin. Alexander. n.d. *O dvorianstve*. Electronic library http://pushkin-lit.ru/pushkin/text/zametki/o-dvoryanstve.htm. Last accessed January, 2024.

Pushkin, Aleksandr Sergeevich. 2010. *Izbrannoe*. Vol. 2. Moscow: ROSSPEN.

Reyfman, Irina. 1999. *Ritualized Violence Russian Style: The Duel in Russian Culture and Literature* Stanford, CA: Stanford University Press.

Rosen, Nathan. 2002. "Up the Down Staircase in 'The Queen of Spades'." *SEEJ* 46, no. 4: 711–26.

Semenko, Irina. 1995. "The 'Author' in *Eugene Onegin*: Image and Function." Translated by by Sona Hoisington. *Canadian-American Slavic Studies* 29, no. 3–4: 233–55.

Todd, William Mills. 1986. *Fiction and Society in the Age of Pushkin: Ideology, Institutions and Narrative.* Cambridge, MA: Harvard University Press.

Vol'pert, Larisa. 1998. *Pushkin v roli Pushkina. Tvorcheskaia igra po modeliam frantsuzskoi literatury. Pushkin i Stendal'*. Moscow: Iazyki russkoi literatury.

Whitehead, Claire. 2006. *The Fantastic in France and Russia in the Nineteenth Century: In Pursuit of Hesitation*. London: Legenda.

6

(Un)Reading and the "Gappiness" of Context

Toward a New Cognitive Reception Theory

Katherina B. Kokinova

DEFINITIONS AND QUESTIONS

This chapter focuses on the act of reading metafiction, examining the specific textual strategies that works of instructive metafiction impose on their readers, the literary practices and policies that are used to gain and hold power in the text or to engage a reader. "Unreading" will be preliminarily defined as underreading. Vladimir Nabokov's dictatorship in fiction[1] will serve to probe both his theory of reading and the (im)possibilities of metanarrative. The role of gaps and context in the act of reading and their interaction with the reader will constitute the nodal points of discussion. Akin to that, an important aspect of the examination will be the reading—blindness relation. The main objective here is to find out *how textual context models metafiction.*

Elaborating on Hamilton and Schneider's suggestion about the roots of cognitive criticism in reception theory (2002, 640–658), the aim is not only to illuminate the commonalities between these two frameworks but, more importantly, to map a prospective way they can complement each other. Thus, this interdisciplinary study aims to find out how cognitive science and reception theory could work together and thus to outline a new cognitive reception theory. This theoretical undertaking will probe a contextualization through reading metafiction, which is, paradoxically, "both narcissistically self-reflexive and yet focused outward, oriented toward the reader" (Hutcheon 1980, 7). Moreover, this is even more intensified in *instructive metafiction* (metafiction that gives instructions).[2] The term "instruction" stands for an implicit or explicit guideline, provided within or about a piece of metafiction, an anticipatory rule that seeks to guide the interaction with the work. Nabokov seems particularly appropriate because of the pointed self-consciousness of his oeuvre. That is why I will examine a paradigmatic example from his instructive metafiction. The short story under discussion—"The Vane Sisters" (1951)—poses the intertwined problems of narration and reading.[3] Reception theory deals with the interaction between reader and text, defining the reader as a textual structure and a structured act (Iser). Cognitive approaches to literature themselves are an intersection of literary criticism and cognitive science and represent a diverse array of methods[4]. Curiously enough, uniting the perspectives of the implied reader and the findings of cognitive psychology still remains unaccomplished. However, reception theories and cognitive literary studies seem to complement rather than contradict each other in terms of their findings on perception. Furthermore, marrying these two approaches should allow us to rethink and reevaluate their separate contributions. The main background question will be whether effecting a settlement between cognitive literary studies and reception theory might result in, to employ a notorious metaphor, recognizing the elephant as a whole and being able to prove it. My hypothesis is that the cognitive literary and the reception-theory approaches could make good partners because they provide a comprehensive framework for examining textual strategies. Besides, the findings of cognitive psychology, primarily studying the way we think (including *perceive*), could be enhanced by reception theory, focusing on the way we *read*. Thus, bridging the distance between the two disciplines might enable bringing the reader and the text as a whole to the fore; the reader as figured in the text and the text as produced within the reader. A prospective additional benefit of the study of readers of narratives is to learn how to be better readers of life.

THE READER ON THE CREST OF CONTEXT (A MEETING)

The focus here is on one nodal aspect of the reader—text interaction, namely the relation between the reader and the textual context. How are contextual models being built, and what are their functions? The mutual mind-reading of reader and text seems bare in metafiction: the reader as the context for the text and the text as constructing the reader from the gap (*Leerstellen*). Following Iser, I will understand "gap" as the fundamental asymmetry between text and reader that gives rise to communication in the reading process. This act of mutuality between text and reader, then, is a deed accomplished through reciprocal and endless construction, and is pointedly visible through multiple levels of "embedded intentionality" (Zunshine) in metafiction. This literary mind-reading illuminates context as perception. The reader acts as the implied context for the text, which "has in mind" a figure with whose "horizon of expectations" (*Erwartungshorizont*, Jauss) it can play. That way, the metafictional text imposes its terms and engages, even captivates, the reader within them.

"Context" is often understood as the concomitant cradle, the circumstances for something to be understood, agreed upon, that is, the shared obviousness. It is derived from the Latin *contextere*, to weave together, to join. In addition, it is akin to condition (from Lat. *condicio*, agreement). But what is (supposed to be) agreed upon in fiction, and even more in (instructive) metafiction? If fiction insists on telling stories, metafiction discusses these stories in terms of their writing and reading. That is why the role of the textual context appears as pointedly nodal for the conditioning of reading metafiction. However, it needs to be stressed that context is not a fixed, clear-cut, and stable state, but in Boicho Kokinov's theory, it is "the *dynamic* fuzzy set of all *associatively relevant* [. . .] elements [. . .] *at a particular instant of time*" (Kokinov 1995, italics added). How then are these dynamic relations and associations actualized in metafiction? What are the textual conditions for the constraining of context in it? It seems that the instructions are these very elements that activate a given context. How then do they condition it? What is the place of context in view of the reader-instructions interaction? Moreover, if, etymologically, context is the "woven together," then how do the associatively woven textual schemata give rise to coherence? How is the plurality of meanings being configured? And what is the effect of the context's shifting, cloudy constellation of relations?

In search of answers to these questions, I will study the role of context in the reading process of Nabokov's "The Vane Sisters." First, however, I would like to invite you to revisit one of the most referenced psychological experiments, conducted by Christopher Chabris and Daniel Simons in 1998, entitled "The Monkey Business Illusion," which can be seen on their website[5] (Chabris and Simons 2010). In short, it shows two teams passing a ball while the viewer is asked to count the number of passes; during this concentrated activity, many of us do not notice a passing gorilla beating its chest. When one concentrates on something, one often misses other unexpected elements. This experiment on attention and context will be employed here in order to point out various themes in "The Vane Sisters," as well as some "gorillas," and the "inattentional blindness" to them. Here, I will only sketch out briefly these unexpected–unnoticed elements in view of conceptual clarity, and they will be further developed in the section "Minding the Reader."

Woven Together: Reading #1, Gorilla #1

Perhaps the most visible topic of this short story, told by a Professor of French about two sisters enchanted by the supernatural, and his relations with them, especially if read around Halloween, is the "ghost" theme. The prompts are heavily present and repetitive—poltergeist, umbra, ghost (2), phantom (2), transparent (2), apparitions, spells, spiritualism and spirit (2+1), dead (9), death (7), dying, posthumous, auspices, aura, shade (4), shadow (2), and so on. In addition, the text insists on things being strange (4), odd (4), mysterious (2). All this weaves together the contextual model of "The Vane Sisters" as a haunted story. That way, context can be preliminarily defined as perception, the perceived elements that are brought to the fore. However, it simultaneously causes "inattentional blindness" to other things in the text. And thus, the illusion of attention—even of a careful reader—could leave unseen the instructions and the final twist of the story. Thus, the theme unseen, unnoticed, to which we are "inattentionally blind"—the gorilla—when seen, in turn becomes a new reading with yet another gorilla unread (gorilla #1 = reading #2).

Woven Together: Reading #2, Gorilla #2

A careful reader, caressing details, might first see—in the fore—the numerous alliterations, initials, misspelled words as well as the repetitive use of the following: "letters" (4), "misprints," "logogriphs," "Alph," "alphabetically," "acrostics," and so on. Thus, the letter theme is being woven, illuminating the implicit instructions on letter hunting as the contextual model of the story. An enthusiastic reading along these threads might leave the "ghost" theme unseen (gorilla 2 = reading 1). That is how the reflection of the reader looms over what they see in the text-mirror.

Woven Together: (Un)Reading #n (n>2). How Many Gorillas?

What are the conditions for the activation of context, for the different threads to be woven together? Can it be claimed that the "letter" theme is quantitatively more present (hence, visible) than the "ghost" theme? Or maybe they are interchangeably visible once you see both (similarly to the famous young/elderly lady psychological experiment that plays with changing the elements of focus in order to illuminate two different silhouettes, Boring 1930)? What is left unseen in this case? There should always be yet another gorilla, especially in (meta)fiction, and I will discuss this in the next part. More important for now is that context turns out to be not only perception and interpretation but, to employ Iser's theory, building coherence, a combination of textual schemata, associative connections/relations that are constantly in the process of rearranging.

Thus, context can be redefined as *the dynamic, resinous net of the actualized relations*, the associatively woven textual schemata (a combination of conditions and relations) that give rise to coherence. It is resinous because of its non-liquid, non-solid state. In other words, context can be presented as a *texture*. This concept has been used before (mostly unrelated to reading, though) in several scholarly works, most notably by Peter Stockwell,[6] as well as in Nabokov's *Ada or Ardor* (1969). Here, texture will be preliminarily understood as the disposition or manner of the union of the components of the text, a composite of its closely interwoven elements. In short, that which is formed by the threads of a text's fabric. A texture thus, akin to the idea of the resinous net, illuminates context as related to gaps as well as to the processes of filling them in, but more importantly, of their correlating. Consequently, the contextual model conditions the reading, and I would propose to call reader participation the *texture of reading*. Hence, context can be illustrated also as connecting the dots and transitory seeing of figures and constellations in the text's sky. Yet, different perceivers see different figures; one sees the whole Sagittarius constellation, another—its Teapot asterism; one sees the image of the plow, another—the dipper (see Iser 1974, 282).

The role of textual context and its texture can also be linked to Peter Stockwell's term "literary resonance," which "involves a prolonged response, generating an aura of significance, with sympathetic overtones, from an initially intense moment followed by interference, damping, and decay or persistence" (Stockwell 2009, 19). Similarly, though from a reception-theory perspective, Wai Chee Dimock's *A Theory of Resonance* claims that "[t]exts resonate through time, using noise 'as an apt analogy for . . . interpretative context'" (Willis 2018, 155). In addition to Stockwell's cognitive poetic understanding of "a textured prolonged feeling that can be revivified periodically after the initial experience," resonance is "a tone, an atmosphere in the mind that seems to persist long after the pages have been put down" (Stockwell 2009, 17). In other words, context resonates, and this is an important characteristic that illuminates it as the "take-away message" of a piece of fiction, what remains with the reader beyond the act of reading. This leads to revisiting Kokinov's theory of dynamic context, previously abridged, which reads in full: "the dynamic fuzzy set of all associatively relevant *memory* elements (mental representations or operations) at a particular instant of time" (Kokinov 1995, italics added). Certainly, context would not work without memory, and that is how it piles up on relevant elements to build coherence. Thus, integration and systematic or logical connection or consistency are achieved. That way, context forms a momentary figure to be brought forward for the next stratification of interrelated conditions.

Moreover, literary resonance is also related to *attention* and experiential memory. According to Stockwell, neglected elements (those to which the reader is inattentionaly blind in Chabris' and Simons' terms, or examples of blindness to context in Scharfstein's wording (Sharfstein 1989, 51)) may be the product of "textual patterning." This seems to describe well the work of a contextual model in the reading process, especially with the elaboration "another focused element comes to *occlude* the previously focused figure" (Stockwell 2009, 22, italics in original). This seems to be precisely what happens when one contextual model interchanges with another in the shifting of perspectives, leading to altering readings.

Resonance, prolonged and textured, is the very effect of context. Stockwell himself introduces the notion of texture as a cognitive aesthetic of reading that is synonymous with coherence: "textural experience of reading literature" (2009, 14), "the sense of textuality [which is the abstract feature of a text]," its subjective characteristic (2009, 5, 190)—the configurations between texts and literature in literary works that are essentially heteronomous (non-autonomous). In sum, "[t]extuality is the outcome of the workings of shared cognitive mechanics, evident in texts and readings. Texture is the experienced quality of textuality" (Stockwell 2009, 1). Similarly, the philosopher Stephen Pepper sees texture as inseparable from quality and thus defined as "*the details and relations* which make up that character or quality" (Pepper 1942, 238, italics added). Moreover, "[q] uality always exhibits some degree of fusion of the details of its texture. [. . .] [Fusion] is an agency of qualitative simplification or organization" (Pepper 1942, 243–244). Thus, Pepper explains context as an *indirect* contributor to the quality of texture. Cognitive psychologists, on the other hand, have discovered that context influences not only decision-making but also our memory for events (Kokinov, Petkov, and Petrova 2007, 317–329). And if, following Iser, we consider reading an event, then the inner connections within different text episodes would be differently influenced by context. In other words, content changes with context. Since the act of reading is essentially "thinking the thoughts of another" (Poulet 1969, 55), these thoughts—in the form of the modeled textual context—are imposed on the reader, who is thus entangled in its texture. In line with this comes Pepper's claim that "the texture of perception [integrated by and under the look of the perceiver] [. . .] must be partly made up of the strands carried into it by the activities of the perceiver" (Pepper 1942, 266, 276).

Building on the discussion so far, context turns out to be what is perceived and undergoes reasoning. That is why the texture of reading is the very trajectory of the act of reading; the way context outlines and conditions the movement of the wandering viewpoint (Iser) between the gaps. The implicit, textual metastrategy of modeling the context serves as a good ground for guiding toward certain interpretations. Paradoxically, though, it not only attracts the reader's attention but also distracts it: it functions as a *disciplining factor* and an *attractor*, but also as a *distractor*. That way, only one of the multiple immanent contextual models is realized at a given time. However, concretization (Ingarden) and contextualization are different, even if related processes. The former is accomplished with the completion of reading, while the latter, being a product of context (Hristov 2017), remains always resonating and potentially open for new recontextualizations and new consistency building. The texture of reading allows for the shifting of positions, for (re)interpretation. If concretization is a product of (re)arrangement of the gaps, then context is a function, contingent on the gaps' filling *and* (re)arrangement alike.

Context, a chain of interrelated conditions and relations, may be represented visually as a cloud or a wave. It is stable only at a certain time in contextualization when forming a state of mind or a specific constellation. Therefore, these can be seen, as Vidinsky rightly points out, only *post factum* (Vidinsky 2018). This means that in the act of reading, the context's role is too dynamic to notice and is only perceivable after the concretization is completed. This allows for distancing and opens possible new interpretations. In a sense, a first contextualization is achieved along with the concretization of the work but the effect of it, its role, is reconstructible post-concretization. What is further complicated by fiction, and especially by metafiction, is that context functions not on the level of a word or a sentence, but rather within the wholeness of the work. This means that the dynamic figure/ground relations around gaps appear in combination with the whole multidimensional texture. That is why the illustrations in describing and defining context undergo transformations and alter various metaphors: a resinous net, a wave, a cloud, and so on.

How, then, is the texture of reading conducted, and how is context being constructed? One way to model it could be through employing patterns, repetitions; yet another would be through instructions. We can see both in Nabokov's "The Vane Sisters." However, some contextualizations appear to be easily activated, whereas others remain too subtle. One may think that a text so rich with instructions (even though predominantly implicit) on letter hunting would inevitably activate the letter-awareness contextual model for the story. Nevertheless, many readers stay unaware of the final twist. This may be due to the ghost theme (very active throughout different parts) or due to the subversive role of irony embracing many of the instructions. That way, it turns out that context, even if carefully constructed, may be subverted by irony. Another explanation might be that the multiplicity of contextual models disrupts the act of reading. There are at least two competing contextual models—contextual model 1, built in parts 1, 3, 5 (the "ghost" theme) vs. contextual model 2, built in parts 2, 4, 6 (the "letter" theme)—which come together in the final, seventh part of the story. Following Kokinov's, Petkov's, and Petrova's results from a cognitive experiment on the degree of internal connectivity of the coalition representing the episode on the outcome of the reconstruction process ("the more [. . .] links between the elements of the episode [. . .], the higher the number of details we recall, and the lesser the intruded elements and the context influence," Kokinov, Petkov, and Petrova 2007), and judging by the acrostics missed by many readers, I would argue that one of the models has a "stronger" effect than the other. Or better yet, for very few readers, they are interchangeable. That way, readers can switch between the models. This, in turn, leads to gorillas/ gaps left unseen and unread. Along the same lines is Iser's argument on gaps, pointing up to context:

> There is no longer a definitive frame of reference by which to judge the events of the narrative—such a frame has to be produced during the acts of comprehension [context—KK]. Without this central orientation, the segments of the perspectives tend to be more *densely interwoven*, for the meaning arises not so much from what the individual perspectives represent, as from the continual transformation of what they make conceivable. (Iser 1978, 205, italics added)

A more important aspect, though, would be the ability not only to switch but also to combine them both. Or better yet, in line with Vidinsky's view on the importance of *distance* in the transformation of a context (Vidinsky 2017, 16), for the interwoven contextual models to work, it would be essential to see them in their *continuity* together. In addition, if the fictional is an attribute of context, then the communicatory structure of the fictional text could be further explained by Iser's notion on the role of negativity:

> Blanks and negations denote the missing links and the virtual themes along the syntagmatic and paradigmatic axes of the text. They make it possible for the fundamental asymmetry between text and reader to be balanced out, for they initiate an interaction whereby the hollow form of the text is filled by the mental images of the reader. In this way, text and reader begin to converge, and the reader can experience an unfamiliar reality under conditions that are not determined by his own disposition. Blanks and negations increase the *density* of fictional texts, for the omissions and cancellations indicate background, and so the formulated text has a kind of unformulated double. This "double" we shall call negativity. (Iser 1978, 225–226; italics added)

> [. . .] the function of the blanks is dual in nature: on the syntagmatic axis of reading they constitute the links between the perspective segments of the

> text; on the paradigmatic axis they constitute the links between negated norms and the reader's relation to the text. The intimate connection between the two functions is the basic condition that gives rise to the interaction between text and reader. (Iser 1978, 216)

That way, one may speculate that textual context as a function of the text (the paradigmatic axis of reading) interacts with the reader (the syntagmatic axis), thus modeling the texture of reading. This might explain why

> the interplay between the syntagmatic and paradigmatic axes of the reading becomes of increasing relevance. It will be remembered that the syntagmatic axis ranges the perspective segments into a theme-and-horizon order. Here *the blanks are the missing links between segments on the one hand, and vacancies on the other, arising whenever a segment loses its thematic relevance and forms a background for the next thematic segment.* (Iser 1978, 215; italics added)

Might this sentence be employed as another definition of context? Iser further argues:

> We have called this process syntagmatic because it relates to the structure (*changing perspectives*) and not to the contents, which are inevitably transformed through this interaction. Now the negation of the contents leads to additional blanks, for the contents are not only subjected to the theme-and-horizon structure, but this subjection also takes place under the explicit provision that they are negated. These blanks therefore have *a restrictive effect on the way in which the segments may be combined, and a selective influence on the meaning to be produced* by the reader's acts of ideation. (Iser 1978, 216, italics added)

Thus, texture—constituting context's ontological characteristic—is illustrated by context's functional characteristic—resonance. Closely related to the reading event are memory and attention. That way, the details and relations outline the trajectory of the reading process. It is interesting to note that both context and gaps alike act restrictively for perception. That is why in the next part, the trespassing from text to context will be discussed in comparison to the contextualization of the reader as a gap and the role of "gappiness" in reading (meta)fiction (Bernaerts et al. 2013).

MINDING THE READER: THE READER CONFRONTS THE GAP (A CLASH)

Carefully crafted, "The Vane Sisters" illustrates Nabokov's training program for the reader. However, it seems to fail with many readers, including the learned editors of the *New Yorker*, who notoriously rejected it for publication. Where does the problem with this failed reception come from? What ways of reading should one have to really appreciate this story? Does it play along with and prepare only the most devoted readers? If it isn't enough to be a good reader in Nabokov's understanding, what is the good reader of this story, maybe overly abundant with contextual models and thus in a sense overly *gappy*? These are the questions I will focus on in the following part.

Mind the Letter: Letters (Are) Matter!

Style is matter to Nabokov and perhaps that is why it points out the importance of letters in this story, requiring a specific *texture of reading*. The explicit training program in paying attention to letters is particularly visible in parts 2, 4, 6, and 7.

The art of caressing details/letters evolves from arranging (and misplacing) the students' copybooks alphabetically (Nabokov 2002, 621)—typically done in *dictionaries*—through letter play: "Death was not better than D minus, but definitely better than Life minus D" (Nabokov 2002, 622) to peek into "miraculous misprints," and "logogriphs" (Nabokov 2002, 626). There is much alliteration that should activate resonance and moreover, a good reader shouldn't fail to notice the abundance of eccentricity of "mis-shapen or illicitly connected words" (Nabokov 2002, 626) in the final paragraph of part 4:

> "A*l*ph" was a pRophetic sequence of the initia*l* *l*etters of Anna *L*ivia P*l*urabe*ll*e (anotheR sacRed RiveR Running thRough, oR Rather aRound, yet anotheR fake dReam), whi*l*e the additiona*l* h modestly stood, as a pRivate signpost, for the word that had so hypnotized MR. PoR*l*ock. [hither→hitler] (Nabokov 2002, 626, emphasis added on *l* and R. Dear reader, please imagine it was added on a, p and h as well! [KK])

After this pointed alph-abetical reference, there follows the seemingly most explicit instruction on letters and acrostics. This might lead a very curious reader to check right away—before actually getting there by linear and thorough reading!—"the first letters of the words in its [the short story's] last paragraph" (Nabokov 2002, 626). It may even seem impossible to miss this, and yet many—even learned—readers do. Perhaps it's neither just a matter of the training program for the reader nor only of knowing Nabokov's way of writing well. What, then, are the conditions that lead to a failed reception? In a letter to Katharine White of the *New Yorker*, Nabokov writes: "I start preparing the reader for the last paragraph by describing the kind of thing millions of cranks have done with Shakespeare's sonnets—reading the initial letters of the lines to see if they made some esoteric sense" (1989, 117). Indeed, he does prepare the eager reader well, explicitly and implicitly, persistently from beginning to end. It even seems that he considers the letter-hunt for "sacramental words" (Nabokov 2002, 629) in part 6 even more instructive than the above-quoted "prophetic sequence of the initial letters" in part 4.

There are many poems employing the trick of an acrostic. However, this technique is transposed to a whole different level, genre, and context in "The Vane Sisters," and as Nabokov himself states, "[t]his particular trick can be tried only once in a thousand years of fiction" (2002, 669). Style is more than having an artistic sense; "'style' *is* matter" (Nabokov 1989, 116). The literal use of letters in this story as if serves to demonstrate the full meaning—literally and literarily—of being "a man of letters."

The Reader and the Gap

Reading backward, diagonally, or up and down is not something a reader would normally do, even a good one. Furthermore, it is empirically tested that readers usually "misread" (unread), which is, in a sense, to succeed in reading by predicting, even misspelled/scrambled words if the first and last letters are in place (Rawlinson 1976, notoriously turned into a popular, augmented, meme). However, there are way too many implicit and explicit instructions in the story for (re)reading single letters in all possible directions, *provided that* (on *condition* that) one's mind is open and prepared. So, what kind of reader would fondle a letter play, a trick on the micro-level of the single word/letter while having in mind the bigger picture? Who is capable of shifting perspectives, reading simultaneously several contextual models (understood as the relevant threads of a texture, traceable *post factum*)?

The unsaid, the half-said, and the "disnarrated" (Gerald Prince) play a huge role in this story. All skills for filling the gaps (*Leerstellen*) need to be awakened. "I notice, of course, only those clues that I am prepared to notice" (Booth 1961, 305), and hence, this story demonstrates the power of knowledge and instruction: the more trained and willing the reader, the more pleasure and rewards they will get. "Nabokov's fiction offers a course of instruction in illicit connections, a series of lessons for the hermeneutic *Bildung* of a 'perverse amateur'" (Naiman 2010, 8). This story models its good reader from the gap while at the same time the reader fills in the gaps in the act of reading because the reading process is essentially an act of gap-filling:

> The gaps, indeed, are those very points at which the reader can enter into the text, forming his own connections and conceptions and so creating the configurative meaning of what he is reading. Thanks to the "vacant pages," he can reflect, and through reflection create the motivation through which can experience the text as a reality. (Iser 1974, 40)

What are the gaps in this story, then? The figures of absence and transparency as well as of artistic presence serve to mark the gappiness in the texture of reading. Even D.'s character, presented *initial*ly, evokes death, absence, emptiness, and vainness. It is no wonder, then, that one of the means for gaping at the reader would be Sybil, whose name means "go-between." Thus, the text has the reader in mind from I [eye] to "meaning. Everything seemed yellowly blurred, illusive, lost" [me Sybil] (Nabokov 2002, 631). The *essential sitelessness of the reading act* (Stewart 1996, 55) constructs a contractual contact (cf. Stewart 1996, 10). That is how a "transacted gap" is opened "between reader and read" (Stewart 1996, 18–19). Stepping into this very gap, occupying this vacancy, this gap, in turn, fills them in, and the reader themselves begin to serve as a gap for/in the text: "The blanks and vacancies thus chart a course for reading a text by organizing the reader's participation with their structure of shifting positions" (Holub 1984, 94). This constitutes the *syntagmatic axis* in the text, explained by Iser's concept of *wandering viewpoint*, which is "a means of describing the way in which the reader is present in the text" (Iser 1978, 118).

The discussion of the role of "gappiness" in reading fiction (Bernaerts et al.) evokes a distinction between several degrees of gappiness:

- Information gaps (omissions) in the text;
- Existing information that is unavailable for the reader—reconstructible or non-reconstructible (blind spots). In this case, it is most visible how reading is a form of blindness;
- Available information that is cloudy, non-transparent for the reader (needs dictionary/translation)—unreading, "blind reading" (Caracciolo 2013, 81–106); this is how the readers get sorted and some don't get through. Thus, some texts, like the story I am discussing, can be unread. Unreading (Herbert Schwaab) is different from non-reading and is rather "a form of reading that is guided by experience instead of interpretation." (De Valck and Teurlings)

It seems that "The Vane Sisters" falls into the third degree of gappiness. It turns out that an acrostic also acts as a gap in the text—it being simultaneously present and invisible. And that is why the peak of the story is the hidden acrostic—paradoxically—acrostically exposed all the time. Just like the gorilla beating its chest. One needs to reread the text without actually reading it, or to reread it, unreading it. The text, minding the reader reveals the outline of the relation between the reader and the gap. As a "silent partner" (Stewart 1996, 10), they take the position of a gap. Thus, the reader acts as a void for the text to pass through, a good conductor of images and words.

The requirements for the reader—incidentally, a word used very loosely! (Nabokov 1980, 3)—of this story seem too many already, almost as many as to someone who made themselves void of themself so that they can take the presence of the Other (text). But isn't that characteristic of a *translator*? This is one who makes themself gappy, letting the text pass through them. Not only do they perceive and read the text, but, rather, they process it in a way of simultaneous reading and writing, a double act of coalescing with the text—once as being the text and then taking the pouring text in (essentially, rereading). Only that way they could simultaneously embroider letters while having the whole work in mind. Only then could they shift between contextual models.

Essentially, a good translator makes themself a blank page, a screen on which the author projects their images and words. This is the one who transforms, masters, and recreates the gappiness of the story, they themself being a gappy creature. They are an invisible presence, "a miraculous feeling of the words being there, written in invisible ink and clamoring to become visible" (Nabokov 1980, 379) on the blank pages. The liminality of the reader makes them astraddle, bridging the gap as a translator does. A reader may skip or omit something, unlike the translator who ought not to leave out anything that was uncomprehended. This is how the reader-translator takes the place of the gap which has waited there for them to be filled in.

However, it's not advisable to use the word translator very loosely here. There are three kinds of translators according to Nabokov's typology:

> [1] the scholar who is eager to make the world appreciate the works of an obscure genius as much as he does himself; [2] the well meaning hack; and [3] the professional writer relaxing in the company of a foreign confrere. The scholar will be, I hope, exact and pedantic: footnotes—on the *same* page as the text and not tucked away at the end of the volume—can never be too copious and detailed. The laborious lady translating at the eleventh hour the eleventh volume of somebody's collected works will be, I am afraid, less exact and less pedantic; but the point is not that the scholar commits fewer blunders than a drudge; the point is that as a rule both he and she are hopelessly devoid of any semblance of creative genius. Neither learning nor diligence can replace imagination and style. (Nabokov 1981, 319)

It seems that all three may err in one way (or another) but what's most likely the good translator suitable for the gap position in this Nabokovian text is the one to forget themself, to make themself transparent, to be a genius (i.e., talented), to be knowledgeable, and to possess the gift of mimicry, to "be able to act, as it were, the real author's part by impersonating his tricks of demeanor and speech, his ways and his mind, with the utmost degree of verisimilitude" (Nabokov 1981, 319). In short, they are supposed to be void of themselves in order to allow the manifestation of a double self. In addition to providing a new explanation for the well-known characteristic of Nabokov's good reader—the one in the mirror—this might further explain the mysterious requirement for a dictionary in good reading.

Having stated all that, I mind the possibility of unreading it as I haven't translated "The Vane Sisters" yet. Paradoxically enough, after translating it, I might have a different gappy reading, which would only prove the proposed thesis. Thank Logos, it seems close to untranslatable to me. Have a gappy reading down the rabbit hole!

(*Note.* All gaps in (the logic of) this part were placed intentionally, for there's always another gorilla unseen . . .)[7]

NOTES

1. "I am the perfect dictator in that private world" (Nabokov 1990, 69).
2. For more on instructive metafiction and its rules and roles, see Kokinova (2023).
3. Spoiler alert. There are certain key aspects of this story that will be discussed here and hence the reader unfamiliar with the text of "The Vane Sisters" will be deprived from a virgin pleasure of experiencing it.
4. For an up-to-date bibliography on cognitive approaches to literature see Lisa Zunshine's page on Academia.com: https://www.academia.edu/17855983/Bibliography_for_Cognitive_Literary_and_Cultural_Studies_in_progress_updated_regularly.
5. Please take three minutes to see http://www.theinvisiblegorilla.com/videos.html. For a discussion of the experiment, see Caracciolo (2013).
6. See Pepper (1942); Stockwell (2009); and, most recently, Vidinsky (2018).
7. This research project was conducted thanks to the generous support of the Center for Advanced Study (Sofia) and its Advanced Academia Fellowship program (March-July 2018). It was also undertaken in loving memory of my father Boicho Kokinov. I am grateful for the constructive criticism, questions, and suggestions made by Bogdana Paskaleva, Diana Mistreanu, Todor Hristov, and Vassil Vidinsky on its very first drafts.

BIBLIOGRAPHY

Bernaerts, Lars, Dirk De Geest, Luc Herman, and Bart Vervaeck, eds. 2013. *Stories and Minds: Cognitive Approaches to Literary Narrative*. Lincoln, NE: University of Nebraska Press.

Booth, Wayne C. 1961. *The Rhetoric of Fiction*. Chicago: Chicago University Press.

Boring, Edwin. G. 1930. "A New Ambiguous Figure." *American Journal of Psychology* 42: 444–445.

Caracciolo, Marco. 2013. "Blind Reading. Toward an Enactivist Theory of the Reader's Imagination." In *Stories and Minds: Cognitive Approaches to Literary Narrative*, edited by Lars Bernaerts, Dirk De Geest, Luc Herman, and Bart Vervaeck, 81–106. Lincoln, NE: University of Nebraska Press.

Chabris, Christopher, and Daniel Simons. 2010. *The Invisible Gorilla and Other Ways Our Intuitions Deceive Us*. New York: Crown.

Hamilton, Craig A., and Ralf Schneider. 2002. "From Iser to Turner and Beyond: Reception Theory Meets Cognitive Criticism." *Style* 36, no. 4: 640–658.

Holub, Robert C. 1984. *Reception Theory: A Critical Introduction*. London: Methuen.

Hristov, Todor. 2017. "*Kontekst, golemi danni i individualizirane na potrebitelite.*" *Piron* no. 14: 15. http://piron.culturecenter-su.org/todor-hristov-context-big-data/.

Hutcheon, Linda. 1980. *Narcissistic Narrative: The Metafictional Paradox*. Waterloo, Ont.: Wilfrid Laurier University Press.

Iser, Wolfgang. 1974. *The Implied Reader: Patterns of Communication in Prose Fiction from Bunyan to Beckett*. Baltimore: Johns Hopkins University Press.

Iser, Wolfgang. 1978. *The Act of Reading: A Theory of Aesthetic Response*. London: Routledge and Kegan Paul.

Jauss, Hans Robert. [1970] 1982. *Toward an Aesthetic of Reception*. Minneapolis: University of Minnesota Press.

Kokinov, Boicho. 1995. "A Dynamic Approach to Context Modeling." In *Proceedings of the IJCAI-95 Workshop on Modeling Context in Knowledge Representation and Reasoning*, edited by Patrick Brézillon and Samy Abu-Hakima, 1–11. LAFORIA 95 (11).

Kokinov, Boicho, Georgi Petkov, and Nadezhda Petrova. 2007. "Context-Sensitivity of Human Memory: Episode Connectivity and Its Influence on Memory Reconstruction." In *International and Interdisciplinary Conference on Modeling and Using Context*, edited by Boicho Kokinov, Daniel C. Richardson, Thomas R. Roth-Berghofer, and Laure Vieu, 317–329. Heidelberg: Springer. https://doi.org/10.1007/978-3-540-74255-5_24.

Kokinova, Katherina. 2023. "Instructing the Reader of Metafiction: Nabokov & Gombrowicz." *Narrative* 31, no 2: 117–137.

Nabokov, Vladimir. 1980. *Lectures on Literature*, edited by Fredson Bowers. London: Weidenfeld and Nicolson.

Nabokov, Vladimir. 1981. *Lectures on Russian Literature*, edited by Fredson Bowers. London: Weidenfeld and Nicolson.

Nabokov, Vladimir. 1989. *Selected Letters 1940–1977*, edited by Dmitri Nabokov and Matthew J. Bruccoli. San Diego: Harcourt Brace Jovanovich.

Nabokov, Vladimir. 1990. *Strong Opinions*. New York: Vintage Books.

Nabokov, Vladimir. 2002. *The Stories of Vladimir Nabokov*. New York: Vintage Books.

Naiman, Eric. 2010. *Nabokov, Perversely*. Ithaca, NY: Cornell University Press.

Pepper, Stephen C. 1942. *World Hypotheses. A Study in Evidence*. Berkeley: University of California Press.

Poulet, Georges. 1969. "Phenomenology of Reading." *New Literary History* 1, no. 1: 53–68. https://doi.org/10.2307/468372.

Prince, Gerald. 1988. "The Disnarrated." *Style* 22, no. 1 (Spring): 1–8.

Rawlinson, Graham E. 1976. "The Significance of Letter Position in Word Recognition." Unpublished PhD Thesis, University of Nottingham.

Sharfstein, Ben-Ami. 1989. *The Dilemma of Context*. New York: New York University Press.

Schwaab, Herbert. 2013. "'Unreading' Contemporary Television." In *After the Break. Television Theory Today*, edited by Marijke De Valck, and Jan Teurlings, 21–34. Amsterdam: Amsterdam University Press.

Stewart, Garrett. 1996. *Dear Reader. The Conscripted Audience in Nineteenth-Century British Fiction*. Baltimore: The Johns Hopkins University Press.

Stockwell, Peter. 2009. *Texture. A Cognitive Aesthetics of Reading*. Edinburgh: Edinburgh University Press.

Vidinsky, Vassil. 2018. "Postfaktum za konteksta i izlishnoto." *Piron*, no. 16: 21. http://piron.culturecenter-su.org/vassil-vidinsky-post-factum-on-context/.

Willis, Ika. 2018. *Reception*. Abington: Routledge.

7

Re-visioning Despair

The Medical Gaze in Sologub's The Petty Demon

Kelly Knickmeier Cummings

This chapter utilizes social cognition, the study of the cognitive processes and mental mechanisms that underlie social interactions, to examine Fyodor Sologub's novel *The Petty Demon* (1907) and its protagonist Peredonov. The plot follows the psychological deterioration of Peredonov and the onset of his schizophrenia, a disorder that affects a person's ability to think, feel, and behave clearly. Sologub's narrator assumes a *medical gaze* that catalogues the extent to which Peredonov interprets reality and social interactions abnormally, becomes increasingly paranoid, and eventually commits arson and murder. At the same time, the narrator and Sologub move the reader from revulsion toward Peredonov to feelings of compassion toward him, even as he commits his worst deeds. Social cognition offers a frame of reference that can help make sense of this affective shift over the course of the novel. This affords a deeper understanding and re-visioning of Sologub's commentary on the nature of evil, the emotional and social dimensions of human experience, and the Symbolist milieu.

DEFINING THE MEDICAL GAZE

Sologub's narrator employs a medical gaze because he practices medical observation. He documents the signs and symptoms of illness to determine the cause and diagnosis of Peredonov's psychological deterioration. Gaze in this case refers to "an act of selecting what we consider to be the relevant elements of the total data stream available to our senses" (Misselbrook 2013, 312). Practitioners use this data to make diagnoses, prognoses, and treatment plans. Thus, a medical gaze is the process by which a physician "reads" a patient's signs and symptoms of illness and translates or mediates the "mystery"—a contagion, injury, or disequilibrium—into a narrative and action plan toward restoration and/or resolution. I make the case throughout this chapter that the medical gaze of a physician and the penetrating gaze of a Symbolist poet share these creative acts of deciphering, decoding, naming, and narrating to make the invisible visible.

The concept of the medical gaze was interrogated by Michel Foucault (1926–1984) in *Madness and Civilization: A History of Insanity in the Age of Reason* (1961) and *The Birth of the Clinic* (1963) as commentary on the exercise of power within social systems. Foucault was concerned with how doctors used their knowledge to wield power, selecting pieces of a patient's story to fit a "biomedical paradigm, filtering out non-biomedical material" to such an extent that it became an abuse of knowledge and power (Misselbrook 2013, 312). Since the time of Foucault's criticism, practitioners better understand the sociocultural and symbolic contexts of medicine. Kleinman identified "medicine's symbolic reality" and acknowledged "the acts of ordering, naming, interpreting, and offering therapy for illness are aspects of symbolic reality common to both the sick individual, the healer, and their society" (1973, 208). O'Callaghan asserted that psychiatry today values this "wider biopsychosocial gaze that is missing in Foucault's medical gaze" while also maintaining necessary "narrow diagnostic classificatory systems" when determining a diagnosis (2022, 1796). In this chapter, my use of the medical gaze employs this wider, contextual lens.

The narrator in *The Petty Demon* deploys a medical gaze. He notes many spiritual, psychophysiological, sociocultural, and socioeconomic aspects of Peredonov's distress. We as readers are invited to partake in this "total data stream" to make sense of the world and characters and to make sense of the meaning and import of Peredonov's illness for ourselves. By extension, Peredonov becomes our patient, too. Thus, a medical gaze is an opportunity for authors like Sologub to play with the affective nature of symbolic reality.

By rendering Peredonov an object of medical observation, Sologub capitalizes on the similarities between the goals of the physician and the goals of Symbolism as an aesthetic school. Kennedy argued that "medical observation and its authority are useful because they enable the reading of less tangible realities, in an allegorical reading of character" (2010, 19). Kennedy defined the visual field of the physician as "a formalized and rigorously policed structure of knowledge imposed upon the messy stuff of human interaction" (2010, 70). A physician is trained in this structured knowledge to read, interpret, translate, and diagnose something that is otherwise occult to the patient and their community. The assumption is that a physician's training in this cache of structured knowledge, when applied thoughtfully and responsibly, can have positive outcomes for individuals and society and make otherwise invisible things accessible.

This was similarly the business of Symbolism, though it accorded with a different cache of knowledge: to use poetic form to create innovative symbols with the hope that the alchemy of creation and contemplation could provide a transformative experience for author and reader alike. This alchemy would facilitate access into less tangible, hidden, or transcendental realities. The assumption was that this process of spiritual and physical experimentation at the intersection of life and creation could alter materiality, lead to transfiguration, or access states of being that exist beyond human sense. The quest was often framed as a rediscovery and recovery of one's divinity.

In his 1893 manifesto on Symbolism, Dmitri Merezhkovsky (1865–1941) maintained that "[c]haracters can . . . serve as symbols" and "symbols express the unrestricted aspect of truth" (Cioran 1983, 12). As will be elaborated upon in a later section, Symbolists founded this narrative in the ancient Gnostic myth of Sophia. Years later, in his memoir *Necropolis*, Vladislav Khodasevich (1886–1939) called this retrospectively unsuccessful, priestlike quest the "philosopher's stone of art."

Both forms of observation—the medical gaze of the physician and the penetrating gaze of the poet—result in a process of symbolic naming and, therefore, are creative acts. Poets (certainly Symbolist ones) and physicians can "see" truths that lie hidden to others and can use this wisdom to create narratives for us to read, if not enact. Ronald Peterson proposed that "a symbol connotes a sign that needs to be deciphered and therefore invites the participation of the reader or a viewer to penetrate the mystery" (1993, xi). By drawing upon the labor of medical observation, a clinical form of seeing, knowing, and representing, Sologub invites us as readers to participate in deciphering, decoding, and naming both Peredonov's illness and the symbolic reality of his novel.

The medical gaze assumed by Sologub's narrator makes available to us a particular kind of creative practice: medical observation and diagnosis. In doing so, Sologub makes medicine's "modes of knowledge a transparent medium to the spiritual view beyond, to make the invisible visible" (Kennedy 2010, 89). The following sections analyze how Sologub accomplished this through an intentional spectacle of social signals to activate his readers' "capacity to make sense of intentional behavior in terms of mental states" (Spaulding 2018, 1)—what psychiatrists call *Theory of Mind* (ToM) or *mind-reading*—to discuss and propose what it may have been that Sologub intended for his readers to see and comprehend.

PEREDONOV'S ILLNESS

The Petty Demon follows the life of Peredonov, a schoolteacher in a provincial Russian town, who has learned of an opportunity for promotion to inspector. Peredonov's enthusiasm that he could exert influence and control over others and garner immediate respect is overshadowed by anxieties that others will be jealous, wish him harm, and may even denounce, if not murder, him. These anxieties are not unfounded, at least in the beginning: Peredonov is deeply flawed, consumed by petty desires, insecurities, and delusions of grandeur. He is unkind to his students and his fiancée Varvara, thinks poorly of others, and generally assumes a selfish outlook.

The novel portrays Peredonov's relationships and interactions with friends, neighbors, students, local government officials, and several women. As it progresses, Peredonov's inflated ego leads him to perceive slights where none exist, fueling his paranoia and driving him to manipulate and abuse those around him in a desperate attempt to maintain his sense of superiority. The novel delves into Peredonov's increasingly erratic behavior and the consequences it brings not only for himself but also for those who are unfortunate enough to be caught in his path. This is the fate of his student Sasha Pilnikov, a strikingly beautiful adolescent in the process of discovering his sensuality and the effect it has on others. The narrator details the extent to which Sasha, under the influence of a sensual woman, Liudmila, clandestinely but innocently experiments with performing gender identities and roles. In a warped interpretation of the Symbolist myth of Sophia, Peredonov launches a smear campaign against Sasha, Liudmila's muse, insisting he is a girl in disguise.

As Peredonov navigates the social hierarchy of the town, the rumors he spreads, and various (mis)perceptions, he obsesses over maintaining his status until he descends into madness. In his mind, he is stalked by a small furry demon, the *nedotykomka*. He reads sinister intent among people and within inanimate objects. In the end, Peredonov kills his friend Volodin, confident that Volodin has designs on his now wife Varvara and the future position of inspector, though neither are actualities. Varvara lied about Princess Volchanskaya securing Peredonov's promotion. Volodin's murder is completely unnecessary.

Sologub's narrator diagnoses Peredonov's illness as the mind's impaired perception or awareness of itself and the world: "His sensibilities were dull and his consciousness was an apparatus for corruption and destruction" (1983, 97). This assertion does not localize Peredonov's ailment to a specific part of his temporal body. Rather, the disease is found in his consciousness, defined as an apparatus: the technical equipment or machinery needed for a particular activity or purpose, in this case, for the processing of impressions and perceptions. Peredonov's consciousness—the means through which his ability to recognize and comprehend environmental stimuli and then make behavioral decisions—has been disabled. "Everything that reached his consciousness was transformed into something vile and filthy," the narrator tells us (97). "He was immediately taken with deformities in objects and rejoiced over them" (97). Peredonov is not awake but rather asleep in the mire of small-minded, delusional, and mundane material concerns.

Social knowledge is a basic human need, and Peredonov has lost it. Understanding "the why" of changes in our environment, especially another person's behavior, is one of the qualities that separates humans from other living beings, and it informs social cognition, all "the mental processes involved in perceiving, attending to, remembering, thinking about, and making sense of the people in our social world" (Moskowitz 2005, 3). The conflicts that arise from Peredonov's distorted social perceptions drive the plot and are recorded through the narrator's medical gaze.

As his illness progresses, Peredonov's anxieties about a potential life-changing promotion agitate him. Peredonov fears denunciation, even from a cat. "Whom was [Peredonov] trying to discover? Denouncers. They were hiding behind all objects, speaking in hushed whispers and laughing. His enemies were besieging Peredonov with an entire army of denouncers" (178). The natural world around him is just as menacing as people are. "For some reason the sun kept hiding behind the clouds. Was it spying on him?" (212).

Peredonov's descent into madness serves as a critique of the society in which he lives, highlighting the hypocrisy and moral decay that permeate every level of existence. Varvara lied about the Princess's promise. The townsfolk gossip. Out of jealousy, they form a vulgar mob that comes close to injuring Sasha. Sologub's characterization of this small-town Russian life has credibility. For many years before becoming a successful poet, Sologub worked as a provincial schoolteacher himself, supporting his sister, experimenting with poetic forms, and waiting to escape to another way of life. Sologub uses the novel and Peredonov's illness to explore the destructive nature of the small-mindedness he detested.

Sologub extends Peredonov's individual sociopsychological decline as an allegory of the *byt* (everyday life), *poshlost'* (philistinism), and economic and social stagnation of Russian society at the turn of the twentieth century. In his preface to the second Russian edition of *The Petty Demon* in 1908, Sologub asserts, "it is about you that I have written my novel" (27). He claims, "everything that relates to the narrative incidents, the everyday life, and the psychology in my novel is based on very precise observations" (27). For these reasons, I approach Sologub's novel as he told us he intended, at least in his second preface—Peredonov as an allegory for Russian society—but I take things a step further. Sologub's assertion is that a pathological time demands a medical gaze in which, in his own words, "the deformed and the beautiful are reflected in it with equal precision" (28).

PEREDONOV'S DIAGNOSIS

Sologub's narrator attributes the root cause of Peredonov's warped motivation and behaviors to his failed search for higher meaning and purpose:

> Yes, Peredonov was striving for the truth after all, according to the general law of every conscious life and he was oppressed by the striving. He himself was not conscious of the fact that like all people he was striving for the truth, and for that reason his anxiety was obscure. He couldn't find the truth for himself and became muddled and was perishing. (1908, 228)

The illness Peredonov suffers from is his state of *not* being awake and aware, a faulty consciousness. Peredonov longs for understanding, insight, and a better life, but his perception is impaired. Depression, anxiety, anger, and restlessness have slowed his mind's processing speed and made things blurry: "Either his gaze would be fixed on something far off, or it would wander strangely. It seemed as though he were constantly scrutinizing an object. This caused objects to double before his eyes, freeze, and then pulsate" (178).

Peredonov is driven mad by the longing to see something more than the monstrous. The narrator tells us that "[s]pectres had divorced Peredonov from the world. His eyes, crazed and dull, wandered without pausing on objects, just as though he were constantly seeking to look beyond them, beyond the objective world, and was searching for the apertures" (242). Peredonov's own gaze—his capacity to navigate "the total data stream available to our senses" (Misselbrook 2013, 312)—is completely defunct.

The deterioration of Peredonov's mental state facilitates Sologub's interrogation of the "health" of Russian society at the turn of the twentieth century, a historical moment characterized by a loss of equilibrium. As a methodological approach to the novel, social cognition makes consonant two seemingly divergent readings of the novel: an *applied,* scientific-empirical interpretation and a *theoretical,* metaphysical interpretation of Peredonov's symptoms. Both the medical and the Symbolist worldviews Sologub employs in *The Petty Demon* produce the same diagnosis—madness. The questions are how and why?

SOCIAL COGNITION AS METHODOLOGY: PEREDONOV'S THEORY OF MIND

Though Symbolism and social cognition are distinct fields—the former an aesthetic practice and theurgic worldview and the latter a scientific discipline—they both probe and interrogate the complexities of human thought, emotion, and social interaction. Social cognition shares common ground with the aesthetic and literary objectives of Symbolism. Both approaches delve into the lived experiences and subjectivity/objectivity of the human mind/psyche to explore such things as consciousness, memory, motivation, creativity, perception, and aesthetic and psychic impact. Both social cognition and Symbolism are concerned with representation and the categorization of associations, as well as archetypal and universal themes and how these things impact and drive behavioral choices. They both engage with transcultural and transcendental aspects of human experience.

Social cognition interprets social and emotional information and then regulates behavioral choices based on this acquired social knowledge; it is a process of reflective reasoning, which assigns meaning to others' thoughts and intentions (Tal and Rankin 2014). As an area of study, it focuses on how people process, store, and apply information about other people and social situations (Hunt, Borgida, and Lavine 2012). The brain employs mental mechanisms to first interpret other people's emotions, thoughts, and intentions to then determine one's own behavioral response through social signals, such things as facial expressions, eye gaze direction, cues, and personality traits (Frith 2008, 2034). A person's behavior is driven by the relationship between situational opportunities and individual desire, extrinsic and intrinsic motivation. Social cognition discloses that "the world is filtered through a personalized lens" (Moskowitz 2005, 4).

Theory of Mind (ToM) is a psychological concept that refers to the ability to attribute mental states to oneself and others and the capacity to understand that other individuals have their own perspectives, thoughts, and feelings different from one's own. Sometimes called mind-reading, ToM is a result of constant stimulation, but it is often not a conscious activity. Zunshine suggested that it is "the neural basis of interpersonal subjectivity" (2008, 68). Sologub maximizes this potential for interpersonal subjectivity by engaging various readers or social interpreters. My discussion of ToM will start at the center of the novel—Peredonov and his increasing inability to read others—and will then work outward through concentric circles of readers, from characters to the author himself to his contemporaries to us.

In documenting Peredonov's social disconnection and delusions, Sologub's narrator gives us an impression of reliability as we learn more about Peredonov's ToM. From the beginning, the narrator questions the accuracy of appearances and consistently reports on the protagonist's emotional state and that of his community: "it seemed as though people were living peacefully and harmoniously in this town. Even happily. But it only seemed that way" (33). Next, the narrator questions the quality of Peredonov's vision as it is mediated through lenses: his small, stealthy, dull eyes, his spectacles, his paranoia, his consciousness. Peredonov's friends challenge the credibility of his fiancée Varvara's connection with the Princess and question whether Peredonov and Varvara are cousins. Peredonov is immediately angry and defensive. His friend Rutilov encourages him to think of other possible partners, his sisters perhaps. Peredonov takes this to a delusional conclusion: "Yes, everyone is in love with me here" (34).

These first few paragraphs of the novel set up the ToM that shapes Peredonov's world. Most of the novel is structured around dialog with insightful commentary from the narrator. This active reporting of Peredonov's inner thoughts, attempts at dating, awkward social life, and intensifying paranoia and maliciousness is a strategic documentary style that reinforces the reliability of the narrator and the sense of direct observation, much like the clinical notes of a physician in a medical case study recording the statements and expressions of a patient.

Peredonov occasionally does attempt, but completely fails, to understand the behavior of others. Like all individuals, he has an "implicit personality theory," "an organizational structure that contains the attributes associated with a specific person type and the relationships (causal interconnectedness) between those attributes" (Moskowitz 2005, 169). When Peredonov thinks about his actions, however, he is often focused on the mechanics of an action and/or social interaction. That is, he processes social interactions and causal interconnectedness at a low level.

This can be seen when Peredonov makes his rounds to the homes of the various local officials and administrators. Peredonov does not recognize obvious juxtapositions of a person's public-facing behavior and words relative to their private home life. He cannot process that appearances are not what they always seem or that title and rank often carry with them performative qualities. In the case of the mayor Skuchaev, the living quarters are "cozy, calm and cheerful" but the front receiving rooms were "strained and severe" and deliberately uncomfortable (92). The public prosecutor Avinovitsky's public persona is fierce and frightening, but he looks upon his son with warmth and pride (99). Peredonov misreads both object and person perceptions, while others work hard to understand him. Skuchaev stares at Peredonov "with melancholy perplexity" (94) because Peredonov's social signals are peculiar.

In this novel-cum-medical case study, Peredonov occupies a confining and self-prescribed, delimited space, in which he interprets mundane or innocent actions as evidence of a plot against him. His limited ToM leads him to assume everyone shares his vices and intentions: "[p]eople who were alien and hostile to Peredonov lived everywhere and some of them even now might be plotting ill against him" (123). Peredonov doesn't weigh and consider other people's motivations in situations beyond a projected reflection of his own disordered desires. He escalates acts of violence. Peredonov cuts one of Varvara's dresses into shreds, thinking the flounces were put there to deceive and conceal. He stabs out the eyes of playing cards to stop their mocking and winking. He falsely accuses students of misbehaving and watches with satisfaction as parents discipline them.

OTHER CHARACTERS' THEORY OF MIND

In contrast, numerous characters in the novel study Peredonov's words and actions carefully and often adjust their own behavior to match his level of engagement and/or seek to pacify or serve him. The implication is that their ToM is more sophisticated. Volodin, for example, intuits when Peredonov is happy or unhappy and adjusts his sociobehavioral response accordingly. Varvara chooses many of her actions in avoidance of irritating or angering Peredonov. Vershina, who repeatedly lures Peredonov into her home to entice him into marrying her young tenant Marta, can often guess his state of mind: "it seemed as though he were insulted by the fact that not everyone understood him as well as Vershina did" (41). We are told that she loves power (278) and that she regularly contemplates and weighs Peredonov's motivations (88). Peredonov senses her effect on him. "In her figure he had the illusion of something ominous: a black witch standing there, emitting a spellbinding smoke and casting spells" (179). Is the effect Peredonov experiences in Vershina's presence magic, or his discomfort in being the focus of studied analysis?

Marta has a very high level of ToM. Though Vershina continues to throw Marta in the path of Peredonov as a potential fiancée, her sophisticated ToM renders Marta a binary complement to Peredonov. A clear example is her ability to intuit Vershina's needs.

> "I feel like something tart to eat."
> "Would you like some bilberries and apple? I'll bring it," Marta said, quickly getting up.

"Yes, please bring some."
Marta ran out of the room. Vershina didn't watch her go. She had grown accustomed to calmly accepting Marta's obliging ways as something to be expected. (181)

Marta is sensitive to Vershina's every word and action, indicating her keen awareness and alert perception of others' needs, behaviors, and motivations. Marta is situationally aware of people, objects, and environmental stimuli at any given moment. The implication is that Marta will be a good wife.

We also see a high level of ToM associated with others when Peredonov calls on various people. Nadezhda Vasilievna Adamenko works hard to make her guests comfortable and to pick an interesting topic of conversation:

> The guests had to be entertained, and [she] thought that the most pleasant and comfortable conversation for a teacher of the Russian language would be a conversation about the state of pedagogy, about the reform of the gymnasia, about the raising of children, about literature, about Symbolism and about the Russian journals. She touched on all these topics, but received nothing in response other than perplexing rebuffs which revealed that her guests were not interested in those questions. (76)

Simultaneously, Nadezhda begins to play a game with her younger brother and ward, who remains hidden behind a door. Her ToM is at a high enough level that she can hold more than one conversation. One verbal and "unbearably boring for her" (77), all while privately and nonverbally communicating with her brother through hand signals and stifling her laughter.

Liudmila Rutilov is another example of a community member with a higher level of ToM than Peredonov. When looking at her perceptions, interpretations of others, and behavioral responses, an opportunity to consider ToM from a Symbolist perspective, informed by a Gnostic worldview, becomes available. The next section investigates this complementary approach to social cognition through Liudmila's ToM.

SYMBOLIST LIFE-CREATION AS METHODOLOGY: RESTORING SPIRITUAL CLEAVAGES

Peredonov's perceptions are inaccurate and warped according not only to a medical interpretation, but a metaphysical one as well. Sologub knew Peredonov's world, having worked as a provincial schoolteacher himself. For this reason, *The Petty Demon* becomes a unique and informative example of life-creation. The pursuit of life-creation (*zhiznetvorchestvo*) was a quest for art and life to bridge the gap or cleavage between the spiritual (noumenal) and material (phenomenal) worlds that Symbolists hoped would lead to transformation. Life-creation was an attempted re-creation of life through art that would facilitate transcendence into higher, sacred realms, where beauty suffused everything and suffering faded away. Symbolists sought to achieve a humanistic ideal—a personal integration of knowledge, compassion, and action in the world—through aesthetics, poetry, the undertaking of a creative dream, or the action of loving a muse or paragon.

Cioran described this tendency in art: "[t]he salvation of mankind lay in the search for a new spiritual idealism" (1983, 9). Vladimir Soloviev (1853–1900) became a leading exponent of this divine quest in aesthetics as he debated the extent to which art and the pursuit of beauty were effective measures against the "real" threats of degeneration, decay, despair, materialism, and vulgar utilitarianism at the *fin de siècle*:

> And man, as one who belongs to both worlds, can and must by an act of rational contemplation concern himself with the divine world, and finding himself yet in a world of contention and vague apprehension, he must enter into communication with vivid images from the kingdom of glory and eternal beauty. But in particular, this positive although incomplete knowledge or penetration into the reality of the divine world is characteristic of poetic creativity. (Cioran 1977, 44)

Soloviev asserted in 1889 that "we should define beauty as the *transformation of matter through the embodiment in it of another supra-natural principle*" (Soloviev 2003, 36; emphasis is Soloviev's). This notion of beauty extended the new natural eschatology and psychopathology of modern society into the realm of aesthetics. "Beauty is indeed a fact," Soloviev insisted, "a product of real natural processes perfected in the universe" (2003, 37). To demonstrate this in terms of materialism, Soloviev compared a piece of coal to a diamond: made of the same substance, "a diamond, which, although of lowly content, is a perfected and finished expression of its Idea of stone-made-lucid" (2003, 41). He added that "the criterion of aesthetic worthiness is the greatest perfected and multifaceted embodiment of this ideal moment of a given substance" (Soloviev 2003, 40). The story Soloviev told here is an ancient alchemical one of the transmutation and transfiguration of material dross into spiritual gold. "The aesthetically beautiful," Soloviev surmised, "should lead to an actual improvement of reality" (2003, 30). He proposed that an artist facilitates this process of transformation.

Sologub's Peredonov is the opposite of Soloviev's artist, and there is no new industrial, economic, or social vitality being added to the provinces where he lives. His everyday life is defined by dross and a lack of opportunity for growth, mobility, or change. Even if he wanted to pursue Beauty, the raw material for it is unavailable. The chance for self-improvement was never actual; the Princess made no reliable promises. Peredonov's hope remains an illusion, rumor, and deception. Coal *unexcavated* from *byt*; a diamond *in potentia* but never to be realized. Mental illness becomes the force that transforms. Absent are the necessary raw materials for transformation into Beauty. Peredonov is instead "burnt up." His schizophrenia is a further fall, or descent, into the material and phenomenal world.

The story of Sophia became the core archetype in the Russian Symbolists' creation of myth, and it offers a method for restoring spiritual cleavages (Cioran 1977). Sologub engages with a ToM rooted in the idea of Sophia. Restoration and salvation—excavation of divinity from matter—are inevitable, perhaps imminent, Symbolists asserted, if people could only see—that is, value and perceive—Beauty, or Sophia, the mediator between God and creation, in themselves, one another, and their sociohistorical moment. The story of Sophia is the eruption of the need for God's self-reflection. In Gnostic myth, she is an emanation of eternal light from the Godhead. Shattered fragments of her divinity were scattered throughout dark, painful, and slumbering creation. The salvation of humankind can be achieved through awakening and transcendence: the initiate must deny their earthly physicality and recognize the indwelling spark of immaterial light (the presence of Sophia). In death, if one possesses this knowledge, their divine spark can return to the one, true, and good Godhead.

Underpinning the Sophia myth is the idea of cleavage: cleavage between perfection and distortion, matter and spirit, good and evil, salvation and damnation. To this list can be added yet another: legitimate insanity and the madness of true belief. The diagnostic distinction between insanity and divine madness is ancient. This discourse about spiritual (noumenal) versus material (phenomenal) madness was complemented by a rich cultural history of holy fools and the persistence of magical thinking and shamanistic initiation rites and practices within human thought: the very things that the new discipline of anthropology was exploring at the turn of the twentieth century. This longing for restoration of wholeness was the concern of many artists at the *fin-de-siècle,* which lent itself to what I will call a *metaphysical* ToM. Instead of practicing social cognition and mind-reading from a cognitive basis rooted in social information, this was a *philosophical* or *spiritual* ascription used to interpret others, an attempt to attribute occult knowledge and/or the spark of divinity in one another. Often the "metaphysical" was performative, as in the case of Valerii Briusov's (1873–1924) Mephistophelean pose. Sologub engaged a medical gaze to complicate and interrogate such an idiosyncratic, theoretical, and tenuous ToM.

Dmitri Merezhkovsky set out the social signals of this metaphysical idealism:

> the three major elements of the new art [are] a mystical content, symbols, and the expansion of artistic impressionability . . . only a creative faith in something infinite and immortal can ignite the soul of man, create heroes, martyrs and prophets . . . People have need of faith, they need inspiration, they crave a holy madness in their heroes and martyrs. (Cioran 1983, 9)

The lens of social cognition and an analysis of characters' levels of ToM provide an applied approach to quantifying such a qualitative and metaphysical assertion in the following way: Peredonov embarks on a rather mundane quest to find a bride, his Sophia, if you will. This quest provides Sologub an opportunity to introduce the reader to using their own ToM to observe and evaluate diverse iterations of courtship, marriage, partnership, and parenting, all while witnessing Peredonov's repeated inability to apply even basic levels of ToM in the situations himself.

Every woman Peredonov interacts with is a potential partner for himself or a friend. If he attempts to ascribe at least one attribute to a person, and with any consistency, it is marital and/or romantic intention. Even Peredonov's obsession with punishing his students functions as a plot device by which he gains access to familial homes, affording him the opportunity to observe and evaluate diverse iterations of marriage, partnership, and parenting. While the narrator makes it beyond clear that Peredonov lacks the motivation, capacity, and level of ToM to accurately weigh and measure these firsthand experiences, the narrator does provide us with a direct, methodical medical gaze into numerous case studies of provincial married life. At the same time, as we have seen, several women characters in the novel are given higher levels of ToM than Peredonov regarding the pursuit of love and potential marriage.

Peredonov seeks marriage and career advancement, very ordinary and mundane human longings. Carl Jung argued that neurosis results from "the suffering of a soul that has not found its meaning" (Stephens 1994, 125). Peredonov corresponds to this condition. His attempts at finding a bride and his eventual marriage to Varvara do not lead to masculine and feminine completeness according to a Solovievian worldview nor to a happy and successful domestic life.

THEORY OF MIND AND THE SOPHIA MYTH

Sophia embodies a dual personality in the system of Valentinian Gnosticism, where she plays the binary role of Hagia Sophia (Holy Wisdom;

in the world of spirit) and Sophia Prunikos (Wisdom the Whore; in the world of matter) (Carlson 1996). Sophia Prunikos embodies folly and distortion. Several women in the novel encapsulate aspects of Sophia Prunikos, Liudmila and Varvara especially. Liudmila, for example, attempts transformation through her lavish and sensual experiments with Sasha Pilnikov, but they do not lead to transcendence of the material world or even the consummation of desire. "I know there's nothing to hope for here, but all I want is for him to caress me a little, any old way," Liudmila blushes and cries (170). Liudmila occupies a depressing and hopeless existence, much like Peredonov's, but she has not gone mad nor lost her ability to interact meaningfully with others. Though Liudmila pursues beautiful and sensual things, it remains the case that her sexuality and longing do not offer transformation, transfiguration, or theurgic potential, merely seduction and pleasure.

Liudmila embodies material deception and a ToM sophisticated enough to manipulate others: "with the irresistible persuasiveness of falsehood" (268) she convinced the headmaster that Sasha was an innocent child. Peredonov's accusation that Sasha has been seduced by her is true, but the narrator confirms the upside-down emanation of Sophia's divinity when she descended into matter. "Liudmila's tender rapid babbling purled on and on, and the chimerical construct of Peredonov's falsehood dispersed in smoke" (269), which the reader knows is actually its inverse: truth. Liudmila's chimera is true: Sasha is not really a girl, as Peredonov insists, though Sasha does explore his sexuality and gender performativity under Liudmila's influence. With her encouragement, Sasha assumes the costume of a geisha. This experiment is successful only in that people are fooled, but not as genuine transformation. The raw material of humanity's divine spark remains buried, awaiting excavation.

Much like Liudmila, Varvara also embodies aspects of Sophia Prunikos. Varvara is a distorted contradiction: her body is perfection, but her face is pockmarked and grotesque, her disposition rude and coarse. Screaming matches lead to migraines and indifference: "she had already grown accustomed to a disorderly and vulgar life and couldn't restrain herself from indecent escapades. She had long since ceased to have any respect for herself or for others" (276). Varvara's small-mindedness contributes to Peredonov's demise. She repeatedly deceives him and finds satisfaction in the mundane existence of their provincial town.

The consequence of the "fall" into matter is a faulty consciousness: a state of unseeing and unknowing. The world Peredonov perceives is combustible, a version of hell, and he wants to take revenge. But revenge upon Sophia Prunikos is futile. According to Peredonov's metaphysical ToM, all women in the text are iterations of Sophia Prunikos. This is what stands behind his behavioral choices toward all women throughout the novel, even the *nedotykomka*. It is to stop her, the tiny demon of dust, from hiding in the stage curtains that leads Peredonov to set fire to and destroy the theater.

PEREDONOV'S PROGNOSIS

Spiritual, physical, and psychological restoration were not available to Peredonov. His mental illness and his neuroses fuel his inner cleavage, and he remains at war within himself. In this, he did not differ that much from numerous Russian Symbolists whose experiments in life-creation were unsuccessful. Such experiments may not have led to arson and murder, but several experiments resulted in unhappy, if not tragic, endings, as was the case with Nina Petrovskaia's (1879–1928) suicide. In turning a medical gaze unto his character Peredonov, Sologub turned a medical gaze unto himself and his contemporaries.

Masing-Delic points to a lack of ontological certainty as the foundation of Peredonov's fear of being observed (1978, 117). He is disconnected from others and all sense of hope. For all their embracing of Soloviev's idealism, Sologub's contemporaries felt the weight of such anticipation. The Symbolist Zinaida Gippius (1869–1945) felt sympathy for Peredonov because she could relate to his metaphysical anxiety (Gippius 2003). Another contemporary, Alexander Blok (1880–1921) also saw his own anxieties reflected in the novel: "Peredonov is *each of us*, or if you like, I will say it more gently: in each of us there exists Peredonovism" (Greene 1985, 36; emphasis is Blok's).

Russian Symbolism embodied a dynamic psychology, expressed as a cultural myth of narrativity, an ideology. The movement concerned itself with the nature of being, the ontology of evil, and to what extent the mind and body are perhaps faulty or perhaps theurgic apparatuses. Their penultimate goal was to resolve the cleavages between the macro and micro, spiritual and material realms. Sologub transposed this larger, metaphysical concern upon the cultural and historical context of late Imperial Russia. The clash between traditional values and modernity is reflected in Peredonov's struggles, as well as the limited opportunities for average, educated people against an age of increasing speed, modernization, and social, political, and economic disequilibrium and extremism.

Taking account of these theoretical and applied considerations of real and imagined lives, Sologub is again encouraging the reader to engage their own ToM to evaluate Peredonov's actions. The reader walks away from Sologub's novel more sympathetic than not toward Peredonov.

> All things were strangely and surprisingly concealed behind the darkness as though a different nocturnal life, that was incomprehensible and hostile to man, had awakened in them. Peredonov walked softly along the streets and muttered:
>
> "You're wasting your time following me. I'm not going to do anything bad. Brother, I'm only concerned about the good of my work. Really." (174)

Peredonov intuits his own helplessness. We read of his steady decline and seem to "get it": to comprehend Peredonov's struggle, his anxiety, and apprehension. We feel the weight of the conditions and environmental stimuli (or lack thereof) that drive Peredonov's (in)actions. He commits murder, but it doesn't seem entirely his fault. We can understand the daily grind and social immobility as an affront to our individual humanistic ideal, as well as the pursuit of the idea of the stone-made-lucid put forth by Soloviev.

THE READER'S THEORY OF MIND: OTHER-IMAGINING AND PERSPECTIVE-TAKING

By focusing on Peredonov's mental deterioration, Sologub invites us to decipher its mysterious cause and to apply a diagnostic process. Sologub engages our own vision fields and summons us to employ a medical gaze. Engaging our own ToM and considering *The Petty Demon* from such a vantage point reinforces the extent to which Sologub's novel is an example of life-creation, even if, at the same time, it challenges the viability of Symbolist tenets. What opportunities does this offer us as readers?

Rosenthal and Foley aptly characterized Peredonov as "impervious" (1982, 52). Impervious to restoration through the theoretical principles of Symbolism and impervious to restoration through an applied "folk psychology," or ToM, of our own. Peredonov does not have a high level of ToM, or what Judith Mills called "independence of mind," unlike Liudmila, Nadezhda, Vershina, or Marta (1984, 21). These female characters are varying degrees of impervious to gossip and the sociopolitical conditions of provincial Russia and demonstrate "control over self, situation, and destiny" (Mills 1984, 21). Peredonov, on the other hand, remains susceptible to the *byt* and *poshlost'* of his community. His world is mechanistic, and he is often referred to as puppet or doll-like. When he does create, it is rumor and lies.

Peredonov's life is uninspiring, perhaps stifling. Strive as he might, his consciousness cannot perceive divinity behind the mask of matter:

> The mystery of eternal transformation of impotent matter into a force that annulled the bonds of death was forever veiled from him. A walking corpse!

> He was possessed of an incongruous combination of nonbelief in the living God and Christ with a belief in sorcery! (201)

In this way, Sologub effectively articulates that the Russia he as an author sees around him could not become worse, could not be a more complete expression of a manifestation of evil. Firstly, Sologub's Russia may in fact be the full extension of Sophia Prunikos' downward fall, descent, and emanations into corrupt matter. Stephen Hutchings similarly outlined how Sologub used provinciality as the ground zero for Gnostic transcendence (1996, 675–76). Secondly, the narrator gives us constant reports of Peredonov's presenting symptoms of schizophrenia. The school physician and the anticipated medical examination are lax; though rumors spread about his growing madness, the police chief knows that he has gone insane, and expulsion from the school looms.

The reader becomes the most informed about Peredonov's condition and is invited to diagnose him. The reader's other-imagining or perspective-taking—"imagining what another person is experiencing" or "what we would experience if we were in another person's situation" (Malbois 2023, 91)—is privileged and welcomed. The ToM of the reader is engaged, and sympathy and empathy toward Peredonov and his community are invited. The reader cannot help Peredonov and his community, but perhaps one's affective empathy is activated while reading the text. Could our own altruistic behavior be motivated, if not toward others, then at least toward ourselves? While the characters in the novel experience very little to no sympathy for one another, Sologub's readers have the potential to counteract the "evil" of callousness they witness in the characters by caring for themselves, others, their own communities, and the greater world. Sologub's engagement of the readers' ToM while watching these characters is the key that Sologub uses to unlock this realization and uncover a truth.

In drawing from both medical and metaphysical fields of vision in his novel, Sologub asserts that the only thing that remains for Peredonov and Russian society is the opposite of evil: hope, love, and the (seemingly inaccessible) promise of restored wholeness. Sologub's optimism is that all that remains is an ascent. This would indeed be a maddening and torturous hope, but hope nonetheless. According to a process of other-imagining and perspective-taking throughout the novel's journey, readers are the ones left holding altruistic responsibilities.

To explore the sympathy which one may or may not have for Peredonov, let us return to the framework of social cognition. Per Malbois, sympathy and empathy are not emotions but are rather a "type of emotional experience" (2023, 85). Regular emotions are focalized around particular objects (a specific person or thing lost, or a fear of danger attributed to an object or activity). Other-oriented emotions like empathy and sympathy have objects of focus related to someone else. The feeling of empathy involves perspective-taking or emotion sharing. Therefore, it is *with* another. Sympathy is felt *for* another. They represent a "reaction of concern" (Malbois 2023, 85). Do we as readers experience a reaction of concern at moments for Peredonov and other characters? Or experience surprise, distaste, and even discomfort for or with them?

Several scenes of whipping and beating are quite graphic and unsettling, and numerous characters take pleasure in cruelty toward one another. It is sad when Marta's brother Vladya cannot take his fishing rod home because he made room for Peredonov to be comfortable in the cart; Peredonov responds with animosity and vague threats. We feel relief any time Marta can get away from Peredonov, be it freedom outside with her brother or betrothal to another man. Pity arises regarding Varvara: she beats herself with nettles because her friend fooled her into thinking it's a beauty routine. She *wants* to be married to Peredonov, but her social standing doesn't improve as a married woman. She remains hopelessly vulgar. Volodin's voice and persona might be annoying to us in real life if indeed he regularly bleated his words like a sheep. A reader may feel anxious for Sasha at the masquerade: will attendees find out the geisha is him, a young man, and will the angry and envious mob harm him? Peredonov is socially awkward and gullible from the start; his situation only gets worse. We are the ones who must observe and process all this awkwardness and social discomfort as it unfolds.

If Sologub does want us to feel sympathetic to Peredonov and his community, we need to consider how and why. Sologub's narrator relies upon our own functioning consciousness, our ToM. Sologub may have sought to engage our neurobiology of emotion. Immordino-Yang stated that "our biological survival and our socio-cultural survival are housed or controlled and felt by the very same neural systems in our brain"; she continues, explaining that: "when you feel inspired by another human being's mental qualities, you literally are feeling that inspiration on the substrate of your own biological survival. Your biology and your sociality are completely, at this point, intertwined with one another" (2011). This is to say that one's sympathy and empathy are evoked.

Sologub's narrator invokes a medical gaze. This "shift in vision," per Kennedy, "crucially produces a shift in understanding, in passion, and thus in sympathy. Morality in this tradition is the affective knowledge produced by the visual relation between seer and seen" (2010, 91). Sologub portrays Peredonov's illness from within and grants us privileged access to his spiritual and sociopsychological disequilibrium. This medical gaze and re-visioning of Peredonov's despair, when made a spectacle available for medical observation, "shifts the narrative's tenor from judgement of evil to a kind of sympathy at the moment of its dissolution" (Kennedy 2010, 103).

CONCLUSION

The medical gaze of Sologub's novel offers at least two worldviews or positionalities in its pragmatic application. The discussion thus far has engaged two diagnostic approaches in the interpretation of the consequences of Peredonov's quest for truth and his inability to access it: a metaphysical approach founded on the philosophical, qualitative, and theoretical Symbolist worldview of Soloviev, and a sociopsychological approach founded in the scientific, quantifiable, and practical worldview of social cognition and attendant historical conditions. Despite these divergent approaches, both arrived at the same diagnosis: madness. Through a reading grounded in cognitive studies, Peredonov remains allegorical and extreme, but at the same time becomes more relatable and realistic through a medical gaze. The viewpoint of social cognition offers an opening to draw lessons from a quintessential Symbolist novel and apply them to everyday life, from fin de siècle Russian society to our own at the beginning of the twenty-first century. We are invited to decipher, decode, diagnose, and narrate—that is, to create—a better world.

BIBLIOGRAPHY

Carlson, Maria. 1996. "Gnostic Elements in the Cosmogony of Vladimir Solov'ev." In *Russian Religious Thought*, edited by Richard Gustafson and Judith Kornblatt, 49–67. Madison: University of Wisconsin Press.

Cioran, Samuel. 1977. *Vladimir Soloviev and the Knighthood of the Divine Sophia*. Waterloo: Wilfrid Laurier University Press.

Cioran, Samuel. 1983. "Introduction." In *The Petty Demon*. Translated by S. D. Cioran, 9–25. Ann Arbor: Ardis

Frith, Chris. 2008. "Social Cognition." *Philosophical Transactions of the Royal Society B* 363: 2033–39.

Gippius, Zinaida. 2003. "Slezinka Peredonova." *Sobranie sochinenii*. T. 7. *Myi i oni. Literaturnyi dnevnik*. Publistika 1899–1916 gg. Moskva: "Russkaia kniga". http://az.lib.ru/g/gippius_z_n/text_1908_slezinka.shtml.

Greene, Diana. 1978. "Structure and Meaning in Sologub's 'Petty Demon'." *Ulbandus Review* 1, no. 2: 26–36.

Greene, Diana. 1985. *Insidious Intent: An Interpretation of Fedor Sologub's The Petty Demon*. Columbus: Slavica Publishers.

Hunt, Corrie, Eugene Borgida, and Howard Lavine. 2012. "Social Cognition." In *Encyclopedia of Human Behavior*, Second ed., edited by V. S. Ramachandran, 456–62. Oxford: Elsevier.

Hutchings, Stephen. 1996. "Plotting against Abstraction in Russian Literature's Provincial Hell: Fedor Sologub's Aesthetics of Embodiment." *The Modern Language Review* 91, no. 3: 655–76.

Immordino-Yang, Mary Helen. 2011. "Embodied Brains, Social Minds: How Admiration Inspires Purposeful Learning." November 8, 2011. TEDxManhattanBeach. https://www.youtube.com/watch?v=RViuTHBIOq8.

Kennedy, Meegan. 2010. *Revising the Clinic: Vision and Representation in Victorian Medical Narrative and the Novel*. Columbus: Ohio State University Press.

Kleinman, Arthur. 1973. "Medicine's Symbolic Reality: On a Central Problem in the Philosophy of Medicine." *Inquiry* 16: 206–13.

Malbois, Elodie. 2023. "What is Sympathy?: Understanding the Structure of Other-Oriented Emotions." *Emotion Review* 15, no. 1: 85–95.

Masing-Delic, Irene. 1978. "'Peredonov's Little Tear'—Why is it Shed?" *Scando-Slavica* 24: 107–24.

Merezhkovsky, Dmitri. 1975. "On the Reasons for the Decline and On the New Tendencies in Contemporary Russian Literature." In *The Silver Age of Russian Culture: An Anthology*, edited by Carl Proffer and Ellendea Proffer, 3-5. Ann Arbor: Ardis.

Mills, Judith. 1984. "Expanding Critical Contexts: Sologub's *Petty Demon*." *SEEEJ* 28, no. 1: 15–31.

Misselbrook, David. 2013. "Foucault." *British Journal of General Practice* 63, no. 611: 312.

Moskowitz, Gordon. 2005. *Social Cognition: Understanding Self and Others*. New York: Guilford Press.

O'Callaghan, Aoife. 2022. "'The Medical Gaze': Foucault, Anthropology, and Contemporary Psychiatry in Ireland." *Irish Journal of Medical Science* 191: 1795–96.

Peterson, Ronald. 1993. A *History of Russian Symbolism*. Amsterdam: John Benjamins Publishing Company.

Rosenthal, Charlotte, and Helene Foley. 1982. "Symbolic Patterning in Sologub's *Melkij Bes*." *SEEEJ* 26, no. 1: 43–55.

Sologub, Fedor. 1983. *The Petty Demon*. Translated by S. D. Cioran. Ann Arbor: Ardis.

Soloviev, Vladimir. 2003. "Beauty in Nature." In *The Heart of Reality: Essays on Beauty, Love, and Ethics*, edited and translated by Vladimir Wozniuk, 29-66. Notre Dame: University of Notre Dame Press.

Spaulding, Shannon. 2018. *How We Understand Others: Philosophy and Social Cognition*. New York: Routledge.

Stevens, Anthony. 1994. *Jung: A Very Short Introduction*. New York: Oxford University Press.

Tal, Shany-Ur, and K. P. Rankin. 2014. "Cognition, Social." In *Encyclopedia of Neurological Sciences, Second Edition*, edited by Michael Aminoff and Robert Daroff, 814–17. Oxford: Elsevier.

Zunshine, Lisa. 2008. "Theory of Mind and Fictions of Embodied Transparency." *Narrative* 16: 65–92.

8

Autism in Nabokov's *The Defense*

Brett Cooke

LITERARY EVOLUTION

What is it like to read Nabokov's novels, especially the way a first-time reader reads them? At what point in *Pale Fire* (1962) do you first suspect that you have in your hands not a critical edition of an actual poet's masterwork but the ravings of a homicidal schizophrenic instead? Or that Humbert Humbert is seducing you into tolerating pedophilia in *Lolita* (1955)? That in *Invitation to a Beheading* (1935–1936) you are unable to wake yourself from a lurid, depressing dream? Or viewing the world from the perspective of an autist, that of the chess master Luzhin, in *The Defense* (1929–1930)? The subjective experience of the naïve reader is the point of literature, and it likely pertains to all of us. I suggest that something highly salient to our evolution is at hand. Furthermore, that something will help us understand the peculiar style of that novel which shapes that experience.

My question is prompted by B. R. Tilghman's "What Is It Like to Be an Aardvark?" (1991). This seminal article really ponders the nature of human experience. Upon first reading it, my reaction was openly derisive. One might think, so I said to my book club at the time, that this question was posed by a human being for others of the same kind and that one or the other, perhaps even both, would already know the answer . . . Worse was Tilghman's conclusion: if you want to know what it is like to be a human being, you should read novels. Novels, really? Aren't they fiction? How silly . . . Only later did I realize that there was a point to Tilghman's suggestion, that we might have something valuable to learn about our cognition from novels, one of our best media not only for depicting the experience of subjectivity but also for imparting and even developing it. I will illustrate this point with Nabokov's first popular success, published serially in Paris in a Russian émigré journal, *Sovremennye zapiski*, as *Luzhin's Defense*. Since the author supervised its translation as *The Defense* (1964), I will examine the latter as the canonical version.

Given all swipes at Freudian psychoanalysis that Nabokov made in the forewords to the English translations of his novels, one might think that the writer would be opposed to any psychological appreciation of his works, especially one that emphasizes unconscious forces that would appear to deprive the writer of control over his text. Nevertheless, Nabokov's work as a professor of literature gives us clear reason to suspect that his work as a novelist serves to develop our understanding of our psychological capacities, somewhat along the lines Tilghman suggests.

Perusing Nabokov's lectures on literature, one notices how the writer-turned-professor acknowledged cognitive findings achieved by other writers. Indeed, he contended that "all novelists of any worth are psychological novelists" (1973, 174). It appears that his benchmark was not the psychology of any particular school, but rather his own introspective impressions of how we actually think. Nabokov spoke of his appreciation for Tolstoy's representing the passage of time in a manner close to our experience (1981, 141). He inferred from Proust's *Swan's Way* that memory renders a more accurate and richer picture of the past when it is passive, evoked by involuntary associations (1980, 208, 246, 248). He chided Joyce's use of the stream-of-consciousness "device" for representing words as passing in an even flow, when, playing with the English term, he jested that it is more likely that some will take more time to get around the rocks (1980, 289, 363).

Nabokov perceived an evolutionary character, at least in terms of cultural progress, to literary history. Speaking about Tolstoy's depiction of childbirth in *Anna Karenina*, he wrote:

> the whole history of literary fiction [. . .] may be said to be a gradual probing of deeper and deeper layers of life. It is quite impossible to imagine either Homer in the ninth century B.C. or Cervantes in the seventeenth century of our era [. . .] describing in such wonderful detail childbirth. The question is not whether certain events or emotions are or are not suitable ethically or esthetically. The point I want to make is that the artist, like the scientist, in the process of evolution of art and science, is always casting around, understanding a little more than his predecessor, penetrating further with a keener and more brilliant eye—and this is the artistic result. (1981, 164–65)

Nabokov sensed how writers learn from each other. In his view, a great work of art often develops not only new styles and themes but also ever more valid perspectives on human subjective experience. Clearly, what Nabokov envisions here is largely a one-way process, that is, progress, whereby knowledge gained is retained and then in turn serves as a stepping-stone for the next stylistic and thematic innovation, which more importantly constitutes a valid new insight into our shared psychology, including what it is like to be a human being. He even implies that literature changes us. In his *Lectures on Literature*, Nabokov pronounced that "every new type of writer *evolves* a new type of reader" (1980, 316; my emphasis). Given his lifelong study of butterflies and characteristic care with precise language, Nabokov's reference to evolution bears consideration; does he have natural selection in mind?

To test Nabokov's notion, let us ponder first that there may be a form of evolution at hand, not just as a matter of cultural development, and second that this consideration involves a force that drives much of our behavior. Per the so-called "Theory of Mind" (ToM) that Tighlman refers to, we generally can guess the internal states of others. We usually behave as if we were able to correctly read the minds of others, though this is literally impossible in the complete sense. ToM is an important cognitive function since the major selection pressure on us is exerted by human competitors. Consider the advantages of being able to correctly distinguish allies from enemies, and to discern the latter's intentions in advance. Our intuition of the emotional states of others is characteristic of social species such as our own, among whom political interrelationships are particularly intense and vital (Miller 1997, 316).

Such "natural psychology" is a crucial portion of the biological heritage we term human nature, the set of behavioral proclivities genetically inherited and shared by typically developing people. Due to social competition, one may expect an escalating demand for insight into the mentation of others. According to Robert Trivers (2011), to deter those who would deceive us, we develop means of detecting cheaters, who, in turn, seek more subtle ways of gulling us, while at the same time we may attempt to conceal our intentions, and so forth—leading to an escalation of cognitive needs and therefore capacities.

Gaining a competitive advantage in natural psychology is crucial to our inclusive fitness. Hence, these features may be predicted to wax, along with our interest in each other and in ourselves. Keep in mind that members of our species are in constant competition with each other: as long as we interbreed, there is no escape, no conclusive success. As a result, there is selection pressure for larger brains capable of supporting "Machiavellian minds." It follows that we will continually seek to increase our limited epistemic access to others' thoughts and feelings, to become more perceptive readers of the thin slices of their minds we have access to in reality on the one hand, and to weave ever more nuanced consciousness in ourselves as models for our fellow human beings on the other, as well as to develop countermeasures in deception and its penetration—but never obtain ultimate insight.

Speculating further, the major cap on this otherwise potentially unlimited escalation is the capacity of our brains and the somatic requirements for growing them. Nicholas Humphrey suggests that this selection pressure for ToM and self-consciousness drove massive changes in our species, including but not limited to bipedalism, extended childhood, and shared parental care (Humphrey 1983).[1] This amounts to much of what we recognize to be human nature. Running up against physical limits, I further suggest that our cognitive adaptation to the stresses of social life was accelerated by the development of culture, shared acquired behavior. This process, in turn, was further accelerated with the invention of art, which over time has exhibited a growing impulse for novelty, increasing the range of available behavioral variation, generating and preserving ever more diverse examples of nevertheless plausible human actions. A further boost was provided by the invention of fiction, which also demands novelty, but always within the bounds of verisimilitude to our potential behavior. The result is that we consume narrative to learn about what we are capable of doing and what it might feel like to experience something else, whether it is encountering battle for the first time, like Nicholas Rostov or Pierre Bezukhov in Tolstoy's *War and Peace*, carrying out what was planned to be a cold-blooded murder in Dostoevsky's *Crime and Punishment*, or throwing oneself under a moving train near the end of the former's *Anna Karenina*. Innovative novels like Nabokov's push the envelope yet more by conveying more unusual frames of mind; each of them should be regarded as an experiment probing our psychological potentials. Of course, we now have clinical means of conducting psychological inquiry, but art and fiction once played a leading role in this endeavor and, indeed, continue to do so. That this can be effective is suggested in *The Defense* since Nabokov appears to accurately describe autism more than a decade before that syndrome was first clinically identified. Furthermore, this probing is conducted via narrative; we do not merely learn about ever more unusual but nevertheless valid mental capabilities, much as we might do with formal reports, but rather the text also leads us to experience them, to see the world from the eyes of those so afflicted. For instance, what does it feel like to be autistic? My suggestion is that we get some sense of this by reading *The Defense*.

In this view of literature, mere novelty does not suffice. New modes of narrative must also provide cognitive insight if they are to contribute to fitness. They succeed only insofar as we recognize them as a plausible rendition of our actual or potential experience. Precisely how we think is a matter still beyond our clinical reach, but novels like *The Defense* seemingly bring us closer to the mark; they get us to note something we recognize in others and also in ourselves. Providing information that would have been useful at least in the historical context of human evolution, works of art attract our interest.

The explosive development of subjectivity evident in modern literature ultimately stems from our capacity to detect agency and to follow the gaze of other organisms as a means of anticipating their actions, a capacity noted not just in small children but also in several species. We can never know all of what another person is thinking, but we are wise to imagine it as best we can. Literature is a means of opening our minds about minds, others' and our own. Omniscient narration, indirect discourse, and stream-of-consciousness are trials at constructing more penetrating models of human perspectives. They exercise and amplify our capacity to simulate often alien states of mind. Subjectivity also increases readers' emotional investment and retention, contributing to other adaptive benefits of the text.

According to Blakey Vermeule, "Innovations in narrative technique are driven by the need to ratchet up pressure on our mind-reading apparatus" (2010, 98). The mental effort required may place a cap on this process, a limitation perhaps reached with multiple levels of intentionality in novels like those by Virginia Woolf, which, as Lisa Zunshine suggests, push "our mind-reading ability [. . .] to its furthest limit" (2006, 27).

AUTISM

Inasmuch as novels are particularly suited to modeling minds, autism is an ironic choice of theme for *The Defense*. The essence of autism is a deficit in imagining what other people are thinking. Simply put, metamentality is the core subject of novels; roughly speaking, autism is the reverse. According to Lisa Zunshine, this is *Why We Read Fiction* (2006). Being unable to sense how others are feeling and anticipate how they are likely to react constitutes a severe disadvantage in social politics. Facial expressions and other forms of body language remain unintelligible; we sense this late in the novel when Luzhin attends a silent film but is unable to discern the characters' intentions from the actors' actions, gestures, and expressions (191).[2] Lacking this capacity, the autist may feel clueless in society and prefer to remain content in his separate psychological realm, a penchant which gave this neurotype its name.

The view provided of Luzhin's childhood in the opening chapters strongly suggests the protagonist suffers from a mild form of autism.[3] It is evident on the opening page that he always has been a difficult child, one resistant to change in his environment, such as beginning to attend school.[4] His parents are apprehensive in imparting this news. On the one hand, Luzhin is usually unresponsive; on the other he is subject to violent tantrums, often for no apparent cause. He rarely talks (49). And when he does, it is mostly in the form of monosyllabic replies (78) or clumsy phrases (83). There is little or no emotional bond between Luzhin and his parents, or almost anyone else for that matter. He has no friends either as a child or as an adult. Other children pick on him at school. Apparently, something singles him out for victimization. There is little sign of imaginative play. Rather, he prefers to sit in a dark corner of the playground, away from other children, every day of the school year, for at least 250 recesses in all (29).

Luzhin also exhibits the repetition compulsion and self-stimulation often witnessed with autists. He bites his nails, fidgets, and fiddles with things; he wears out the label on his hat with incessant drumming (35, 16, 73, 78, 83, 107). Strolling around St. Petersburg, he always takes the same route, going out of his way to distance himself from the hourly cannon shots (many autists are sensitive to loud sounds), while taking care to step on the pavement lines (21). Both as a child and as an adult, he repeatedly sharpens pencils and contents himself with drawing straight lines and geometric solids (47, 48, 207). His few interests comprise patterns, as in math puzzles, wallpaper, carpet colors, and especially chess (33, 37, 32, 51). To be sure, neurotypical (non-autistic) people engage in many of these activities, but not so many; diagnosis focuses on their quantity, combination, and strength of expression.[5] As Luzhin's future mother-in-law exclaims, "there's something downright abnormal there" (112).

Luzhin's autistic symptoms continue to appear as an adult. The high intelligence that some autists like Luzhin possess often delays diagnosis, and it is common for parents to be confused and in denial, like Luzhin's parents; worse, he is their only child (Frith 2003, 11). Yet more, autism had not yet been defined in 1929 when Nabokov wrote his novel; nevertheless, there is remarkable consistency and sensitivity to detail in his description of Luzhin as being neurodiverse. Luzhin shows little facial expression and avoids eye contact; his future mother-in-law complains that he "talks with his back!" (112). At times, he appears to be deaf, probably because his mind is elsewhere; he has trouble understanding simple statements, which must be repeated to him (13, 228). His speech is strange, and he often parrots the words spoken to him, all characteristics of autism (87). His wife remarks, "Oh, Luzhin, [. . .] what you do to the language" (108, 204).[6] Luzhin rarely poses questions to others: it seems that he is simply not interested in them (88). His statements are often inappropriate. Some of his responses to questions posed out of mere politeness are ridiculously long and detailed, providing information nobody requests, such as when he informs his future mother-in-law that he suffers from hemorrhoids (106).[7]

Luzhin neglects his appearance, evincing more of the social disadvantages of autism. Autists are less self-conscious; they think little of how people regard them. Luzhin rarely bathes, washes his linen, or changes his razor (126, 94). Once out of his parents' care, and abandoned by Valentinov, his manager, his clothes become shoddy and out of fashion (84, 86, 106, 108, 118).

Luzhin is inclined to solipsism, whereby little exists outside of chess (139). Being blind to the fact that other people have minds is the essence of autism. At one point, he asks his wife whether she is real (130). He never learns how to embrace her, albeit, in Nabokov's and our minds, she must have tried to guide him. Luzhin is uninterested in women and compliant as a teenager when Valentinov forces a celibate lifestyle on him. As with most other autists, he somewhat adapts to society and, especially, to life with his wife. However, it is unclear, indeed, it seems highly unlikely, whether he ever consummated their marriage. Only with great difficulty does she manage to develop outside interests in Luzhin, but he is quick to drop them and revert to chess. Later, she realizes that he will never change (233). Such appears to be the case with autism. Yes, he suffers a nervous breakdown during a tournament, but Luzhin is not, as other readers have posited, "mad," just overwhelmed and exhausted (Downey 2004; Purdy 1968–69). He is neurodiverse: there may be adjustments to be made, but there is no cure.

Let us posit that our capacity for grasping, let alone enjoying, narrative constitutes the opposite of autism. Fiction draws on and develops our ToM. But what of those who have been born lacking that capability? Although often otherwise high-functioning, autists have trouble with story comprehension. The reverse case is found in those with Williams Syndrome, people who are severely cognitively impaired but highly social, well able to grasp narrative with good ToM (Boyd 2009, 190). This is not to say that we come into the world with fully developed natural psychology, but rather that most of us possess the innate potential to develop it. Healthy infants rapidly learn to distinguish other human beings from other parts of their immediate environment, to take an interest in them, and actively to establish means of interpersonal communication: note how they stare at your eyes. How do babies know what eyes are and that they warrant attention? It stands to reason that eye contact is crucial to parent-infant interaction and the consequent development of ToM. Narrative plays a partial but often helpful and important educational role in developing our metamental skills; perhaps significantly, children naturally take great interest in stories. How much about ourselves can we learn from fiction? It may be a lot. Tilghman is onto something.

Natural psychology is a product of natural selection, presumably for the reasons of intrasocial politics as described earlier. Notably, the interpersonal intuition and empathy such politics entail are conspicuously missing with cases of autism, which is believed to be largely genetic in origin in as many as 80 percent of cases. Boys, for instance, are four times more likely to be diagnosed with it than are girls.[8] With 90 percent of identical twins, if one has autism, so does the other, albeit to varying degrees of severity (Frith 2003, 65, 71). Nabokov's portrait of Luzhin anticipates the recognition of autism by Leo Kanner in 1943. Certainly, such people had always been around, probably regarded as "odd."[9] The consistency of Nabokov's characterization with recent descriptions may be taken as an indication of the effectiveness of his artistic insight, something commonly attributed to great writers. It also suggests the productive thinking long performed by the arts in advance of modern clinical science.

One important contradiction to Luzhin's autism is that he is capable of deception. This requires the capability of "false belief," of being able to imagine the *erroneous* thoughts of others. Luzhin pretends to be asleep when his mother looks in (43), conceals a piece of chocolate (51), hides his chess interests from his parents, and, most extremely, plays hooky from school for a week so that he can play chess at his aunt's apartment (52). Later Luzhin fakes a toothache and hides chess columns to peruse in his wife's absence (234).[10] These behaviors can be regarded as instances of the "masking" common among autists to conceal their neurodiversity (Price 2022). However, Luzhin also places tacks on his French governess's seat (16) and practices magic tricks (35), thus anticipating how *other* minds might think something other than what he knows to be the truth. He sets traps for his chess opponents, though not always with success (134). Due to the sheer potential complexity of chess, where no one can either calculate all its virtually innumerable positions, players try to discern their opponents' intentions. Such guesswork is faulty: Turati anticipates Luzhin's "defense," a planned sequence of moves in chess, and surprises him with an unexpected opening in their climactic match.

Autism does not follow a consistent pattern. Nabokov's depiction may have some inconsistencies, but those afflicted can be very diverse, and it should be remembered that the writer could not have known what autism is. Crucial here is whether readers perceive Luzhin to be plausible as a person. Significantly, Luzhin was found by his initial readership to be "lovable"; as Nabokov noted in his foreword to the English translation, "there is something in him that transcends the coarseness of his grey flesh and the sterility of his recondite condition" (10). It may be that the writer trains us to read humanity *into* his character by getting us to see the world through Luzhin's eyes. More on this later.

CHESS AND AUTISM

It is commonly thought that Nabokov based his protagonist on chess players who themselves may have been somewhat autistic. The efficacy of Nabokov's psychology may be seen in how Luzhin compares to other players who were thought to be insane. A gifted player, Nabokov once long held off the reigning world champion, Akimba Nimzovich, during one of the latter's simultaneous matches (Rogers 1983, 223). A student of the game and highly cognizant of its history, Nabokov probably was aware of how many players were struck down by chess, whether by the incredible demands posed on minds by its great complication, the ego-dystonic qualities of chess, and/or the insecure lifestyle forced on its greatest practitioners.[11] We can look at known examples, but who knows how many other oddballs the writer encountered in chess clubs?

Nabokov's protagonist pays for his immortality in chess by withstanding social alienation (few appreciate his genius), self-neglect, and the pressures of tournament play, culminating in a mental breakdown and hospitalization. While no great chess players have committed suicide, Luzhin shares important facets of their pathologies.[12] Both Akiba Rubinstein and Alexander Alekhine were obsessed with chess to the point of shutting out the world. At one point in the novel, Luzhin wonders, "[w] hat else exists in the world besides chess?" (139). Nabokov mentioned Alekhine as one of his models for Luzhin (Field 1967, 177). Luzhin's antisemitic mother-in-law suspects that the protagonist's "real name is Rubinstein or Abramson" (107). Rubinstein became paranoid; he would go out of his way to avoid meeting strangers.[13] He later spent thirty years in an insane asylum. Wilhelm Steinitz and Lionel Kieseritsky, loser of the "Immortal Game" cited in the foreword to the English translation, also ended up this way (Johnson 1985, 89). Alekhine developed a rampaging megalomania and married obvious mother-figures, women his senior by an average of over twenty years; so did Richard Reti. The same has been said of Luzhin (Johnson 1985, 108n18). Somewhat like Luzhin, who reads a supposed metaphysical "repetition" in the environment near the end of the novel, Steinitz imagined himself playing—and winning—a match with God (Bowen n.d.).

Perhaps it is not that chess causes insanity, but rather that certain personality types are attracted to chess by its bounded rules and clear outcomes. This seems to be the case with Luzhin, whose pathology predates his introduction to the game. Nabokov probably modeled him after the mode of an *idiot savant*, someone who is magnificently proficient in one sphere, often a materially useless one like chess, and incurably dysfunctional in most others. Luzhin can assess a chess position with a single glance.[14] But other, seemingly simple, cognitive functions befuddle him. He can neither remember the address of his future in-laws, nor provide it to taxi drivers without reading the rest of their invitation card (118).

Autism may be adaptive; it often bears some advantages, especially in terms of extraordinary concentration, grasp, and memory. It may be beneficial for chess players and others to shut out the world. Nabokov associates Luzhin's symptoms with his unusual gift for chess. But those same gifts are inappropriate elsewhere. When someone who doesn't know the game at all asks whether there are moves that are always strong, Luzhin expresses his one deep interest by discussing the issue at tiresome length (121). When his future wife asks Luzhin how long he has been playing chess, he replies with a detailed calculation down to the number of days (87). And, as already noted, in response to a polite question about his health, he replies that he suffers from hemorrhoids (106).

FOILS

Lest the reader fail to see how neuro*un*typical Luzhin is, Nabokov juxtaposes him with some activities which, by contrast, give relief to his mindblindness. One is the silent film screening he attends near the end of the film that we already noted. Another is a parlor game wherein one player leaves the room, then tries to guess what was said in his absence. Both require the mind-reading capacities that autism largely lacks.

Another tactic is to contrast Luzhin's perspective with that of several characters who are neurotypical. The major foil to the chess master is his father, the first to discern the depth of his son's difference. Why does Luzhin elder *have* to be a novelist, a career that consists of modeling subjective states? But then Ivan Luzhin writes juvenile literature, which generally involves very penetrable levels of intentionality; in popular narratives, characters wear their hearts on their sleeves, making it easy to distinguish protagonists from antagonists.[15] Nabokov includes several passages of Ivan's indirect discourse, including how the father is basing his current novel on his son, only the young boy is a composer prodigy, one resembling Wolfgang Amadeus Mozart. That his hero will die young expresses latent filial tensions (78). The elder Luzhin emotionally pulls for one of his son's chess opponents, being unable to beat him himself (68).

Another contrast is provided by Luzhin's very emphatic wife, a woman who exudes sympathy for suffering animals (105). With her, too, Nabokov devotes several passages to her *erlebte Rede*, offering the reader an intimate view of *her* mind. Perhaps it was because she was a Russian émigré like Luzhin and, already twenty-five, in need of a husband that she latches onto the unattractive chess master, but her emotional generosity plays a major role in their match. She also claims superior metamental capacities; at one point, she warns her husband: "I can see every thought—so behave yourself" (162). But she can't—and he doesn't.

A third foil is Luzhin's mother-in-law, who is acutely aware of the expectations of privileged Russian émigré society. Her statements and reported thoughts consistently reflect just how out of place Luzhin is in their milieu. She opposes their marriage by raising objections to her obstinate, perhaps desperate, daughter, all in vain.

As Julian Connolly adroitly noted, Nabokov's

> elaborate narrative shifts expose the fundamental difference between the relatively limited perspectives of his characters and the relatively unlimited perspective of that other which surrounds and gives life to the characters—the author himself. Nabokov's art celebrates a freedom of movement in consciousness that is inaccessible to his invented characters. (1992, 96)

Nabokov creates in his protagonist a cautionary tale of how not to be. As his mother-in-law exclaims of Luzhin, he's "not a real person" (108). Per Connolly's observation, if there is any ideal we should gain from Nabokov's novels, it is one of seamless mental dexterity, a capability of reading and responding appropriately to any social situation, never showing one's awkwardness. Luzhin regularly fails at this.

AUTHOR VS. READER

Much of *The Defense* is constructed to give readers some experience of being autistic, of being restricted to a different consciousness. The likely consequence is that if neurotypical readers are going to be able to make sense of Nabokov's novel, they will have to compensate by practicing a greater degree of metamentality. This dynamic is intrinsic to all narratives, but Nabokov stretches his readers further by making them do more of the task of mind-modeling on their own; he provides fewer hints as to what other characters are thinking than normally are provided. The wonder is that it works: according to Nabokov's foreword, this novel exudes a greater "warmth" than his other Russian language works (10). Perhaps this comes from hard-working readers, almost certainly not from the unusually obtuse protagonist.

There is little dialogue. All cited speech is compressed together, with few attributions as to who said what, and never elucidated by paragraphing. Mixed in are many snatches of disconnected and rarely completed conversations. To make sense of the events described, readers have to connect the scarce dots with longer and more speculative lines of their own.

Secondly, most characters lack first names, at least until the last line when the reader escapes Luzhin's world, when we learn that he is Aleksandr and can deduce from his patronym that Luzhin *pere* must have been an Ivan. This denies the reader some sense of their unique personalities. It definitely impedes the task of tracing actions and the agencies that motivate them. All four women lack names entirely, except as we can surmise their surnames from that of their husbands; we never learn one for Luzhin's in-laws. Instead, the major characters are identified by family stereotypes, the "father," the "fiancée," or later "the wife," and so on, a device that further bleeds them of any distinct psychologies. They appear more as pale phantoms who are tangential to Luzhin's narrow world. Of course, they are as real as any fictional personages are; it is just that readers have to imagine more to perceive them as such. After all, no narrative portrait is ever complete; even in the case of the most tiresome description, there always will be blanks to be filled in by effective readers, just more of them in the case of *The Defense*. Presumably, as with other metamental tasks, neurotypical people do this based on their internal models of what other minds are like, checking it against their consciousness of themselves.

Yet more, in Nabokov's *The Defense* these other characters contribute to the impersonality of the text by calling Luzhin "Luzhin." Even the protagonist's father and wife address him that way at home (18, 203). (Sharing his surname, one wonders what they call themselves.) As if this were not a sufficient impediment, on several occasions Luzhin is asked for his name and patronym. This question normally elicits an immediate response from a Russian: few select their own names; patronyms are automatically determined by the father's given name, much as happens with surnames. But there is no response to fill the silence (120, 127, 197). Nabokov makes readers acutely aware that something is missing.

Nabokov's characters appear to be faceless. Yes, of course, all people have faces, but autists are less likely to notice them; they rarely look. Few facial features are provided in the novel, even less so are emotional gestures and body language. Neurotypical people notice and interpret these, as it were unthinkingly, without effort and usually effectively, but Nabokov largely confines us to the perspective of an autist. Indirect eye gaze is a common symptom of autism. Those afflicted appear simply to not be interested in others. When Luzhin's name is reported in the newspapers, a former classmate is unable to recall what he looks like (31). Perhaps Luzhin was always looking in another direction.

Unmoored by Nabokov's denial of individual personal names and facial descriptions, the reader is further disoriented by the writer's (intentional, no doubt) run-on sentences and sloppy paragraphing, which characterizes most of the text. Events and topics are not sorted out by punctuation and indents; rather, they are mashed together, resulting in a continual blurring of the narration that the reader must overcome to keep track of who is doing what, let alone imagine why. An extreme example of this happens when Luzhin attends a soiree at the Berlin apartment of his future in-laws, a scene which slides into the chess tournament he plays in on the next day—and then back to the same apartment the following evening, a series which conveys Luzhin's distracted mind (121–23). Earlier, Nabokov blends two conversations at a resort to slide us seamlessly from a tournament in 1912 to his first conversation with his future wife in 1928; Luzhin does not appear to notice the introduction of his interlocutor. Like a castling move which dramatically changes the focus of a chess position, this passage allows Nabokov to leap across sixteen years (71). Events are blurred into one another; late in the novel, Luzhin confuses a visit to a photographer with one to a dentist and then to the passport office (242–44). A similar effect is achieved when Nabokov interweaves a scene where the wife is reading an editorial about current politics (a topic she is trying vainly to interest Luzhin in) with his thoughts about a chess position (yes, his real obsession) (223–24). It is likely that modern readers follow Luzhin's chess career, having read this far mostly through his eyes, but would they care about Berlin politics of, say, 1928?

In the meantime, the First World War and the Bolshevik Revolution pass mutely in the background, reflecting Luzhin's disinterest in anything besides chess. Nabokov's intended audience in 1929, fellow Russian émigrés, would be acutely aware of the events that recently denied them their homeland. They must have been interested in current developments in the USSR, something Nabokov tantalizes them with in scenes where Luzhin's wife entertains a tiresome visitor from the Soviet Union, a woman who boasts about the superiority of life there yet urgently wants to go shopping while she is in Berlin.

Nabokov encourages us to become as obsessed with chess as his hero. Chess pieces melt away in his prose to become incorporeal forces contending in some abstract realm. Luzhin's climactic match with Turati is imparted in an extended but intense paragraph that conveys the sheer excitement of chess; this passage is replete with musical terms, which impart Luzhin's synesthesia while immersed in the game.[16] When captured and taken off the board, pieces regain their ordinary material form (136–40). Meanwhile, Luzhin repeatedly perceives chess combinations elsewhere in his real environment, seeing the world through the lens of the game (91, 99).

Another commonly used device is the provision of half-dialogues, where we only read what is said by one party to a conversation. The reader must imagine what is being said by the other; this increases the task of modeling the consciousness of both. This is common in film and in theater when a character talks on a phone with an unheard caller; a case in point here is when Luzhin eavesdrops on a violinist's phone conversation during a concert intermission (41–2). However, in Nabokov's novel, there are many other instances when both parties are physically present, when readers might expect a give-and-take exchange—but hear only one side of the conversation. Related to this is a passage where a chess match is described entirely from the point of view of Luzhin's opponent, making the latter into more of a passive and clueless victim (56). We might term this scene a half-narration.

Nabokov occasionally takes other personages out of Luzhin's world entirely. As with autists, the chess master's limited consciousness does not adequately recognize alien agency. Objects around him appear to move on their own, independent of human intention. "A crystal ashtray came down between them" (120). "Shoes, ties and socks appeared" (170). "The chairs moved with the sound of throats being cleared" (178). Invisible hands hold crowns above the bridal couple's heads during their Orthodox wedding (179). At a lesser degree of impersonality, we are often informed that an undefined actor did something: "someone closed the door so that the music would not catch cold" (202). Surrounding people are viewed as phantoms (140, 176, 179). Luzhin senses that "someone—a mysterious, invisible manager—continued to take him from tournament to tournament" (95).[17] Isn't this what Nabokov is doing to us?

Another variant to Nabokov's practice is to describe a series of actions in exacting detail but at the same time deprive readers of any information as to why. The latter is forced to imagine the motivations of the pale characters involved. As already noted, one example of this is the passage that describes Luzhin's visit to the cinema, where Nabokov reports the silent and, for the protagonist unintelligible gestures he witnesses on the screen (191). Readers are confronted by similar "just the facts" scenes in the text, where consequential events are described bereft of the intentions that motivated them: these include both Luzhin's nervous breakdown and suicide. We have to surmise the psychological factors on our own.

Indeed, reading *The Defense* is a challenge with its many narrative innovations. Luzhin repeatedly evokes consequent cases of estrangement, as when "the asphalt hit him in the back" (249). Often readers must deduce what really is going on, as in this case where Luzhin fell on a Berlin sidewalk. More seriously, earlier, when he is ten years old, it is understandable that Luzhin is oblivious to the sexual affair his father is conducting with his aunt, let alone how this double betrayal by both her husband and her sister contributes to his mother's distress and early death. Effective readers cannot be so blind.

Nabokov's vibrant imagery often distracts from the narrative; readers may get lost in the lurid details of what often amounts to poetic prose.

What difference does it make to Luzhin that there was a raspberry floating in his father's glass of milk (65)? Or that an artificial bird was bobbing on his mother's hat as she ascended the stairs of their house (24)? It appears that Nabokov is giving us some semblance of what life is like for autists: they are easily overwhelmed by sensory information (Price 2022, 60, 114). They prefer predictable environments, much as Luzhin seeks "simplicity, harmonious simplicity" (36). He tries to identify patterns around him, a means of organizing and thereby simplifying information, making it easier to be coped with, such as when Luzhin counts the iterations of goose imagery on the wallpaper of his room (32).

Not only does Nabokov deny readers simplicity and narrative orientation, but his text often lacks connectives. Unable to model the intentions of others and thereby anticipate their actions, the chess master and readers are sometimes surprised by unexpected encounters. The result is paranoia. Luzhin begins to imagine an unseen opponent ready to crush him according to some sort of repeating pattern. True, he is right to sense that Valentinov is luring him back to chess, but he imagines his former manager to be only part of a larger, looming threat. Autists are much more likely than the normal population to experience paranoia, even hallucinations, and perhaps with good reason, as they are vulnerable to manipulation and exploitation by others (Neff n.d.; Price 2022, 129). This happened with Valentinov earlier. Being less able to read their social milieu, autists must be apprehensive, especially in gatherings where the task of modeling other minds is multiplied. For them, gatherings are difficult to endure, even menacing (Price 2022, 74). Add to this Luzhin's experience of being bullied at school; he is understandably intimidated by groups (71). Autists, therefore, typically prefer focused tasks like games to free social interaction (Price 2022, 127). Nabokov imparts Luzhin's disorientation and distress at an émigré ball with chaotic narration of how he gets lost in the swirling crowd, seeks refuge by sitting down silently in a corner—much as he used to do in his schoolyard—and runs into a former schoolmate and tormentor, Petrishchev (196). Luzhin flees in now total panic; his terminal paranoia has already set in.

It is often difficult to anticipate where Nabokov is taking us. Several scholars have tried to discern plot rhythms, such as Luzhin's urge to go "home" at the end of the first chapter, in the middle of his first match with Turati, and finally at his suicide.[18] Perhaps, as Leona Toker suggests, it is just a ruse on the part of the author, one intended to tempt readers into seeking patterns that do not exist in the text, let alone in the world (1989, 86–7). Starting with the ball, Luzhin misapplies what little natural psychology he possesses and, indeed, falls into a trap of his own devising in the final pages. On a similar note, scholars have noticed that the "Immortal Game" cited in the English foreword as a model for the novel does not figure in the text, except by means of encouraging egregious projective reading, precisely what Nabokov often tries to catch with his many snares (Johnson 1985; Parker 2017). Apparently, he was still at it when he had his novel translated three decades after its Russian publication. Reading Nabokov, we have to be on our toes and wary about our author's intentions.

Another challenge to readers is posed by how Nabokov will often slide from the indirect discourse of one character to that of another, sometimes in the course of the very same paragraph. One instance is that same émigré ball, where the perspective almost imperceptibly slips from Luzhin, lost in the swirling crowd, to the thoughts of his wife, seeking him, to that of those surrounding her (193–96). It is all the more difficult for us to model who is thinking what and why, but, inasmuch as this is the most popular of Nabokov's Russian novels, apparently most of us manage to muddle through, and indeed enjoy *The Defense*. This resembles the cognitive workout Lisa Zunshine perceives in *Lolita* (2006).

In many ways, the reader is required to practice mental dexterity, including a subtle natural psychology, to live up to Nabokov's ideals. In effect, we have to evolve as readers, perhaps not in the biological sense, but surely in metamental terms. Otherwise, we cannot read *The Defense* properly.

NOTES

1. Michelle Scalise Sugiyama reminds us of the considerable somatic energy and parental investment required to build the gray matter that enables metamentality; this was likely developed by a "tandem process" of "extended provisioning of offspring and encephalization," "each driving the other in a 2 million-year-long feedback loop" (2005, 21). The adaptive demand for Theory of Mind capacities required nothing less.

2. All citations to *The Defense* are listed by page number only.

3. Mild forms of autism used to be termed Asperger's syndrome. For the purposes of this study, I have not attempted to distinguish between the two, using the term "autism" loosely. Recently, these terms have been collapsed into autism spectrum disorder, perhaps as occupying opposite poles as "low-" and "high-functioning." The latter is discerned with people who have superior IQs (Hosseini and Molla 2024). Luzhin's mastery of chess suggests he is one.

4. Common symptoms of autism are based on Frith (2003, 2–5), Janzen (2003, 8), and Price (2022).

5. The *Diagnostic and Statistical Manual of Mental Disorders*, Fifth Edition, defines autism as exhibiting "persistent deficits in social communication and social interaction across multiple contexts, as manifested by all of the following: deficits in social-emotional reciprocity, in nonverbal communicative behaviors used for social interaction, and in developing, maintaining and understanding

relationships" (Hess 2022). *The Defense* provides evidence for all three symptoms in Luzhin's behavior. It should be kept in mind that there is an enormous variety in the expression of autism. Autists cannot be stereotyped; they exhibit different combinations and degrees of symptoms. Devon Price, himself an autist, claims that autists are more diverse than neurotypicals (2022, 21).

6. Regarding Luzhin's unusual and deficient language, see Roth-Souton 1990.

7. A chess player, Luzhin has spent most of his life in a sitting position, overweight and out of shape. Still in his early thirties, he already walks with a cane and suffers shortness of breath at the least exertion, such as when he climbs stairs. Autists commonly neglect their physical fitness (Price 2022, 90, 102). Of course, these symptoms are shared by many neurotypical people.

8. Devon Price argues that female autism is underdiagnosed due to gender stereotypes (2022, 35, 53).

9. Uta Frith suggests some fictional characters in narrative as likely autists; one is Sherlock Holmes (2003, 17).

10. It might be objected that Luzhin reads fiction by Arthur Conan Doyle and Jules Verne, but often it is to discern patterns (33, 167).

11. That chess is dangerous to the ego is suggested in one strikingly Freudian passage where Luzhin imagines himself as a nearly immobile pawn: "trembling and stark naked," surrounded by "huge pieces, megacephalous, with crowns or manes" (236). At a minimum, there is no element of chance, hence no acceptable excuse for losing a game.

12. Nabokov acknowledges the similarity of Luzhin's suicide to that of Curt Carl Alfred von Bardeleben, a prominent chess player in Berlin, who apparently leaped out of a window in his apartment in 1924. From Nabokov's note, it does not appear that they were personally acquainted (1971, ix).

13. Parker compares Luzhin to Rubinstein (2017, 447).

14. Perhaps, in Nabokov's mind, Luzhin inherited his special talent and neurodiversity from his maternal grandfather, an obscure composer.

15. This is conveyed by the title of Sophia Wege's wonderful study of popular narrative, "The Reader Is Always Right" (2019).

16. Regarding musical terminology in this passage, see Boyd (1987, 583).

17. Boyd (1987) suggests a supernatural dimension to the many phantoms of this sort who appear in *The Defense.*

18. See especially Boyd (1987) who links such patterns to the inclusion of Luzhin's father and maternal grandfather, who shares some of the protagonist's monomania, in the text.

BIBLIOGRAPHY

Bowen, Peter. n.d. "The Most Dangerous Game: The Perilous Path of Bobby Fischer and Other Chess Players." https://bleeckerstreetmedia.com/editorial/the-most-dangerous-game.

Boyd, Brian. 1987. "The Problem with Pattern: Nabokov's *Defense." Modern Fiction Studies* 33: 575–604.

Boyd, Brian. 2009. *On the Origin of Stories: Evolution, Cognition, and Fiction*. Cambridge, MA: Harvard University Press.

Connolly, Julian W. 1992. *Nabokov's Early Fiction: Patterns of Self and Other*. Cambridge: Cambridge University Press.

Downey, Glen. 2004. "The Relentless Combination: Chess and the Patterns of Madness in Vladimir Nabokov's *The Defense*." *The Antigonish Review* 121: 147–53.

Frith, Uta. 2003. *Autism: Explaining the Enigma*. Malden, MA: Blackwell.

Hess, Peter. 2022. "DSM-5 Revision Tweaks Autism Entry for Clarity." https://www.spectrumnews.org/news/dsm-5-revision-tweaks-autism-entry-for-clarity/.

Hosseini, Seyed Alireza, and Mohammed Molla. 2024. "Asperger's Syndrome." Excerpt, https://pubmed.ncbi.nlm.nih.gov/32491480/.

Humphrey, Nicholas. 1983. *Consciousness Regained*. Oxford: Oxford University Press.

Janzen, Janice E. 2003. *Understanding the Nature of Autism*, 2nd ed. San Antonio: Therapy Skill Builders.

Johnson, Donald Barton. 1985. *Worlds in Regression: Some Novels of Vladimir Nabokov*. Ann Arbor: Ardis.

Miller, Geoffrey F. 1997. "Protean Primates: The Evolution of Adaptive Unpredictability in Competition and Courtship." In *Machiavellian Intelligence II: Extensions and Evaluations*. Edited by Andrew Whiten and Richard W. Byrne, 312–40. Cambridge: Cambridge University Press.

Nabokov, Vladimir. [1964] 1990. *The Defense*. Translated by Michael Scammell. New York: Vintage Books.

Nabokov, Vladimir. 1971. Foreword to *Glory*. Edited by Vladimir Nabokov and translated by Dmitri Nabokov, ix–xiv. New York: McGraw Hill.

Nabokov, Vladimir. [1973] 1981. *Strong Opinions*. New York: McGraw-Hill.

Nabokov, Vladimir. 1980. *Lectures on Literature*. Edited by Fredson Bowers. New York: Harcourt Brace Jovanovich/Bruccoli Clark.

Nabokov, Vladimir. 1981. *Lectures on Russian Literature*. Edited by Fredson Bowers. New York: Harcourt Brace Jovanovich/Bruccoli Clark.

Neff, Megan Ann. n.d. "Schizophrenia vs. Autism." https://neurodivergentinsights.com/misdiagnosis-monday/shizophrenia-vs-autism.

Parker, Luke. 2017. "The Gambit: Chess and the Art of Competition in *The Luzhin Defense*." *Russian Review* 76: 438–57.

Price, Devon. 2022. *Unmasking Autism: Discovering the New Faces of Neurodiversity*. New York: Harmony Books.

Purdy, Strother B. 1968–1969. "Solus Rex: Nabokov and the Chess Novel." *Modern Fiction Studies* 14: 379–95.

Rogers, William N. 1983. "Heroic Defense: The Lost Positions of Nabokov's Luzhin and Kawabata's Shûsai." *Comparative Literature Studies* 30: 217–30.

Roth-Souton, Danièle. 1990. "Language Deficiency as Luzhin's Defense and Vladimir Nabokov's Metaphor for Exile." *Revue française d'études américaines* 45: 149–60.

Scalise Sugiyama, Michelle. 2005. "Reverse-Engineering Narrative: Evidence of Special Design." In *The Literary Animal: Evolution and the Nature of Narrative*.

Edited by Jonathan Gottschall and David Sloan Wilson, 177–96. Evanston: Northwestern University Press.

Tilghman, B. R. 1991. "What Is It like to Be an Aardvark?" *Philosophy* 66 (257): 325–38.

Toker, Leona. 1989. *Nabokov: The Mystery of Literary Structures*. Ithaca: Cornell University Press.

Trivers, Robert. 2011. *The Folly of Fools: The Logic of Deceit and Self-Deception in Human Life*. New York: Basic Books.

Vermeule, Blakey. 2010. *Why Do We Care about Literary Characters?* Baltimore: John Hopkins University Press.

Wege, Sophia. 2019. "The Reader Is Always Right: Biopoetic and Cognitive-Aesthetic Aspects of Karl May's Adventure Novel *Winnetou I*." In *Evolution and Popular Narrative*. Edited by Dirk Vanderbeke and Brett Cooke, 132–55. Leiden: Brill Rodopi.

Zunshine, Lisa. 2006. *Why We Read Fiction: Theory of Mind and the Novel*. Columbus: Ohio State University Press.

9

Provocation and Pre-Diction

Terrorist Realism as a Narrative Mode in the Russian Empire 1862–1914 (Particularly in Andrei Bely's Petersburg*, 1913)*

Michał Mrugalski

Throughout this chapter, I will try to explain and contextualize a scene from Andrei Bely's *Petersburg* (1913), while trying not to explain it *away* because—as a staff member of the Russian embassy put it in Joseph Conrad's *The Secret Agent* (1907)—for an act of terror to be efficient, it must defy all mundane explanatory categories and never stop bewildering or energizing the general public (1920, 42–45). For literary modernists, literary works of art are more fit to convey the experience of shock and terror than other kinds of discourse since their literariness depends on defying routine. Once a work does not shuffle the reader's and the protagonist's perceptive and thought patterns, it not only ceases to communicate terror but altogether loses its distinctive feature of literariness, which in modernism equals unpredictability that invigorates and alarms the reader.

The following fragment of Bely's *Petersburg* baffles the reader while showing how a subject exposed to the threat of terror and provocation deals with words (he does it in a top-down fashion, by way of simulation). A revolutionary catches fragments of conversations on a boulevard, integrating them into a "gossip of the Nevsky" prospect, his own projection of reality:

> "Do you know?" came from somewhere to the right and expired in the accumulating rumble.
> And then to the surface again came:
> "They're going to . . ."

"What?"
"Throw . . ."
[. . .]
"Who at?"
"Who, who," came an echoed whisper from afar; and then the dark suit spoke.
"Abl . . ."
And, having spoken, the suit moved on.
"Ableukhov?"
"At Ableukhov?"
But the suit finished what it was saying somewhere over there
. . ."Abl . . . oody wish you'd try to splash me with a . . . cid . . . just you try . . ."
[Abl . . . eika menia kk.. .isla.. toiu . . . poprobui . . .]
And the suit hiccupped.
But the stranger stood still, shaken by all he had heard:
"They're going to? . . ."
"Throw? . . ."
"At Abl . . ."
"Oh no: they're not going to . . ."
[. . .]
[T]here came from another crossroads:
"It's time . . . pravo, indeed it is . . ."
The stranger heard not *pravo* (indeed) but *provo-* and himself completed the word:
"Provocation?!"
Provocation began to go on a spree along the Nevsky.
Provocation altered the sense of all the words that had been heard: with provocation did it endow the innocent "indeed [pravo]"; while it turned "I bloody wish" [Abl . . . eika] into the devil knew what:
"At Abl . . ."
And the stranger thought:
"At Ableukhov."
He had simply of his own accord attached the preposition 'at' [v]: by the appendage of the letter a and the letter t an innocent verbal fragment had been changed into a fragment of dreadful content; and what was most important: it was the stranger who had attached the preposition.
The provocation, consequently, lay in him; and he was running away from it: running away—from himself. He was his own shadow. (Bely 2005, 25–26)

The provocation comes from inside the subject (who, as an accomplished revolutionary, has had experiences with factual provocation) to establish, or at least shape, what is recognized as real in the outside world. I contend that Bely foreshadows one of today's more influential theories of cognition, known as "enactive inference." Enactive inference,[1] occupies a dominant position in contemporary neuroscience and cognitive theory. "Predictive coding," "predictive processing," and "active inference" all fall under the umbrella of "enactive inference," which holds that all that we perceive and act upon is merely the brain's simulation of some hidden causes of our internal states; the brain infers the causes from stimuli by relying on prior embodied experience. Thus, our top-down models of reality are assumed to be reality itself. The bottom-up flow of sensory input modifies these models only when it significantly undercuts the anticipated simulation. The theory relies on the subject's management of energy; top-down cognition and economizing are energetically cheaper.

In this chapter, I will place the productive, world-making provocation, which renders Bely's discourse representative of the whole genre of Terrorist Realism (henceforth TR), in the context of literary and political history with the aim of demonstrating that the history of literary forms cannot separate itself from the history of ideas, understood also as a history of mindsets, and *vice versa*, the history of how people think cannot forgo literary devices, lest we become blind to forms and think empty thoughts. In the second step, I will propose a model of TR as a particularly telling case of Modernist narrative. This model, which relates to cognitive narratology, has a structuralist communicationist foundation and an enactive inference-based superstructure. According to the model, the opening scene from Bely is realistic in terms of cognition in general and in terms of cognition in conditions of terror and provocation in particular. Pinned in a tight corner, cognition as a matter of life and death (survival is the primary function of cognition in enactive inference) betrays its homology with Modernist and proto-Modernist poetics.

TERRORIST REALISM AS A MINDSET AND LITERARY MODE

Acts of "individual terror," aiming at scarring and disorienting decision-makers and not anonymous crowds, occurred all over Europe during the protracted nineteenth century, eventually sparking the start of World War I, but nowhere were they such a crucial social issue, occupying both outcasts and pillars of society, as in the Romanov Empire, including the Kingdom of Poland (Anemone 2010; Baranov 2000; Frank and Gruber 2012; Budnickii 2000; Dietze 2016; Geifman 1993, 2005, 2010; Mogil'ner 1999; Patyk 2017, 2023; Safronova 2014). The development of the political strategy of terrorism in the Romanov Empire went hand in hand with, or even was preceded by, the creation of a large number of narrative texts expressing—emphatically or as an abhorring illustration of a crisis—the frame of mind in which an act of terror could not only become acceptable but glorified.

The corpus of these narratives of terror, conspiracy, and provocation contains many significant works: alongside Bely, we have Dostoevsky's *Demons*, narratives by Leo Tolstoy, Anton Chekhov, Leonid Andreev,

Stanisław Brzozowski, Andrzej Strug, or—on a global scale—Joseph Conrad. But the actual terrorists' proclamations also use narration, fabricate, and relativize their reference to reality with regard to their effect (they provoke facts rather than state them while oftentimes retaining the form of a report).

Those texts, both belletristic and belligerent, are endowed with specific characteristics due to their thematic and formal orientation toward violent activities and their psychological underpinnings. The description of these characteristics firstly enables a cultural-historical reinterpretation of the evolution of the literary discourse of the Romanov Empire between 1862 and 1914. It sheds new and local light on the more universal processes, encompassing the literature of the West, of tying together literariness and unexpectedness and the ensuing mounting up intricacy that culminates in avant-garde tendencies. Secondly, the narrative mode, by virtue of its foregrounding of the expected and the unexpected, provides new insights into the narrative construction or reproduction of cognition ("percepts," see Schmid 2017) since, in the framework of enactive inference, probability and expectation, employed in the service of survival, likewise take center stage. Thirdly, this historical narrative mode influences how terrorism is conceptualized and experienced even today (e.g., Twitter gossips that Putin's carriage, pardon, limousine was pelted with bombs). Fourthly, this mode brings to light the workings of the economy in narrative texts, economy meaning in TR not only the actions involved in producing, exchanging, and consuming goods and services, but also, in the spirit of enactive inference, the budgeting of energy according to the probability distribution of events in the environment. The description of TR's aesthetic and cognitive efficacy should accordingly focus on the economy understood as the distribution of goods and the distribution of energy. Destitution motivated political terror and its mental and discursive expressions, while the distribution of energy formed their (narrative) shape. The main issues of terrorist tactics pertain to energy: how to release the energy of the people while introducing disorganization to the system of power.

The fact that the poetological or narratological question reciprocates the ideo-historical and economical ones is already evident in the term "terrorist realism" (TR), which draws on Roman Jakobson's conception of "revolutionary realism in literature." Jakobson describes "revolutionary realism" as a kind of abrupt reversal of semantic hierarchies while describing an apparently familiar phenomenon (Jakobson [1921] 1987, 22). With this formulation, Jakobson relates what has become the established concept of estrangement (*ostranienie*), which justifies or explains literary evolution, specifically to narrative, social upheavals, and hypothesizing about the make-up of the outward world, upweighting or downweighing the significance of particular sensations for the assessment of a situation, akin to today's enactive inference. Enactive inference similarly correlates the sudden shift in the explanatory model of reality (identified with reality), conducted in the wake of a prediction error unaccounted for by the model, as "a reality effect."

By adapting and shifting Jakobson's term, I claim that it refers not to "revolution" in all its ambiguity, but specifically to "the individual terrorism" of the *sztyletnicy* (dagger fighters), *Narodnaia volia* (the People's Will), the party of the Socialist Revolutionaries, or the Polish Socialist Party—to what is known in the West as the "Russian method" (Patyk 2018, 230). I primarily seek to avoid confusion with the Marxian concept of "revolution" as an expression of the mature class consciousness of the proletariat, able to recognize its interests: the difference with Marxism lies at the heart of the most striking characteristics of TR—instead of the scientific-objective view of historical processes, which supposedly characterizes the Marxism of the Second International, TR focuses on the theme and technique of provocation, using violence and fabrication to force the transition to the desired state. The reader should not experience maturity and a stable scientific worldview; rather, they should encounter the antithesis of these qualities. These include acceleration, hasty conclusions, premature commitment to beliefs inferred from inadequate clues, impatience, and general anxiety, confusion. This frame of mind is made conspicuous through the dynamization of the narrative perspective, which foregrounds shifting attention and hectic hypothesizing, that is, re-hierarchization and reinterpretation of the percepts. The poetics thus refer—affirmatively or disapprovingly—to concrete political and ideological positions, along the lines of Blanquism, populism (*narodnichestvo*), anarchism, irredentism, etc.

The conflict between Marxism and populism dominated the social life of the Empire, at least among the Westernized intelligentsia (see Mrugalski 2021). While the Marxists adhered to economism and thus regarded the laws of economics, which they claimed to know, as the ultimate explanans of history, the populists perceived the economy as only one, albeit important, aspect of the development of society. For the populists, it is individual conscience, not economic processes, that initiates change in history. The Marxists "knew" that the Russian Empire, like the rest of the world, had to go through the whole cycle of capitalist development before it could make a qualitative leap into the realm of communist freedom. The rural population of the Empire must be transformed into the industrial proletariat before it acquires the ability to govern itself and humanity. The populists, on the other hand, wanted to save Eastern Europe from the horrors of capitalism, did not want to wait for the full development of industry, and so they relied on the tactics of conspiracy, provocation, and individual assassination, leading to a sudden outbreak of general all-destructive violence followed by a final renewal of life, taking a new form inspired by the traditional rural community.

In my attempt to translate populist economics into aesthetic and narrative conventions, I will draw on the work of the sociologist Leon Winiarski, who was forced to flee the Russian Empire in 1885 as a result of the persecution of the first Polish workers' party, "Proletaryat." Despite its name, the party—as Rosa Luxemburg (1895–1896, 459–70) pointed out—had a Blanquist, populist disposition, as it did not plan to assist in the prenatal development of proletarian class consciousness but formed conspiracies and even an alliance with the Russian terrorist organization The People's Will. As a privatdozent in Geneva, Winiarski worked on extending the economic theories of the Lausanne School, sometimes called the Mathematical School (Léon Walras, Vilfredo Pareto), to society as a whole, with particular attention to aesthetics. In lucid French prose, backed up by mathematical formulae, Winiarski conveys, alongside or perhaps through the general tenets of the Lausanne School, views that correspond to populist terrorism, such as the recognition of individual genius as the only factor of social change, as opposed to society, which is conservative by default. He also expresses a view, typical of both terror and Modernist art theory, that the utility, the enjoyment, of a state is directly proportional to the effort required to achieve it, as if Winiarski could not fully accept the Lausanne School's doctrine that the marginal utility tends to diminish after passing a threshold—too much of a good thing may be taxing.

Winiarski expresses this invitation to, or justification of, the energetic potlach in equations derived from Lagrangian/Hamiltonian mechanics. These equations reveal an economic or energetic rationality behind the anti-Marxist Eastern European left. Winiarski accepts the Lausanne School's basic tenet that the ultimate source of value is not labor, as Marx and classical economists in general would have it, but utility or rather a belief in utility.[2] Accordingly, Winiarski argues that it is not the production of goods but the transformation of energy that provides the most general explanation of both physical and social realities. Energy, by definition, changes form, so that the aesthetic energy of enjoying beauty can be transformed into the political action of throwing bombs, or vice versa—a transformation that Lagrangian mechanics can describe. Moreover, these equations make Winiarski's theory compatible with the current theory of enactive inference as a way of understanding sentient behavior. In the last subchapter, I try to use Winiarski's aesthetics to adapt enactive inference to Modernist poetics regarded under the aspect of cognition, which becomes particularly salient in TR. Winiarski's theory serves here as a source of inspiration for how to adapt contemporary enactive inference to Modernist art, as the deliberations on art conducted in this framework are superficial in their emphasis on the adaptive value of artistic creation and their disregard for art's specific mechanisms.

CLASSICAL BASIS: COMMUNICATIONISM

The model of TR that I propose combines the classical communicationist approach with postclassical enactive inference. This model provides a framework for characterizing the complicated formal relationship between terrorism and narrative works of art. Acts of violence and utterances can be aligned with one another at a more general level of communication, since both are to be understood as acts of communication (Deitze 2016; Hilbrenner 2022; Schmid and de Graaf 1982). The narratological model hinges on the cultural-historical thesis that terrorists and their opponents (the secret police) generally communicate through provocation, which includes both acts of violence and counterfactual statements; accusing the other side of provocation is the preferred means of provoking. Moreover, the act of verbal and violent communication, understood as a provocation, shares with the fictional discourse specific traits that are their exclusive preserve. The authors of TR explore precisely these disturbing similarities between apparently polar opposite forms of communication, either in order to amplify the cause of the terrorists or to counteract it. For the sake of the affect (threat, terror) and mindfulness (awareness) that terrorist communication mobilizes, classic "communicationism" in narratology is supplemented with cognitivist elements. Consistent with the prevailing view (Olson 2011), I position "classical" (Structuralist) narratology as a base upon which newer, "postclassical" approaches to narrative can build. As TR foregrounds provocation, permanent ambiguity, and even fear-induced paranoia, of all cognitive approaches, enactive inference is arguably one of the most well-suited to describe the provocative discourse.

The narratological point of reference is furnished by the Polish school of literary communication ("Warsaw Structuralism," see Balcerzan 1971; Bartoszyński 1971), which draws on Viktor Vinogradov (1930), Valentin Voloshinov ([1928] 1973), and Roman Jakobson ([1960] 1987). According to the United Nations Consensus Scientific Definition (Schmid 2012), acts of terrorism are acts of communication that can be characterized by the presence of a division into "direct targets" and "main targets." In violent communication, direct targets serve only as the generators of messages addressed to the main targets (dead politicians cannot be scared into making concessions). As a rule, in the context of the Russian Empire, this split in the receiver entity corresponds to the split in the emitter entity, divided, in the spirit of provocation and conspiracy, into an authentic and a counterfactual sender. In order to generate revolutionary energy, maintain conspiracy, disorient the antagonist, and increase general uncertainty, the actual historical terrorists created imaginary senders: the Revolutionary Central Committee (as the sender of the first terrorist manifesto "Young Russia," actually penned by the imprisoned student Zaichnevskii), Bakunin and Nechaev's *Narodnaia raspravа*, and so on. In fictional narratives, the terrorist groups are usually presented as revolving around at least one strong manipulative character who fulfills the role of an "author" affecting the borders of the factual. So, the groups are necessarily split into narrators (emitters) and audience, whose members appear as actors for another audience (including victims or receivers), both inside and outside the diegetic world. TR models within its safe "as if" mode the relationship between the counterfactual and the factual, a distinction which provocation upsets to the point of delirium. Dostoevsky, Brzozowski, Bely, and Conrad, inspired by real-life master manipulators Sergei Nechaev and Evno Azef, construe their fictional provocateurs as fabulists restlessly shifting the limits of the factual by self-fashioning and staging simulacra of reality. The actual terrorists—the models for the writers—fabulated while confabulating with comrades and foes and penned proclamations designed to blur what the case is. If authors wanted to actively impact reality as authors, then they did it by presenting activists as authors. Dostoevsky's caricature of Nechaev, Petr Verkhovenskii, is a bad author, planning to release unprecedented revolutionary energies by spreading among the people the legend he invented of the hidden *real* tsar embodied by the aristocratic Nikolai Stavrogin (1974, 325). He probably draws inspiration from the characteristic Russian cultural association of popular rebellion with political usurpation. Pugachev, the leader of the great popular uprising that many terrorists referred to, supposedly was Peter III, miraculously rescued.

It is precisely this split in the communicative entities between direct and indirect participants that allows the act of terror to be set side by side with the literary work, which always has an implicit and an explicit reader or author too. According to Balcerzan (1971), literary narrative texts are the only type of utterances that necessarily represent the process of sending and receiving alongside the diegetic world, that is, they obligatorily divide their entities into inner- and extratextual, fictional and factual. Likewise, Foucault argues that only *authored* texts show discontinuity between the fictional speaker and the empirical writer; the "author" function, which is fundamental to fiction, operates precisely in this hiatus (Foucault [1970] 1981, 58–59).

If the division of communicative instances and the reflexive representation of this division are the most fundamental characteristics of literature, then literariness overlaps with the societal and cognitive functions of literature, that of communication, whatever the aim of a work. An overflow of aesthetic energy into political spheres, as postulated by Winiarski, does not seem so implausible from a narratological perspective, as well.

Provocation—the main topic of TR novels—pertains not only to manipulative utterances aimed at gaining actual advantage, but also to actual killing, which affects the mental world models and compels adversaries to respond (Zugzwang).

The actions of the terrorists and their adversaries thus inscribe themselves in the basic situation of communication, which consists of exchange. An action on the part of the sender is supposed to provoke a reaction so that the receiver in turn adopts the position of the emitter. For example, the desired reaction to an attentat—as stated in the first terrorist manifesto Petr Zaichnevskii's "*Molodaia Rossiia*" (Zaichnevskii [1862] 1997, 144)—is a wave of reprisals that arouse hostility between the people and the government and thus raise awareness of the two sides' hostility. This terrorist tactic suits particularly well the description in terms of information theory, which equates entropy with informativeness (Shannon 1948): the bomb is nothing else than a message *sub specie* the discharge of energy. Due to the information's unalienable affective and sensorimotor components, this type of information must now be positioned as a compound that cannot be reducéd to the intelligible or the noetic. The bombastic message is directed at the body, and its salience is closely related to the body's survival in the most uncertain environment.

POSTCLASSICAL SUPERSTRUCTURE: INFERENTIAL ENACTIVISM

Inferential enactivism accounts for the energetic aspect of the communicative process, that is, the origin and the transformations of energy engaged in the provocative exchange. This theory adds the active body to the structuralist model, making it appear that energy is a matter of life and death. This is especially pertinent in the context of terrorist provocations, propaganda, and outright violence. Winiarski's social mechanics of beauty are apt to form a bridge between inferential enactivism and the study of art and literature because of the emphasis on physical action: "All the phenomena of beauty," wrote Winiarski ([1898–99] 1967, 193), "have as a common substratum the nervous [system's] movement of persons who feel [ressentir] it, or the nervous and muscular movement of persons who materialize [réaliser] and embody the phenomena in art." The energy that drives the neurological motions is, incidentally, "sexual energy," which is sublimated into many artisanal, cultic, and creative forms (Winiarski [1898–99] 1967, 196).[3]

The starting point of inferential enactivism is the assumption that cognition has a primarily life-sustaining function (Seth 2021, 7). Surviving comes down to an organism sharing energy and, by extension, information (described in terms of entropy) with its surroundings without breaching the Markov blanket, the border between the two (Parr et al. 2022, 54–55; Winiarski [1898–99] 1967, 186–88). As with Winiarski, in enactive inference, these exchanges and transformations of energy are expressed in the equations of Hamiltonian mechanics; these equations are also proposed to be comparable to information theory's notions of informativeness (Parr et al. 2022, 50ff). Probability is inferred using Bayes' theorem (Parr et al. 2022, 9; Friston et al. 2006); I demonstrate such a Bayesian inference further in this text with an example from Dostoevsky's *Devils* (1872).

Why probability? Inferential enactivism follows Helmholtz's understanding of the relationship between the brain and perception as the result of the former's "unconscious inference" (1867, 3rd volume; Friston and Stephan 2007). The subject perceives its own projections as appearances of the external and internal worlds. The brain, enclosed within the cranium, "infers" from the electrical stimuli reaching it by relying on previous similar situations what their cause might be and what it should most likely prepare the body for. The world turns out to be a sum of assumed—with different probabilities—causes of sensations coming from outside and inside the body (the inner and the outer world as the hypostasis of probabilistic hypotheses). The subject is immersed in their own hypotheses as to the true nature underlying sensations.

As for Lagrangian/Hamiltonian mechanics and entropy, the brain is generally assigned the role of manager of energetic resources; for the sake of economy, the brain opts in a predictable environment for automatism of reactions, so that awareness amounts to a state of exception that arises in moments of threatening uncertainty as the need for decision-making arises. The brain tries to minimize "suprisal" or prediction errors. While perceptual predictions flow predominantly "top down," prediction errors flow "bottom up" (Friston 2005; Solms 2021, 142): the frugal brain only conveys upward the portion of the incoming information that does not meet expectations or the presumptions of the model (Hohwy 2013; Clark 2015, 23). These prediction error signals disrupt habitually-based automatism and trigger awareness; the brain then uses the prediction errors to update its predictions (model).

Model and signal synchronization can take place in one of two ways: either the subject modifies the model to fit the environment, or the environment is purposefully changed to fit the model. Informative sensation processes arise in the embodied mind as a result of the incessant activity of this body; in other words, perceptions and emotions are solicited and not simply had (Parr et al. 2022, viii).

Prudent (anticipatory) reliance on prior experiences becomes relevant for literature, especially Modernist and proto-Modernist writing, because literary utterances play with habit and spontaneity, anticipation and surprise, bringing together the familiar and the unexpected. The familiar acts as a background against which a pattern (startling juxtapositions of words in poetry or events or perspectives in narrative) becomes noticeable as a prediction error. When phenomena go beyond "mechanical" pattern detection, awareness and "seeing" take their place. In the context of enactive inference, estrangement and narrative eventfulness can be regarded as artistically designed sequences of prediction errors. TR highlights specifically the close connection between prediction, event, and estrangement by virtue of its general uncertainty, produced by all-suspected provocation in deed and word.

There are at least two significant ways that inferential enactivism docks onto traditional narratology. In the beginning, it aids in clarifying and operationalizing the concepts of estrangement and eventfulness. Second, it offers a fresh, energizing perspective on literary and manifesto-like communication as two modes of knowledge exchange that go beyond dry sparsity. Here, excess is reasonable in the same way that awareness ("seeing" the error) triumphs over instinctive reactions (recognizing one's own predictions).

According to Iurii Lotman, a champion of classical narratology, without surprisal there cannot be eventfulness and significance in narrative. It is common knowledge that Lotman considers the event and the plot (a series of events) to always be transgressive. Compliance with the norm is uneventful (Lotman 1977, 231). While translating Shklovskii's theory of estrangement into the language of structural semiotics, Lotman correlates the norm with expectation and event with surprisal:

> A device is viewed in terms of the general conception of [slow perception,] and the de-automatization of form as *the relation between expectation and the text*. Thus for Shklovskii a device is the relation of an element of one syntagmatic structure to that of another, and consequently it includes a semantic element.[4]

In the enactive inference jargon: When a text doesn't match the expectation, one explanatory hypothesis (model) replaces the previous one that didn't explain a strange pattern. The re-coding of the text occurs as a result of the perception of an error. This translation or transition of the subject from one explanatory framework to another produces both significance and eventfulness; an impression that the reader has had an experience. Reading rewards.

Significance is always an effect of a re-coding, a translation from one series to another, just as "[a]n event in a text is the shifting of a person across the borders of a semantic field" (Lotman 1977, 233) (or As Michel De Certeau put it: "What the map cuts up the story cuts across" (1984, 129)). It is in connection with this transgression that Lotman calls the event "a revolutionary element opposing accepted classification" (1977, 234) and the plot "the 'revolutionary element' in relation to the world picture" (1977, 238). Revolution means here, as in Jakobson, a reversal of percepts and values. No wonder, then, that the Devil tells Ivan Karamazov: "If everything on the Earth was reasonable, then nothing would ever happen" (Dostoevskii 1976, XV:77); by the way, the Devil, this hallucination or projection, expresses only what Ivan could have expected him to, given that he himself already told Alesha that "the world stands on absurdities [*neleposti*], and without them, perhaps nothing at all would have happened" (Dostoevskii 1976, XIV:221). Ivan and the devil, who hypostasizes Ivan's own interpretations of eventfulness as a major aspect of reality and experience, echo the words of Dostoevsky's "Man from the Underground" who stated that in the rationally organized future world "there will no longer be any actions or adventures" (Dostoevskii 1973, 113).

In terms of communication theory, prediction also applies to our relationships with other people, including those who wish to provoke or kill us. In relation to "mutual prediction," Andy Clark speaks of "self-fulfilling psychosocial knots and tangles" (Clark 2023, 76), which sums up much of TR.

Rainer Paris's communication-based theory of provocation, apparently modeled on individual terrorism, involves the adaptation of a model of reality to account for a prediction error. A model of reality based on habit is updated when the provocation "elicits a reaction that, in the eyes of the third party, morally discredits and unmasks [the provoked opponent, i.e. the indirect target]."[5] Discreditation entails a vehement adaptation of a model in view of a flagrant prediction error. According to communicationism and structuralism, the third party in literary works can be found inside and outside the text, and both instances—direct and indirect recipients—are involved in an energy transformation, that is, adapting their models of reality. Manipulating reality in a manner that is as unpredictable as possible is where provocative violence begins; provocation amounts to "a deliberately committed but unexpected violation of norms intended to draw an opponent into open conflict" (Paris 2015, 49).

The impact of the initial violation determines how successful violent provocation will be; the degree to which the provocateurs force the updating of beliefs relies on how much of the social system's balance they disrupt. This is the economy of terror's logic, which is also evident in Modernist art, especially avant-garde work: the more energy and surprise expended by the sender, the more potent the provocation is in connection to the recipient. Furthermore, Winiarski's mathematical formalisms and active inference show that this paradoxical economy of effort is the foundation of our existence as living, feeling, and cognizing organisms.

If we express the communicative situation of TR in terms of energy transfers, the initial provocation, the opening of the exchange, appears as a great influx of energy; the larger the influx, the greater the surprise or the unsettling of the system's equilibrium. Winiarski points out that, according to Lagrangian/Hamiltonian mechanics, every disturbed system tends toward regaining equilibrium. However, it is incorrect to equate balance with stagnation and dullness, in contrast to unscientific intuition. Active inference also warns us that the organism's quest to minimize free energy "should not be equated with a rigid repertoire of responses (e.g. automatic homeostatic responses), but rather the opposite [. . .]. We can develop open-ended repertoires of novel behaviours to pursue our original homeostatic imperatives" (Parr et al. 2022, 60). Sentient organisms enjoy *minimizing* free energy or *accounting* for prediction error and *not a minimum* energy; their tendency is a change, coping and not a stable state. According to Winiarski, equilibrium simply means the most energetically possible state of the system: "The supreme principle of Dynamics, that of Lagrange, tells us that each material system tends to produce, at the moment of establishing equilibrium, the maximum energy compatible with the existing conditions" (Winiarski, [1898–99] 1967, 168).

Monopolies are the single factor preventing the economic system from achieving the maximum amount of energy (Winiarski [1896] 1967, 96); doubtless, analogous inhibitions apply to the field of art. The imperative is to remove artificial constraints so that nature might flourish freely, which is typical of *narodnichestvo*, anarchism, and, in the case of Winiarski's economy, anarcho-capitalism. Enactive inference suggests that there are environmental constraints or preferences that are built into organisms and prevent them from becoming excessively energy- and information-consuming machines. However, "if one removes both ambiguity and prior preferences, the only remaining imperative is to maximize the entropy of observations (or states [. . .]). This may be interpreted as uncertainty sampling (or keeping one's options open)" (Parr et al. 2022, 36). According to the mathematical formulae of active inference, the most fundamental motivation of organisms is the desire for new information, no matter the cost. They pursue the *activity* of minimization, that is, difficulty, and not a minimum or a *state* of equilibrium. I contend that the realm of art may be where the most basic impulse may be acted upon by virtue of the nonexistence of the constraints placed on organisms by the need to survive in a factual reality.

Winiarski's and active inference's equations (Winiarski [1898–99] 1967, 169 and Parr et al. 2022, 28) clearly demonstrate that the larger the effort (biological energy transformed by an individual) or entropy (in each case, the subtracted values), the larger the jouissance, pleasure, utility, or simply the total energy of the system (the positive values), since outcomes are supposed to tend toward zero or minimum, respectively.

Effort in Winiarski and entropy in active inference must be sufficiently high to balance off energy or a partial pleasure (see Winiarski [1898–99] 1967, 191; Parr et al. 2022, 60–61). Thus, it turns out that minimizing free energy may be understood as striving for maximum entropy (randomness, informativeness).

> The agent is striving to *increase* entropy [. . .] of the agent's (approximate posterior) belief. [. . .] [T]he imperative to explain things as accurately as possible but also 'keep options open' and avoid committing to any specific explanation unless this is necessary—that is, the *maximum entropy* principle (Jaynes 1957). (Parr et al. 2022, 60)

The agent thus invests energy in maintaining their own uncertainty. In terms of aesthetic equilibrium, Winiarski explicitly says that the intensity of pleasure is proportional to the expenditure of energy or money:

> The fundamental law of mathematical economics, which can moreover be deduced from Lagrange's general equations of motion, is the following: equilibrium in the satisfaction of needs is only established when the intensity of the last satisfied desires is proportional to energy (or money) expenditure. (see Winiarski [1898–99] 1967, 198)

The fundamental urge for spending or informativeness, which in my opinion equates to the sense of aliveness underpinning and guiding all cognitive processes, can be freely pursued in art, particularly TR, a discursive formation foregrounding dealing with uncertainty under the threat of death. Additionally, the energetic potlatch has essential adaptive benefits outside of art, particularly for top-down modeling, since the organism can educate itself to create and test ideas in response to perplexing patterns. Enactive inference proponents underline the critical importance of having the capacity to create counterfactual justifications for the enactment of the factual. In this regard, art is given a key role (Clark 2023, 277).

TR texts, on the one hand, belong to art's sanctuary, where the subject can enjoy and live out energetic expenditure and uncertainty, not fearing immediate consequences, such as being too exhausted to react to a sudden threat. On the other hand, they contain instructions for formulating and testing models, their diegetic worlds full of Gestalt switches triggering eventfulness, deep meanings, and aesthetic pleasure. "In narratological enactivism, the revisions of prediction throughout the narrative provide the outline of a plot trajectory" (Kukkonen 2019, 20). TR both models in a particularly prominent way the cognitive processes of its communicative instances (A) and directs the process of reading (B); in the second case, TR makes the reader a participant in the communicative process, that is, a part of the model. To flesh out the idea:

A. Conrad shows in *Under Western Eyes* (1911), in reference to a Russian terrorist plot, how our assessments of the world are founded on the consistency of the discourse in stories we regard as credible (probable): the experienced revolutionary woman clears the hero Razumov, who is guilty, from suspicion because, according to the cognitive and narrative ways she is used to using to recount the ways of the world, the hero does not fit the description of the culprit. Sophia Antonovna "drew her conclusions from the tale," conclusions full of "maybe," "A man like that would be," "People said he was," "if he had been once before," "as seemed certain," to eventually arrive at what she calls "conclusive evidence." The exonerated culprit Razumov "meditated in silent astonishment upon the queer verisimilitude of these inferences" (Conrad 1947, 276). Sofia Antonova with her queer, eventful inferences exemplifies—as Conrad's narrator puts it in a paratextual preface—"the Russians' extraordinary love of words"—resulting in "The illogicality of their attitude, the arbitrariness of their conclusions, the frequency of the exceptional, [which] should present no difficulty to a student of many grammars" (Conrad 1947, 276).

An example from Dostoevsky's *Devils* illustrates how enactive inference approximates Bayes' theorem as a way of accommodating observations in beliefs about reality. The mentally disturbed, disoriented governor exclaims upon seeing a fire started in a town district: "If anything burns, it is nihilism!" (Dostoevskii 1974, 395). What makes him so certain? If we substitute the elements from the diegetic world into Bayes' formula, we see that the probability of a nihilist's presence (N) given a fire (F) equals the product of the probability that there is a fire given the presence of a nihilist and the probability that a nihilist is present at all, divided by the probability that a fire breaks out in general: $P(N \mid F) = (P(F \mid N) * P(N))/P(F)$. The denominator has a great value since the narrator claims (Dostoevskii 1974, 394) that the sight of a fire in a Russian town is too widespread to require a description, having in mind probably the wooden architecture. So, to arrive at such a high level of certainty $P(N \mid F)$, in the governor's perturbed mind the probability of meeting a nihilist must be extremely high, just as the probability that he or she starts a fire. The governor must be paranoid when assuming such a high saturation of society with nihilist-arsonists (the adversary disoriented him successfully). If the governor's insanity is obvious to a reader not acquainted with Bayes' theorem, so obvious that my explanation amuses them as superfluous and pompous, it is because the reader spontaneously approximates the theorem without much theorizing.

B. The emitting instances of TR demonstrate how they model the reading process through an apparent play with genre schemata. In order to persuade the reader to embrace a set of expectations that he then abruptly fails to meet, Dostoevsky plays with components of established genres (gothic novel, crime story, and *Geheimbundroman*).[6] This also applies to Ivan Turgenev and Nikolai Chernyshevsky, who were Dostoevsky's greatest rivals in terms of literary representations of political violence. In Turgenev's *On the Eve* (1860), what the other protagonists and the reader initially take to be Insarov's gothic-novel-styled personal vengeance ends up being a selfless national struggle for Bulgaria's liberation. The auctorial narrator of Chernyshevsky's *What Is to Be Done?* (1862) comments on his own play with readers' expectations as he introduces elements of romances and detective stories.

The love of words and literary conventions, fanned by the frequency of the exceptional and unexpected, coincides, paradoxically, with the soberest nihilism. This is exactly what the fragment of Bely's *Petersburg,* quoted at the beginning, shows. To understand Bely, one should frame nihilism as a cognitive attitude and observe its development. Turgenev depicts nihilism as a kind of materialistic Cartesianism: methodical doubt, constantly weighing up what is "real" and what is just an "illusion" fostered by tradition. Subsequently, in TR, the reader's mediums (characters and narrators) bet on what seems more likely or, conversely, more daring, more improbable—and for that very reason more effective (and as such expectable from the provocateurs). With time, the methodical doubt expands from the level of the represented world to the level of representation. In Bely, we see how narrative prose about nihilism reaches a stage where the discourse no longer only labels or signifies imaginary stimuli; this is, by the way, the stage at which all previous analyses of predictive processing in literary fiction arrive (see Pianzola et al. 2021). Lexemes here act as the actual stimuli (albeit already in Dostoevsky's *Devils* the governor's paranoia is triggered by a specific nonsensical verbal formation "*flibust'ery*"). Instead of signifying or alluding to the extero- or interoceptive flow, narrative uses its words, in their perceptible, physical form, with their sounds, connotations, and energy, as both perceived qualities and perceptual categories.

If the words are perceptible and cause perceptions that are explainable in words, the reader is prompted to take on a hallucinatory attitude. As the external and interior communicative situations start to intersect, the reader is forced to consider the permeable boundaries of fiction and provocation that allow for shooting energy from one level of communication to the next. The assumption of the porosity of the boundary on the one hand explains why the literary evolution accompanied so closely the development in actual political violence and on the other hand reinforces the model of TR that joins structuralist communicationism with enactive inference; the object of this inference is precisely what is on the other side of the boundary (Markov's blanket, Derrida's *hors-texte*) and why it is so exciting and instructive.

NOTES

1. I borrow the notion from Ramstead et al. (2020); Venter (2021) speaks of "free energy enactivism"; on combining active inference with enactivism, see also Downey (2017); however, Di Paolo et al. (2022) warn against "conflating" enactivism and active inference. Generally, on the notion of predictive processing and enaction seen in cognitive science and neuroscience (see Friston 2012; Seth 2013), philosophy (see Hohwy 2013; Clark 2015), and narratology (Kukkonen 2014, 2016, 2017, 2018, and 2019; Caracciolo 2014, 2016; Popova 2015; Irving 2016).

2. Active inference specifically focuses on "beliefs" in their activating role: "in Active inference, . . . expected free energy is a functional of beliefs about states, not a function of states" (Parr et al. 2022, 53).

3. Unless a translation is cited, all translations are my own.

4. Lotman ([1970] 1977, 232) translation altered in accordance with Lotman (1970, 281; emphasis added).

5. English translation quoted after Patyk (2023, 11), altered in accordance with Paris (2015, 49).

6. The trailblazing studies of Dostoevsky's indebtedness to popular genres were done by Grossman (1925, 20–63).

BIBLIOGRAPHY

Anemone, Anthony, ed. 2010. *Just Assassins: The Culture of Terrorism in Russia*. Chicago: Northwestern University Press.

Balcerzan, Edward. 1971. "Perspektywy 'poetyki odbioru'." In *Problemy Socjologii Literatury*, edited by Janusz Sławiński, 79–95. Wroclaw: Ossolineum.

Baranov, Aleksandr. 2000. "*Revoliucionnyi terrorizm kak fenomen russkoi kul'tury kontsa XIX – nachala XX veka*." PhD diss., Rossiisskii gosudarstvennyi gumanitarnyi universitet.

Bartoszyński, Kazimierz. 1971. "Zagadnienie komunikacji literackiej w utworach narracyjnych." In *Problemy Socjologii Literatury*, edited by Janusz Sławiński, 127–48. Wroclaw: Ossolineum.

Bely, Andrey. 2005. *Petersburg. A Novel in Eight Chapters with a Prologue and an Epilogue*. Translated by David McDuff. New York: Penguin Books.

Belyi, Andrei. 1981. *Peterburg. Roman v vos'mi glavakh s prologom i epilogom*. Moskva: Nauka.

Budnickii, Oleg. 2000. *Terrorizm v rossiiskom osvoboditel'nom dvizhenii: ideologiia, etika, psikhologiia*. Moskva: Rosspen.

Caracciolo, Marco. 2014. *The Experientiality of Narrative. An Enactivist Approach.* Berlin: De Gruyter.

Caracciolo, Marco. 2016. "Cognitive Literary Studies and the Status of Interpretation: An Attempt at Conceptual Mapping." *New Literary History* 47(1): 187–207.

de Certeau, Michel. 1984. *The Practice of Everyday Life.* Translated by Steven Rendall. Berkeley: University of California Press.

Clark, Andy. 2015. "Embodied Prediction." In *Open MIND: 7(T)*, edited by Thomas Metzinger and Jennifer Windt, 1–21. Frankfurt am Main: MIND Group.

Clark, Andy. 2023. *The Experience Machine. How Our Minds Predict and Shape Reality.* Dublin: Allen Lane.

Conrad, Joseph. [1907] 1920. *The Secret Agent. A Simple Tale.* London: Metuhen & Co.

Conrad, Joseph. 1911. *Under Western Eyes.* London: Dent & Sons.

Di Paolo, Ezequiel A., Evan Thompson, and Randall D. Beer. 2022. "Laying Down a Forking Path: Tensions between Enaction and the Free Energy Principle." *Philosophy and the Mind Sciences* 3, 2. https://doi.org/10.33735/phimisci.2022.9187.

Dietze, Claudia. 2016. *Die Erfindung des Terrorismus in Europa, Russland und den USA 1858–1866.* Hamburg: Hamburger Edition.

Dostoevskii, Fedor. 1973. *Zapiski iz podpol'ia.* In *Polnoe sobranie sochinenii*, vol. V, 99–179. Leningrad: Nauka.

Dostoevskii, Fedor. 1974. *Besy.* In *Polnoe sobranie sochinenii*, vol X. Leningrad: Nauka.

Dostoevskii, Fedor. 1976. *Brat'ia Karamazovy.* In *Polnoe sobranie sochinenii*, vols XIV–XV. Leningrad: Nauka.

Downey, Adrian. 2017. "Radical Sensorimotor Enactivism & Predictive Processing – Providing a Conceptual Framework for the Scientific Study of Conscious Perception." In *Philosophy and Predictive Processing: 11*, edited by Thomas Metzinger and Wanja Wiese, 180–95. Frankfurt am Main: MIND Group.

Foucault, Michel. [1970]. 1981. "The Order of Discourse." Translated by Ian McLeod. In *Untying the Text: A Post-Structuralist Reader*, edited by Robert Young, 48–79. Boston: Routledge.

Frank, Michael, and Eva Gruber, eds. 2012. *Literature and Terrorism: Comparative Perspectives.* Amsterdam: Rodopi.

Friston, Karl. 2005. "A Theory of Cortical Responses." *Philosophical Transactions of the Royal Society of London. Series B, Biological Sciences* 360(1456): 815–36.

Friston, Karl. 2012. "A Free Energy Principle for Biological Systems." *Entropy* 14(11): 2100–121.

Friston, Karl, James Kilner, and Lee Harrison. 2006. "A Free Energy Principle for the Brain." *Journal of Physiology* 100(1–3): 70–87.

Friston, Karl, and Klaas Stephan. 2007. "Free-Energy and the Brain." *Synthesis* 159(3): 417–58.

Geifman, Anna. 1993. *Thou Shalt Kill: Revolutionary Terrorism in Russia, 1894–1917.* Princeton: Princeton University Press.

Geifman, Anna. 2005. *La mort sera votre dieu! Du nihilisme russe au terrorisme islamiste.* Paris: Table Ronde.

Geifman, Anna. 2010. *Death Orders: The Vanguard of Modern Terrorism in Revolutionary Russia.* Santa Barbara: Praeger Security International.

Grossman, Leonid. 1925. *Poetika Dostoevskogo*. Moskva: GAKhN.
Hilbrenner, Anke. 2022. *Gewalt als Sprache der Straße. Terrorismus und die Suche nach emotionaler Gemeinschaft im Russischen Reich vor 1917*. Stuttgart: Franz Steiner.
Helmholtz, Hermann. 1867. *Handbuch der physiologischen Optik*. Leipzig: Voss.
Hohwy, Jakob. 2013. *The Predictive Mind*. Oxford: Oxford University Press.
Irving, Dan. 2016. "Presence, Kinesic Description, and Literary Reading." *CounterText* 2(3): 322–37.
Jakobson, Roman. [1921] 1987. "On Realism in Art." In *Language in Literature*, edited by Krystyna Pomorska and Stephen Rudy, 19–27. Cambridge: Harvard University Press.
Jakobson, Roman. [1960] 1987. "Linguistics and Poetics." In *Language in Literature*, edited by Krystyna Pomorska and Stephen Rudy, 62–94. Cambridge: Harvard University Press.
Jaynes, Edwin. 1957. "Information Theory and Statistical Mechanics." *Physical Review* (106)4: 620–30.
Kukkonen, Karin. 2014. "Presence and Prediction: The Embodied Reader's Cascades of Cognition." *Style* 48(3): 367–84.
Kukkonen, Karin. 2016. "Bayesian Bodies: The Predictive Dimension of Embodied Cognition and Culture." In *The Cognitive Humanities: Embodied Mind in Literature and Culture*, edited by Peter Garratt, 153–67. London: Palgrave Macmillan.
Kukkonen, Karin. 2018. "The Fully Extended Mind." In *The Edinburgh Companion for Contemporary Narrative Theory*, edited by Zara Dinnen and Robyn Warhol, 56–65. Edinburgh: Edinburgh University Press.
Kukkonen, Karin. 2019. *4E Cognition and Eighteenth-Century Fiction: How the Novel Found its Feet*. Oxford: Oxford University Press.
Lotman, Iurii. 1970. *Struktura khudozhestvennogo teksta*. Moskva: Iskusstvo.
Lotman, Iurii. 1977. *The Structure of the Artistic Text*. Translated by Ronald Vroon. Ann Arbor: Michigan University Press.
Luxemburg, Rosa. 1895/96. "Der Sozialpatriotismus in Polen." *Die Neue Zeit* 14(2): 459–70.
Mogil'ner, Marina. 1999. *Mifologiia "podpol'nogo cheloveka." Radikal'nyi mikrokosm v Rossii nachala XX veka kak predmet semioticheskogo analiza*. Moskva: NLO.
Mrugalski, Michał. 2021. "Energieformen und Kraft des Lesens. Erweiterte Kognition und revolutionäre Gefühle in Lev Tolstojs 'Das Göttliche und das Menschliche'." *Poetica. Zeitschrift für Sprache- und Literaturwissenschaft* 52: 58–95.
Olson, Greta, ed. 2011. *Current Trends in Narratology*. Berlin: De Gruyter.
Paris, Rainer. 2015. *Der Wille des Einen ist das Tun des Anderen*. Weilerswist: Velbrück.
Parr, Thomas, Giovanni Pezzulo, and Karl Friston. 2022. *Active Inference. The Free Energy Principle in Mind, Brain, and Behavior*. Cambridge: MIT Press.
Patyk, Lynn. 2017. *Written in Blood: Revolutionary Terrorism and Russian Literary Culture, 1861–1881*. Madison: University of Wisconsin Press.
Patyk, Lynn. 2018. "Dostoevsky's Terrorism Trilogy". In *Terrorism and Literature*, edited by Peter Herman. Cambridge: Cambridge University Press.
Patyk, Lynn. 2023. *Dostoevsky's Provocateurs*. Chicago: Northwestern University Press.

Pianzola, Federico, Giuseppe Riva, Karin Kukkonen, and Fabrizia Mantovani. 2021. "Presence, Flow, and Narrative Absorption: An Interdisciplinary Theoretical Exploration with a New Spatiotemporal Integrated Model Based on Predictive Processing." *Open Res Europe* 1(1): 28.

Popova, Yanna. 2015. *Stories, Meaning, and Experience. Narrativity and Enaction*. New York: Routledge.

Ramstead, Maxwell, Michael Kirchhoff, and Karl Friston. 2020. "A Tale of Two Densities: Active Inference is Enactive Inference." *Adaptive Behavior* 28(4): 225–39.

Safronova, Iulia. 2014. *Russkoe obshchestvo v zerkale revoliutsionnogo terrora: 1879–1881 gody*. Moskva: NLO.

Schmid, Alex. 2012. "Revised Academic Consensus Definition of Terrorism." *Perspectives on Terrorism* 6(2): 158–59.

Schmid, Alex, and Janny de Graaf. 1982. *Violence as Communication: Insurgent Terrorism and the Western News Media*. London: Sage.

Schmid, Wolf. 2017. *Mentale Ereignisse. Bewusstseinsveränderungen in europäischen Erzählwerken vom Mittelalter bis zur Moderne*. Berlin: De Gruyter.

Seth, Anil. 2013. "Interoceptive Inference, Emotion, and the Embodied Self." *Trends in Cognitive Science* 17(11): 565–73.

Seth, Anil. 2021. *Being You. A New Science of Consciousness*. London: Faber.

Shannon, Claude. 1948. "A Mathematical Theory of Communication." *The Bell System Technical Journal* 27(3): 379–423.

Sławiński, Janusz. 1971. "Socjologia literatury a poetyka historyczna." In *Problemy Socjologii Literatury*, edited by Janusz Sławiński, 29–52. Wroclaw: Ossolineum.

Solms, Mark. 2021. *The Hidden Spring: A Journey to the Source of Consciousness*. London: Profile Books.

Winiarski, Léon. [1896] 1967. "Deux théories d'équilibre économique." *Essais sur la mécanique sociale*, edited by Giovanni Busino, 76–97. Genève: Librairie Droz.

Winiarski, Léon. [1898–99] 1967. "Essai sur la mécanique sociale." In *Essais sur la mécanique sociale*, edited by Giovanni Busino, 162–290. Genève: Librairie Droz.

Venter, Elmarie. 2021. "Toward an Embodied, Embedded Predictive Processing Account." *Frontiers of Psychology* 12. https://DOI=10.3389/fpsyg.2021.543076.

Vinogradov, Viktor. 1930. *O khudozhestvennoi proze*. Moskva & Leningrad: Nauka.

Voloshinov, Valentin. [1928] 1973. *Marxism and the Philosophy of Language*. London and New York: Seminar Press.

Zaichnevskii, Petr. [1862] 1997. "Molodaia Rossiia." In *Revoliutsionnyi radikalizm v Rossii: vek deviatnadtsatyi*, edited by Evgeniia Rudnitskaia, 142–50. Moskva: Arkheograficheskii tsentr.

10

Mass Shooters as Underground Men of the Twenty-first Century

Irina Meier

As the nineteenth-century novelist and philosophical thinker who was particularly concerned with the complexity and scope of individual human experience, Fyodor Dostoevsky spent the majority of his life developing a portrait of the Underground Man: his development, attempts at self-actualization, and dénouement. The tragedy of the Underground Man in *Notes from Underground* (1864) lies in his inability to adapt and co-exist with others in modern civilization, which he perceives as the dehumanization of human experience. As Dostoevsky argues, the overly rationalized, utilitarian social models that emphasize extreme individualism contribute to the atomization of society, where people seek only self-interest and pleasure at the expense of genuine human connections. The craving for a meaningful life beyond the void of a modern lifestyle manifests in a highly self-aware individual in the form of existential despair because traditional beliefs have already disintegrated in his value system; whereas alternatives are not sufficient to satisfy his need for fundamental aspects of human existence, such as meaning and purpose of life, hope, personal intimacy, and moral responsibility. As a result, the Underground Man is headed toward destruction or self-destruction. Dostoevsky writes:

> Civilization merely develops man's capacity for a greater variety of sensations, and . . . absolutely nothing else. And through the development of this capacity, man may yet come to find pleasure in the spilling of blood. Indeed, this has already happened. ([1864] 1992, 25)

Indeed, torn by their internal conflict from over-intellectualizing the human experience, at least two of Dostoevsky's underground men left their physical underground to spill the blood of others and their own: Rodion Raskolnikov in *Crime and Punishment* (1866) killed the pawnbroker Alyona Ivanovna, her sister Lizaveta, and Lizaveta's unborn child to prove his own exceptionalism and affirm the self-granted authority to take others' lives; Nikolai Stavrogin's decisions in *Demons* (1872) led to multiple murders and suicides, including his own, done in his name. As underground men, they possessed an enhanced sensitivity to rewards and pleasure received from morally ambiguous and even morally reprehensible behavior. At the critical time of decision-making, their minds got locked in the rigid state of decreased cognitive flexibility and, through an unraveling inner dialog, these underground men self-rationalized killing because they lacked solid ethical principles and strong human connections to counterbalance their yearnings for transhumanism.

PSYCHOLOGY OF THE UNDERGROUND MAN

The mindset and rigidity of the underground men's cognitively-twisted visions of reality, exacerbated by the fragmentation of modern society, parallel the psychology of today's mass shooters and their neurological processes in the moment of decision-making. Their behavior illustrates the rationality-within-irrationality principle proposed by Link and Stueve, when in instances of violence "psychotic symptoms [. . .] are experienced as real, violence unfolds in a 'rational' fashion" (1994, 143). By presenting his characters' voices and perspectives as entire worldviews, what Mikhail Bakhtin called heteroglossia, Dostoevsky exposes the altered, rigid realities of his underground men as fully developed and paradoxically harmonious in their contradictory pictures of the world. As Bakhtin points out:

> The hero interests Dostoevsky not as some manifestation of reality[. . .] the hero interests Dostoevsky as a *particular point of view on the world and on oneself,* as the position enabling a person to interpret and evaluate his own self and his surrounding reality. (1984, 47)

In his analysis of a mass shooter's mind from the neurological point of view, psychiatrist Mark Goulston (2015) explains the process of decision-making through the concept of triunal rigidity, which describes a state in which the brain locks itself in one version of reality being unable to realign to the changing environment. According to James Gross (1998), the strategy of cognitive reappraisal plays an essential role in developing cognitive flexibility in regulating emotions. Reappraisal, as opposed to suppression, involves recognizing negative thought patterns leading to tunnel vision and learning how to short-circuit cognitive loops. Although the mental make-up and motivations of mass shooters are influenced by a wide range of social, psychological, and environmental factors, some clearly exhibit some similarities: rumination on negative emotions, failure of cognitive reframing, intellectualization, aversion to humankind, internal conflict between self-imposed alienation and a need for human connection, and existential angst—all of which characterize the Underground Man as a psychotype.

The Underground Man as a psychotype has the following distinct characteristics:

1. Constant internal conflict and self-contradictory patterns of thought and behavior.
2. Self-imposed alienation.
3. Intellectualization of human experience. Heightened sense of consciousness and self-awareness that leads to social paralysis instead of prompting positive changes.
4. A sense of boredom that results in moral ambiguity and existential experimentation with others and oneself. Enhanced sensitivity to both positive and negative stimuli, including humiliation of others and oneself.
5. A fear of public and personal mockery.
6. Bitterness and resentment toward one's own environment and social order that comes from an intense desire for individual freedom and autonomy.
7. Existential angst and messianism that result from questioning the meaning and purpose of existence.
8. An intense desire for human connection and self-sabotage of any potential intimacy out of self-loathing and fear of rejection.

Following Dostoevsky's lead to explore underground men's versions of realities as interpretations of their own identities, I intend to examine the personal journals, manifestos, and interviews of four shooters in order to explore their metaphysical movements of consciousness and uncover their self-portraits, altered realities, and inner dialogs to rationalize and justify their planned rampages. I examine three cases in particular: Eric Harris and Dylan Klebold (1999 Columbine High School massacre), Seung-Hui Cho (2007 Virginia Tech shooting), and James Holmes (2012 Aurora, Colorado shooting).

During the Columbine High School massacre on April 20, 1999, two twelfth-grade students, eighteen-year-old Eric Harris and seventeen-year-old Dylan Klebold, killed thirteen people and wounded twenty-three others with a semi-automatic pistol, shotguns, and a carbine rifle, and subsequently killed themselves. They also planted self-made bombs that failed to detonate properly. Harris and Klebold left behind their personal journals and video tapes documenting their actions. In the Virginia Tech shooting on April 16, 2007, an undergraduate student, twenty-three-year-old Seung-Hui Cho, killed thirty-two people and wounded seventeen others with semi-automatic handguns, and also subsequently shot himself. Prior to the killing spree, Cho sent out a multimedia package containing his manifesto, photographs, and videos. In the 2012 Aurora shooting on July 20, 2012, a former doctoral student in neuroscience at the University of Colorado in Denver, twenty-four-year-old James Holmes, killed twelve people and wounded fifty-eight others with a shotgun, a semi-automatic rifle, and a handgun in a Century 16 movie theater during the midnight screening of *The Dark Knight Rises*. He also planted homemade explosives in his apartment. After the attack, Holmes surrendered to the police in the parking lot, and in August 2015 he was sentenced to twelve life sentences without parole and 3,318 years in prison. Hours before the shooting, Holmes mailed a notebook with his plans and theories to his psychiatrist. Similar to Cho, he posed for selfies with guns so that these images would be shared by the media for posterity after the shooting. All four shooters exhibited psychological characteristics of the Underground Man.

SELF-IMPOSED ISOLATION AS A WILL TO INDIVIDUAL FREEDOM IN MODERN SOCIETY

The Underground Man voluntarily withdraws into the physical and existential underground. He sees that a way to individual freedom lies through solitude as an inevitable outcome of rebellion against the social order and rules of the world. This self-imposed isolation, as Dostoevsky demonstrates, inevitably leads to exceptional egoism and self-centrism. The Underground Man starts his path of social isolation with a nihilistic rejection of all societal norms and conventional truths, whether material or ethical. He finds participating in society meaningless because an individual does not choose these activities, but they are imposed on him against his will. The Underground Man believes that accepting the rational needs of society as necessary is amoral and incompatible with human dignity and individual freedom because every person has an immeasurable and incomparable value a priori, regardless of the socially enforced virtues such as status, talent, wealth, and so on. that people earn by being active participants in modern society. According to the Underground Man, people have an inherent need to prove to themselves "that men are still men, and not piano keys," even by creating "destruction and chaos" if needed, to affirm their will to freedom (Dostoevsky [1864] 1992, 34–35).

In the media, mass shooters are often portrayed as ostracized loners who take revenge on others for their involuntary alienation. However, after a closer look, it becomes clear that isolation is more often their own choice. As soon as the Underground Man gets a small inheritance, he quits his job; Raskolnikov from *Crime and Punishment* abandons his university studies despite his dismal financial state and without any particular reason; and the Aurora shooter Holmes dropped out of his doctoral program simply because he did not want to retake his comprehensive exams.

In their writings, all four shooters demonstrate strong contempt for meaningless social structures and order, hatred toward other people, whom they see as empty-headed followers and enablers of the unjust system, and intolerance of overly structured modern civilization that impedes human freedom. Holmes told his psychiatrists about his hatred of both "sheeple" (a combination of sheep and people) and their "shepherds" (Reid 2018, 72). Cho expressed his resentment for false Christianity and the hedonism of the wealthy whom he called snobs and accused of being incapable of sacrifice: "You will never give up a single can of your Bud Light, a shot of your cognac, or a half-drop of your own precious blood for another human being, only fuck the shit out of him and lie afterwards" (2014, 1–2). The social system, in his eyes, granted rich people undeserved status and thus labeled them a success and him a loner with anxiety and depression—that is, a failure. Harris and Klebold rebelled against social norms mostly as "typical" juvenile delinquents by engaging in underage drinking, drug use, stealing, vandalism, and hacking into the school computer system to find other students' locker combinations, until their revolt took a turn toward destruction and chaos and they felt the need to affirm their individual freedom by asking their older friends to purchase guns and detonating self-made explosives. Being a high school student, Harris also directed his hostility at popular students, school athletes for their focus on good physical shape and environmental concerns, Star Wars fans for being boring, and anyone else "with [their] set standards and shit" (2014, 2–3).

ACUTE SENSE OF CONSCIOUSNESS AND FEAR OF REJECTION

When meeting with his former schoolmates, the Underground Man, too, was visibly resentful about the accomplished and wealthy lifestyle that one of them, Zverkov, enjoyed since their younger years: his popularity in school and success in studies (that the Underground Man chalks up to his "influential connections" and an unexpectedly inherited estate of two hundred serfs), "his barrack-room successes as a lieutenant," "the wild life he was leading," and "his advances in the service" (Dostoevsky [1864] 1992, 72–73). The Underground Man is sensitive to status. As a person of acute consciousness, he despises the social success that Zverkov, whom he views as intellectually limited, gained by conforming to societal standards. The Underground Man voluntarily withdraws from active participation in society, but he is envious of the social validation that others, whom he considers mediocre, receive.

The Underground Man sees his heightened self-awareness concurrently as an illness that makes him spiteful and as proof of his own exceptionalism. His acute consciousness emerges from suffering, forces him into asking questions about the dystopian system of rational utilitarianism that requires people to abandon their individuality, and prevents him from existing harmoniously in it: "[i]n a crystal palace [suffering is] unthinkable: suffering is doubt, negation, and what kind of crystal palace would it be if doubt were possible in it?" (Dostoevsky [1864] 1992, 39). The Underground Man calls himself an anti-hero whose mission is to remind people of "living life" because others are too scared of their own will to freedom and their own desires, had their hands got untied: "I have in my own life merely carried to the extreme that which you have never ventured to carry even halfway" ([1864] 1992, 152). At the same time, the Underground Man is entirely unable to show his vulnerability in direct interaction with another person because his biggest fear is to be challenged or, even worse, ridiculed, which is why he writes a manifesto as a declaration of his own extraordinary condition: "it will somehow be more solemn when put down on paper [. . .] more impressive [. . .]" ([1864] 1992, 46). In his mind, the Underground Man constructs an altered reality in which he is intellectually superior to others because in reality the Underground Man is a social outcast and an emotional cripple who desperately tries to belong.

All four shooters wrote a sort of manifesto with both explicit and implicit references to their heightened consciousness that made them different from their conformist peers. Cho mentioned his tortured consciousness, while the rich "have never felt a single ounce of pain in [their] hedonistic lives" (2014, 2). Harris wrote that only he and Klebold had self-awareness and fully comprehended their own position in the world and everyone else's function in keeping the mechanism moving. In their eyes, this philosophy of the world and themselves got them rejected by society (Harris 2014, 1, 3). Klebold explained his depression and suffering by his hyper-awareness ("overdeveloped me") and everyone else's ignorance. In his worldview, his power and his unhappiness both originated in his excessive thinking: "[m]y realm of thought—Time, Space, & THOUGHT. Thought is the most powerful thing that exists—anything conceivable can be produced, anything & everything is possible, even in your physical world" but "[a]wareness signs the warrant for suffering" (Klebold 2014, 4, 7). A "crystal palace" metaphysical dilemma in which conformism is rewarded and doubts are punished also bothered Holmes. In his notes, he traced the mythological history of those who were expelled from society for daring to seek more knowledge about the world: Adam and Eve banned from the Garden of Eden, Prometheus sent for eternal torture by the Greek gods, and Goethe's Faust condemned for selling his soul to the devil (Holmes 2015, 15).

In their critique of modern civilization, in which people are encouraged to set shallow goals and lead overly regulated lives, Harris and Holmes also echoed "the Unabomber" Ted Kaczynski's anarchic primitivism. Kaczynski, too, fits the psychotype of an Underground Man. Kaczynski (2018) argued that industrial society had been methodically eradicating human freedom through total control as an intrinsic condition for its existence. In his journal, Harris claimed that the real goal of education was "[to tame] all the young people into good little robots and factory workers that's why we sit in desks in rows and go by bell schedules" (2014, 2–3). Fixating on the disciplining and policing role of social institutions that Kaczynski and the Underground Man criticize, Harris held similar beliefs that education in modern society "drains or filters out a little bit of human nature" (2014, 4). He also mirrored Kaczynski's drive to go back to an earlier and more natural lifestyle: "just thinking if I want ALL humans dead or maybe just the quote-unquote 'civilized developed and known-of' places on Earth, maybe leave little tribes of natives in the rain forest or something" (Harris 2014, 4).

Like the Underground Man who is skeptical of the socially assigned standards of morality, in an interview with forensic psychiatrist Dr. Reid, the Aurora shooter Holmes accepted that killing people was "legally wrong." Since laws are rules that are created and enforced by social institutions to regulate people's behavior, Holmes saw murder as a socially unacceptable but not necessarily metaphysically impossible choice. In his eyes, civilized society teaches that killing is unacceptable because it emanates from societal rational needs by infringing on individual freedom to will. Holmes accepted that he killed out of his own self-centered urge: "it was necessary to do what was in my best interest" (Reid 2018, 69).

Dostoevsky wrote *Notes from Underground* as a critique of Nikolai Chernyshevskii's theory of rational egoism, and Holmes serves as a real-life rebuttal to the concept developed by the Russian populist. The theory of rational egoism states that rational needs also always satisfy a person's self-interest, but the Underground Man is irrational: he acts purely out of his inner need, even when it brings him and others great discomfort. He confesses that the ability to act according to one's own will might be a good enough rationale even for deliberate madness (Dostoevsky [1864] 1992, 35). When arrested, Holmes had newly dyed bright red hair, a detached demeanor, and appeared mentally ill. In combination with the false rumors that emerged of him referring to himself as the Joker, he chose to enter a plea of not guilty by reason of insanity as his defense strategy in court.

Even in the most structured, perfect, and stable society, the crystal palace, Dostoevsky argues, where "[a]ll human actions will [. . .] be classified [. . .] mathematically, like a logarithm table," someone will inevitably emerge with a proposition to "smash all this good sense to smithereens with one hard kick, to the sole end of sending all these logarithms to the devil and living a while again according to our own stupid will!" ([1864] 1992, 27–28). And, Dostoevsky continues, a person like this will surely have followers. Cho called Harris and Klebold martyrs in his manifesto; Harris and Klebold were inspired by Timothy McVeigh, who was responsible for the 1995 Oklahoma City bombing and wanted to outdo him. Holmes mentioned that he previously read Ted Kaczynski's work.

MESSIANISM AND INTELLECTUALIZATION OF HUMAN EXPERIENCE AS SYMPTOM OF COGNITIVE RIGIDITY

According to Dostoevsky, underground men are paradoxically divided: one part of them is drawn to nihilism (rejection of all norms and values), and the other strives for apocalypticism (suffering and self-annihilation). For Dostoevsky, there are essentially only two ways in which the unresolved inner will to freedom and the acute consciousness of underground men can be actualized: through Godmanhood and Mangodhood. The only acceptable way of soul salvation for Dostoevsky is via Godmanhood, by accepting Jesus Christ because, in Jesus Christ, man and God are united in harmony. In Mangodhood, man realizes that he is free, free of any laws and morals, free of any power, including divine power, to become God himself. If there is no God, he is God. If there is no God, no higher truth, and no higher laws, then everything is permissible, absolutely everything. For Dostoevsky, this is a path of destruction and false messianism. It either leads to murder, like with Raskolnikov, or to suicide, like with Stavrogin and Kirillov. Alexei Kirillov is Stavrogin's pawn in his Mangodhood games of power and manipulation in Dostoevsky's *Demons*. Inflicted with nihilism and moral relativism from Stavrogin, Kirillov kills himself in the ultimate act of overcoming the fear of God in death and, therefore, his own humanity: "God is the pain of the fear of death. He who overcomes pain and fear will himself become God" (Dostoevsky [1872] 1995, 115).

Messianic urges often accompany underground men in their spiral of becoming a Mangod, but all of them see their mission differently, ranging from heroic fantasies to theories of transhumanism. The Underground Man dreams about calling for a duel or slapping his former schoolmate to prove his worth and saving the prostitute Liza by helping her develop heightened consciousness (Dostoevsky [1864] 1992, 130). Raskolnikov develops an elaborate theory about ordinary and extraordinary people, according to which extraordinary people are "benefactors and founders of mankind" and "master[s] of the future" who pursue goals of the higher order and therefore, can give themselves the right "to step even over a dead body, over blood" in order to say "a new word in their environment" (Dostoevsky [1866] 1993, 260–261). The rest, "master[s] of the present," serve as reproductive material that can be disposed of to help an extraordinary person reach their messianic goal. Raskolnikov assigns values to people: men v. lice. While confessing his murder of the pawnbroker to the prostitute Sonya Marmeladova, whom he views as his fellow moral transgressor at the bottom of the social ladder, he asks her to validate his idea by calling the pawnbroker a louse and placing a higher value on the life of Katerina Ivanovna, who is stricken by humiliating poverty, than on the well-off lawyer Luzhin who flaunts his money and social status to demonstrate his superiority.

The messianism and resentment toward the powerful and mighty of the world that distinguish most of Dostoevsky's protagonists also characterize today's mass shooters. According to the psychologist Dr. Peter Langman (2009), Cho saw himself as the revolutionary leader of the underprivileged and humiliated. In his manifesto, he compared himself to Moses who would "spread the sea and lead [his] people" and die like Jesus Christ "to inspire generations of the weak and the defenseless people" (Cho 2014, 1). Cho imitated the anger of God from the Old Testament who had had enough and was prepared to punish "Descendants of Satan Disguised as Devout Christians" for their downfall and betrayal (2014, 1). Harris spewed out indignant rhetoric that was similar to Cho's rant about "all high and mighty . . . [who] can just come up and tell [him] what to do" (1998, 7).

Similarly, cognitively distorted beliefs about themselves and the world around them drew the shooters to ideas of overcoming. "I am the law, if you don't like it, you die," Harris wrote in the section "Philosophy" on his web page (2014, 13). Harris and Klebold wanted to possess the godly powers of life and death and saw their shooting spree as Judgment Day when the weak die while the strong survive: "I want to grab some weak little freshman and just tear them apart like a wolf, show them who is god" (Harris 2014, 9). On the day of the shooting, Harris wore a white T-shirt that had "Natural selection" printed on his chest. Harris often expressed thoughts of his own moral superiority similar to Raskolnikov's, albeit in a juvenile, immature form: "I feel like God and I wish I was, having everyone being OFFICIALLY lower than me. I already know that I am higher than most anyone in the fucking welt [German: world] in terms of universal Intelligence" (2014, 2).

Self-righteous, intellectually misguided, but rational in his irrationality, Holmes had an elaborate theory of human capital, similar to that of Raskolnikov. As Dr. Reid (2018) points out, he held on to it even after his arrest and after being on antipsychotic medications for some time. Raskolnikov, too, believes in the validity of his theory almost until the last pages of *Crime and Punishment*. In the interview with Reid, Holmes confessed that he would kill again if given an opportunity. He devoted several pages of his notebook to the drawings of stick-figures for visual demonstration of human capital transactions, in which he operated with the assigned values of zero, one, infinity, and minus infinity because "[a] ll men are uncreated equal" (Holmes 2015, 5). Holmes also explained his theory to his ex-girlfriend Gargi Datta via text messages. Unlike Sonya, one of Dostoevsky's saintly sinners, who immediately recognized Raskolnikov's unhappiness and the depths of his downfall and responded with empathy and mercy, Datta tried to engage in an intellectual debate with Holmes (futile business with underground men!) that led nowhere. In Holmes' cognitively distorted reality, an individual could increase their own human capital by taking another person's life/value: each life was worth one point, and as soon as a person died, their value equaled zero. In his gamified version of human experience, he mocked modern society, which also assigns points, albeit less bloody ones, for completing educational, social, and professional milestones.

Holmes created his own symbol of Mangodhood that he called "Ultraception" (figure 10.1). Holmes drew it in his bedroom calendar under July 19 and repeatedly in his journal. The symbol consisted of a circle (or zero) around an infinity symbol (lemniscate) and a big number one going through the middle, signifying the self-contained and self-perpetuating conflict between good and evil that can be resolved only through death. In his journal, above the symbol, Holmes wrote that he could not sacrifice his soul to "rehabilitate the broken mind," and therefore, "[t]here [was] one more battle to fight with life. To face death, embrace the longstanding hatred of mankind and overcome all fear in certain death" (2015, 14). He mirrored Kirillov's desire to transcend his humanity and relieve his acute consciousness through overcoming the fear of death, but for Holmes, the transgression had to be done through homicide, by gaining human capital and thus, transcending into God.

Klebold's path to Mangodhood also lay through overcoming his human flaw—fear of death and uncertainty: "About 26.5 hours from now

Figure 10.1 James Holmes' Symbol Called "Ultraception." *Source*: Holmes 2015, 3.

the judgment will begin . . . It's interesting, when I'm in my human form, knowing I'm going to die. Everything has a touch of triviality to it" (2014, 14). Klebold was deeply depressed and felt happiness only when he was close to the resolution, his suicide. Unlike Harris and Holmes, Klebold was seeking suicide as his ultimate transgression more than homicide. Langman (2009) claims that according to multiple witnesses, Klebold showed mercy several times during the spree, letting people whom he liked live, while Harris did not show pity for anyone. In the crime tandem of Harris & Klebold, Harris was an enraged, pleasure-seeking nihilist and Klebold a depressed, self-destructive maniac. In his journal, Harris was writing a "shitlist" of people to kill, while Klebold in his was drawing hearts visualizing loneliness and unrequited love. They were both teenagers who were narcissistic, self-righteous, and filled with self-hatred, but their death drives were different in their essence. Klebold's drawing resembling the Cross of Salem (pontifical cross carried before the pope) reflected his thoughts about Mangodhood symbolizing authority and significance (figure 10.2), but his drawing of Kolovrat (neopagan, neo-Nazi Slavic religious symbol) that typically refers to an endless cycle of life and death symbolized the force of destiny. Despite his claims for Mangodhood, Klebold also remained fatalistic. (See figure 10.3.)

While discussing his theory of transhumanism with Dr. Reid, Holmes claimed that even his potential death sentence executioner could get a point for his life, provided he believed in this theory (Reid 2018, 203). Indeed, intentionality, another symptom of messianism, was equally important for Harris and Holmes. For Holmes, the killing had to be intentional to ensure human capital transfer (Reid 2018, 89). Harris expressed anger toward those whose bravery was accidental. Both Harris and Holmes proudly called themselves men of action (Harris 2014, 1; Reid 2018, 97). "Like James Bond," Holmes clarified in his interview after the arrest (Reid 2018, 97). The Underground Man, however, believes that men of

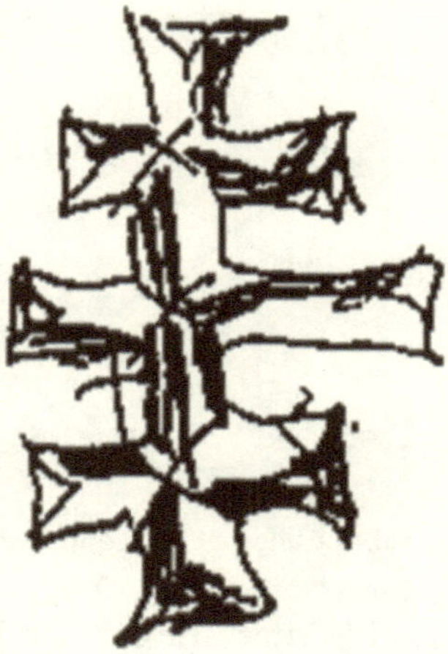

Figure 10.2 Dylan Klebold's Drawing Resembling the Cross of Salem. *Source*: Columbine Record 1998, 495.

Figure 10.3 Dylan Klebold's Drawing Resembling Kolovrat. *Source*: Columbine Records 1998, 497.

acute consciousness are always idle because they remain doubtful of their own importance in the world, while men of action act because they have no doubts about their righteousness. The Underground Man is aware of his own danger to society. He recommends keeping underground men "well reined in" because "a man like [himself] may be capable of sitting in his hole for forty years without a word, but once he comes outside and breaks out into speech, he'll talk and talk and talk" (Dostoevsky [1864] 1992, 42). As soon as Raskolnikov exits his underground, he kills. So did Harris, Klebold, Cho, and Holmes. Readers leave the Underground Man at a turning point. Dostoevsky finishes *Notes from Underground* with the Underground Man's rant about "generalhumans," who forgot the taste of living life, and his decision to stop writing "from Underground" ([1864] 1992, 153). Dostoevsky as the narrator adds the last word that despite his resolution, the Underground Man "went on writing" ([1864] 1992, 153). Perhaps, he kept writing with blood.

ENHANCED SENSITIVITY TO MORALLY AMBIGUOUS BEHAVIOR AS A PSYCHOPATHIC TRAIT

Underground men are bored most of the time, which is why their minds are activated by ethically positive and negative actions equally. Raskolnikov in *Crime and Punishment* takes care of his dying friend and the friend's dying father, saves a drunk girl in the street from being raped by a stranger, and helps Sonya's family with Marmeladov's funeral by giving away the last money he had, all while developing a theory to justify the murders he was about to commit (Dostoevsky [1866] 1993, 537, 46–50, 185–186). Underground men often express their will to freedom through emotional manipulation because it brings immediate gratification. The Underground Man's desire "to wield unlimited power over his [friend's] soul" overpowers even his need for friendship: as soon as his authority is validated, he starts resenting his friend for his weakness (Dostoevsky [1864] 1992, 80).

The Underground Man enjoys the aesthetics of his own loathsomeness and considers this ability a refined intellectual trait developed by his acute consciousness. Moreover, he possesses such a heightened sensitivity to cognitive stimuli—both positive and negative in nature—that he finds pleasure in doing intentionally despicable acts as well as in savoring his own humiliation afterward:

> I would feel a certain hidden, morbid, nasty little pleasure in the acute awareness that I had once again committed something vile that day [. . .] and I would gnaw and gnaw at myself in silence, tearing and nagging at myself until the bitterness would finally begin to turn into a kind of shameful, damnable sweetness and, in the end—into a definite, positive pleasure! (Dostoevsky [1864] 1992, 7)

Underground men exhibit several traits that Ramplin and Ayob (2017) distinguish in psychopathy, such as proneness to boredom and need for stimulation, impulsivity, controlling and manipulative behavior, lack of empathy, and impaired moral responsibility. Because of his paranoid, narcissistic, and antisocial personality traits, Langman (2009) classified Harris as a psychopathic shooter. Harris believed that "everything that happens in our world is just that, a HAPPENING. Anything else is relative to the observer, but yet we try to have a 'universal law' or 'code' of what is good and bad" (2014, 6). Harris also mentioned that he thought about becoming a marine "to do good" (2014, 10).

Holmes, too, claimed that he did not believe in absolute good and absolute evil. During a text conversation with his ex-girlfriend in which he explained his theory and expressed his desire to kill people, Holmes also wrote: "I am not inherently evil, Gargi, my outlook on destroying life is plan B. I also found a purpose for 'good'" (Reid 2018, 59–60). Holmes enrolled in the doctoral program in neuroscience to find a scientific explanation for the violent thoughts that his brain had been producing since he was a child. Holmes, like the Underground Man, also searched for the reasons for his inner conflict and unhappiness: the eight pages in his notebook, right between his philosophical wandering and the actual planning of the rampage, contain one question: "Why?" written dozens of times.

ALTERNATIVE COGNITIVE REALITIES AND LACK OF COGNITIVE REAPPRAISAL

The delusions of his characters are exactly what Dostoevsky brought to light. Bakhtin (1984) pointed out the polyphony of voices and consciousnesses that distinguish Dostoevsky's prose. Dostoevsky narrated stories of underground men in their own voices as these stories played out through their own eyes: not "the hero's reality but the hero's self-consciousness, as a reality of the second order" (Bakhtin 1984, 49). In the realities of Dostoevsky's characters and modern underground men, it is always the hero versus the rest of the world. The hero is misunderstood, bullied, humiliated. He craves revenge for his misery and affirmation of his extraordinariness. The myopic reality that they themselves create serves as the fertile ground for the violence that brews inside of them. The life story of any underground man is a story of humiliation:

> It was sheer torture, a continuous intolerable sense of humiliation at the idea, which turned into a constant and direct feeling, that I was nothing but a fly before all that fine society, a revolting, obscene fly—more intelligent, more cultivated, nobler than anyone else, that went without saying, but a fly nonetheless, forever yielding the way to everyone, humiliated and insulted by everyone. (Dostoevsky [1864] 1992, 61)

The Underground Man's brain is locked in a cognitive loop of negative thoughts, unable to reframe its reality in a constructive manner. Similarly, the mass shooters' manifestos and personal journals reveal alternative, skewed versions of reality that are often not supported by the facts of their biographies or witnesses' testimonies, but grounded in their own metaphysical philosophies and self-perceptions.

Holmes had a similar episode of misinterpreting reality with his psychiatrist Dr. Fenton when she accidentally misspelled his name on the prescription. The mistake was fixed, but Holmes got very upset. He expressed his disappointment in a short email: "An inconvenience Fenton. Holmes." with the subject line "<(o.X)>Q(o.O)Q." When she asked him what this meant, he explained that the Qs were "his fists punching her in the eye." However, in a post-massacre interview with Dr. Reid, he said that the Qs symbolized her punching *him* in the eye (Reid 2018, 66–67). Just like the Underground Man, the primary offense that Dr. Fenton committed, as it played out in Holmes's mind, was to hint at his insignificance by misspelling his name. And in his myopic reality, this was, of course, intentional. In his interviews, Holmes demonstrated paranoia on multiple occasions. For example, he claimed that during his last appointment with the psychiatrists, Dr. Feinstein wore a fake sling on his injured arm to evaluate the level of his empathy, and a knife was hidden in the sling (Reid 2018, 82).

The media often tells stories of continuous bullying in the lives of mass shooters. Although bullying indeed took place in some of those cases, bullying was not the nudge that sent Harris, Klebold, Cho, and Holmes over the edge. Langman (2009) claims that he found only one incident when Harris was physically bullied by being pushed into lockers, but Harris constantly talked about people mistreating him. In his videos, Cho also repeatedly complains about being insulted or hurt by others (McAskill 2007), but according to witnesses' accounts, when other students tried to befriend him, he was unresponsive to their attempts. Klebold was uncomfortably shy and quiet, but he was not disliked by his peers, and Harris was fairly charismatic. However, Harris and Klebold were provocateurs. They gave Nazi salutes and yelled "Hail Hitler!," talked about killing black people and Jews, vandalized other students' homes, built explosives, and acted confrontationally, which caused a negative reaction from their peers. Harris often punched walls in anger and picked fights. Klebold cursed at teachers, threw things across the classroom, and slammed the door as he stormed out (Langman 2009, 13–14). Nevertheless, in his journal, Klebold complained:

> no girls (friends or girlfriends), no other friends except a few, nobody accepting me even though I want to be accepted, me doing badly & being intimidated in any & all sports, me looking weird & acting shy—BIG problem, me getting bad grades, having no ambition of life, that's the big shit. (2014, 3)

NEED FOR HUMAN CONNECTION AND SELF-SABOTAGE OF POTENTIAL EMOTIONAL INTIMACY

Underground men resent their peers and feel aversion toward all of mankind while at the same time craving everyone's approval and respect: "now I despised people, now set them above myself," the Underground Man confesses (Dostoevsky [1864] 1992, 51). Underground men desperately want to be accepted but cannot sustain any of their relationships because, as Dostoevsky argues, they lack a strong moral and spiritual foundation to conquer their own pride. Dostoevsky sees the rootlessness of his underground characters as the cause of their moral ambiguity and urges to sabotage any potential intimate connection to others. The Underground Man reveals to Liza that he lost his family as a young boy and was placed in a boarding school by his distant relatives. He connects his lack of empathy with a lack of love as a child. Both Raskolnikov and Stavrogin grow up without a father. They constantly search for "safe" companions (the prostitutes Liza and Sonya, the mentally and physically disabled Maria) who cannot leave them or, even worse, laugh at their darkness.

For underground men, sudden feelings of anger or disappointment toward any developing human connections emerge as their visceral reaction to the fear of being ridiculed. The Underground Man pushes away the prostitute Liza who sees in him, like Sonya in Raskolnikov, his potential for goodness, feels his pain from alienation, and therefore discerns his vulnerability, which is the Underground Man's biggest fear. Throughout his life, the Underground Man has terrifying memories of being laughed at for his physical appearance as a child and frightening fantasies of others laughing at him as an adult, "roaring with laughter [. . .] as loudly as their healthy throats permit" (Dostoevsky [1864] 1992, 11). "I was [. . .] morbidly afraid of looking ridiculous," he confesses (Dostoevsky [1864] 1992, 51). His schoolmates' drunken giggles set him off during dinner. The mere thought of Liza, a prostitute, laughing at him for his need for human connection turns him aggressive toward her.

When Stavrogin presents his confession to the priest Tikhon and intends to distribute it publicly, he does not look for repentance. Instead, he wants others to be amazed or terrified at his ability to transgress conventional morality in the most loathsome crime. Stavrogin is terrified of being pitied and ridiculed for his confession, which is why he becomes agitated when Tikhon sees his crime as ordinary and "uncomely" (Dostoevsky 1995, 710). The reason why underground men are so afraid of being ridiculed is because they are filled with self-hatred. They cannot tolerate their own vulnerability and, as a result, disrupt any potential intimacy.

Just like the Underground Man, who continues to seek social validation by imposing himself on his former schoolmates while despising them, all four shooters longed for social acceptance regardless of their aversion to others. "Oh the happiness I could have had mingling among you hedonists, being counted as one of you, only if you didn't fuck the living shit out of me," wrote Cho in his manifesto (2014, 1). Klebold was terrified of abandonment and was afraid he would lose even Harris when they graduated from high school. In the interviews, Holmes used the metaphor of "nuclear winter" to describe suppressing the feelings of anger out of fear of hurting other people or driving them away (Reid 2018, 23–24).

Rootlessness was at the heart of the shooters' alienation. Cho was an immigrant from South Korea who was conflicted about the traditional values that his parents preached and his own Americanized views. Harris blamed his father, who was an Air Force pilot, for uprooting the family and moving it around from Kansas to Ohio to Michigan to New York and finally to Colorado. In the Basement Tapes, he said that every time he was forced to start from the very bottom of the social ladder. Holmes was also traumatized by moving around California with his family. In the interview with Dr. Reid, he recalls the first time he tried to cut himself with a piece of cardboard was when the van was driving away from their former home (2018, 15). In his notebook, Holmes called it "parasuicide" (2015, 30).

Like Dostoevsky's underground men, both Cho and Holmes reportedly saw prostitutes before their shooting sprees. The story of one of them, Monica Hall, was quite similar to the story of two meetings that the Underground Man had with the prostitute Liza: frightened by his own vulnerability and agitated by a spark of fear and self-hatred, he started acting aggressively with her. Hall revealed that Holmes behaved "like Jekyll and Hyde" during their two meetings: the first time he was "sweet and friendly," whereas the second time he was aggressive and violent (Daily Mail 2012).

Since underground men view their violence as an aesthetic expression, the mass shooters were not afraid to be perceived as ugly, loathsome, or repulsive. More than anything, they were terrified of being viewed as mediocre, tasteless, and laughable. Therefore, they did everything to demonstrate their intelligence, hyper-awareness, and monstrosity in their manifestos and photographs, featuring an excessive number of guns and body armor to be commemorated by the media for posterity because, heaven forbid, anyone would see them as a brainless and farcical cliché of the Godman. "I HATE PEOPLE and they better fucking fear me if they know what's good for 'em," Harris hid his insecurity behind his rage (2014, 8). Holmes shot seventy people during his rampage, but there is only one of his victims he remembered—a man in the front row of the movie theater who appeared to be smiling: "When I was gonna leave, going towards the exit, I just looked back and saw that he was smiling." It was odd, he thought. Was it really a smile? A grimace? Was he wounded? Frozen in his seat? Relieved that the auditorium was suddenly quieter? Holmes didn't think about shooting him because "it would have been really personal to shoot a person who's smiling at me" (Reid 2018, 123–124).

The shooters' fear of ridicule came from their self-hatred, which manifested through negative inner dialog, self-harm, and anxiety. Cho wrote a poem called "Spear me down, Heaven" in which he revealed a "wish to annihilate [him]self" (Gangloff and Adams 2007). As Langman

(2009) describes Cho, he was a quiet loner with "poverty of speech" who listened but avoided talking. He was diagnosed with anxiety, selective mutism, and major depressive disorders. Klebold cut himself to find emotional relief. Harris revealed that his anger came from low self-esteem: "I have always hated how I looked, I make fun of people who look like me, sometimes without even thinking sometimes just because I want to rip on myself. That's where a lot of my hate grows from" (2014, 8). Harris had a chest deformity known as pectus excavatum, which made him self-conscious when changing for his gym class because some students laughed at him. In his journal, Holmes wrote an entire list of body parts he hated about himself as a possible explanation for his "broken mind," including his teeth, nose, ears, and penis. After breaking up his "friendship with benefits" with Gargi, Holmes felt even more depressed and hopeless. He told Dr. Reid (2018) that only his "mission" brought him hope. His mission was to kill as many people as possible, which he believed would allow him to recover from depression and prevent him from committing suicide (Reid 2018, 68–69).

HOW RIGID IS THE COGNITIVE RIGIDITY OF MASS SHOOTERS?

In order to find a satisfactory explanation for mass shootings, society often tries to find a single defining factor that propelled a person to cross the line from metaphysical rebellion to actual violence, whether it was bullying, or ostracization, or family dysfunction, or psychological issues, or the availability of guns. However, regardless of psychological predisposition or sociocultural context, every single underground man is left with the ultimate decision to determine his own path. Bakhtin writes: "Dostoevsky always represents a person on the threshold of a final decision, at a moment of crisis, at an unfinalizable—and unpredeterminable—turning point for his soul" (1984, 61). No life is predetermined and finalized throughout its duration. Human nature is unpredictable and, therefore, tragic. It is the existential uncertainty that truly tests individual will to freedom through inner dialog with the world and oneself. Mass shooters as underground men face the challenge of navigating the cognitive rigidity of their consciousness but fail to successfully adapt to the conflicting demands of individual freedom, morality, and personal responsibility that modern society issues to them.

If every mass shooter was "unfinalizable" and "unpredeterminable" until the very second when they walked into a school building or a movie theater and pulled the trigger, was there a chance to sway them toward a different choice? In other words, how rigid was their cognitive rigidity?

Holmes admitted that he first hoped that his psychiatrists knew about his urges without him explicitly telling them and that they would stop him. Later, he had a fantasy of the FBI stopping him right before the rampage. As Holmes stepped out of his car outside the theater on the day of the shooting, he said he called the number of a mental health hotline at the university he previously saved on his phone "to see if [he] should turn back." It was one last chance to "stop the mission" and back out. But there was silence on the other end, and the call ended after nine seconds: "There was still a chance it wouldn't [happen] when I was in my car. [Up to that moment], I was still skeptical." After the call ended, he knew he was "really gonna do this" (Reid 2018, 115–116).

Holmes' story demonstrates that there was potential for his cognitive reappraisal until the moment when the final decision to proceed with the rampage was made. Throughout their lives, despite continuous self-sabotage, underground men of the twenty-first century seek empathy and human connections. Their failure often comes from their inability to accept even the possibility of their own ordinariness: "either a hero, or mud; there was no middle" (Dostoevsky 1998, 66). Their violent outbursts, which leave trails of blood and suffering behind in an attempt to say "a new word in their environment," do not shake even one brick in the foundation of modern society. As Bakhtin (1984) notes, Dostoevsky does not finalize the identity of his characters and does not provide the answer to the question "Who is he?" but he reveals the characters' answers to the questions "Who am I?" and "Who are you?" For Dostoevsky, only human connection takes underground men from their metaphysical underground, and only inner dialog opens up the possibility of finding a suitable resolution to the dialectic existence of different intellectual and moral urges in a person's psyche. Likewise, in modern society, the drive to empathy and human connection remains the only satisfying alternate value system for underground men that can help reframe their existential angst by providing adequate answers to questions regarding the meaning and purpose of life and deter them from violence against others and themselves.

BIBLIOGRAPHY

Bakhtin, Mikhail. 1984. *Problems of Dostoevsky's Poetics*. Edited and translated by Caryl Emerson. Minneapolis: University of Minnesota Press.

Cho, Seung Hui. 2014. "Manifesto." *SchoolShooters.info*. Accessed January 6, 2024. https://schoolshooters.info/sites/default/files/cho_manifesto_1.1.pdf.

"Dark Knight Killer Became Obsessed with One Prostitute's Red Hair and Freaked Out Before Sex on Another Just One Week Before Massacre." 2012.

Daily Mail, July 30, 2012. Accessed May 23, 2024. https://www.dailymail.co.uk/news/article-2181025/James-Holmes-Denver-Dark-Knight-killer-paid-prostitute-sex-just-week-massacre.html.

Dostoevsky, Fyodor. [1864] 1992. *Notes from Underground*. Translated by Andrew R. MacAndrew. New York: Bantam.

Dostoevsky, Fyodor. [1866] 1993. *Crime and Punishment: A Novel in Six Parts with Epilogue*. Translated by Richard Pevear and Larissa Volokhonsky. New York: Vintage Books.

Dostoyevsky, Fyodor. [1872] 1995. *Demons: A Novel in Three Parts*. Translated by Richard Pevear and Larissa Volokhonsky. New York: Vintage Books.

Gangloff, Mike and Duncan Adams. 2007. "Cho Poem Was Entry in 2006 Virginia Tech Event." *The Roanoke Times*, August 29, 2007. https://roanoke.com/archive/cho-poem-was-entry-in-2006-virginia-tech-event/article_b864ad17-c4eb-550e-aa1b-c9939385a284.html.

Goulston, Mark. 2015. "Inside the Mind of a School Shooter: A Case of Triunal Rigidity." *Psychology Today*, October 20, 2015. https://www.psychologytoday.com/us/blog/just-listen/201510/inside-the-mind-school-shooter

Gross, James J. 1998. "The Emerging Field of Emotion Regulation: An Integrative Review." *Review of General Psychology*, 2 (3): 271–299.

Harris, Eric. 2014. "Journal." *Schoolshooters.info*. Accessed January 7, 2024. https://schoolshooters.info/sites/default/files/harris_journal_1.3.pdf.

Holmes, James. 2015. "Notebook." Annotated by Dr. Jeffrey Lieberman. *The Marshall Project*. Accessed January 7, 2024. https://www.themarshallproject.org/documents/2091448-james-holmes-notebook-annotated-by-dr-jeffrey.

Jefferson County Sheriff's Office. *Columbine High School Shootings Investigations Records*. Released May 15, 2000 and modified April 3, 2019. https://www.jeffco.us/3832/Columbine-Records.

Kaczynski, Theodore John. 2018. *Industrial Society and Its Future*. Westminster, CO: Pub House Books.

Klebold, Dylan. 2014. Journal and Other Writings. *Schoolshooters.info*. Accessed January 7, 2024. https://schoolshooters.info/sites/default/files/klebold_journal_1.2.pdf.

Langman Peter F. 2009. *Why Kids Kill: Inside the Minds of School Shooter*s. New York: Palgrave Macmillan.

Link, Bruce G. and Ann Stueve. 1994. "Psychotic Symptoms and the Violent/Illegal Behavior of Mental Patients Compared to Community Controls." In *Violence and Mental Disorder: Developments in Risk Assessment*, edited by John Monahan and Henry J. Steadman, 137–159. Chicago: The University of Chicago Press.

MacAskill, Ewen. 2007. "Virginia Tech Killer Sent Statement and Tape to TV Network." *The Guardian*, April 19, 2007. https://www.theguardian.com/media/2007/apr/19/broadcasting.usnews.

Ramplin, Steve and Gloria Ayob. 2017. "Moral Responsibility in Psychopathy: A Clinicophilosophical Case Discussion." *BJPsych Advances* 23 (3): 187–195.

Reid, William H. 2018. *A Dark Night in Aurora: Inside James Holmes and the Colorado Mass Shootings*. New York: Skyhorse Publishing.

11

Russian Cognitive Approaches for Studying Genres of Contemporary Electronic Communication

Interpreting "Sincere Conversations" in New Media

Anna Novikova and Julia Lerner

The study of new genres of communication mediated by different media technologies requires researchers to develop new methodological approaches. First and foremost, this concerns the conceptualization of the interactive possibilities of new media, which are transforming even familiar genres of communication. The Russian-language academic discourse on this topic focuses mainly on applied issues of media enterprise efficiency and new approaches to journalistic practice.

In this chapter, we offer a perspective on the interactive potential of new media, focusing on how it develops the speech genre of sincere conversation (also called "heart-to-heart talk"). In order to analyze and heuristically evaluate sincere conversations on YouTube, we will draw on the concepts developed by Yurii Lotman, who argued that in certain periods, culture is constructed through the monologue model as the main form of communication, while in other periods, the dialogue model comes to the fore (2022, 16). We will also use Erving Goffman's approach to analyzing interaction, in particular his understanding of frames and forms of talk as significant frameworks for understanding society, power relations, perception of hierarchy, and patterns of emotional culture.

What is significant for us is that in new media, the traditional form of dialogue is augmented by the real-time participation of virtual audiences. Interactivity complicates the communicative model of this genre, while at the same time enhancing the element of spectacle and increasing the degree of authenticity. This is achieved through the use of various media influence tools. The most obvious of these are related to technology: the ability to ask questions of the guest during the broadcast, to comment at any time, and to circulate a link to the broadcast or recording on social networks, adding one's own interpretation of what one has heard.

But we want to focus on more traditional tools of interactivity, particularly metaphors, both verbal and visual. On the one hand, they have been quite well studied as tools of cognitive communication, both in art history as well as in cognitive linguistics and psychology (for example, researchers who use the concept of "interpretive repertoire" (Potter and Weatherall 1987) to study different communities). On the other hand, the influence of the interactivity of new media on the impact of metaphor in communication is rarely considered. In this chapter, we reflect on how metaphors become markers of a common language in digital interactive space and form virtual communities. We also raise the issue of how a metaphorical visual image fits into a sincere conversation, which commonly relies on verbal metaphors, turning it into a polylogue.

At the same time, we try to follow the approach to textual analysis proposed by Lotman in his later works and reconstructed by one of his students, Suren Zolyan (2022, 117): an approach that describes not only the text itself but also the processes of text formation, interpretation, and communication around the text. The multi-level approach proposed by Lotman will allow us to better understand how the "social imagination" of Russians is formed. We understand social imagination, according to Charles Taylor, as the ways in which "people imagine their social existence, how they interact with each other, how relationships between people are formed, how expectations that are usually fulfilled arise, as well as the deeper normative perceptions and images that underlie these expectations" (2004, 23).

Through the observation of text formation, we focus on the genre of sincere conversation itself in its various mediatized modalities, particularly the YouTube talk show format. In the *interpretation* phase, we consider the key metaphors used by the interlocutors not only as vessels of emotion but also as the core of narratives through which people seek to find confirmation of the validity of their life choices.

In analyzing the communicative potential of these shows, we consider metaphors as cognitive nodes of meaning that assist a moral interpretation of crisis situations and turn participation in public sincere conversations into a form of political action. This multi-level approach allows us to see metaphors as a means of interaction, and the density of metaphors in the conversations as an invitation to viewers to interact not only in interpersonal empathy but also in community building. This becomes possible because, in the interactive space of digital media, metaphors serve as markers of a common language, allowing viewers to engage in interaction through interpretation, commentary, and replication of quotations and ideas. At the same time, the very understanding of metaphors in similar ways and their common use in narratives delineates the boundaries of communities.

THEORETICAL APPROACHES TO THE STUDY OF METAPHORS

Since the core of our study is the analysis of metaphor, it is necessary to briefly describe the theoretical approaches to metaphor research on which we draw. First of all, there is cognitive rhetoric, which considers metaphor as one of the main mental operations that facilitate cognition of the world. This approach is associated with the names of George Lakoff and Mark Johnson, founders of the theory of conceptual metaphor (1980), and Mark Turner, founder of cognitive rhetoric in literary studies, and author (with Gilles Fauconnier) of the theory of conceptual integration (1998). Despite the fact that these approaches were developed on the basis of literary analysis, the researchers found (Turner 1991, 22) that they could serve as a basis for a variety of possible theories.

In our analysis, we will concentrate on a cognitive approach that does not focus on a rigid division of metaphors according to formal features but analyses their semantic similarity. In the opinion of Nina Arutyunova, a metaphor in the broad sense is "any way of indirect expression of thought" (1990, 296–297). This approach considers not only comparisons but also hyperboles, periphrases, phraseological phrases, and so on. as metaphors. It also allows us to speak of visual metaphors, which are very different in terms of both the mechanisms of metaphorization and interpretation. Researchers of film language, such as Sergei Eisenstein (2000, 80–86), Yurii Lotman, and Yurii Tsivian (1994), have devoted much thought to this problem. They are often referred to in Russia in the study of video media but are not associated with the research of media linguists. For the study of video and multimodal media, it seems important to us to combine these approaches.

There is also no generally accepted explanation for the question of which visual images can be regarded as metaphors, especially since visual metaphors have been less studied than linguistic metaphors. In our analysis, we rely on the definition of Noël Carroll (1996), who considers a visual image to be metaphorical when there is a fusion of two different realms of experience. This definition is convenient because it allows us to focus on editing as a tool for metaphorizing the screen spectacle, which includes YouTube shows.

Sergei Eisenstein considered not only representational metaphors, in which new meaning is created by the juxtaposition of two frames (a simple example from the silent era is the image of a woman in the stance of a snake, followed by a frame of an actual snake), but also metaphorical mise-en-scène, which assumes that the viewer will make generalizations for himself (a technique the director uses repeatedly in *Battleship Potemkin*). Also, in the book he was working on in 1937, Eisenstein reflected on the greater effectiveness of "metaphors of verb order" (2000, 268), i.e. those that transfer from subject to subject properties selected from the field of activity (for example, the scene on the Odessa steps in the same film uses the metaphor of "roaring stones," with stone lions seeming to grimace in a painful roar). In the mid-1990s, Lotman and Tsivian, discussing cinema as a symbolic system, spoke of the montage style of cinematic thinking (1994, 169). And even though the talk shows on YouTube only marginally inherit the traditions of cinema, it would be a mistake not to consider integrative processes in the simultaneous perception of verbal and visual metaphors when watching these on-screen spectacles, as researchers who choose genres with more diverse video sequences do (Fauconnier and Turner 2002; Fahlenbrach 2016).

By focusing on the number of metaphors in public open conversations on Russian YouTube in the first half of 2022 (i.e., the first months of the full-scale war on Ukraine), we follow researchers who have studied the frequency of metaphor use in times of crisis. For example, Christ'l de Landtsheer, who studied the use of metaphor in Dutch political discourse between 1831 and 1981, showed that the frequency of metaphor use correlates with periods of crisis (1991). The same was confirmed by studies of Russian media discourse during the August 1998 crisis, conducted under the supervision of Anatolii Baranov (2000). They also showed that the frequency of the use of metaphors increased sharply at the height of the crisis. Thanks to these studies, we can say that the increase in the use of metaphors in open conversations during this period is not a coincidence, but a natural phenomenon, the analysis of which will allow us to come closer to understanding the sociocultural processes in Russian society.

CONVERSATION SHOWS ON YOUTUBE AS A TEXTUALLY GENERATIVE GENRE

Sincere conversation is a particular form of communication that involves the public expression (through oral or written speech) of issues of private life, self-analysis, and disclosure of a person's inner emotional and intimate life. The manifestations of this type of communication/conversation can be found in various private as well as institutional contexts: diaries and autobiographies, all kinds of formal and informal statements, bureaucratic inquiries, and therapy sessions. In all of them, different implementations of the framework of "sincere conversation" can be observed.

The genre of sincere conversation, also called "heart-to-heart conversation," has been known since ancient times and is reflected in the literature of various epochs and cultures. In Russian literature, "sincere" or "frank conversation" existed in the form of oral stories and religious books. In his book about eighteenth- and nineteenth-century biographical prose, Dmitry Kalugin (2015) notes that biographical and autobiographical genres take on special significance at moments of transformation, when opposing forces compete for the right to produce conceptions of human life and its purpose. In such times, these texts become important documents that, through their language, constitute new models of the subject.

Soviet ideology used this genre to educate the new man. Dar'ia Dimke (2018, 134–164) writes how the format of sincere conversation served as an important vehicle for the pedagogical/educational model of communist society. Resistance to Soviet ideology was also developed through a type of sincere conversation—the "kitchen conversation." By the second half of the twentieth century, heart-to-heart talks or "sincere conversation" became the basis for the genre of radio and television conversations and documentaries (Sergei Muratov 1983). Sergei Muratov notes that in the late 1980s, in the wake of perestroika, television began to make extensive use of heart-to-heart conversations in the television studio to make public, through personal and family stories, many painful historical and political issues, the public discussion of which was forbidden in the USSR.

After the collapse of the USSR, one-on-one radio and television conversations on philosophical and scientific topics on Russian television were replaced by shows based on American models: with hosts, guest experts, and an audience in the studio (such as the Phil Donahue and Vladimir Pozner's show (1986–1987), *Theme* (1992–2000), *About It* (1997–2000), and *Voice of the People* (1999–2002)). From 2000–2001 with the collapse of NTV, the Russian media sphere began to return to strict state control. Many journalists moved to internet publications, which were less dependent on the authorities at this historical moment. This led to the emergence of an alternative platform in the Russian segment of the Internet, which some scholars consider marginal and insignificant, while others consider it critical and oppositional to the ruling authorities (Kiriya 2021).

The genre of sincere conversations became particularly popular in the Russian segment of YouTube in the 2010s, when several important shows appeared, with long studio interviews lasting 1.5 to 2 hours, and sometimes even longer, as their main format. One of the first and most popular was journalist Yurii Dud's YouTube channel "VDud." The main difference between these channels and their TV predecessors, as noted by Russian researchers (Podosokorsii 2018, 2020), was not necessarily their length, but the more informal nature of the conversation and the vocabulary used. Thus, the formats of open conversations on YouTube have been inherited from both TV and radio talk shows, as well as open "kitchen conversations" in their friendly or educational versions.

In the present analysis, we focus on two Russian YouTube talk shows: Katerina Gordeeva's show *Skazhi Gordeevoi* and Vyacheslav Manucharov's show *Manuchi's Empathy*. Both talk shows were created before the war with Ukraine, but their formats underwent significant changes after February 2022.

In September 2020, Katerina Gordeeva, known for her civic activism, created the YouTube channel *Skazhi Gordeevoi*. The format that Katerina Gordeeva offered to the viewers filled the American talk show format with the communicative features of the Soviet "kitchen conversations," which served the purpose of channeling dissatisfaction with the public situation into a private, emotional conversation (Ries 1997). The conversations in this program did not resemble traditional interviews between a journalist and an expert, but rather therapeutic conversations in which the journalist assumed the role of a psychologist and the guest expressed their own personal emotional experiences rather than their professional competence.

At the beginning of the war with Ukraine, the popularity of the *Skazhi Gordeevoi* show skyrocketed. We associate this with the fact that the format allowed political emotions related to opposition to the war, disagreement with the official discourse on the "Special Military Operation," personal and family experiences of a difficult past, patriotism, and the possibility of emigrating from the country to be made public. In their dialogues, the host and her guests began to present acceptable forms of verbal expression for the emotional shock suffered by a section of society, while at the same time fulfilling a therapeutic task (Lerner and Novikova 2024). As both researchers and engaged listeners to these interviews, we noticed that the frank accounts of the show's guests contained a lot of metaphor. We also found important the range of people Katerina Gordeeva invited to her show. They included not only scholars and experts who have traditionally conducted "intra-cultural dialogues" in the twentieth century (Bibler 1991). In the era of new media, which significantly changes the nature of communication processes and creates a more trusting relationship between speakers and the public, the task of conducting such dialogues often passes to a new type of public figure—"influencers." This is forcing even professional journalists (Katerina Gordeeva in particular) to adjust their choice of public personas for frank interviews, inviting many actors and singers, pop psychologists, and popular journalists.

There is also a YouTube channel with similar candid conversations but with different content—the show *Manuchi's Empathy*. This channel was launched in 2018, and by 2022, the number of subscribers had grown dramatically to over one million. In their conversations, the participants also use a lot of metaphors and tell stories from their families' lives, recalling the same crises in the country's life as Gordeeva's guests. At the same time, however, they maintain the legitimacy of the Russian government's military and political decisions and stress the sincerity of their position.

Vyacheslav Manucharov, the host of *Manuchi's Empathy*, is not a journalist, but an actor and director of variety shows. The host and his star guests (from the very beginning, the show invited mainly popular artists) are people who are used to relying not on professional expertise but on intuitively chosen images, especially metaphorical ones. From the outset, their main aim was not to analyze facts, but to present the emotions aroused in them by the events discussed (mostly in social life). In the context of the military actions, the guests of this show, just like Gordeeva's guests, began to express perceptions and images related to the war and the deterioration of international relations, but reflecting the perceptions and expectations of a different segment of Russians.

The differences between the two shows are thus primarily defined by the political views held by the guests of the show on the eve of the war, as well as those they develop immediately after the war has started. We propose that this political vision should also be seen as a cognitive and emotional disposition that provides the framework for interpreting not only the thoughts expressed, but also the metaphors that "package" the unreflected attitudes that the guests are unable or unwilling to talk about directly. Metaphors become a tool with which the direct participants in open conversations fuse personal emotions into political ones, while the audience (mediated participants), interpreting these metaphors in a certain way, recognize "their own" and identify "strangers."

These groups do not yet intersect in direct dialogue, but they conduct asynchronous dialogues with each other, hoping to communicate their positions not only to each other but also to the undecided part of Russian society and the world community.

METAPHORS BASED ON PSYCHOLOGICAL TERMS AND DISEASE METAPHORS

Among the imagery used by the cognitive theory of metaphor, one of the most typical is the relationship between "top and bottom." In this case, human well-being—happiness, health, success—is perceived as the "top," while the "bottom" is associated with grief, humiliation, illness, impurity, and death. The metaphors used in the public conversations we analyzed are well within this tradition. However, the understanding of "health" and "illness" in our case is primarily based on the terms of modern popular psychology. The therapeutic frame associated with the genre of sincere conversation has long been unfamiliar to the Russian mass audience.[1] Therefore, it was important for us to note and reflect on the fact that Gordeeva's guest interviews contain many metaphors that play with psychological terms.

In the program *Skazhi Gordeevoi*, we find such metaphors in the talk of two public psychologists—Liudmila Petranovskaia and Marina Meliia. Both of them use professional terms not only in their narrow professional sense but as generalized "diagnoses" when describing the "illnesses" of society:

> Russians perceive sanctions as a confirmation of their world view. I see strategies of attachment here [. . .] a lot of it seems vindictive-sadistic combined with paranoid. That is the strategy. I have observed it in some foster children with very difficult biographies. (Petranovskaia)[2]

In this statement, the professional vocabulary is used metaphorically, modeling the attitude to the social situation. The worldview of a Russian person is presented by the speaker as "bottom," and economic sanctions confirm this. People with different views are described through the image of an "orphan," whom the psychologist sees as mentally ill—angry and vengeful. A conversation with Ludmila Petranovskaia, published on March 25, 2022, is rich in such metaphors. She talks about the intergenerational trauma of Russian families, about moral panic, and about the experience of identifying with the aggressor. She also talks about the particular psychotype of those in power in Russia:

> All these people who are making decisions now, they do not understand NGOs because of their psychotype, they do not understand Ukrainians either—they do not have the ability, they lack that thing they need to understand people who stand for certain ideals. (Petranovskaia)

In her opinion, those Russians who have ideals are at the "top" while the existence of ideals among the opponents is not expected. Below we will see that the guests of the show *Manuchi's Empathy* disagree with this and claim that it is they who are guided by ideals.

The psychologist and coach Marina Meliia describes the situation in very similar terms, although her interview was recorded in the autumn (published on October 4, 2022). She, too, defines the state of Russian society in terms of "top" and "bottom." At the "bottom" are people "who are under a kind of anesthetic, who simply do not want to see, analyze, or understand what is going on." And at the "top" are those who, thanks to "commitment therapy" (she uses this metaphor to describe those who, like herself and her colleagues, are involved in charity work and helping others), are able "not to feel victimized" (Meliia).

Pop-psychological metaphors are also used by public figures who have no expertise in psychology. For example, the journalist Svetlana Sorokina, in her reflections (published on 11 March), combines the pop-psychological notion of "a complex person" (we are talking about cognitive intellectual sophistication) with the metaphor of "a brand on the forehead": "The complex man exists. It's just that he's in the minority, he's relegated to the periphery, and he has a brand on his forehead, an enemy of the people. Complex people are now branded" (Sorokina). Referring to medieval public punishments for crimes, she is also echoing the memory of Stalin's repressions (she also uses the metaphorical expression "enemy of the people"). Sorokina uses the opposition "center–periphery" and shows how people close to her in spirit have been pushed from a "central" position to a "peripheral" one. The war against Ukraine appears here as a transformative force.

Sorokina also uses metaphors, and the traditional "dungeon" metaphor of the "top-bottom" opposition is used to illustrate the state of moral failure of society: "Some crap has crawled out of the dungeon," she says of her compatriots who support the war. And she contrasts them with "incredible treasures"—other compatriots who have survived much turmoil but have retained their kindness.

Dmitrii Muratov, a journalist, editor-in-chief of the opposition newspaper *Novaia Gazeta* and Nobel laureate, reflects on the difference in attitudes between the younger and older generations, also using medical and psychological metaphors, but in his case describing the opposition between "inside and outside": "Our nervous system is not above the skin, it is under the skin. But for the young it is still the other way round," "they (the young) have a different kind of empathy." And the behavior of Russian President Vladimir Putin, due to "resentment," "strong psychological damage," and "self-induction," are internal driving forces hidden behind external aggressiveness and self-confidence (Dmitrii Muratov).

Pop psychology metaphors and disease metaphors, like most of the emotional metaphors that Zoltán Kövecses (2004, 49) wrote about, can be described as metaphors of the interplay of forces. Such emotions are related to actions and can be perceived as events. Therefore, we think it is possible to consider these sincere conversations on YouTube as political actions. In this case, it is not only the presenter and her guests who are actors, but also the users of the new media, who experience emotions alongside the speakers, interpret the metaphors, and post their sympathy or disagreement in the comments under the video or on their personal page when reposting.

MYTHOLOGICAL METAPHORS AND THE IMAGE OF THE HOMELAND

While opposition speakers try to rationalize their emotions and create emotional communities through psychological metaphors and moral evaluations, the supporters of the Russian government, it seems to us, try to give pragmatic state interests a moral value through sincere conversations. This task is achieved, in particular by transforming the notion of "motherland" into a concept of a higher order, that is, into a conceptual metaphor (Evans and Green 2006, 38).

For example, Ilze Liepa uses the technique highlighted by Fauconnier and Turner, "movement from the many to the one," to create a conceptual metaphor:

> I love the Russian village so much. I think it is very important that we admire things beyond the works of the Italian masters. And that we see the joys, something so touching when we see these old houses. [. . .] I wanted to understand that Russia is huge, that these fields are ours, our vastness, that this is our beautiful country! (Liepa)

Individual old houses scattered over a large area create a collective image of the "Russian village," which evokes a "poignant feeling," and one can sense a reference to the traditions of Romantic literature, which gives a special appeal to the inconveniences of life and the joy of suffering.

Another version can be seen in an interview with Polina Agureeva, for whom the conceptual metaphor of home is linked to the history of her ancestry (Cossack): "What is the feeling of motherland? It is to feel that you are a link in a huge chain of historical events in your country. To be responsible every day for everything that happens in your country." In this case, conceptual integration is achieved through a sense of "getting to the essence of things" and "strengthening meaningful connections," another model described in Fauconnier and Turner's theory (2002, 310–312).

The transformation of the notion of "motherland" into a concept through the "strengthening of meaningful connections" can also be found in the conversations of Katerina Gordeeva's guests. Film critic Liubov' Arkus talks in detail about the repressions to which her parents and husband were subjected, and then explains why she does not want to emigrate:

> [t]his is my country. I will take it with me wherever I go. It will torture me even more. And it tortures me a lot! Because I can't reconcile myself with what's happening. [. . .] I have to understand what ails my country. (Arkus)

In both cases, the conceptual metaphor of home is linked to the symbolic action of taking responsibility. For both women, responsibility is associated with painful emotions—for Polina Aguryeva because her concept of responsibility differs from that of many of her friends. Liubov' Argus characterizes this responsibility as torment, but not associated with specific people, but rather with the disease of the country. For Agureeva, the action arising from this responsibility is to travel to Donbass. For Arkus, it is continuing the work of her charitable foundation.

Another type of metaphor, common to the open conversations in the *Manuchi's Empathy* show, is found exclusively among speakers who support the political decisions of the Russian government. These are metaphors based not on personal associations or family memories but on the mythology of Russia's "special path" (Dubin 2000). We may even say that they have a pop-religious character. They combine biblical motifs with concepts from other religious and occult traditions. The singer Liubov' Kazarnovskaia, for example, speaks of "Holy Russia," "Heavenly Russia" as "the spiritual center of the planet," and then immediately promises the West punishment, "which in the East is called the law of karma" (Kazarnovskaia). Diplomat Maria Zakharova suggests looking at all the actions of the modern Western elite through the metaphor of barbaric destruction: "We are the only ones left trying to preserve Christian values. In the West, all this is gone, everything is in pieces, in rags, everything has been torn apart" (Zakharova). In this case, the metaphorical description of emotions is also linked to actions, namely destructive actions. But they feel that it is not they who are subjecting the world to these acts but others, particularly the West.

Most of these images are taken from the works of the nationalist philosopher Alexander Dugin (1993), whose ideas began to gain popularity among the elite in the mid-1990s and now claim the status of the ideological mainstream. Behind the pop-religious metaphors of the guests on *Manuchi's Empathy*, it is easy to see the clichés of Soviet propaganda culture. This is most obvious when the conversation shifts from describing an actual emotional state to talking about the motherland. The Soviet experience of describing the motherland is vividly analyzed by Irina

Sandomirskaia (2021). In describing the Soviet collective consciousness, she discusses the notion of the motherland as an ideological icon. According to her, the construction of the community as a political whole within it is built through a metaphorical reinterpretation of the relationship between kinship and motherhood. "Native discourses" are artificially elevated to the status of national symbols, a censored version of the symbolic universe. We believe that the religiosity proclaimed today by the Russian authorities and the cultural elite that supports them elaborates on these Soviet clichés, thus smoothing over the contradictions between archaic and modern notions of morality.

For example, none of Viacheslav Manucharov's interviewees explicitly states that they support the war. On the contrary, each of them expresses, in one way or another, that the war has been a painful development for them. The actress Polina Agureeva explains the necessity of this war with pop-religious metaphors—war as a "struggle with sin," with "the darkness within oneself" (Agureeva). The other speakers try to transfer painful emotions to others. The ballerina Ilze Liepa transposes the collective image of the West, using the metaphor of a "rotten tree covered in a beautiful shell" (Liepa). And media manager Margarita Simon'ian compares the reluctance of some of her fellow citizens to make an icon of the motherland to a congenital disease: "There are people who have no sense of the motherland at all. I know such people, but I cannot understand them. It is an underdevelopment of the fetus, probably during pregnancy" (Simon'ian).

Therefore, the analysis of metaphors allows us to suggest that the statements describing the political emotions of Russians in the first months of the war are formed at the intersection of three cultural paradigms: Western post-Freudian emotional culture, Soviet propaganda culture, and the religious and mythological culture associated with Dugin's Eurasianism. Each of these paradigms is characterized by a set of familiar metaphors which, in the process of communication, enter into complex dynamic processes of integration, of which Turner and Fauconnier have written, creating mixed mental spaces that build new structures of meaning. Or, if we refer to Lotman's logic, this leads to "explosions" in culture and complicates mutual understanding both within the community and of the processes taking place within it from the outside.

At the same time, each of the opposing communities values the sense of mutual understanding to which they aspire, particularly through the use of similar metaphors. However, oppositional speakers recognize themselves as a minority that has found itself "at the bottom" of the culture (while continuing to assess the majority's feelings as "lower"). While those who support the government's decisions present themselves as "at the top," emphasizing their unanimity in every way: "[a]ll my friends are involved in our military operation, they are all of one mind," "it is very important for us that we are all of one mind here." "It seems to me that there is no guile in this conversation. As it is, so it is! This is how we are" (Liepa).

And yet, this desire is unlikely to be fulfilled, as it is hardly possible to achieve a "unified spirit" in Russia with such a diversity of options for integration. Nevertheless, in these frank YouTube conversations, we see a different version of emotional culture from the Western one. Whereas in Western society, therapeutic emotional culture is intertwined with market and consumer logic (Illouz 2008), the contemporary Russian version of emotional culture tends to diminish self-awareness and return through nostalgia to the Soviet collective mythology, supplemented in some cases by conservative pseudo-religious fantasies of "Russian togetherness."

We believe that the methodological approach we propose can be applied to the analysis of other media formats, as it allows us to identify both commonalities and cultural differences in the conceptualization of emotions through metaphors. It also allows us to trace how the characteristics of different media platforms, genres and modes of communication both reflect and influence social expectations.

VISUAL METAPHORS IN SINCERE CONVERSATIONS ON YOUTUBE

As an example of the impact of the audiovisual media format, let us consider the use of visual metaphors in talk shows. In most cases, the format we are considering does not imply the use of rich video sequences. A significant part of *Skazhi Gordeevoi* and *Manuchi's Empathy* is limited to the plastic metaphor of mise-en-scène, which refers to "kitchen" (in Gordeeva's case) or "salon" (in Manucharov's case) conversations. However, since some of Gordeeva's programs that we analyzed were filmed not only in a studio but also in the guests' homes, at work, or in public places, it is possible to demonstrate how visual metaphors expand the range of possible interpretations of sincere conversations on YouTube.

While the metaphors we analyzed above appeared in the conversations spontaneously, at the initiative of the guests of the show (both Katerina Gordeeva and Viacheslav Manucharov rarely use metaphors in questions), visual metaphors were mostly deliberate and reflected the emotions of the authors of the show—presenters, cameramen, and editors. For example, a conversation with journalist Svetlana Sorokina in her home is accompanied by close-ups of things: a beautiful chandelier, statuettes, houseplants, and animals. Each detail speaks of a well-established everyday life, and together they become a metaphor for the motherland that the heroine is unwilling to leave. In this case, the metaphor of the "home as nation" is created according to the model of "from many to one," as seen in verbal metaphors. The space of the house, shown in the frame, is contrasted with the story of "the crap that crawled out of the dungeon." Thus, the visual metaphor of the house and the story about the heroine's perception of what happens outside the doors of the house are treated as the classic opposition "inside-outside," forming a mixed space (a blend, as defined by Fauconnier and Turner).

A similar model of the opposition "inside-outside" appears in the conversation with Dmitrii Muratov, the editor-in-chief of *Novaia Gazeta*, which takes place in his office. The walls are decorated with posters of the front pages of prominent editions of the newspaper from different years. On the screen of an old computer is a video of a speech by Anna Politkovskaia, the journalist who was murdered for political reasons in 2006. The office, which is at the same time a museum, a space of collective memory, can be seen as a metaphor for the past, as part of the opposition "inside-outside." In the interview, it is contrasted with the metaphor of the future, which, according to Dmitrii Muratov, everyone dreams of: "Russia will be open to the world. The borders will be temporary. [. . .] There will be an atmosphere like during the World Cup" (Dmitrii Muratov). The image of the past, associated with the Chechen wars, and the image of the future, destroyed by the war with Ukraine, form a backdrop against which Muratov (a Nobel Peace Prize winner) appears as the hero of an epic, fighting a dragon that grows new heads.

In the conversation with the sociologist Greg Yudin, the metaphor of the "past" is not the room in which the presenter talks to her interlocutor, but the outside world, the park in which they walk. The Museon Art Park on Krymskii Val in Moscow, near the New Tretiakovka building, which after the collapse of the USSR became a graveyard for many monuments to Soviet-era political figures, can be seen as David Lowenthal's "landscape of memory" (1975). The camera shows us monument after monument, according to the logic of conceptual integration "from many to one," turning this district of Moscow, and with it the whole country, into a metaphor of "intertemporality," which Greg Yudin describes in his interview: "[i]t doesn't seem to me at all that this strange, protracted intertemporality in which we find ourselves can be regarded as a continuation of the Soviet one" (Yudin).

At the same time, Yudin describes the beginning of the war with Ukraine using the metaphor of the leadership's "sabotage" against its own country: "[e]verything we see now is an enormous sabotage of the country" (Yudin). And the prospects for the future—through metaphorical comparisons with the events of a century ago—include "civil war," "terror," "explosion from within." As a result of cognitive integration, one gets the feeling that the entire history of Russia is an "intertemporal period" between two "explosions."

As censorship intensifies, the authors of the series *Skazhi Gordeevoi* increasingly complicate and expand the possibilities of interpreting open conversations by metaphorizing the visuals (in particular, by stringing together verbal and visual metaphors that require the viewer to interact not only through emotional involvement in the conversation and interpretation of individual metaphors, but also through multimodal, intersemiotic decoding of the spectacle). This happens, for example, in the episode with the writer Alexander Arkhangelskii, where a significant part of the conversation takes place in a Russian cemetery in Nice. The tombstones refer the viewer to the life stories of the emigrants buried there in past centuries. They are constantly brought up in conversation by the guest and the presenter. In the dramatic clashes of the past, the viewer can see a metaphorical representation of the suffering of the present. This world of suffering is juxtaposed with the seemingly carefree life of the French Riviera, as shown in the shots of the streets and seafront of Nice. The second example is a conversation with the actor and director Veniamin Smekhov, the flow of which changes according to the memorable places in Moscow that the film crew takes their guest to. In addition to visual metaphors related to urban space, poetic metaphors play an important role in this issue. The actor reads many of his favorite poems. He chooses them so that the emotional images of the past resonate with the contemporary experiences of the audience. In these two episodes, visual and poetic metaphors, metaphorical mise-en-scène, and montage techniques become a full-fledged Aesopian language through which the authors convey to the audience what they cannot speak directly. But in order to interpret these metaphors, the viewer must engage in an active interpretive interaction with the multimodal text.

THE ROLE OF METAPHORS IN COMMUNITY BUILDING

As a way of conclusion, we would like to reiterate that Lotman's three-level system of analysis, which we have used, seems to us essential for the study of contemporary interactive media. It contributes to the global methodology of studying media genres in the context of the contemporary intertextual culture of knowledge and communication. At the same time, this approach is particularly sensitive to the Russian communicative linguistic context, so it can be useful for interdisciplinary analysis, as we will illustrate in the third stage of our textual analysis (according to Lotman). We propose here to conceptualize the effect of metaphors as cognitive nodes of personal and collective meanings.

It seems to us that the guests of these shows, when talking about their personal destiny, the destiny of their community, and the common historical memory, describe themselves as "communities of fate." Viktor Vakhshtain (2019) writes about the "community of fate" and discusses it with Max Weber, Georg Simmel, and Peter Baer. In his work, he compares Simmel's model (according to which the totality of previous life choices and assigned historical events makes one part of a certain community of fate) with Baer's model, according to which fate is a real external threat, the confrontation of which makes a community a community, and Weber's model, according to which fate is a shared historical memory, updated by political power for nation-building.

It seems to us that the sincere conversations, especially those that took place at the very beginning of the war against Ukraine, amidst the mass emigration of opposition journalists, human rights activists, and other citizens with an active anti-war stance, illustrate the beginning of the formation of new discursive practices, marking the moment of a further division of the political whole in Russia. They reflect the formation of several "communities of fate" that simultaneously create discourses and need discourses to support their decisions. Of course, this process is not only manifested through metaphors. The interviews as a whole are emotional, self-reflective narratives about the fracturing of society and personal identity as a result of political events and war.

All the guests talk about what they felt and did in the first days after the outbreak of hostilities in Ukraine and what they observed in their immediate environment. Some of them publicly acknowledged their shame, fear and horror, guilt and responsibility, anger and hatred, resentment and disappointment; others felt pride in a country that was once again playing an important role in world history, a sense of unity with like-minded compatriots, indifference and contempt for those who have gone into exile, pity for ordinary Ukrainians who have fallen victim to corrupt authorities, and bewilderment toward foreigners—all this emerges as both a personal choice of public figures and a form of collective therapy, as well as a declaration of ideological theses that are important to the speakers.

The extended metaphors related to memories of childhood and family history in the context of the country's history, and the mystical sense of love for the country used by public figures in *Manuchi's Empathy*, allow us to see in these conversations signs of the formation of a "community of fate," close to Weber's understanding of the "community of fate" as the foundation of the nation. This understanding, which is the most political of the three and has negative connotations from the past (the ideology of Nazism) and the present (contemporary Chinese ideology), is also important for the protagonists of Gordeeva's interviews. In their monologues, they also refer to their families' experiences, inscribing them and themselves in the history of society. In almost all the interviews, there are references to certain tragic events in Soviet history and their impact on the family. However, unlike the protagonists who support state policy, the anti-war speakers see their unity as emotional rather than institutional. Narratives about the historical trauma of past generations and metaphorical comparisons of past and present are more often used to explain the personal and collective experience of living through the current political crisis.

The metaphors used by Gordeeva's protagonists, which draw on the concepts of pop psychology, are more indicative of the formation of this community according to Simmel's model. For this model, it is precisely the previous life choices that determine personal memory and morality that are of paramount importance. In our case, these are the choices made by liberal intellectuals in the 1990s. At that time, they partly inherited the values of the Soviet intelligentsia (reflected today in the metaphorical images of the motherland and the nation) and formed a negative view of the troubled Soviet past. This prevents them today from agreeing with the propaganda calls of the Russian authorities to restore Russian-Ukrainian unity based on the Soviet model. We see both in the metaphors they use to describe their motherland. The new community that emerges from this foundation in response to an urgent external threat is also close to Baer's model. The primary social glue for it is the feelings people are experiencing at the moment. These are reflected in the sickness metaphors and psychotherapeutic metaphors that are used to describe and discuss the possible actions generated by these feelings and metaphors: emigration, social activities inside or outside the country, mutual aid, and so on.

Thus, the ritual of sincere conversation on YouTube as a communicative action consolidates community experiences through the formation of a set of shared metaphors and shapes common attitudes toward military events among community members with similar political views, even if they live in different parts of the world.

Although the viewers of *Skazhi Gordeevoi* did not participate directly in the YouTube conversations, we observed that they continued the discussions started by the speakers in the comments under the YouTube video or in reposts on social networks. This, it seems to us, was one of the reasons why Gordeeva herself and a significant number of her interlocutors were declared "foreign agents" by the Russian Ministry of Justice within a year of the start of the war. And Ilze Liepa was stripped of her Lithuanian citizenship for her participation in *Manuchi's Empathy*. We believe that these are important confirmations of the communicative and political importance of these open emotional conversations. The phenomenon of public discussion of personal choices reflects the personalized and emotional nature of the representation of political experience that is particularly characteristic of today's mass media culture. These sincere conversations help both hosts and guests, as well as viewers, to experience themselves as communities of individuals united not only by historical memory, but also by the commonality of personal existential choices that shape identity in a time of fracture and transformation. The very format of sincere conversation in digital media becomes a metaphor for authentic political communication of the new reality, while it is filled with different meanings for particular emotional moral communities and social groups.

NOTES

1. In particular, one of the authors of this chapter, Julia Lerner, has written about "therapeutic culture without psychology" in the Russian media (Lerner and Zbenovich 2013).
2. All unmarked translations are our own.

BIBLIOGRAPHY

Agureeva, Polina. 2022. "*poezdka na Donbass i kul'turnaia elita.*" Interview by Viacheslav Manucharov. *Empatiia Manuchi*, YouTube, August 16, 2022. https://www.youtube.com/watch?v=DLXzx-vDC1w.

Arkhangel'skii, Aleksandr. 2023. "'*Nashi rebiata' – eto obman.*" Interview by Katerina Gordeeva. *Skazhi Gordeevoi*, YouTube, April 11, 2023. https://www.youtube.com/watch?v=AX3JM81Db9E.

Arkus, Liubov'. 2022. "*Esli u tebia net dostoinstva, tebia u sebia net.*" Interview by Katerina Gordeeva. *Skazhi Gordeevoi*, YouTube, April 18, 2022. https://www.youtube.com/watch?v=8yyD1R7sLP8.

Arutiunova, Nina. 1990. "*Metafora i diskurs.*" In *Teoriia metafory*, edited by Nina Arutyunova, 5–32. Moscow: Progress.

Baranov, Anatolii 2000. "*Metafory v politicheskom diskurse: iazykovye markery krizisnosti politicheskoi situatsii.*" In *Sprachwandel in der Slavia. Teil 1*, edited by Lew Zybatow, 103–128. Frankfurt am Mein: Lang.

Bibler, Vladimir. 1991. *Mikhail Mikhailovich Bakhtin ili poetika kul'tury*. Moscow: Progress.

Carroll Noël. 1996. "A Note on Film Metaphor." *Journal of Pragmatics*. 6 (26): 809–822.

Dimke, Dar'ia. 2018. *Nezabyvaemoe budushchee: Sovetskaia pedagogicheskaia utopiia.* Moscow: Common Place.

Dubin, Boris. 2000. "*Zapad, granitsa, osobyi put': simvolika "drugogo" v politicheskoi mifologii sovremennoi Rossii.*" *Monitoring obshchestvennogo mneniia*. 6 (50): 25–34.

Dugin, Aleksandr. 1993. *Apologiia natsionalizma. Politicheskaq artiomiia, evraziistvo i natsionalizm*. Moscow: URSS.

Goffman, Erving. 1981. *Forms of Talk*. Philadelphia: University of Pennsylvania Press.

Eco, Umberto. 1986. *Semiotics and the Philosophy of Language*. Bloomington: Indiana University Press.

Eisenstein, Sergei. 2000. "*Obraz i metafora.*" In *Montazh*, 80–86. Moscow: Muzei kino.

Evans, Vyvyan and Melanie Green. 2006. *Cognitive Linguistics: An Introduction*. Edinburgh: Edinburgh University Press.

Fahlenbrach, Kathrin, ed. 2016. *Embodied Metaphors in Film, Television, and Video Games: Cognitive Approaches*. New York: Routledge.

Fauconnier, Gilles and Mark Turner. 1998. "Principles of Conceptual Integration." In *Discourse and Cognition: Bridging the Gap*, edited by J. P. Koenig, 269–283. Stanford: CSLI Publications.

Fauconnier, Gilles and Mark Turner. 2002. *The Way We Think: Conceptual Blending and the Mind's Hidden Complexities*. New York: Basic Books.

Illouz, Eva. 2008. *Saving the Modern Soul: Therapy, Emotions and the Culture of Self-Help*. Berkeley: University of California Press.

Yudin, Greg. 2022. "*Eto diversiia protiv strany.*" Interview by Katerina Gordeeva. *Skazhi Gordeevoi*, YouTube, April 8, 2022. https://www.youtube.com/watch?v=BNTDs8x2Zwk.

Kalugin, Dmitrii. 2015. *Proza zhizni: russkie biografii XVIII-XIX vv.* St. Petersburg: Izdatel'stvo Evropeiskogo universiteta v Sankt-Peterburge.

Kazarnovskaia, Liubov'. 2023. "*Emigratsiia, protivostoianie, Rossiia i Evropa.*" Interview by Viacheslav Manucharov. *Empatiia Manuchi*, YouTube, March 5, 2023. https://www.youtube.com/watch?v=ZfK8_2EesqI.

Kiriya, Ilya. 2021. "From 'Troll Factories' to 'Littering the Information Space': Control Strategies Over the Russian Internet." *Media and Communication* 9 (4): 16–26.

Kövecses, Zoltán. 2004. *Metaphor and Emotion: Language, Culture, and Body in Human Feeling*. Cambridge: Cambridge University Press.

Lakoff, George and Mark Johnson. 1980. *Metaphors We Live By*. Chicago: University of Chicago Press.

de Landtsheer, Christ'l. 1991. "Function and the Language of Politics: A Linguistic Uses and Gratification Approach." *Communication and Cognition* 24 (3/4): 299–342.

Lerner, Julia and Anna Novikova. 2024. "From Moral Therapy to Political Defiance: Public Self-Reflections on Russian YouTube." *The Russian Review* 83 (1): 51–65.

Lerner, Julia and Claudia Zbenovich. 2013. "Adapting the Therapeutic Discourse to Post-Soviet Media Culture: The Case of *Modnyi Prigovor*." *Slavic Review* 72 (4): 828–849.

Liepa, Ilze. 2022. "*Styd, dvoinoe grazhdanstvo i lichnyi vybor.*" Interview by Viacheslav Manucharov. *Empatiia Manuchi*, YouTube, November 1, 2022. https://www.youtube.com/watch?v=EMkrYDB2DTU.

Lotman, Yurii. 1996. *Stat'i po semiotike kul'tury i iskusstva*. St. Petersburg: Akademicheskii proekt.

Lotman, Yuri. 2000. *Semiosfera*. St. Petersburg: Iskusstvo-SPB.

Lotman, Yuri. 2022. "Lecture at Tartu State University, March 13, 1981." *Slovo.ru: Baltic Accent*. 13 (2): 10–23.

Lotman, Yurii and Yurii Tsivian. 1994. *Dialoga s ekranom*. Tallinn: Aleksandra.

Lowenthal, David. 1975. "Past Time, Present Place: Landscape and Memory." *Geographical Review* 65 (1): 1–36.

Meliia, Marina. 2022. "*Planirui khudshee, nadeisia na luchshee. I ver' v chudo.*" Interview by Katerina Gordeeva. *Skazhi Gordeevoi*, YouTube, October 4, 2022. https://www.youtube.com/watch?v=IGc1a3WnwEw.

Muratov, Dmitrii. 2022. "Peculiar Way the Good and the Evil Were Decided." Interview by Katerina Gordeeva. *Skazhi Gordeevoi*, YouTube, March 7, 2022. https://www.youtube.com/watch?v=8CW-WAJq0ts.

Muratov, Sergei. 1983. *Televizionnoe obshchenie v kadre I za kadrom*. Moscow: Iskusstvo.

Petranovskaia, Liudmila. 2022. "*Eto istoriia pro otrezanie obratnykh sviazei.*" Interview by Katerina Gordeeva. *Skazhi Gordeevoi*, YouTube, March 25, 2022. https://www.youtube.com/watch?v=UN529dZLQE8.

Podosokorskii, Nikolai. 2018. "*'Litso s ekrana': V chem sekret populiarnosti tok-shou vDud'?*" *Nauka televideniia* 14 (3): 151–166.

Podosokorskii, Nikolai. 2020. "*Evoliutsiia Iuriia Dudia: Ot populiarnogo videoblogera do obshchestvennogo deiatelia.*" *Nauka televideniia* 16 (4): 65–82.

Potter, Jonathan and Margaret Wetherell. 1987. *Discourse and Social Psychology: Beyond Attitudes and Behavior*. London: Sage Publications.

Ries, Nancy. 1997. *Russian Talk: Culture and Conversation During Perestroika*. Ithaca: Cornell University Press.

Sandomirskaia, Irina. 2021. *Kniga o rodine: opyt analiza diskursivnykh praktik*. Vienna: Wiener Slawistischer Almanach Sonderband.

Simon'ian, Margarita. 2023. "*Galkin, Urgant, blokirovka YouTube i ukhod s RT.*" Interview by Viacheslav Manucharov. *Empatiia Manuchi*, YouTube, February 19, 2023. https://www.youtube.com/watch?v=08Ba1hRJaFE.

Smekhov, Veniamin. 2023. "*Beregite vashi litsa.*" Interview by Katerina Gordeeva. *Skazhi Gordeevoi*, YouTube, December 29, 2023. https://www.youtube.com/watch?v=6gD-rmCdS1Y.

Sorokina, Svetlana. 2022. "Complicated People are Now Stigmatized." Interview by Katerina Gordeeva. *Skazhi Gordeevoi*, YouTube, March 11, 2022. https://www.youtube.com/watch?v=uNiPZC0jikY.

Taylor, Charles. 2004. *Modern Social Imaginaries*. Durham, NC: Duke University Press.

Turner, Mark. 1991. *Reading Minds: The Study of English in the Age of Cognitive Science*. Princeton: Princeton University Press.

Vakhshtain, Viktor. 2019. "*'Soobshchestvo sud'by': k voennoi istorii idei.*" *Sotsiologiia vlasti* 31 (4): 12–52.

Zakharova, Mariia. 2022. "*Pugacheva, Vajkule, Dozhd' i EKHO.*" Interview by Viacheslav Manucharov. *Empatiia Manuchi*, YouTube, December 12, 2022. https://www.youtube.com/watch?v=BBr1sN4Qo0I.

Zolyan, Suren. 2022. "Yurii Lotman: On the Problems of Language and Linguistics." *Voprosy iazykoznaniia* 1: 106–119.

12

Dream (Re)Interpretation

Metaphors and Story Schemas in Meaning Creation

Anna A. Lazareva

According to cognitive theories, dreaming is a process of thinking, which means dream content (as a reflection of cognitive processes in the brain during the dream state) is based on language, metaphors, cultural concepts, and narrative forms (Hall 1953; Foulkes 1978; Kilroe 2001, 107; Walsh 2022). Therefore, dream interpretation is regarded as eliciting these concepts and metaphors from the dream content (Hall 1953, 275; Lakoff 2001), disentangling the dreamer's thoughts and thus revealing personal concerns (or even cultural processes that can be represented in the form of transformations of cultural models in individual dreams) (Mageo 2021; Mageo 2022, 33; Lohmann 2021; Sheriff 2021). This approach is based on the idea that dreams are experienced in the form of a story, and dream reports tend to preserve this original form (Friesen 2019, 176–184). For example, acknowledging that "the verbal dream report will also enhance the narrative organization of the dream text," Patricia Kilroe considered that a dream report "reflects the narrative structure of the experienced dream," so "we do not necessarily impose a narrative structure on the dream" (Kilroe 2000, 135). At the same time, many other scholars concentrate on the sociocultural nature of narratives about dreams and point out that remembering dreams is a "retrospective reconstruction" of the actual dream experience influenced by language and culture (Kilborne 1981, 175; Mannheim 1991, 48). In other words, we cannot deny that stories about dreams (like any other narratives) are products of waking cognitive processes (remembering, verbalization, etc.). But how can we measure to what extent these processes distort the actual content of dreams? Which parts of a dream plot are constructed, and which are experience-based?

Citing Bartlett (1932, 206), Ronald Casson pointed out that remembering is constructive because "Not all stimuli are stored in memory; rather, schemata are employed to provide 'a general impression of the whole' and to construct (or reconstruct) 'probable details'" (Casson 1983, 430). Wallace Chafe proved that any verbalization is interpretive, and talking about something recalled from memory is a creative activity because the same thing can be verbalized in a different way on different occasions (Chafe 1977, 219–237). The difficulty in the analysis of how dream memories are structured in a narrative form (and therefore inevitably distorted) arises from the fact that the dream experience is inaccessible to research. So, how can we research the processes of constructing a narrative about a dream? Peer Bundgaard and Frederik Stjernfelt claimed that *cases of alternate schematizations where the same situation or the same object is referred to in two or more different ways* make the process of applying cognitive schemas particularly clear (Bundgaard and Stjernfelt 2010, 63). Similar conclusions were made by Jane Hill, who, analyzing narrative structures, noticed, "the analyst should always try to imagine all the other ways that the story might have been told, and to ask why particular rhetorical choices occurred as against those which did not" (Hill 2005, 173). To regard alternative ways the story about a dream can be told, I analyzed different records of the same dream reinterpreted several times.

After a dream is interpreted, its description is transformed. For example, having compared stories about dreams recorded right after the dreamer woke up and then after those dreams were interpreted as predictions of real events, Evgenii Safronov showed that once a dream is linked to a real event, its description shortens—the irrelevant plot details that cannot be connected to the waking life event tend to be reduced (Safronov 2016, 53–59). Having analyzed conversations about dreams during psychoanalytic sessions, Anssi Peräkylä and Jörg Bergmann noticed that the interpretation of a dream supposes redescription of the dream scene using key words that emphasize the connection between the dream and the real world (2020).

In my previous works, devoted to revealing narrative structures of prophetic dream stories, I proved that certain invariant forms of a dream plot suppose a certain logic of dream interpretation. I described these invariants as a system, showing their interconnections and hierarchical levels (from selecting several general structures underlying most of the stories about prophetic dreams to their more specific variances applicable to smaller sets of narratives). For example, "*An object is damaged or lost in the dream. After that, something bad happens to its owner in real life*" is a general plot schema. "*Someone's house is destroyed in the dream. The dweller of the house dies in real life*" is a more specific plot schema (applicable to a smaller group of narratives), which can be regarded as a variant of the general schema. Therefore, I conceptualized this system of invariants as a certain "language" (narrative grammar) lying at the core of the collection of narratives I researched. I presented this system of invariants in the form of a motif index of folklore narratives about prophetic dreams that were recorded in the Eastern Slavic regions during twentieth to twenty-first centuries (including my field research in the Poltava region of Ukraine conducted during 2012–2018) (2020, 187–231, 2023).

The current chapter advances my previous research. Based on the revealed narrative grammar (system of invariant structures) of Eastern Slavic prophetic dream stories and drawing on the conclusion that each narrative form supposes a specific meaning, this paper examines the process of dream interpretation as a process of shaping the dream story in a culture-specific form. I claim that while interpreting dreams, the dreamer not just modifies their plot descriptions but gives a shape (a certain story schema) to dream content. Therefore, dream reinterpretation supposes molding a dream plot into a new invariant structure that corresponds with a new meaning. Considering the process of dream narrative construction, I started with the fact that culture-specific narrative forms can be imposed on dream memories.

The research draws on the idea that popular dream interpretation supposes constructing the dream plot so it goes back to a cultural model—folklore samples (invariants) of prophetic dream stories presupposing certain semantics of the dream (Lazareva 2023, 166–169). Since meaning is based on understanding (Lakoff and Johnson, 1980, 197; D'Andrade 1984, 102–103), in other words, meaning does not exist without an interpreter who elicits and defines it, I am going to consider dream interpretation as a process of meaning-making through conceptualization and narrative construction. Prophetic dream stories based on folk interpretations of dreams as harbingers of the future can serve as clear examples of how the narrative is constructed, since the dreamer (guessing what the dream could mean in changing circumstances) can attribute to the dream imagery different meanings. Analysis of how dream memories become molded into a stereotypical story about a prophecy and how the dream plot changes when it is reinterpreted will help us understand how interpretation and verbalization (remembering) of a dream plot are interconnected.

RESEARCH MATERIAL

I conducted a series of in-depth interviews with a woman born in 1943 in the town of Myrhorod who had a special secondary education, worked at a plant, and retired. She lived her whole life in Myrhorod (Poltava region of Ukraine), where the interviews with her were conducted. In an interval of a year, the informant made two different descriptions of the same dream that she considered prophetic and interpreted as a prediction of future events. The first record was made in August 2015, and the second in June 2016. The interpretation of the dream changed several times, depending on the changing circumstances.

The goal is to analyze how the informant makes sense of her dream experience by applying different story schemas (drawing on different conceptual metaphors) while retelling its plot. In other words, I regarded how alternative interpretations of a dream entail different schematizations of the story about the dream.

RESEARCH METHODS

Structural-Semiotic Analysis

In my previous works, I proved that the structures of stories about prophetic dreams (narratives containing a description of a dream plot and its interpretation corresponding to folk beliefs) differ significantly from other types of dream narratives. The main idea of a prophetic dream story is to compare the dream plot (the "event" of the dream) with life events (the semantics of the dream plot).

Revealing these story schemas of prophetic dream narratives, I use structural-semiotic analysis, which implies that form (the structure of a dream plot) is connected to its meaning (the structure of the real-life event: actual or hypothetical). Therefore, I regard the plot structure of a prophetic dream story as a sentence (the combination of symbolic units according to culture-specific narrative grammar) that allows the interpreter to connect dream imagery with the prophetic message ascribed to the dream. This method of applying structural-semiotic analysis to describe and systematize structures of prophetic dream plots having similar semantics was described in detail in my previous works (Lazareva 2023). In the current chapter, I use this method to show how the informant was structuring her stories about a dream to render the description of the dream plot in a form that supposes a specific meaning.

To understand how the informant applies narrative grammar (narrative construction principles) of prophetic dream stories to interpret a dream, I will compare the structures of the narratives in question with the previously revealed structures of stories about prophetic dreams collected in Eastern Slavic regions from the end of the nineteenth century to present (Lazareva 2020, 187–231, 2023).

Since I am going to show the process of making sense of dream imagery, the current research is based on the ideas of cognitive linguists who regarded speech production and comprehension as mutually connected processes (Fillmore 1976, 23; Chafe 1977). So, story schemas are considered representations of mental structures embedded into the language, as Casson formulated: "linguistic forms bring schemata to mind and schemata are expressed in 'linguistic reflexes'" (Casson 1983, 432–433).

Analysis of Metaphors as Cognitive Schemas

Most of the invariants of prophetic dream stories I revealed can be regarded as metaphors if we use George Lakoff's definition of "conceptual metaphor" (Lakoff 1993, 222–223). George Lakoff wrote that metaphors provide an understanding of one domain of experience (which he named a "target domain") in terms of a different domain of experience (which he defined as a "source domain"). Also, a source domain structure corresponds with the structure of a target domain (for example, if we talk about love in terms of a trip, we define the relationship as moving together and problems in the relationship as obstacles on the way (Quinn 1987, 175–176; Lakoff 1993, 206–208), and so on). In this chapter, I turn to conceptual metaphor theory to show the processes of looking for correspondences between dream imagery and waking life events and (re)constructing the narrative about the prophetic dream to emphasize such correspondences. Lakoff wrote that "our everyday system of conventional metaphor is employed whenever an interpreter interprets a dream" (Lakoff 2001, 273). However, in analyzing dream content, he was more interested in making assumptions about the hidden meaning of dreams based on the idea of dreaming as a form of thought which (as other forms of thinking) makes use of conceptual metaphor (Lakoff 2001, 273–274). Since the research question of this paper is how people construct prophetic dream narratives during dream telling, I don't regard the question of what dreams mean or why the dreamer had a certain dream. I am interested in how people use metaphors for reasoning about dream meaning and, therefore, for constructing stereotyped narratives about dreams that came true. Therefore, I analyze conceptual metaphors used to describe and interpret dream plots the same way researchers analyzed how people use metaphors to describe life events/situations and reason about them (Lakoff 1993; Quinn 2005).

THE DREAM

Let's look at the first record of the dream made on August 15, 2015. The informant told this story while answering the question of whether she had prophetic dreams. She noticed that she had good intuition and provided several examples (of anticipations and prophetic dreams) that proved her ability to anticipate future events.[1] The following narrative was among these stories:

The Dream about the Broken Roof

I have neighbors, the Sidorenko,[2] who live right behind my house. [. . .] And there is a sick girl. She is not a girl . . . [The informant made a pause] She is already . . . She is already sixty . . . more than sixty years old. Well, she's like that . . . [The informant sighed]. So, I had a dream . . . She sometimes breaks her arm, then her leg. They sometimes scold her and sometimes treat her kindly, this way and that. But she respects me (well, her name is Nadia) because I have never shouted at her, I have never quarreled with her. Why would I quarrel with her? Well, yes, I deal with her tactfully. And she respects me more or less. However, there is nobody around whom she doesn't despise and hate. As for me, she calls me "Ninka, Ninka" [Nina – is the informant's name]. That is how she calls me [the informant laughed].

I had a dream . . . There is their house. Their house has been divided into two parts: one was for the parents and the other for the children. After the parents had died, one sister [Nadia] occupied their half, and the younger sister [Vera] remained with her family [in the other part of the house]. And Nadia stayed on the part where the hall, bedroom, kitchen, and bathroom were situated – that all is on that side. And the parents appointed the middle daughter [Liuba] as Nadia's caregiver. Well, there were conflicts over the inheritance in the family. Her name was Liuba. And this Liuba was registered in her parents' house. She also had a house over there on Khmelnytskyi street. But she gave that house to her daughter: her family is there. Aunt Liuba moved here and lived with this Nadia. They had a huge hall, a bedroom, a kitchen, a toilet, and a bathroom for the two of them. Wasn't that too much for two people? So what? Nadia needs a separate room. Well, there was such tension between the sisters. Oh, I thought, "Lord! If only everything were normal!" But here is Nadia, how she exasperated everyone! Well, Vera was at work, those guys were all at work, and Liuba was constantly, as it turned out, with her. And there were scandals, scandals, scandals. Her [Liuba's] daughter also didn't do well–there were troubles [in the daughter's family]. This Liuba helped me a lot when I was sick and helped other neighbors. Well, she was like an ambulance.

And I had a dream that this house . . . its roof *on that half, where Liuba and Nadia lived* . . . As if there was a hurricane at night and *it had blown the roof away*. I came out here on the corner, looked at this house, and thought, "Gee, how didn't it blow off the whole roof?" Such a big solid house and the roof was blown off! And where was that roof? I couldn't see where it had fallen. *But it was clear that it had fallen, and I heard the voices of that sister, Vera, and her husband, Seryozha. He said, "I have started to repair it."* What? I was silent. I didn't tell anybody about that dream. Why would I do that? Somebody could say that I . . . [wished them something bad]. And we kept waiting. There was a woman who helped me with my documents [Galina]. [. . .] I told her about my dream, and she said, "Oh, Nina, it will probably be trouble there!" And everyone . . . Well, who . . . [with whom the dreamer discussed this dream] for some reason, thought that something bad would happen to Nadia. Because she broke her arm twice, and her leg. Well, she is like that. She barely walks. She can fall down somewhere, and–bang!–she has already broken her arm or leg. They are constantly looking after her.

After some time . . . [The informant described in detail how Liuba used to work without rest despite having health problems] She had a fair every day: either Nadezhda [Nadia's full name] would demand care or her daughter would bring her children here–such a hubbub! They were always noisy! And bang! [pause] Liuba's blood pressure had risen, and she had a stroke.

She got to the hospital, but the doctors couldn't understand what was wrong with her. No result. Well, that all cost money. They put her from one department to another, dragged her back and forth, and she wound up in intensive care. [The informant made a pause and sighed.] And I told Galina, [the informant said quietly, highlighting the citation of her own words] *"You see, the roof is blown away. That means a sore head"*. She answered, "Wow, you are really something!" *I said, "But the house remained intact. Let's hope it meant that Liuba would be ill, but she would recover and come back"*. [A pause] Well, we kept waiting, and she returned. She was in serious condition but returned. And again all these stresses, and this Nadia, these quarrels. Consequently, she soon had a stroke again. This time, it was a severe stroke. [Pause] She got to intensive care again. [The informant talked about the financial problems that Liuba's family faced since they had to pay for her treatment and described how she helped her neighbors by lending them her last sum of money and sharing some food when Vera needed to spend with her sister all night long in the hospital. Liuba underwent brain surgery. Right after, while her relatives were trying to take her home from the hospital, Liuba felt bad and was taken to intensive care again.] Some time passed (it was on Tuesday) when Vera came and cried. I said, "Vera!" Well, I didn't tell her about my dream. "Everything should work out. Everything should be fine." We had just finished talking, she ran home crying. [The informant criticized the doctors, who decided to discharge Liuba from the hospital too soon, right after the surgery.] Soon, she called me and said, "Liuba passed away." That is that. (Lazareva 2018, 84–86)

Having applied Labov and Waletzky's method (1967) to analyze dream narratives, Laura Cariola distinguished in dream reports units that have real-life orientation: usually embedded in the beginning of a narrative, descriptions of real life introduce events of the past that could have caused the dreamer to see particular imagery (2008, 16–20). However, speaking about prophetic dream narratives, instead of an inclusion of

Table 12.1 Central Structural Units of the First Narrative (According to Labov and Waletzky's Narrative Analysis Method)

	Reality Event story	*"Dream Event" story*
Orientation	The informant describes the neighbors' house and their family. There was tension between the two sisters—Liuba and Nadia.	The dreamer sees the neighbors' house.
Complication	Liuba got ill. Doctors tried to cure Liuba.	The roof of the house was broken by a hurricane. The neighbor was trying to fix the roof.
Resolution	Liuba died.	N/A
Evaluation	Liuba was a very good person (not like her selfish sister Nadia). The dreamer didn't think that something miserable was going to happen to Liuba. And when she got ill, the informant hoped that she would get better. She considers that Liuba got sick and died because of constant stress caused by problems in her family and conflicts with Nadia.	This dream is bad. Something bad might happen in the neighbors' family.
Coda	"That is that"	The dreamer didn't remember whether the neighbor managed to fix the roof.

Source: Generated by the Author.

autobiographical units, we can discern two elaborated plot lines: dream event story and reality event story. Each of them has its own structure, sometimes a very detailed one, with an introductory part, complication, and so on. For example, it may be described that way (see table 12.1).

However, such a description would be an oversimplification because the dream story and the real event story are not two parallel plots mechanically combined into one story. They are inextricably linked with each other.

The general line of the narrative is the unexpectedness of Liuba's demise anticipated in a dream that was misinterpreted. The narrative can be divided into two parts: (1) the initial interpretation of the dream, and (2) the interpretation of the dream after Liuba became ill, and the conclusion revealing that both interpretations weren't right. In each of these parts, the correlation between the dream plot and hypothetical reality is presented in different ways.

The First Part

The informant started her dream narrative by speaking about the eldest sister, Nadia, and then emphasized the contrast between her and Liuba. Nadia was characterized as a selfish person with a bad temper (the informant called her "a girl" as if she were a selfish child), demanding a lot from her family. Whereas Liuba was presented as a good person who was helpful to others and put other people's needs first: not only was she her oldest sister's caregiver, but she also helped her daughter and her neighbors—"*She was like an ambulance.*" Whereas Nadia occupied the best part of their parents' house, Liuba left her own house to her daughter.

There are several false starts at the beginning of the description of the dream plot. The informant several times started with the words "*I had a dream that . . .* ," but instead of proceeding to speak about what she dreamt, she went on speaking about the structure of the neighbor's house. It shows that she considered this information important to understanding the interpretation of the dream plot. Why? The informant described in detail how the neighbor's house was divided between their family—and which family member lived in which part of the house. Then, speaking about the dream plot, she pointed out that the roof collapsed over the place where Nadia and Liuba lived. On the one hand, it could represent the ongoing conflicts in the family: the informant mentioned the tension between Liuba and Nadia (*Nadia exasperated everyone; there were scandals*). If we regard the house as a symbol of the family (something is wrong with the house—something is wrong in the family), we can connect the roof broken above this part of the house with this conflict situation that resolves in the story. The idea is that these constant conflicts were leading to something bad ("Oh, I thought, 'Lord! If only everything were normal!'"). On the other hand, the clarification over whose part of the house the roof fell on is important for connecting the dream plot with a hypothetical future event. The metaphor "*an object as a symbol of a group of people (most often—family)*" can be frequently traced in the narratives about prophetic dreams (see table 12.2). In such narratives, an element of the object symbolizes a family member, and its destruction (or detachment from the object) symbolizes the death (or in some narratives—departure) of a family member. A house as a symbol of a family is a very common metaphor, reflected not only in dream interpretation but also in cultural beliefs. For example, in the Poltava region of Ukraine, people believed that reducing the size of the house could cause the death of a family member (Miloradovich 1992, 171).

According to Lakoff, the metaphorical description of a target domain inherits the structure of the source domain—he described linking one event structure with another as a "mapping" (1993, 215). In this story, the "mapping" of the dream plot (source domain) onto the hypothetical future event (target domain) manifests itself in "mapping" the structure of the house onto the structure of the family, different rooms inside the house onto people who lived there, the condition of different rooms onto the future of people living there, the bad condition of the room (the roof was broken over it) onto a bad prognosis for a person who lives there. Therefore, we can extend the structural correspondence between the house and the family by relating certain parts of the house with certain family members who live in these parts. So did the informant when she interpreted her dream the first time. (See table 12.2.)

Since Nadia was the oldest family member and she was ill (the informant twice pointed out that she broke her leg and her arm twice: "She can fall down somewhere, and—bang! —she had already broken her arm or leg"), initially, the dreamer thought that something bad would happen to Nadia. It's typical of prophetic dream stories to mention that initially the dreamer attributes the malign meaning of a dream to the oldest or ill family member. Pointing out that everyone with whom she discussed this dream "thought that something bad would happen to Nadia," the dreamer emphasized that it was the most probable event.

Liuba's illness that follows that dream can be regarded as an unexpected resolution of the first plot line. Liuba was presented as a victim of the selfishness and bad temper of her elder disabled sister, which made her feel stressed and, therefore, provoked high blood pressure and a stroke. The next part of the story represents a new round of dream interpretation.

The Second Part

The second part begins by mentioning that the doctors couldn't give Liuba a correct diagnosis. In this period of uncertainty, the informant turned to this dream plot again, trying to make a more optimistic prognosis about the future in the changed circumstances. This time, instead of suggesting that this dream predicted death (as followed from the initial logic of

Table 12.2 An Object as a Symbol of Family or Household

An Object Loses Its Part in a Dream		*A Family Loses Its Member* in Reality
House	wall, corner, roof (ceiling), stove	death of a family member
Stove	element of the stove, pot standing in the stove	parting with a family member, divorce:
Body	tooth, hair, finger, arm, leg	
Clothing	sole of the shoe, detail of the wristwatch	the son leaves for the army the daughter moves to her husband
Tree	fruit, tree branch	

Source: Expanded version of Lazareva (2023, 182 Table 1)

interpretation), the dreamer highlighted dream plot details that could be regarded as benign signs. She re-conceptualized the dream imagery, rendering it into another narrative structure. The invariant structure "*if an object is damaged in the dream, a particular person, represented by the object, gets ill or dies in real life*" (based on the metaphor "*an object as a symbol of a person*") is also very common for prophetic dream stories. An object that symbolizes a person (most often a house, a stove, or a tree) is damaged or lost, which is interpreted as a prediction of the death or illness of the person (most often its owner) (see table 12.3).[3]

In this case, the interpretation of the dream is more of a mapping of reality onto the dream plot: the real events define the new understanding of the dream. The fact that Liuba's brain had been damaged "clarifies" the dream plot about the damaged roof of the house where she lived. Since the head is the top part of the body, Liuba's illness was linked to the damage to the roof—the top part of the house. Then the dreamer swaps the target and source domain again, making a prediction of the future, based on the "house is a body" metaphor (instead of "house is a family"). So, the structure of the house is "mapped" onto the structure of the body of the ill woman. Since the house symbolizes the body, its parts are body parts. So, the roof (the top part of the house) signifies the head (the top part of the body):"You see, the roof was blown away. That means a sore head." Therefore, the destruction of the roof corresponds with a stroke.

This new conceptualization brings out new plot details that were not important during the first interpretation. The dreamer emphasized that the whole house stood intact and the damaged roof could be fixed. The man who lived in that house (Vera's husband) was going to fix the roof

Table 12.3 An Object as a Symbol of a Person

An Object Is Damaged or Lost in a dream		A Person Dies/Gets Ill in reality
House/Stove	destroyed	
	in decline, needs renovation	
	is dirty	
Tree	is cut down	
	withers	
	disappears	
Personal Item	is lost	
	drowns in a river	
	breaks into small pieces	
	is rotten	
Heavenly Body	dims (doesn't shine)	

Source: Generated by the Author.

in the dream (*I heard the voice of Vera's husband, Seryozha. He said, "I have started to repair it"*). If the house is the body, the roof is the head, and a broken roof means a stroke, then the mending of the roof symbolizes treatment. See the words of the same informant reasoning about the meaning of a damaged house in another dream:

> If a house somewhere begins to collapse or is rotten, and you are sure that it will collapse—it means the death of the owner: either illness or death. [. . .] I dreamed that a crack appeared and the plaster was crumbling. I looked at it—there was a firm good wall beneath [the crack]. I said, "It's okay. We will scrape it off." Well, I got sick but survived.
>
> I often dreamed that the pipes were rotten or something else. And I was asked, "Did you try to repair it?" I said: "Yes, the workers were repairing." And they answered me, *"If the house is being repaired, you will be working."* (Lazareva 2018, 69)

The damaged state of the house or its destruction in a dream is regarded as bad signs in Slavic folklore, regardless of which of the metaphors the dreamer refers to ("house = family" or "house = body"). In other words, the conclusion that the destruction of the roof signifies a sickness of the head and the idea that renovating the house means healing and recovery don't literally correspond with oral dream books. Strictly speaking, these interpretations cannot be regarded as conventional. However, the logic the informant implemented to make sense of the dream is based on traditional models of dream interpretation. The informant extends the metaphor "house is a body" referring to its "unused" parts (Lakoff and Johnson 1980, 52–53). For example, the damaged state of the house or its destruction signifies illness or death in "oral dream books" (corresponding with the damaged state of an ill body or the destruction of a corpse). The "unused" parts of the metaphor are the elements of the house, which can be mapped onto specific parts of the body, or improvements to the house, which could stand for curing. Employing these "unused" parts of the metaphor allows the dreamer to interpret the dream in a positive way. If "house is the body," then "roof is the head," and "repairing the house is curing."

Sliding from one metaphor (house is a family and its parts are family members) to another (house is a body, hence its parts can be regarded as body parts) drastically changes the interpretation of the dream (see figure 12.1).

Lakoff and Mark Johnson noticed that a metaphor that "allows us to comprehend one aspect of a concept in terms of another [. . .] will necessarily hide other aspects of the concept [. . .] that are inconsistent with that metaphor" (1980, 10). In the case of dream interpretation, the new metaphor allows the dreamer to draw attention to the words about a

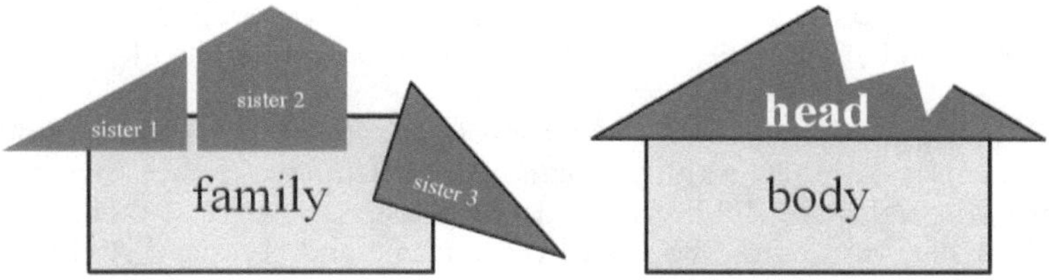

Figure 12.1 The Symbolism of the House and Its Parts Depending on the Metaphor Used to Interpret the Dream. *Source*: Generated by the Author.

renovation of the house, which can be interpreted as an auspicious sign. The details that were crucially important during the initial interpretation are not significant in this new framework. The dreamer didn't interpret the fact that the roof collapsed over the part of the house where Liuba lived with her older sister, which, according to the metaphor "house is a family," could mean that Liuba will "depart" from her family like a piece of the roof departed from the house (in other words, die). So in the new circumstances, when it is about the life of her friend, the dreamer is more creative and imaginative in interpreting her dream plot, not passively referring to the traditional ways of conceptualizing such kinds of dream images but intentionally looking for alternative ways to understand them.

The abrupt resolution of this story (*Liuba passed away. That is that.*) correlates with the common idea (expressed directly by some of my informants) that a bad dream will inevitably come true, no matter whether you believe it or not or how you want to escape the bad prognosis.

THE SECOND RECORD OF THE DREAM ABOUT THE BROKEN ROOF

The first text was recorded right after the death of the dreamer's friend. Let's compare it with the narrative about the same dream recorded next year, on the 24 of July 2016:

> Yesterday was a year after my neighbor had died. There were three sisters. The middle one died. It has been a year. And before it happened, I had a dream [. . .] I came out to my yard (well, in a dream) and took a look at the roof [of the neighbors' house]. There was no slate left on half of the roof. So, I looked out and thought, "Wow! What a hurricane there was last night!" The roof went down like that. But the rafters were standing. *I thought, "Well, it might be broken."* Then I heard the voice of their son-in-law (apparently, someone had asked, "What happened to you?"). *And he said, "Yes, I fixed it a little, but . . .* [the informant paused, trying to remember exact words heard in the dream, but ended the phrase with a generalization.] *In general, it's hopeless."*

I didn't tell anyone about this dream. Absolutely. And I thought, "Something must happen in that house." [The informant paused and sighed.]

Some time passed (in general, I won't speak for a long time), and the middle sister . . . She had this [health problem]: her pressure was either lowered or increased. And these children, this crippled sister . . . Oh . . . Well, it was hard for her, very hard. She would come to me and cry. [. . .] And as for that dream . . . I didn't tell anyone about it. I thought that something would happen to that sister [Nadia]. May God forgive me for thinking like that! Nothing happened to that one [Nadia], and this one [Liuba] was like this. As a result, she ends up in the hospital. [Pause] Bad, bad, bad. She felt bad. Then she got a little bit better. But [right after she returned from the hospital] her daughter already left her small child with her, notwithstanding that she shouldn't have bent over because she had had a stroke. Then Nadezhda shouted: "I wish you were dead!" [The informant told in detail how Liuba was taken to the hospital the second time and how she lent her last money to the neighbors]. [. . .] And I thought to myself: "Everything might go well. She has got nervous, that's all." In short, it lasted, but eventually, she passed away. So much for the roof!

The description of the dream plot is much more coherent than the previous one. In this case, the real event (Liuba's death) is a source domain—a lens through which the informant understands her dream, interprets and verbalizes it. Although the informant noted that she initially thought the dream boded ill for Nadia, she didn't discuss all the wrong interpretations. So, she didn't mention the details of the dream plot that corresponded with them. The informant omitted the thorough description of the neighbors' house structure and didn't mention that the roof fell over Nadia and Liuba's part of the house. Also, she didn't say that the house wasn't completely ruined—only the roof was damaged and might be fixed, which could have been interpreted as a good sign.

Whereas the first description of the dream plot didn't have a resolution, so the final part of the dream was open to interpretation, the end of the second version of the dream description is very clear. After the dreamer noticed that the roof was broken, she heard a speech from the man living there. The informant altered the neighbor's initial phrase. In the first version of the plot, he said that he had started to repair the roof (*I heard the voice of Vera's husband, Seryozha. He said, "I started to repair it"*). And in the second one, represented in a dialogic form, he answered that he couldn't fix the roof (*And he said, "Yes, I fixed it a little, but . . . In general, it's hopeless"*). The last words represent the main idea of the story. Since the house is a metaphor for the body and its renovation is a metaphor for healing the body, the impossibility of repairing the roof represents the inability to cure the disease. As it was impossible to fix the roof (in other words, the house was completely ruined because you cannot live in the house without a roof), it turned out to be impossible to save the woman.

CONCLUSION

This chapter was devoted to the analysis of versions of a dream plot that may seem similar at first glance. In each of them, the central image is the same: the damaged roof of the neighbors' house. The slight discrepancies in the descriptions could seem like a result of random memory errors. However, as it has been shown, a dream plot structure is always consistent with the dream interpretation. The dream interpretation process supposes structuring the description of a dream so that it coheres with cultural models and the dreamer's ideas about how the dream plot is connected to reality. Each small plot detail that was mentioned (or not mentioned) by the dreamer influences how the dream plot is interpreted.

The dreamer might be confused about choosing plot details to describe and pay attention to. For example, was it meaningful which part of the house was damaged? Was the neighbor still going to fix the roof, or did he acknowledge that he failed to fix it? It turned out to be impossible to answer such questions without filling in the missing parts of the dream memories, which means constructing a plot that implies a certain meaning (in the case of prophetic dreams—a prediction that the dreamer regards as the most probable or desirable). The subtle changes in the plot description demonstrate how the informant shifts between different metaphors and story schemas—forms of description that imply different meanings for the dream imagery. Since each narrative structure of the dream plot (as well as each mentioned detail) leads to a certain logic of dream interpretation, the informant fills the gaps in her memories and structures the story about the dream differently in different circumstances. Each new description of the dream plot allowed the dreamer to "elicit" a new meaning.

Analysis of the interpretation of the dream as foretelling the future makes it more evident because the dream plot, being connected to hypothetical events in the future (that do not always meet predictions and expectations), transforms in response to changing circumstances. As we have seen, on each step of interpretation, the informant turned to a new story schema:

1. In a dream, an object loses its part. In reality, a family loses its member (a family member dies or leaves the family);
2. In a dream, an object is damaged but then fixed. In reality, a person gets ill but then is successfully cured and gets better;
3. In a dream, an object is ruined. In reality, a person dies.

These schemas imply alternative ways of describing the dream plot, paying attention to some details while ignoring others, therefore ascribing to the dream plot disparate meanings (alternative interpretations). At the initial stage of the dream interpretation, the neighbors' house was regarded as a symbol of their family. This metaphor implied a certain hypothetical meaning of that image—"there will probably be trouble"—which can be regarded as a self-censored way to refer to the traditional prognosis of "death in the family." However, since the informant didn't know who would die (it might be someone old whose death would be natural and predictable), she didn't try to impose any structure and meaning (that deviated from the most typical ones) on this plot. At the next stages of dream interpretation, the informant constructs her dream narrative based on the changing circumstances: the illness of the neighbor, who was the informant's friend, and then her death. During her friend's illness, the informant proceeded to construct connections between the dream, reality, and desirable future events. The house is no longer connected with a concept of family. Therefore, a detached piece of the roof is no more regarded as a family member who would be detached from the family. The damaged house is regarded as a metaphor for the ill body. Consequently, its damaged part is interpreted as a symbol of the part of the body that needs healing. The dreamer found dream plot details that can be "mapped" onto favorable changes in the future—the damaged head can be healed like the broken roof can be repaired. So, the dreamer recalled the man going to fix the roof in the dream. The more the informant wanted to adjust the plot of her dream to a benevolent interpretation, the more "imaginative" (Lakoff and Johnson 1980, 53) metaphors she applied. The informant extended the traditional logic of dream interpretation, using unused parts of conventional metaphors in a creative way, which makes the story more original, declining from traditional schemas for prophetic dream plots. Therefore, the process of narrative construction is more visible in this case. After her friend died, the dream plot became a stereotypical folkloric story about a prediction of death in a dream.

Initially, the dream plot was a source domain for speculating about hypothetical future events. During the neighbor's illness, the source and target domains switched places. On the one hand, the real event (the illness) caused the dreamer to revise and restructure the dream plot in order to make the prediction more coherent with the actual situation and desirable (so, the real event was a source domain). On the other hand, based on the re-conceptualized dream imagery, the informant made predictions about the course of the disease (so, the dream plot became a source domain again). After the neighbor's death, this event became the source domain to reason about the dream plot. Making sense of the dream plot, the interpreter constructs a relevant correlation between the dream and reality. In other words, dream imagery and waking life events are "translations" of each other. Dream interpretation is a process of connecting these two domains, finding (or constructing) their correspondences.

Because different patterns can be discerned in (or ascribed to) the same dream, we can conclude that dream memories contain multiple dream plots that can be narrated (and therefore multiple meanings can be ascribed to the same dream). Telling a prophetic dream plot means selecting some details of the memorized dream experience and combining them in the form of a coherent story (reducible to folklore models/conceptual metaphors) that makes sense. If dreaming is a specific form of thought, then dream telling is an extension of this thinking in waking reality, which compares the dream world and the real world and tries to understand them through each other. Therefore, it is quite impossible to separate dream mentation (and, broadly speaking, all kinds of visions or fantasies) from conscious storytelling, which implies a meaning-making process. Not only is there no meaning without an interpreter, but also there is no story without a narrator, who evaluates and explains dream images, reconciles them with one's notions of the meaning (or nature) of dreams, connects them to reality, and therefore turns them into a plot.

NOTES

1. The narratives considered in the paper were translated into English from Ukrainian. Since the purpose of the study is to analyze the process of dream interpretation, the extensive deviations from the main topic (dream interpretation) were replaced by short summaries of the informant's words in square brackets. Previously, much more shortened fragments of these interviews (in the original language accompanied by a translation into Russian) with a brief analytical comment were published in my PhD thesis (Lazareva 2018, 84–88) and monograph (Lazareva 2020, 38–42). Working on the current chapter, I turned to the original audio recordings of the interviews and made another (much more thorough and full) transcript of these texts. This research (a comparison of the two narratives about the same dream) was previously presented at "XII Meletinsky Readings: text in the communication space (folklore section)" (Russian State University for the Humanities, 2020) and at the Joint Meeting of the Society for Psychological Anthropology and the Society for the Study of Psychiatry and Culture "Ecologies of mind. Practices that harm. Practices that Heal" (The University of San Diego, 2023). In the current work, having reviewed and supplemented my prior findings, I have used a cognitive approach to analyze these texts.

2. The identities of the informant and the people she was talking about are withheld (all the last names were either changed or not mentioned).

3. The metaphors "a house is a human body" and "a roof is a head" are also represented in the traditional elements of the design of the houses of the Eastern Slavs and the names of the parts of the house (Krinichnaia 2015, 71–72).

BIBLIOGRAPHY

Bartlett, Frederic Charles. 1932. *Remembering: A Study in Experimental and Social Psychology*. Cambridge: Cambridge University Press.

Bundgaard, Peer and Frederik Stjernfelt. 2010. "Logic and Cognition." In *The Routledge Companion to Semiotics*, edited by Paul Cobley, 79–95. London: Routledge.

Cariola, Laura Annamaria. 2008. "A Structural and Functional Analysis of Dream Narratives." *Dreaming* 18 (1): 16–26.

Casson, Ronald W. 1983. "Schemata in Cognitive Anthropology." *Annual Review of Anthropology* 12 (1): 429–462.

Chafe, Wallace. 1977. "The Recall and Verbalization of Past Experience." In *Current Issues in Linguistic Theory*, edited by Roger William Cole, 215–246. Bloomington: Indiana University Press.

D'Andrade, Roy Goodwin. 1984. "Cultural Meaning Systems." In *Culture Theory: Essays on Mind, Self and Emotion*, edited by Richard Allan Schweder and Robert Alan Levine, 88–119. Cambridge: Cambridge University Press.

Fillmore, Charles J. 1976. "Frame Semantics and the Nature of Language." *Annals of the New York Academy of Sciences: Conference on the Origin and Development of Language and Speech* 280 (1): 20–32.

Foulkes, David. *Grammar of Dreams*. New York: Basic Books, 1978.

Friesen, Ryan Curtis. 2019. *The Nightly Act of Dreaming: Cognitive Narratology and the Shared Identity of Myth*. Liverpool: Liverpool University Press.

Hall, Calvin S. 1953. "A Cognitive Theory of Dreams." *Journal of General Psychology*. 49 (2): 273–282.

Hill, Jane H. 2005. "Finding Culture in Narrative." In *Finding Culture in Talk: A Collection of Methods*, edited by Naomi Quinn, 157–202. New York: Palgrave Macmillan.

Kilborne, Benjamin. 1981. "Pattern, Structure, and Style in Anthropological Studies of Dreams." *Ethos* 9 (2): 165–185.

Kilroe, Patricia. 2000. "The Dream as Text, the Dream as Narrative." *Dreaming* 10 (3): 125–137.

Kilroe, Patricia. 2001. "Verbal Aspects of Dreaming: A Preliminary Classification." *Dreaming* 11 (3): 105–113.

Krinichnaia, Neonila Artemovna. 2015. "*Krysha i cherdak: byt i obrazy*." *Russkaia rech'* 4: 69–75.

Labov, William and Joshua Waletzky. 1967. "Narrative Analysis." In *Essays on the Verbal and Visual Arts*, edited by June Helm, 12–44. Seattle: University of Washington Press.

Lakoff, George. 1993. "The Contemporary Theory of Metaphor." In *Metaphor and Thought*, edited by Andrew Ortony, 202–251. Cambridge: Cambridge University Press.

Lakoff, George. 2001. "How Metaphor Structures Dreams: The Theory of Conceptual Metaphor Applied to Dream Analysis." In *Dreams: A Reader on Religious, Cultural, and Psychological Dimensions of Dreaming*, edited by Kelly Bulkeley, 265–284. New York: Palgrave Macmillan.

Lakoff, George and Mark Johnson. 1980. *Metaphors we Live by*. Chicago and London: The University of Chicago Press.

Lazareva, Anna Andreevna. 2018. *"Simvolika snovidenii v narodnoi kul'ture: fol'klornye modeli i lichnye narrativy."* PhD diss., Gorky Institute of World Literature of the Russian Academy of Sciences.

Lazareva, Anna Andreevna. 2020. *Tolkovanie snovidenii v narodnoi kul'ture.* Moscow: Russian State University for the Humanities.

Lazareva, Anna Andreevna. 2023. "Motif Index of Prophetic Dream Narratives: Methods of Compilation." *Folklore. Electronic Journal of Folklore* 89: 161–190.

Lohmann, Roger Ivar. 2021. "Out-of-body on the Happy Hunting Road: Dialogues between Dreaming and Culture in Papua New Guinea." In *New Directions in the Anthropology of Dreaming,* edited by Jeannette Marie Mageo and Robin E. Sheriff, 137–157. New York: Routledge.

Mageo, Jeannette Marie. 2021. "Metaphors we Dream by: On the Nature of Dream Cognition." In *New Directions in the Anthropology of Dreaming,* edited by Jeannette Marie Mageo and Robin E. Sheriff, 53–71. New York: Routledge.

Mageo, Jeannette Marie. 2022. *The Mimetic Nature of Dream Mentation: American Selves in Re-formation.* New York: Palgrave Macmillan.

Mannheim, Bruce. 1991. "After Dreaming: Image and Interpretation in Southern Peruvian Quechua." *Etnofoor* 4 (2): 43–79.

Miloradovich, Vasilii Petrovich. 1992. *"Zhit'e-byt'e lubenskogo krest'ianina."* In *Ukrayintsi: narodni viruvannya, povir'ya, demonologiya,* 170–341. Kyiv: Lybid.

Peräkylä, Anssi and Jorg Bergmann. 2020. "Practices of Joint Meaning Creation. Dreams in Psychoanalytic Discussion." *The International Journal of Psychoanalysis* 101 (5): 923–950.

Quinn, Naomi. 1987. "Convergent Evidence for a Cultural Model of American Marriage." In *Cultural Models in Language and Thought,* edited by Dorothy Holland and Naomi Quinn, 173–192. Cambridge: Cambridge University Press.

Quinn, Naomi. 2005. "How to Reconstruct Schemas People Share, from what they Say." In *Finding Culture in Talk. A Collection of Methods,* edited by Naomi Quinn, 35–81. New York: Palgrave Macmillan.

Safronov, Evgenii. 2016. *Snovideniia v traditsionnoi kul'ture.* Moscow: Labirint.

Sheriff, Robin E. 2021. "Dreaming Bloody Murder: Women's Dreams of Mortal Threat, True-Crime Culture, and Metonyms of Gendered Vulnerability." In *New Directions in the Anthropology of Dreaming,* edited by Jeannette Marie Mageo and Robin E. Sheriff, 93–113. New York: Routledge.

Walsh, Richard. 2022. "Human Cognition and Narrative Form." In *The Routledge Companion to Narrative Theory,* edited by Paul Dawson and Maria Mäkelä, 369–383. New York: Routledge.

13

Intersections between Language, Social Norms, and Individual Cognition in Natalya Baranskaya's *A Week Like Any Other*

Angelina Rubina

Natalya Baranskaya's novella *A Week Like Any Other* was first published in the USSR in 1969 in a prestigious and politically independent magazine *Novyi Mir* [*New World*]. During this time, often referred to as the "Era of Stagnation," Soviet women continued to carry the heavy double burden of household chores and professional workload, while most husbands refused to participate in household life. A Moscow survey revealed that, out of the women who considered themselves unhappily married during that period, 50 percent were "dissatisfied with the division of labor in their household" (Engel 2004, 243). This double burden found its illustration in Baranskaya's novella, which tells the story of Olga Voronkova, a 26-year-old research scientist. In her daily schedule over the course of one week, the protagonist attends to her two children, her husband Dima, her job at a research institute, as well as a requirement at work to complete an ethnographic survey on women's daily routine habits. Being torn apart between the context of family life, on the one hand, and the work environment, on the other hand, the protagonist and her female colleagues interact with society and the state, while also facing their own fears and aspirations.

Written in the first person in the form of a diary, the novella does not read like a fictional diary with an intricate "external" plotline of murders, love triangles, or mysteries. Its challenges rather come from "mundaneness [*povsednevnost'*]"—"the flow of daily life with all its trivial routine as well as the personal, domestic, and emotional problems confronting the individual" (Natov 1974, 360). Benjamin Sutcliffe compares the exposition in Baranskaya's writing to the style that Roland Barthes denotes as "'zero degree of writing': a 'neutral mode' of realistic representation," which "reveals itself to be far more than art's mirroring of reality" (30). Similarly, Thomas Lahusen describes the novella as "an avatar of 'factography' in the 1960s and 1970s" (208).

Such an ethnographically precise description of the protagonist's life has been recognized by Soviet women and critics. Baranskaya received numerous letters "from grateful women thanking her for telling the truth about their lives" (Heuvel 1990, 775). Critics of Soviet culture "appropriated her [Olga's] diary as their source material, as if *A Week like Any Other* were not a literary text, but an ethnographer's field notes" (Gelfant 1995, 34). While Soviet critics recognized Baranskaya's "sociological acuity and sensitivity to topical issues" more than her "technical abilities as a writer," Western critics did not dismiss her literary merit only because of her focus on *byt* (mundaneness) (Kelly 1994, 399–400).

Ethnographic qualities of the novella have determined previous critical approaches to its analysis. U.S. literary critics have often considered it through both feminist (Marsh 1996) and queer (Fishzon 2017) perspectives, focusing on the overwhelming hardships that Soviet women faced in coping with day-to-day life. Although feminist literary criticism is a common lens for the interpretation of *A Week like Any Other*, the novella itself does not impose any rigid feminist dogma. Nicholas Žekulin says that although the book was initially greeted in a positive way abroad, "more recently, critics have focused on the limitations of its feminism" (242). Moreover, Baranskaya herself expressed a refusal to be labeled a feminist (see Baranskaya 1988, 34 for an interview with Pieta Monks; Lally 1995 for an interview with Kathy Lally). Some critics have also recognized the novella's psychoanalytical angle. Nadine Natov, for example, points out Baranskaya's "interest in a psychological approach" to the life of her protagonist (359). Similarly, Natal'ia Ivanova describes the writing style of the novella as "the physiological sketch" with its depiction of mundane life "day by day, hour by hour" (23).

Although critics have recognized some psychoanalytical elements in the novella, there are no accounts of the systematic role of language and its relations with the state, society, and individual identities in the novella. Addressing this gap, the broader questions of this chapter are: (i) How does the novella depict language—as language created *for* the people or as the language *of* the people, or both? and (ii) What are the effects of different instantiations of language on the protagonist's search for identity? In addressing these broad psychoanalytical questions, this chapter considers the relation between the language of the state ideology and the language of the community and its individual speakers, including the protagonist.

REALIZATIONS OF THE LANGUAGE *FOR* THE PEOPLE

The language *for* the people in the novella is the language of the ethnographic survey that the protagonist and her colleagues need to complete at work. Although this survey has a clearly stated addressee (it is "A Questionnaire for Women"), its creator is not known, as the names of its authors are absent. For example, the protagonist Olga Voronkova notes: "Who thought up this questionnaire? I turn it around but can't see any information on the compilers" (Baranskaya 1990, 7). Later, she learns that the survey was distributed by demographers, who "said that they're carrying out an experiment with these questionnaires at certain institutions where women work" (Baranskaya 1990, 7). However, demographers in this case do not function as the creators of the survey, but rather as nameless transmitters of its language to society. The fact that working women have no choice but to complete the survey suggests that the power of the Soviet state is implied in its distribution and creation.

The language of the survey sets the standard and presents the characteristics for an ideal Soviet woman, the characteristics against which the characters, consciously or not, begin to compare their own lives. Thus, through the survey, the Soviet state attempts to structure women's identities. What functions does an ideal Soviet woman need to perform? How and with what frequency does she need to perform them? Fishzon, for example, points out that such a questionnaire was "probably associated with the regime's pronatalist policies" (557), which is not surprising, because several questions of the survey are related to childbearing. Another implied message of the survey is to emphasize Soviet women's lack of progress "in the context of the society's greater good" (Heldt 1987, 144). Thus, the story of the protagonist's "harried daily life" is legitimized by "the imprint of wider social concern" (Heldt 1987, 145).

Another question on the survey is about the amount of time that respondents spend on housework. The mere presence of such a question creates certain assumptions, and sets the standards and expectations. Is a Soviet woman supposed to fulfill these functions on her own or is anyone, for example, her husband, supposed to help her with them? The fact that the husband is not even mentioned in the questions on household routines signals the state's expectations for the distribution of household duties in the family.

In Lacanian terms, the assumptions created by the language of the survey paint the image of the symbolic Other (capitalized)—an ideal Soviet woman. By painting this image, the survey implicitly pushes its respondents to relate to this image, thus attempting to create in them a desire for this symbolic Other in their search for their real inner *self*. The language of the survey, therefore, operates on its characters as much as they operate on it. In other words, respondents follow the signs while the language of the survey attempts to "speak" them. This language is, like algebra, a structure of relations rather than things, and its function as the Symbolic does not require the name of a specific person that produces it.

Interestingly, in line with Lacanian analysis, this questionnaire addresses the life of a woman, a mother—and not of a sister, a child, a worker, or a man. It implies the woman image (and the mother image) as the first person whom a child sees with their reflection in the mirror on the Imagery stage of the development of their identity.

The symbolic dimension of the language of the survey is that of signifiers with no positive existence in the real world (which the representative function of the sign in a Saussurean understanding would imply). Even though the survey does not directly "push" its readers to follow the norms it creates, the symbolic language of the survey still represents the signifiers with their value telling one where to go (the law-imposing function of the sign in Lacanian terms). In this, the language of the survey resembles Saussurean *langue*—an abstract linguistic system for reference. On a broader cultural scale, the language of the survey also resembles Lotman's understanding of *langue* as a system of ideal rules of social behavior.

The assumptions created by the questionnaire do not skip the women's attention and are not relegated to the unconscious of the respondents. For example, Olga's colleague, Blonde Lusya, says, "I think there is more to this questionnaire than meets the eye. Maybe they'll give us mothers some benefits, eh? Shorten our working day; pay us for the whole time we have off when our kids are sick and not just the first three days, don't you think?" (Baranskaya 1990, 9). However, Blonde Lusya's dreams crash as they face the reality described by another colleague, Dark Lusya, who argues that the purpose of the survey is to encourage women to have more children who would become the building force for the state. Dark Lusya says:

> That's not what it's about. We don't have enough builders, our workforce is too small, that's the point. What will happen? Who will do the building? [. . .] All the building: houses; factories; machines; bridges; roads; missiles; communism. Everything. And who'll defend all this? And who'll cultivate the land? (Baranskaya 1990, 9–10)

Dark Lusya's reply is an example of merging two worlds—the world of physical objects and the world of the abstract, the Symbolic. Building houses and building communism are on the same to-do list that the state imposes on its citizens. Therefore, the language of the survey does not so much focus on the form as it targets the meaning, the purpose of that form (which is the building of communism).

Related to the idea of inscribing social standards on an individual's mind is a discipline that Boris Gasparov calls *the semiotic aspects of social behavior* (16), which he puts at the intersection of structuralist poetics, social psychology, and anthropology. This discipline relies on Iurii Lotman's attention to the relationship between the social norm and its violation in individual behavior. It treats social life as "the realization of cultural codes developed by society" (Gasparov 1985, 16), which implies that social life inscribes social codes on people. According to Gasparov, cultural codes compose systems of "more or less conventional signs that a member of a given society must internalize in order to participate competently in that society's life" (16). Comparing the codes of social behavior to a native language, Gasparov points out that these codes are naturally acquired in the process of practicing social relations and that "[a]ny system with a heightened and deliberate internal organization will tend to play an important role in the process of internalization" (17). Language (in this case, the language of the survey), due to its complex nature, can certainly function as a system that would internalize cultural codes and social expectations in the minds of the members of a society.

Therefore, the language of the survey is supposed to have a top-down effect on its respondents. It's not the society that produces this type of language. This language is rather produced *for* the society and imposed on it, with the norms and ideologies created and distributed by the Soviet state power, as in the Soviet context it seems difficult to divorce official language distribution from state control. The structure and content of the language of the survey influence its readers' worldview, cognition, and experiences, like language, according to the famous Sapir-Whorf hypothesis of linguistic relativity, shapes the way one thinks about reality. The role of this survey is not so much about "measuring the temperature" in Soviet society, nor is it about getting to know more about the real life of Soviet women. It is rather about pushing Soviet women toward a certain way of thinking about their expected way of life and their expected priorities. Such language is not supposed to be representative of the existing reality, nor does it require the name of a definite author as its creator. It is a referential symbolic system of values created by the system of Soviet state power.

REALIZATIONS OF THE LANGUAGE *OF* THE PEOPLE

The language *of* the people in the novella represents a bottom-up effect, which is opposite to the top-down nature of the language of the survey. The language *of* the people is produced by society and reflects the inner nature of this society and its members. In some instances, it manifests itself in people's resistance to and questioning of the ideology (as it is represented in the survey). However, the language *for* the people and the language *of* the people are not two separate units. They interact in such a way that the language *for* the people affects that *of* the people. As a result, the language *of* the people is not uniform in its reaction to the social norms. Individual people do not simply reject the imposed social standards, nor do they unquestionably accept these norms. They are rather torn apart by resisting those norms, on the one hand, and striving to accomplish them, on the other. This internal conflict often restrains the characters from discovering their genuine identity.

One instance of the fluctuation of some female characters in their resistance to, versus support for, the imposed state norms is the reactions of Blonde Lusya and Dark Lusya—two colleagues of the main character. On the one hand, the examples in the section above show that Dark Lusya does not ignore the assumptions created in the survey. As she ironically mocks the survey's role in the building of communism, she also makes these assumptions clear for Blonde Lusya. However, Blonde Lusya still imbibes these assumptions and attempts to justify the state ideology that the survey translates. For example, on Tuesday, Blonde Lusya "flings herself to the defense of the questionnaire" as she remarks: "After all, we must find an answer to our serious, even dangerous, demographic crisis" (Baranskaya 1990, 20). Blonde Lusya's remark shows that the survey, at least to a certain extent, manages to imprint communist pronatalist values onto the minds of its respondents.

The fact that Blonde Lusya and Dark Lusya share the same name does not seem to be a coincidence. In this, they function as two different reflections of the same prototype—the prototype of Soviet society. Their shared name represents the dual nature of society's reactions to the language *for* the people, as well as the dual nature of Russian culture in general. This relates to Iurii Lotman and Boris Uspenskii's work on the semiotics of culture and the binary models of Russian culture, where they argue for the existence of two contradictory spheres of Russian culture ("elevated"—sacred, and "low"—profane) and hence of two contrasting behavioral codes (32–33). This binary typology found its expression in the so-called Russian "double faith" and "doublethink." The Russian invariant cultural plan of doublethink (previously expressed through pagan patterns within Christianity and through the juxtaposition of "westernizers" and "slavophiles," among other things) finds its realization in the novella in the dual nature of Blonde Lusya's and Dark Lusya's reactions to the language *for* the people.

While in the case of Blonde Lusya and Dark Lusya this binary opposition exists between two different people (at least in certain situations), the protagonist Olga Voronkova demonstrates the same opposition, but within a single person. Being torn apart between what she is expected to be, on the one hand, and her search for her genuine identity, on the other, she demonstrates this opposition in her language.

At the beginning of the novella, Olga presents herself to the reader as a reflection of the norms of the world around her: she cares for her husband and her children, she runs the household and works full-time. Olga's reflection of the Soviet norms in her daily behavior resembles the Lacanian mirror phase, or Imaginary (from the French word *image* [reflection]), which suggests that the subject, originally being weak and fragmentary, identifies with the wholeness of their reflected, external form, while this reflection of a subject is not quite what the subject truly is. In Lacan's account, this reflected external form constitutes a baby's reflection of themselves in the mirror (a reflection or projection of the ego described with the lower-case *other*), and it implies pointing to and naming that reflection. Olga's reflected external form is her everyday routine actions, with which she often, consciously or not, identifies herself in her language. In her internal monologues, for instance, she enumerates her children's illnesses, the clothes that she needs to put on them, the food that she needs to buy at the store, and the household chores that she needs to complete over the weekend.

The language that she uses to talk about her chores is not a language of complex sentences, but rather a language of lists and simple sentences, fragmentary and scattered in its nature. Edward Brown argues that the story is a combination of "quick short sentences, incomplete snatches of dialogue, remarks thrown back over the shoulder as one rushes downstairs, anecdotes and one-liners dropped in passing" (320). Brown also notes that the story "is told in a frantic present tense dominated by the verbs for hurrying, worrying, and scurrying" (320). Similarly, Sutcliffe describes women's temporality in Baranskaya's work as "fragmented, cyclical, and self-erasing," arguing that such a perception stems from *byt* and "its magnification of mundane concerns" (38). Thus, with its frantic present tense and its focus on fragmented external objects, Olga's language shows her assumption that her subjectivity exists somewhere "out there" in her daily actions. In other words, her repeated daily actions create a signifying chain for who she is. Olga's identity is inscribed into this daily routine of external objects and repetitive automatic actions even on the level of the structure of the novella—a cyclical Monday-to-Sunday week.

As Olga's internal monologue focuses on external images, these images, in Lacanian terms, create a false signifying chain and cause false self-identification and self-recognition. This results in Olga's difficulty in attaining totality, wholeness, and autonomy, as well as in alienation from her true *self* (or the Real, in Lacanian terminology).[1] One example of such a lack of the feeling of totality and wholeness is apparent in Olga's conversation with her colleagues when they are complaining (even jokingly) about how they would like to exchange certain aspects of their lives with each other. In this dialogue, Olga and her colleagues sound as if they are incomplete, imperfect, and fragmentary the way they are, like a baby in the Lacanian paradigm who sees only parts of themself in the mirror. Moreover, the "three-way exchange" that Olga, Blonde Lusya, and Dark Lusya discuss focuses on the physical sphere of their lives (i.e., on their apartments, bathrooms, appearances, and kids), which also matches the physical nature of the Lacanian mirror phase. For instance, when Dark Lusya says that she could move from her three-room flat into Blonde Lusya's small communal flat, Dark Lusya remarks: "I don't want to, but needs must. I'll lose out on square metres and conveniences—you don't have a bathroom, do you?—but I'll gain on something more important [a Granny]" (Baranskaya 1990, 11).

Olga's detachment from her own true *self* is also clear in the language that she uses to describe her acquaintance with her husband and their honeymoon trip to the seaside in Alupka. In this scene, during a slow walk home along the wide Moscow boulevards, the heroine remembers that happy time, which Lahusen describes as "paradise lost" (213). In her reminiscences about the past, Olga switches from the formerly used "I" to the distant and disconnected "she": "All that was such a long time ago, so dreadfully long ago that it feels as if it wasn't me but some other she . . . It was like this: SHE saw him, HE saw her, and they fell in love" (Baranskaya 1990, 30). In the Russian original, in the phrase "some other SHE," SHE is also capitalized (Baranskaia 1969, 38). Regarding Olga's self-identification, Lahusen notes, "The only time that really counts for Ol'ga turns out to be some sort of epic time of the past, *without any ties to the present*" (212, emphasis added). Thus, this scene not only emphasizes Olga's loss of connection to the present, but it also underscores her detachment from her true *self*, as marked in the pronoun shift.

Beyond the use of language, Olga's detachment from herself is also obvious in the fact that she does not tend much to her physical image. For instance, in her haste to complete all the routine actions, she often forgets to comb her hair or to attach a hook to her clothes.

Olga's female colleagues also encourage her self-identification with her routine behavior. They argue that, compared to their life situations, she is a happy woman with a husband, two sweet children, and a private spacious apartment in a new building. Reacting to this observation, Olga says about herself: "I should be the happiest one" (Baranskaya 1990, 9). In Lacanian terms, her female co-workers represent the figurative mother who, seeing that the baby is looking at its reflection in the mirror, would say: "[l]ook, this reflection is you, this is who you are." They call Olga "a real Soviet woman" and tell her that she is "a good mother and a good worker" (Baranskaya 1990, 12). In this, her colleagues function like the language of the survey, with its top-down delivery of the expected social behavior of an ideal Soviet woman.

Olga, however, seems to question what this definition of a "real Soviet woman" means. She asks herself: "Am I such a good mother? Am I really a praiseworthy worker? And what is a 'real Soviet woman' anyway?" (Baranskaya 1990, 12). These questions suggest that she is trying to resist such subjectivization of her real identity into an externally imposed norm (i.e., the image of an ideal Soviet woman).

One might question the fact whether Olga even cares about these social expectations. However, this Soviet "superwoman" seems to be Olga's point of reference, which is obvious from how she uses her language to talk about herself, her life, and the survey. First, let us turn to Olga's language in addressing the survey. Some of its inquiries were about women's cultural leisure and favorite sports. Natov argues that Olga's ironic responses to these questions show her awareness of the pressure from her everyday routine (361). However, such irony can also be a sign of Olga's self-reproach for not being able to manage her time successfully, as an ideal Soviet woman would. The more Olga goes into the questions of the survey, the less ironic her reactions become. For instance, Olga thinks that the question about days off due to her own and her children's illnesses "inhibits any desire to be witty" (Baranskaya 1990, 6). When Olga discovers how many days she had missed, she thinks: "I don't understand why I feel so awkward, even ashamed. I shrink, avoid looking at people. Why? I'm not guilty of anything" (Baranskaya 1990, 48). Also, while answering the questionnaire, Olga sometimes tries to come up with correct, but not necessarily true, answers, as if, consciously or not, trying to match the standard for an ideal Soviet woman. Thus, Olga's language shows that the top-down effect of the survey's language *for* the people is real.

Not only does Olga's language describing the survey suggest that she uses the ideal Woman as a point of reference, but also her own description of her daily life suggests the same idea. For example, consider Olga's depiction of her constant haste, of her running and running, as if trying to reach the ideal, the unattainable standard of an ideal Soviet woman. For example, describing her day, Olga would say: "I must rush, I mustn't be late. *The others get home by seven*" (Baranskaya 1990, 4, emphasis added).

This suggests that she should get home in time not for her true *self*, but rather to serve her husband and children, like an ideal Soviet woman.

Another manifestation of the presence of an ideal Soviet woman in Olga's mind is her multiple evaluations of situations that involve household chores and childcare. For example, she repeats the phrase "that's not really a good idea" multiple times. Literally, in Russian, this phrase is "*chto nekhorosho* [what is not good]" (Baranskaia 1969, 49), and in Russian, it sounds more like a reproach than a recommendation. A similar effect of self-reproach comes from the phrase "*chto ne polagaetsia* [what one is not supposed to do]," when Olga considers lulling her little daughter to sleep (Baranskaia 1969, 49). The evaluative terms "good," "not good," and "not supposed to" only make sense when they are applied to a certain standard (or ideal?).

Also, in her use of language to describe herself, Olga sometimes turns to the ideal Soviet woman as a point of reference. For example, on Saturday, after her emotional outburst, Olga says to herself: "I already feel ashamed at *having made such a scene*" (Baranskaya 1990, 54, emphasis added). What is lost in the English translation is the semantics of the Russian reflexive verb *raspustilas'* ("*ia tak raspustilas'* [I let myself become less organized, less composed compared to what I should behave like]") (Baranskaia 1969, 50). This verb functions as an indicator of Olga's internal monitor that compares her behavior against the imposed desirable norm. It implies that "such a scene" was not the way an ideal Soviet woman would behave. With the use of the reflexive verb *raspustilas'*, the focus quickly shifts from Olga's inner *self* (which has the right to experience and demonstrate different emotions, outbursts included) to an external norm.

In contrast to the language of the survey, which functions as Saussurean *langue* (an abstract system for reference), the language that Olga (as well as other characters) uses to address these ideal rules matches Saussurean *parole*—a concrete realization of this abstract system in the speech of an individual. The protagonist's dialogues and internal monologues also resemble the interpretation of *parole* as the realization of the real life of a society, in line with Lotman's view of the binary models of Russian culture.

Being exposed to the language of the survey, women do not interact with this language independently of other women. Rather, they engage in an act of shared attention and agency. This involves the same subject (i.e., the theme of the survey), the same place for its distribution (i.e., workplace), the same timeframe within which they need to complete the survey (i.e., one week), and the assumption that each woman needs to complete it.

These characteristics of the women's interaction with the survey follow Michael Tomasello's features of "second-personal engagement" that create "second-personal morality" (48). According to Tomasello, second-personal morality emerges from collaborative acts which have the following qualities: (i) each individual *directly* participates in a social interaction and does not observe it "from outside," (ii) this interaction involves *specific* individuals and not "something more general like a group," and (iii) this interaction happens in the "mutual recognition" of each individual's *equal* second-personal standing (i.e., feeling responsible to one another as a jointly committed "we") (48). Thus, in line with Tomasello's account of second-personal morality, the language of the survey engages its participants in a mutual activity where each one is equally engaged and responsible. Olga and other women engage in discussing the survey questions together (i.e., mutual activity) and evaluate their own responses against the potential responses of their colleagues (i.e., equal engagement and responsibility). For instance, on Friday at work, Olga feels "awkward, even ashamed" about having the highest number of "sick days" missed from work compared to her colleagues (Baranskaya 1990, 48). On the same day, Blonde Lusya asks other women: "What shall I write about the children?" (Baranskaya 1990, 48). She also asks her colleagues, "Have you filled in the questionnaire? [. . .] let's have a look" (Baranskaya 1990, 49). This binds the women as mutually accountable moral agents (in Tomasello's terms of second-personal morality), therefore enforcing the effects of the survey questions compared to the context in which each woman addressed these questions independently of other members of the group.

In summary, the language *of* the people in the novella is the language of individual characters in their evaluations of the world and attempts to discover their genuine identity. While the language *for* the people refers to the symbolic norm imposed on society by the Soviet state in a top-down manner, the language *of* the people reflects real-life situations and the bottom-up reactions to life from individual characters. Characters engage with the language *for* the people not independently of other characters, but rather in an act of shared agency and attention (i.e., where each character is expected to participate and address the same questions). In its essence, the language *of* the people reflects the dual nature of the characters' reactions to the language *for* the people. The conflict between questioning the imposed norm in some situations and aspiring to reach the imposed ideal in other situations results in the protagonist's self-alienation and detachment from her genuine identity. The conflicting nature of the language *of* the people also reflects the dual nature of Russian culture.

AT THE CROSSROADS: IN SEARCH OF ONE'S TRUE *SELF*

Olga's dialogues and internal monologues show that she seems to identify with her everyday routine actions and, in this self-identification, consciously or unconsciously, she also aspires for the unattainable image of an ideal Soviet woman. However, such identifications are external, and therefore they distance Olga from her real inner *self*. Such distancing from the real *self* is expressed in Lacan's rewriting of the famous self-definition of Descartes's "*cogito ergo sum* [I think, therefore I am]") as a form of self-alienation: "I am where I am not thinking" (517). So, only by curing this fantasy about the truth "out there" (i.e., instantiated in the social norms) and by turning to her true *self* can Olga construct her individual subjectivity and come to peace with it.

Olga's *self* gradually begins to show up as the novella progresses, in Olga's actions and in her use of words. On Wednesday, she decides to change her haircut, as if trying to change her familiar (but not genuine) reflection in the mirror. Even in this attempt, she is at first faced with the ruthlessness of the external *female* monitor, who reaches her through the hands of the *woman*-hairdresser who completely ruins her hairstyle, as if trying to impose some external, alien norm onto the main character. Not surprisingly, it is a man, Lenya, who grants Olga the right to find an image in the mirror with which she is happy to identify. She says: "Before me I see a young, funny girl. I smile at her and she smiles back" (Baranskaya 1990, 27). This description, through the contrast between the first and the third-person pronouns, resembles the scene of Olga's reminiscences about her acquaintance with her husband. Like then, the scene at the hairdresser's sounds as if there are now two Olgas out there and as if the one in the mirror truly reflects Olga's genuine *self*. However, in the situation at the hairdresser's, Olga still shifts to the third-person pronoun *she*. This suggests that, although she still tends to detach herself from her genuine identity, this true *self* becomes more and more noticeable. In a similar vein, Beth Holmgren identifies the scene at the hairdresser's as "a moment of freedom and self-investment," as "an essay at recovering identity" (234).

Not surprisingly, it is exactly on the same day, on Wednesday, when Olga says: "I long to walk freely [. . .] to take my time [. . .] to think about where I want to go" (Baranskaya 1990, 29–30). This longing points to how Olga's *self*, confined to the false identification with the routine and the imposed ideals, becomes more vocal in her speech.

With this new haircut, Olga is as if trying to put together the fragmentary and incomplete pieces of her identity. However, the haircut only represents Olga's emerging subjectivity on the level of things and objects, or, in other words, on the level of pointing and naming. Although, in Lacanian terms, she tries to change the mirror image that she used to identify with, she does not quite challenge the symbolic order (i.e., the imposed norm of an ideal Soviet woman as a true point of reference). Does she ever attempt to challenge it?

A hint at Olga's realization about the absence of truth "out there," and an attempt to turn to her inner *self* happens on Friday, when she admits to herself: "I have lost myself, in the pile of work and worry, in the Institute and at home" (Baranskaya 1990, 46). Later, on Sunday, she shows her real *self*—the one that does not want to adhere to the ideal Soviet woman or to identify with the routine. While still in bed with Dima, Olga thinks to herself: "I'm silent. I don't know what I want to say. I just want to talk, and not about vegetables, either. Maybe I want to talk about my thoughts" (Baranskaya 1990, 56). But the only thing that she talks about a moment later is the five rubles that they have left. Thus, her true *self* quickly flashes by in her vague desire to talk about thoughts (as opposed to objects). However, it does not find its expression in distinct elaborations on those thoughts, and Olga's true *self* is quickly subdued by her identification with routine again.

A few minutes later, in the bathroom, another instance of such a challenge of the symbolic order and the imposed social norms occurs when Olga questions the very validity of her way of life as it is. She asks herself: "Or perhaps I don't need this kind of love anymore?" (Baranskaya 1990, 57). However, again, a moment later she drives such thoughts away.

Later during that day, Olga decides to redesign her skirt, which is another attempt by her to turn to her true *self*. However, as with the haircut, the skirt also represents Olga's emerging subjectivity on the level of things and objects, not going beyond that level to the level of language. The symbolic order and the image of an ideal Soviet woman remain unchallenged.

Olga does not completely turn away from her true *self*, though, as she vehemently refuses her husband Dima's suggestion to quit her work at the research institute, a suggestion which she compares to "killing her" (Baranskaya 1990, 60). It is worth noting here that, in asking Olga to turn to the "ordered kind of life," Dima functions like a herald of the top-down language *for* the people. Thus, Olga's true inner *self* does not completely surrender to the "ordered kind of life," as Dima names it, and to the imposed norm.

Where will such a manifestation of *self* take Olga? Will it change anything in her self-perception? Or does it rather remain a simple flash, a hint at the absence of truth "out there"? We might find the answer to this question in Olga's missing hook that she needs to sew back onto her belt. Blanche Gelfant compares this missing hook to the concept of time which "will always be missing" for Olga (35). However, the hook rather functions as a metaphor for Olga's disconnection with her real *self*. The author's choice of the object—the hook—is representative because a hook is something that connects, combines, puts together. Compared, for instance, to a hole in a pocket or a spot on a sleeve, the missing hook as a defect in clothing makes a better case as a symbol of detachment, not just a symbol of a lack of something (for instance, time). Also, the other hooks on Olga's belt, which fall into the wrong eyelets, suggest that the self-identification and the connections that Olga does make between her true *self* and the world are the wrong ones.

At the end of the novella, the hook remains missing. On Sunday night, Olga thinks, "What is the matter with me?"—and replies to herself, "I don't know" (Baranskaya 1990, 62). Thus, Olga's complete connection to her genuine *self* does not happen. Her true *self* remains neglected, and her attention turns to the outside world again. A cultural model of an ideal Soviet woman does not make her seem real to herself. Neither does she feel real by objectifying her routine through the diary of her actions. The disparity between her true, complete, integral *self* and the imposed image of an ideal Soviet woman persists.

CONCLUSION

My proposed psychoanalytical approach to the novella does not only trace the development of the protagonist's self-identification. It also addresses a system of factors that determine the characters' reasoning and self-perception. All these factors are guided by different functions of language, including the language created *for* the people by state power and the language *of* the people who search for their identity. In this search, the protagonist (as well as other characters) demonstrates signs of internal conflict. In some situations, characters' speech and actions tend to resist the norms that the state imposes on them through language. In other situations, however, they succumb to the effects of implicit state propaganda and show signs of aspiration to match the qualities of the imposed norm. This internal conflict remains unresolved for the protagonist.

The internal conflict of women abiding by social norms, on the one hand, and making their own choices, on the other hand, is also present in Baranskaya's evaluation of the role of women. In an interview with Kathy Lally (1995), Baranskaya said that "women should be free to make choices and that they should find the life that satisfies them, not the life society necessarily expects of them." Nevertheless, in the same interview, she was firm in her belief that mothers should not work and should stay at home with their children.

Reading Baranskaya's *A Week Like Any Other* through the different dimensions of language allows us to look at the novella on several interrelated levels. On the level of the symbolic order, this perspective considers the relationship between language and the creation of social norms. On the level of individual characters, this approach captures the use of language in the workings of an individual's mind, as it attempts to search for its true core. Such an approach is informed by different theoretical paradigms and perspectives, including Lacan's psychoanalytical perspective, Saussurean structural linguistics, Tomasello's work on second-personal morality, and Lotman and Uspenskii's work on the semiotics of culture.

NOTE

1. The Real, according to Lacan, is something almost unattainable about the psyche, something that exists no matter whether the subject thinks about it or not. It is the unattainable true core of the inner self, to which a subject constantly and unsuccessfully strives to return. The other two Lacanian dimensions of the psyche include the Imaginary and the Symbolic.

BIBLIOGRAPHY

Baranskaia, Natal'ia. 1969. "*Nedelia kak nedelia.*" *Novyj mir*, no. 11: 23–55.

Baranskaya, Natalja. 1988. "Interview by Pieta Monks." In *Writing Lives: Conversations between Women Writers*, edited by Mary Chamberlain, 25–36. London: Virago.

Baranskaya, Natalya. 1990. *A Week like Any Other: Novellas and Stories.* Translated by Pieta Monks. Seattle, WA: The Seal Press.

Brown, Edward J. 1982. *Russian Literature since the Revolution*. Cambridge, MA: Harvard University Press.

Engel, Barbara A. 2004. *Women in Russia, 1700–2000*. New York: Cambridge University Press.

Fishzon, Anna. 2017. "Queue Time as Queer Time: An Occasion for Pleasure and Desire in the Brezhnev Era and Today." *The Slavic and East European Journal* 61 (3): 542–566.

Gasparov, Boris. 1985. Introduction to *The Semiotics of Russian Cultural History*. Translated and edited by Alexander D. Nakhimovsky and Alice Stone Nakhimovsky, 13–29. Ithaca: Cornell University Press.

Gelfant, Blanche H. 1995. *Cross-Cultural Reckonings: A Triptych of Russian, American, and Canadian Texts.* Cambridge: Cambridge University Press.

Heldt, Barbara. 1987. *Terrible Perfection: Women and Russian Literature*. Bloomington: Indiana University Press.

Heuvel, Katrina V. 1990. "Glasnost' for Women?" *The Nation* 250 (22): 773.

Holmgren, Beth. 2012. "Writing the Female Body Politic (1945–1985)." In *A History of Women's Writing in Russia*, edited by Adele Marie Barker and Jehanne M. Gheith, 225–242. Cambridge: Cambridge University Press.

Ivanova, Natal'ia. 1993. "Bakhtin's Concept of the Grotesque and the Art of Petrushevskaia and Tolstaia." In *Fruits of Her Plume: Essays on Contemporary Russian*

Women's Culture, edited by Helena Goscilo, 21–32. Armonk, NY; London: M. E. Sharpe.

Kelly, Catriona. 1994. *A History of Russian Women's Writing, 1820–1992*. Oxford: Clarendon Press.

Lacan, Jacques. 1966. *Écrits*. Paris: Editions du Seuil.

Lahusen, Thomas. 1993. "'Leaving Paradise' and Perestroika: *A Week like Any Other* and *Memorial Day* by Natal'ia Baranskaia." In *Fruits of Her Plume: Essays on Contemporary Russian Women's Culture*, edited by Helena Goscilo, 205–224. Armonk, NY: M. E. Sharpe.

Lally, Kathy. 1995. "I Am Not a Feminist." *The Baltimore Sun*, May 24, 1995. Accessed March 25, 2024. www.baltimoresun.com/news/bs-xpm-1995-05-24-1995144115-story.html.

Lotman, Iurii and Boris A. Uspenskii. 1985. "Binary Models in the Dynamics of Russian Culture (to the End of the Eighteenth Century)." In *The Semiotics of Russian Cultural History*, translated and edited by Alexander D. Nakhimovsky and Alice Stone Nakhimovsky, 30–66. Ithaca: Cornell University Press.

Natov, Nadine. 1974. "Daily Life and Individual Psychology in Soviet-Russian Prose of the 1970s." *The Russian Review* 33 (4): 357–371.

Saussure, Ferdinand de. 2011. *Course in General Linguistics*. New York: Columbia University Press.

Sutcliffe, Benjamin M. 2009. *The Prose of Life: Russian Women Writers from Khrushchev to Putin*. Madison, WI: The University of Wisconsin Press.

Tomasello, Michael. 2014. *A Natural History of Human Thinking*. Cambridge, MA: Harvard University Press.

Žekulin, Nicholas G. 1993. "Changing Perspectives: The Prose of Natal'ia Baranskaia." *Canadian Slavonic Papers/Revue Canadienne des Slavistes* 35 (3/4): 235–247.

14

Cognitive Aspects of Deixis and Semantic Poetics of Anna Akhmatova and Joseph Brodsky

Denis Akhapkin

Reading poetry is easy because it resonates with our emotions and imagination. Yet, it also demands effort, as nearly every poem exists in a dialogue with tradition—a complex, endless treadmill where Virgil refers to Theocritus, Dante to Virgil, Mandelstam to Dante, and, let's say, Brodsky to them all, requiring background knowledge from the reader. There is a well-known phrase, ascribed to Osip Mandelstam: "[i]f you would read me, you must have my culture" (Brown 1967, XIV). Nevertheless, the mission is practically impossible, as no single reader can retain in memory all potential contexts and pretexts, nor effortlessly grasp all allusions and establish links between traditions. Sometimes it takes years, even for experts, to identify a connection between an image in a poem and another source, and then to build a viable interpretation of this connection. This leads to some questions for cognitive literary studies: how do readers recognize allusions, what occurs when they do recognize them, and what changes when they do not?[1] While I do not intend to fully answer these questions in a brief chapter, I aim to provide initial signposts on the map of prospective research.

My primary area of interest is how specific elements of language can support the use of allusion in a poetic text, directing readers' attention and creating a puzzle to solve, potentially providing pleasure upon its resolution. I'm going to demonstrate, using examples from poems by

Anna Akhmatova and Joseph Brodsky, how such a practice could influence the reading and comprehension of poetry.

The choice of these particular poets is determined by their extensive use of allusions and subtexts, as well as their affiliation with the phenomenon known as "Russian semantic poetics." In this kind of poetry, "something that functions as the author's text on one level becomes a quotation on the next level, allowing for the establishment of new connections that rebuild the poem's scope" (Levin et al. 1974, 71).

Anna Akhmatova (1889–1966) was one of the central figures of the so-called Russian Silver Age, a flowering of poetry and arts in the first quarter of the twentieth century. Perhaps even more importantly, she was one of the few major Russian poets of the era who survived Stalin's terror. In the early 1960s, she became a living legend for the new generation of artists. Having outlived many of her friends and colleagues, she continued to have a poetic conversation with them.

Joseph Brodsky (1940–1996), a Russian-American poet and essayist, Nobel laureate (1987), was one of those young poets who learned from Akhmatova. Brodsky met her in 1961, and she influenced his poetry in many ways.

Allusions, introduced with the use of determiners like "that," "one," and others, are an important part of the poetics of both Akhmatova and Brodsky (Akhapkin 2021, 168–187). This fact is known to scholars, but these quotations are not always identified by a common reader. Therefore, the works of these poets are good material for discussions about different reader strategies for understanding poetic texts that depend on the recognition of allusions.

I use the term "allusion" instead of more common terms like "subtext" or "intertext" because of the extensive semantic connotations associated with both. By allusion, I mean "a brief, indirect, and deliberate reference—in a poem or other medium—to a person, place, event (fictitious or actual), or other work of art" (Wetzsteon 2012, 421). An important part of allusion is the expectation that the audience or reader will grasp the hidden reference.

The tradition of fundamental research on literary subtext as a type of allusion, as exemplified by Kirill Taranovsky (1976) and other scholars, currently lacks studies that fully describe this phenomenon from a cognitive perspective. Specifically, there are very few works exploring the cognitive aspects of allusions and implicit quotes. It is crucial to perceive allusions as intentional textual events crafted by authors who rely on the metacognitive abilities of readers, offering them the opportunity to comprehend (or not) the additional layers of meaning within the text. This type of research is essential due to the pervasive and widespread use of allusion as a rhetorical device.

No doubt, the phenomenon of allusion is one of the central aspects of modern culture. And I don't mean only highbrow poetry or literature. Songs, movies, TV series, etc., constantly use references to other works of art, verbal or nonverbal, and we love to recognize them and discuss them with others. Look at websites like genius.com or the "trivia" section of movie pages on imdb.com, and you will find many explanations of the allusions used by authors (but rarely speculations on how these allusions work). One can observe that the described cases share something in common, not to mention memes/gifs, which are frequently based on allusion.

In one episode of the thrilling TV series *Boat Story*, for instance, when the gang leader searches for the suspected traitor among his friends, the thugs momentarily align themselves at the table, mirroring the figures in Da Vinci's *Last Supper*. We experience a moment of quick recognition, yet not everyone (especially not the chief mobster) can identify in that short moment who is in Judas's place to uncover the identity of the renegade. This revelation will occur in the next episode, though a few spectators may already possess this information. Thus, we witness instances of comprehension, where allusion is acknowledged, but its interpretive potential remains unexplored.

Allusion is at work in different times and genres. In Modernist poetry by T. S. Eliot or Wallace Stevens, allusions contribute to the richness and complexity of the poems. Sometimes, as seen with Mandelstam or Akhmatova, they help authors conceal layers of meaning that are not intended for the eyes of censors in situations of cultural suppression. In more mainstream culture, such as political TV series like *Billions* or *City on a Hill*, allusions are used to underline the characters' similar or differing educational backgrounds, positions they share, or differences between them. In movies by Quentin Tarantino or Aki Kaurismäki, allusions can reveal additional plot twists. In politics, allusions are often employed to emphasize a politician's affiliation with a particular national, religious, or political tradition. And in all these cases, allusions provide the potential reader, viewer, or listener with a sense of recognition or non-recognition, creating a kind of aesthetic "aha-moment."[2]

But the question is, what options do readers and spectators have? Recognize and read the allusion, skip it, or rewind and watch or read again? How do these details impact the overall understanding of a work? Why do we enjoy and discuss this moment of recognition with friends when it occurs?

Discussing the entire phenomenon of allusion poses challenges in addressing these questions. Therefore, it is more valuable to isolate particular, meticulously selected examples and explore how language functions to create nuanced embedded meanings. A good approach would be to find a case where the reader is aware that an allusion exists but is not sure what it exactly is. In other words, there should be some indication in the text that clearly points somewhere without explicitly explaining where precisely.

And Russian poetry of the twentieth century provides us with a few cases where this kind of pointing becomes a feature of the poet's style. Let's consider a small, simple example before delving into cognitive poetics for explanations. There are two lines from Joseph Brodsky's poem "Kellomäki" (1983). In the stanza from which I took the lines, the lyrical persona recalls a winter evening, distant in both space and time. When darkness rises beyond the windows, the time comes:

когда книга захлопывалась и когда
от тебя оставались лишь губы, как от того кота (1, 480).[3]
when a book slammed shut and when,
only your lips leave behind, like the lips of that cat.[4]

There is no direct mention of a cat in the poem except this, so the phrase "that cat" is not anaphoric; it points to a specific cat beyond the text. The reader can infer that this is not just any cat but rather "that cat," singular and unique. The pronoun "that" pointing to nowhere may seem nonsensical in terms of Riffaterre and, in this way, "adds a dimension to retroactive reading" (1978, 139). The reader pauses, whether willingly or not, at the phrase in an attempt to derive meaning from it.

A significant number of readers can easily recognize that Brodsky refers to the Cheshire Cat, a famous character from Lewis Carroll's novel *Alice's Adventures in Wonderland*. The Cheshire Cat is known for its distinctive appearance, depicted with a broad smile and for its habit of disappearing, leaving only its grin ("lips") behind. For this cohort of readers, the solved riddle adds certain characteristics to the image of the lyrical addressee of the poem. For example, it suggests that she is charming, yet mischievous and enigmatic, with a tendency to sudden disappearance. It is also highly probable that resolving an allusion evokes a positive emotion in the reader.[5]

What happens to the other group of readers who are unaware of Carroll's cat and who are unable to establish the reference? Some of them continue to read the poem with a sense of "there is something here that I do not fully understand." Some readers may look for the explanation of the allusion in critical editions, commentaries, or interpretive works. There, they will find traces of the Cheshire Cat. They may not experience the immediate positive "aha" moment while reading the text itself, but instead they spend more time pondering the phrase and the episode. And, of course, there will be readers who do not realize that there is something significant here. Poetry thrives on the strange, and nonsensical phrases find their place in this realm.

However, in this case, readers are still capable of constructing the entire picture of the episode when the lyrical persona is kissing a beloved woman in the dark, and she is, for some reason, compared to a cat. Cats are beautiful creatures, and exploring the various applications of the conceptual metaphor WOMEN ARE CATS can illuminate the scene.[6]

These meditations on two lines of poetry did not answer all the questions we had, but they invited us to bring theoretical and empirical background to explain how we process this kind of allusion. Turning to linguistics and cognitive poetics allows us to highlight that there are at least three important approaches that can help here, and I will explore them in what follows.

The first is the study of deixis. In the example with the cat's lips and in those that follow, we observe the use of small language components: demonstrative pronouns such as *that* or *this*. These pronouns do not function anaphorically by referring to something within the text; instead, they guide us toward an imagined realm outside the text. This is part of the language phenomenon called deixis, and the theory of imagination-oriented deixis can clarify some mechanisms behind allusion.

The second theory is that of conceptual blending, elaborated by cognitive scientists Gilles Fauconnier and Mark Turner. We clearly encounter an intersection of two spaces in the example from "Kellomäki." The first space is described by the author of the poem as the world of a small winter village where lovers live, while the second space is the world of *Alice's Adventures in Wonderland*, inhabited by the Cat and other creatures. Below, I will show how such kinds of spaces can interact and how readers construct them, if indeed they do.

The third approach should help us explain the nature of this "aha" effect and its role in the process of reading and understanding a poem. For this, we will turn to Charles Fillmore, one of the founding fathers of cognitive linguistics, whose ideas about the mechanisms of text comprehension are important for discussing the problem we are dealing with.

DEICTICS IN SERVICE OF ALLUSION

Deixis refers to the linguistic phenomenon in which the meanings of certain words or expressions depend on the context of the conversation for their interpretation. These words, known as deictics, such as *you, they, here, there, this, that, now,* or *then*, rely on the spatial, temporal, and interpersonal context to be fully understood. Deixis helps to locate entities in space and time, as well as establish relationships between the speaker, the listener, and the surrounding environment.

In a canonical speech situation, the listener understands the speaker's message based on the common context and their knowledge. However, in the case of poetry, the situation becomes more intricate, as meaning is influenced not only by the rules of language and poetic conventions but also by a signaling system that guides the reader beyond the text and into their own experiences and the realm of pretexts.

In recent literary studies, there has been a lively debate surrounding deixis as one of the components of the cognitive poetics agenda. Peter Stockwell, in his influential textbook, dedicates a chapter to showcasing how literary studies can benefit from exploring "cognitive deixis" (2002, 41–58). He introduces a classification of deictics and briefly reviews Deictic Shift Theory (DST). Proponents of DST claim that deictics help transport readers into the depicted world, enabling the reader to adopt a specific perspective that evolves alongside the narrative's unfolding events. This mental space created by the narrative exists independently of the reader's actual physical location, allowing for a unique engagement with the text. Throughout a narrative, the deictic center, a focal point influencing perspective, may shift multiple times. It is crucial to note that deictic words in a narrative predominantly direct the reader's attention to characters, locations, objects, occurrences, and relationships within the textual realm (Segal 1995, 15–17).

Stockwell applies the principles of DST to the analysis of works of literature, including "Ozymandias" by Percy Bysshe Shelley. He identifies six categories of deixis (perceptual, spatial, temporal, relational, textual, and compositional) and pinpoints the corresponding words and expressions in the poem. According to Stockwell's hypothesis, deixis helps the reader to create a "cognitively negotiable world" and to modify it in the process of reading (2002, 43–46).

Conversely, there is a question: how "cognitive" this approach to deixis truly is. In this regard, Reuven Tsur, who coined the term "cognitive poetics," argued that although Stockwell uses the adjective "cognitive," he does not push the boundaries of common literary and linguistic studies. Tsur further claimed that there is nothing in Stockwell's toolkit that could not have been used long before the advent of cognitive science. To illustrate this point, Tsur demonstrated how E. M. Forster, in his 1927 book *Aspects of the Novel*, analyzed the shifting point of view in Dickens' works. Tsur's final question is, "In what way is Stockwell's analysis more cognitive than Forster's?" (2008, 598). As argued by Tsur, Stockwell focuses on deictics and the role they play in building the textual world but says almost nothing about the cognitive processes behind them.

I tend to agree with Tsur when he claims that there is nothing in Stockwell's analysis that cannot be accomplished without waving the "cognitive" banner. However, I do find value in Stockwell's incorporation of DST into the discussion of poetry. Furthermore, in order to address another of Tsur's arguments and demonstrate "how cognitive generalizations can be used for handling issues one cannot handle by earlier terminology" (2008, 609–610), one needs to introduce a new emphasis on deixis, along with a clearer explanation of what mental spaces are and how they interact in the process of constructing a "cognitively negotiable world."

The question is how this world changes from actual perception "to 'imagined space,' to the realm of the somewhere or other of pure phantasy, the realm of the here and there of memory" (Bühler 2011, 142). This is a quote from the book *Theory of Language* written by German psychologist and linguist, one of the predecessors of cognitive psychology, Karl Bühler (originally published in German in 1934). From the perspective of cognitive literary studies, the most intriguing type of deixis he introduced in this book is "deixis am phantasma," or imagination-oriented deixis.

In this form of deixis, the deictic signs refer to absent (mental) objects that can be either familiar or unfamiliar to the hearer/reader. The central psychological question, as highlighted by Bühler, is what happens when the attention of the hearer or reader is directed toward *something absent*:

> The initial astonishment at the possibility of imagination-oriented deixis is based on a largely false presupposition. It is not at all the case that imagination-oriented deixis completely lacks the natural deictic clues upon which ocular demonstration is based. Rather, the speaker and hearer of a visual description of something absent possess the same talent and resources that permit the actor on the stage to make something that is absent present and which permit the audience to interpret what is presented on the stage as a mimesis of something absent. (Bühler 2011, 142)

Let me explain the idea using an example from poetry. A couple of years after a breakup with the woman he loved, Brodsky wrote a poem entitled "On Love" describing his dream of their shared happiness. Let's take a look at two lines from the poem where he envisions an imaginary dream space:

Мы там женаты, венчаны, мы те
двуспинные чудовища (1, 366)
We are married and blessed there, we are those
beasts with two backs

Here we observe two deictics of the type we are interested in: *there* and *those*. The first one establishes an imaginary space where the action of the poem takes place, while the second one points to an element in another mental space, highlighting the uniqueness of the object being referred to. These are not just any beasts with two backs but specific ones familiar to the protagonist and the addressee. Are they familiar to the readers? Well, at least to some of them who recall the famous line from Shakespeare's *Othello*, where Iago informs the Duke of Venice: "I am one, sir, that comes to tell you your daughter\and the Moor are now making the beast with two backs" (Shakespeare [1604] 2006, 1.1.115–116).[7]

It seems that there should be a significant difference in the processing of these two deictics. The spatial adverb *there* functions as one of the "deictic elements in discourse which can assist participants in their initial construction of a text-world" (Gavins 2007, 37). This is supported by other world-building elements in the poem, such as *I, you, bedside, light switch, wall,* and *bulb,* all of which evoke the frame of "a bedroom" in the reader's mind. It is unlikely that readers would find this procedure of imagining the possible space *there*, where a separated pair is united in a bedroom, difficult. There are no limitations on how this imaginary bedroom should look or where it is situated—be it a hotel room, a mansion, a city apartment, or a cabin; all settings work. And this operation will be the same for all readers who have basic linguistic and literary competence. As Bühler noted when explaining the peculiarities of using *here* and *there* in fictional texts:

> [a] hearer or reader who has at least passed through his fairy tale period and has practiced it 'there' has as easy a time with the one as with the other. He looks in the distance from his position of actual perception or from an imagined position just as easily and inconspicuously as he follows the instructions of the preterite and the future. (2011, 155)

In a completely different situation with the pronoun *those*, it is evident that readers are expected to imagine not just any beasts, but particular ones. This pronoun functions as an indicator of an allusion, leading to distinct modes of reading that depend on whether we recognize Shakespeare's image or not. It is not a standard procedure like building a text-world using common frames or understanding grammar constructions. In this situation, a reader should have, using Bühler's phrase, the same talent and resources.

A reader of this kind is able to establish a connection where the reference can further enhance the portrayal of imagined blissful love spoiled by the themes of destruction, jealousy, and betrayal by a friend in *Othello*.

Other readers can completely disregard this reference, considering it as a component of the vague imagery of the poetry or as a semantic anomaly. This is a fairly common option. Empirical studies show that grammatical errors and semantic abnormalities in poetry are not perceived by readers as such and do not cause slowdowns in reading (Skulacheva et al. 2021).

Finally, a reader can skip the deictic and process the image of "beast with two backs" as a metaphor with a possible mental projection of animal qualities onto humans, which means in the context of physical love that lovers are wild and untamed in bed. This is a process of so-called conceptual blending or conceptual integration, which I will discuss in the next part of the chapter.

It is essential that in all cases, readers have a spectrum of ideas about the meaning of the poem—be it the simple notion that "it is something about the 'old flame'" or an elaborate interpretation like "Brodsky remembered lost love, with the Shakespearean allusion emphasizing his feeling that his jealousy and impulsivity were reasons for the lovers' separation."

Of course, neither of these interpretations is definitively "right," but it's evident that we are engaging with a complex interplay of constructed mental spaces that could be invoked by imagination-oriented deixis, explicitly demonstrating the presence of an allusion. What is also important is that we are dealing with a specific form of deictic shift. The mental space created by an explicitly noted implicit allusion may exist independently of the reader's actual knowledge and the textbase they construct during reading. At this point, the discussion of deixis starts to be "cognitive," or, better to say, it is entering the area of poetic cognition as Margaret Freeman defines it.[8]

From a pragmatic standpoint, an allusion of this kind functions as a form of presupposition—the preliminary knowledge that the text expects from the reader (Zolian and Lotman 2012, 327). In an experimental design, we can address presuppositions by furnishing readers with the necessary information, or at least with a part of it, in advance.

First approaches to empirical studies of processing of this type of imagination-oriented deixis show that it substantially depends on the level of text immersion. Text immersion, in the realm of cognitive and neurocognitive poetics, refers to the deep mental involvement and absorption experienced by readers when engaging with a text, where they become fully engrossed in the world created by the words on the page. This often leads to vivid mental imagery and an emotional connection with the content.

One of our previous studies demonstrated that a reader's ability to establish reference from lines of a poem to another text, event, or place, which is linked by a deictic, influences text processing: "[w]hen the reader is provided with information that is necessary to establish reference and the level of text immersion is high, a local acceleration in the processing of the deictic expression is observed" (Prokopenya et al. 2021, 54). The full text immersion that is reached when the deictic expression is located in the middle of the poem activates the reader's background knowledge. If this knowledge includes information about the referent of the deictic expression, this referent becomes highly activated in the reader's cognitive system. Thus, reference is established faster, and the reading process is enhanced. Conversely, when the deictic expression is encountered at the beginning of the poem, the reader is not fully immersed in the text yet, therefore deixis is processed as an ordinary referential expression, and there is no substantial effect on text processing.

In general, the results of this study show that a skilled person (in our case, a person with deeper background knowledge) works faster, and this may seem to be commonplace. However, it is not so straightforward, because we'd expect that integrating additional meaning from another text (connected by a deictic) requires additional time and effort.

But every silver lining has a cloud, to rephrase an idiom. The results show that readers with less background knowledge and lower text immersion take more time to process the text. What are they spending this extra time on? Let's take a look at this in light of the theory of conceptual blending.

DEIXIS AND BLENDING

The theory of conceptual integration, developed in a series of publications by cognitive linguists Gilles Fauconnier and Mark Turner, is a cognitive theory that explores how humans creatively combine elements from different mental spaces to form new conceptual connections and derive novel insights. This theory suggests that our minds have the capacity to blend distinct mental spaces, leading to the creation of rich and imaginative ideas. In their seminal book *The Way We Think: Conceptual Blending and the Mind's Hidden Complexities* Fauconnier and Turner showed that the process of conceptual integration is ubiquitous and underlies our capability to learn and build new conceptions. By mental spaces they mean "small conceptual packets constructed as we think and talk, for purposes of local understanding and action. They are very partial assemblies containing elements structured by frames and cognitive models" (2002, 102).

The basic model of conceptual integration assumes four mental spaces: two distinct input spaces representing different domains, a generic space that shares structures with the input spaces, facilitating transfer between them, and a blended space that combines or emphasizes certain elements and connections from the input spaces. Traditionally, these spaces are depicted as four circles with elements inside them and lines that connect related elements. The theory holds significant explanatory and interpretive potential in poetry studies.[9]

Conceptual integration theory may help in understanding how imagination-oriented deixis works in the case of allusion. What happens when the reader encounters constructions like "that X"? Of course, one of the possible answers is "nothing." Bühler raised the question of "whether every reader follows the linguistic instructions exactly or not" (2011, 155) with the obvious answer: "not every." However, if readers notice the deictic reference to an unidentified allusion (and our preliminary research indicates that in many cases they do (Prokopenya et al. 2021)), they are expected to construct a mental space related to it.

One of the poets who most frequently used imagination-oriented deixis to create allusions is Anna Akhmatova. This aspect of her poetics does not escape the attention of critics and scholars. Tatiana Tsiv'ian (2001) noted that in Akhmatova's poems, there often appears a situation of "indefinite undefinable uniqueness," which involves encrypted references where the deictic form implies something specific, yet the reader lacks clues to determine what it might be, like, for example, in the 1929 poem: "Тот город, мной любимый с детства . . . " ("That city, loved by me since childhood . . . "). The poem doesn't mention the city's name, leaving the reader to find the key. Tsiv'ian provides dozens of such examples from Akhmatova's poetry. In all these cases, like in *that cat* case, poems do not contain direct references to a specific *city* (or *contract*, or *evening*). However, a reader acquainted with Akhmatova's poetry and the broader post-symbolist context may have the opportunity to uncover the answers: "In some cases, the reader's knowledge of Akhmatova's 'cryptography' assists in deciphering deixis that is directed towards a text or reality via the text" (Tsiv'ian 2001, 171–172). Let's consider one such case. Here are two lines from Anna Akhmatova's "Poem without a Hero" (1940–1962):

> Это он в переполненном зале / Слал *ту* чёрную розу в бокале (1989, 45)

> It is him, who in an overcrowded room / had sent *that* black rose in a goblet[10]

"Poem without a Hero" is a complex text filled with hidden links and keys that capture the readers' attention. An unnamed character from these lines, designated only by the deictic "he," can be identified by the act of sending a black rose in a goblet. The specific use of the pronoun "that" indicates that a particular rose in a specific situation is being referred to. As such, the pronoun—or, in other terms, the deictic word—functions as a signal to readers, prompting them to search for a reference to construct a mental space from these lines. What is clearly defined here is the set of elements (or space-builders): the lyrical persona, the sender of the rose, the rose in the goblet, and the setting of the overcrowded room.

Operating based on this script, we can understand, for example, that in the context of the Silver Age epoch described in the poem, the act of a man sending a flower to a woman could signify a romantic relationship or a proposal of such a relationship. However, without an additional cue, one still has no idea who all these people are.

Nevertheless, many Russian readers can unmistakably see here an allusion to Alexander Blok's famous poem "In a Restaurant" (1910):

Я сидел у окна в переполненном зале.
Где-то пели смычки о любви.
Я послал тебе чёрную розу в бокале
Золотого, как небо, аи. (Blok 1910, 2)

I was sitting by the window in a crowded room.
Somewhere bows were singing of love.
I sent you a black rose in a goblet
Of Aÿ's champagne, golden as the sky.

Despite Blok's name never being mentioned in Akhmatova's poem, there are other allusions beyond these two lines that also point to him. Blok's "In a Restaurant" has been included in high school anthologies of Russian poetry for many years, and many students, including myself, were assigned to learn it by heart—though, speaking honestly, not all did it. Therefore, some readers will decipher the allusion, while others may not. While any native speaker can easily sense that Akhmatova is indicating something with "that," they might perceive it as a kind of riddle.

In my experience of reading Akhmatova's poetry in class with students, I have observed at least three different reactions to situations of hidden allusions like this. The first, which is rare among students—but might be common among some other populations of readers[11]—can be described as "I am not interested." Readers sense that there is something beyond the text but choose not to invest time or effort in exploring it. This reaction is evident, and I will not discuss it any further.

The second, most common, reaction is when a reader cannot establish the connection but feels that this connection is important. Here are a few excerpts from first-year students' written answers to the question, "how do you think, who is he in this fragment of the poem?"[12]:

"Not knowing [who 'he' is] provokes me to think intensively, to produce multiple meanings and doubt each of them"

"I think that not knowing [who 'he' is] has no negative influence on my perception of the poem. It even stimulates my interest to find the right answer"

"I want to know who 'he' is, especially because the text has a lot of hints!"

The third reaction is when the connection is established. Here is an example of a student's answer:

"The black rose" means Blok. I think that this fragment is more interesting for people who did not recognize this!"

Let's consider schemes of conceptual integrations for the last two groups. This one represents a situation when the connection with Blok is established: figure 14.1.

I have already described the structure of the generic space, which remains unchanged for both cases, as well as the first input space that reflects the surface structure of Akhmatova's lines. The second input space represents the mental space associated with Blok's poem. It repeats the structure of the generic space, filling its positions with details from the poem. The "I" of the poem, the lyrical persona, is associated with Blok since his text is part of an autobiographical series of poems. "You" is a heroine of this cycle, "the Stranger." The crowded room is the suburban restaurant near St. Petersburg, and a rose is a rose.

What happens when a reader creates this blend? The cross-space mapping connects Akhmatova and Blok as poets, and in that role, they both project onto the blend. The reader also projects onto the blend the frame of a date. However, due to the presence of the poets, this date becomes a symbolic poetic encounter in the crowded space of Russian poetry. The rose becomes the quotation itself. It metaphorically carries the poetic essence—like a message from Blok in "In a Restaurant" to Akhmatova in "Poem without a Hero." Therefore, these two lines become a symbol of poetical alliance and the inheritance of tradition. Of course, in the context of Akhmatova's entire "Poem," the image is richer and more complex, but on a micro-level, blending functions in a way that has just been described.

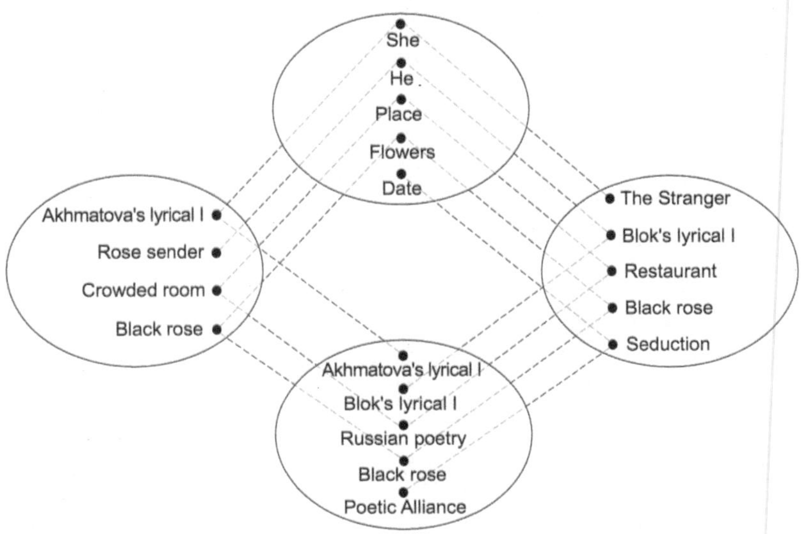

Figure 14.1 Allusion to Blok's Poem Detected. *Source*: Generated by the Author.

And now let's address the situation when the link is not established (figure 14.2).

The generic space and the first input space are the same as the generic space and input space in the previous example because the reader deals with the same lines and the same situational frame. What is most interesting here is that the second input space still needs to be created as well, but it lacks certain definitive building elements. It must be constructed simply because deictics require a specific situation to be considered. However, the reader cannot grasp this situation due to the undetected allusion.

The mental space building here resembles the process of understanding a text in a foreign language by a beginner-level student. Let's picture a reader with elementary English language proficiency encountering a phrase like "In the marshlands, cranes were bugling. They were so loud before sunrise that it seemed as if the birds were circling over the ridge of the hut." In this hypothetical scenario, the reader may lack the understanding of "marshlands," "cranes," "ridge," and "hut" in this context, yet they might infer something like "somewhere some birds were screaming, and it seemed that they were doing something somewhere."[13]

Accordingly, the elements for the second input space will be "someone," "someone," "somewhere" and a "black rose" as a symbol of something. The black rose is the only definite element in this space, because of the deictic in Akhmatova's line.

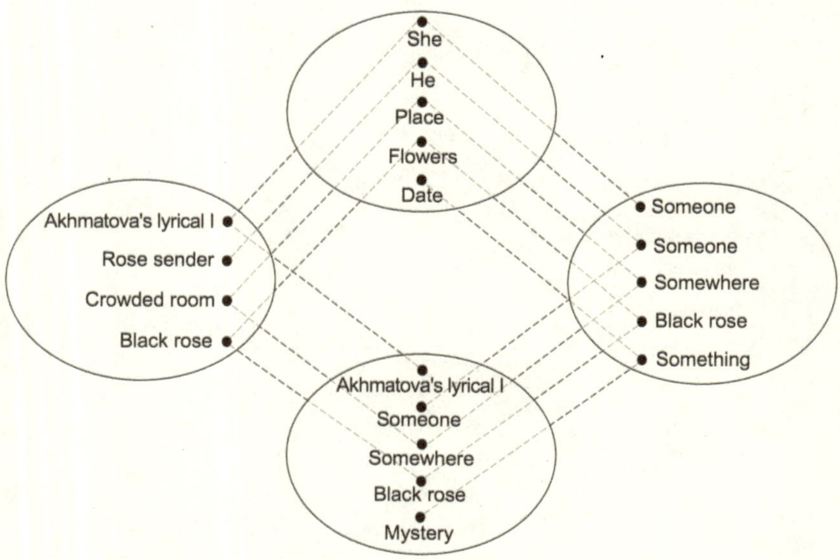

Figure 14.2 Allusion to Blok's Poem Undetected. *Source*: Generated by the Author.

The blend should inevitably be produced due to the presence of two input mental spaces—this is how the mind works, using the title of Fauconnier and Turner's book. In the blend, Akhmatova's heroine receiving the rose from someone creates an atmosphere of mystery. "She wants to be mysterious and tease us with a secret we will never know," some readers may infer from the blend.

Let's return to one of the quoted student's answers. Why could these lines be more interesting for readers who did not recognize the allusion? It seems that in that case we deal with a situation where the reader, using the words of Michael Riffaterre, "at least gets the feeling that the wording of the text, however disconcerting, is no longer gratuitous" (1978, 138).

Returning to the question about the extra time that readers with less text immersion spend on reading, we can suppose that they are trying to build a blended space but lack the necessary elements, thus slowing them down.

LITTLE JACK HORNER MEETS ALLUSION

The theory of conceptual integration offers a way to model the process of constructing meaning from a text. This model can be applied to empirical and experimental studies on allusion processing. But the question remains, what happens next after the blending presented in figure 14.1 or 14.2 is completed? Is there any further difference in text processing between the two possible blending outcomes?

At first glance, it appears that the situation shown in figure 14.1 provides deeper text immersion and richer meanings for the reader. The concealed quotation is reinstated, enabling the exploration of the second level of meaning, which "allows for the establishment of new connections that rebuild the poem's scope" (Levin et al. 1974, 71). On the other hand, in this case, the reader spends more effort on the previous stage, which prepares them to catch the allusion's ball. And by recognizing the allusion, the reader receives a momentary reward.

This process is inevitable. If, for example, you read and remember Hamlet's soliloquy, you automatically recognize "to be or not to be" in a song or advertisement line. But you will hardly cogitate on how the Prince of Denmark's meditations are linked with the advertised product.

Cognitive psychologist Daniel Kahneman postulated the existence of two systems in the mind: System 1 and System 2. System 1 "operates automatically and quickly with little or no effort and no sense of voluntary control" (2011, 20). Among the examples of the work of System 1 provided by Kahneman are language operations involving idioms and clichés, such as "complete the phrase 'bread and . . . '" He also noted that the choice of system, despite being unconscious, depends on the level of expertise. Therefore, one of the exemplary activities attributed to System 1 is "finding a strong move in chess (if you are a chess master)" (2011, 21). In our case, an experienced reader with knowledge of Russian poetry processes the Blok quote almost automatically. They may require additional motivation to pause and reflect on the allusion and its function in the text.

On the contrary, in Kahneman's definition, System 2 "allocates attention to the effortful mental activities that demand it" (2011, 21). Operations of System 2 are impaired when attention is drawn away. In our case, this is what happens when a reader does not recognize the hidden allusion but senses that there is something to uncover here. If immersion is not deep and attention is distracted, a reader may skip the deictics. But if they do not skip them, they engage in voluntary and effortful mental activities. The nature of these activities can be illustrated by using one of Charles Fillmore's ideas.

Fillmore proposed an important theory of text comprehension in his seminal work, "Topics in Lexical Semantics" (1977). Although not frequently remembered by scholars in cognitive literary studies, the theory is essential for discussions about the meanings that readers can or cannot see in a text.

In this work, Fillmore goes beyond the common questions of linguistics such as "what did he say?" (traditional semantics) and "why did he bother to say it?" (theory of speech acts) to explore "settings, beliefs, expectations, memories of personal experiences, and the roles these matters play in the process of figuring out what somebody is talking about" (1977, 80).

To illustrate this, he analyzes an example from a popular magazine—an article describing a speech given at an athletic club by a professional baseball player. In an important moment of the speech, when the speaker took a pause and the audience was silent, the four-year-old son of the speaker approached him. As the article said: "at precisely that moment, a small but amplified voice notified the entire room, in the most lucid idioms, of a common childhood emergency" (Fillmore 1977, 78).

Any adult native speaker of English can understand the context and reason why this situation is funny, as Fillmore notes. What is more interesting is why the article's author uses an indirect description of the occasion. Fillmore proposes an explanation from what he calls the "Little Jack Horner theory of wit." The name of the theory, coined by one of the linguist's students, refers to a well-known English nursery rhyme:

Little Jack Horner
Sat in the corner,

Eating his Christmas pie;
He put in his thumb,
And pulled out a plum,
And said, "What a good boy am I!"

Fillmore argues:

> Young Horner, on discovering the plum, was delighted mainly with himself, and only secondarily, if at all, with the baker. [. . .] If the plum had been sitting right on top of the pie, discoverable without any cleverness or effort on the diner's part, the experience could not have been half so rewarding. (Fillmore 1977, 78)

So, the important point is that readers enjoy indirect passages, and part of the pleasure of reading comes from uncovering small or not-so-small chunks of hidden meaning, allowing them to reward themselves for being "good readers." Recognizing allusions to Lewis Carroll, Shakespeare, and Blok in my given examples offers a "plum" to a reader, and the reward is greater when more effort is made to identify the allusion. It is also important that, in agreement with this theory, the baker's (poet's) intentions and their reconstruction are secondary. Another level of immersion is necessary for delving into the reconstruction of *that "rebuilt poem's scope"* (yes, the phrase sounds familiar!), yet not many readers are eager to reach this level.

WHAT'S NEXT?

Different text processing strategies, like the ones that were discussed in this chapter, are based on psychological mechanisms that cognitive psychology helps us to understand. Hence, one of the benefits that cognitive science offers to literary studies as a whole, and Russian studies in particular, is the recognition of the significant differences between experienced and less experienced readers, and between different levels of reader immersion.

For further empirical research on deixis and other features of literary texts, such as metaphor, parable, and others, it is crucial to understand an existing incongruity. In most experiments, the essential participants are students. Therefore, hypotheses borne out of the introspection of skilled experts in the field are often tested on less experienced readers without discussion of differences between these cohorts of readers. Despite the value of the findings, extrapolating results from one cohort to the general population requires caution, especially when examining complex literary texts.

Cognitive approaches in literary studies and the study of allusions in particular cannot provide the magic key that opens all doors, but they can help us understand which set of keys can help us open a specific door, or, to find *that* door with no lock to lock.

NOTES

1. In the past decades, there has been a growing interest in language and literature studies regarding how readers process various elements of text, including allusions, and why this processing is significant. Various explanatory models have been proposed from the perspectives of pragmatics (Jeffries 2022, 169–181), neuroscience (Jacobs 2015), and cognitive linguistics and poetics (Gronas 2011). While I do not aim to cover all these areas or present an empirical study of the reading process, I will attempt to outline a framework for discussing how allusions can influence reading and understanding.

2. This effect is similar to the perceptual insights in understanding visual art (Muth and Carbon 2013).

3. All references to Brodsky's poetry are taken from the Loseff edition (Brodskii 2017), indicated by volume and page numbers.

4. All poetry translations are my own.

5. Although there is a lack of direct empirical research on the emotional impact of recognizing allusions, it is highly probable that this recognition can be considered a type of insight that produces an "aha" effect. Research on insight situations has shown that resolving other problems that involve an "aha" experience is associated with a primacy of positive emotions in participants' qualitative self-reports (Danek et al. 2014). This primacy has been confirmed in subsequent experiments, where participants were presented with difficult problems and rated their solutions for an "aha" moment and various parameters, including pleasure. The strong correlation was found between pleasure and the global feeling of "aha" (Danek and Wiley 2017). Further exploration of the emotional impact of allusion is needed, though.

6. On the role of conceptual metaphors in poetry, see Lakoff and Turner (1989).

7. In the case of indirect quotations, the implicit reader has an additional goal: to reconstruct missing or imaginary quotation marks (Soshkin 2015, 13). The question is, how do they know that the allusion lies here? Discussion of the author's intention in subtexts has been expanding broadly, but it is evident that in cases where there are no clear marks of allusion, readers and critics may primarily rely on guesswork. Deictics can provide a cue to achieve this goal.

8. While I still use the term "cognitive poetics," following Tsur and Stockwell in their study of deixis in poetry, I find Freeman's notion of "poetic cognition" more promising because it eliminates the redundancy of the adjective "cognitive" in the discussion of language: "[a]s a category of aesthetic cognition, poetic cognition has the potential to provide a theory and methodology for establishing the nature of poetic effects and relating them to human cognitive processes" (2020, 12).

9. See, for example, Freeman (2023).
10. Italics are mine.
11. I use the term "population of readers" proposed by Marisa Bortolussi and Peter Dixon:

> A population is a collection of individuals about which interesting claims might be made. For example, a population might be all undergraduate students in US and Canada; another might be skilled readers of English; still another might be literary critics who have published papers on Borges. (Bortolussi and Dixon 2002, 44–45)

12. Identities of student informants are being withheld.
13. Adapted from a similar example provided in the lectures of the linguist Georgy Bogin (2001, 297).

BIBLIOGRAPHY

Akhmatova, Anna. 1989. *Poema bez geroia* / Sost. i prim. R. D. Timenchika. Moscow: MPI

Blok, Aleksandr. 1910. *"Strashnyi mir." Russkaya mysl'* XI: 1–4.

Bogin, Georgy. 2001. *Obretenie sposobnosti ponimat': Vvedenie v filologicheskuyu germenevtiku*. Tver'.

Bortolussi, Marisa, and Peter Dixon. 2002. *Psychonarratology: Foundations for the Empirical Study of Literary Response*. Cambridge: Cambridge University Press.

Brodskii, Iosif. 2017. *Stikhotvoreniia i poemy*, vol. 2, edited by Lev Losev. Saint Petersburg: Lenizdat.

Brown, Clarence. 1967. "On Reading Mandelstam." In *Mandel'shtam O. Sobranie sochinenii v 3 t.*, vol. 1, edited by G. P. Struve and B. A. Filippova, I–XXVII. Washington: Mezhdunarodnoe literaturnoe sodruzhestvo.

Buhler, Karl. 2011. *Theory of Language: The Representational Function of Language*. Amsterdam: John Benjamins Pub. Co.

Danek, Amory, Thomas Fraps, Albrecht V. Müller, Benedikt Grothe, and Michael Öllinger. 2014. "It's a Kind of Magic—What Self-Reports Can Reveal about the Phenomenology of Insight Problem Solving." *Frontiers in Psychology* 5: 1408. https://doi.org/10.3389/fpsyg.2014.01408.

Danek, Amory, and Jennifer Wiley. 2017. "What about False Insights? Deconstructing the Aha! Experience along Its Multiple Dimensions for Correct and Incorrect Solutions Separately." *Frontiers in Psychology* 7. https://doi.org/10.3389/fpsyg.2016.02077.

Fauconnier, Gilles, and Mark Turner. 2002. *The Way we Think: Conceptual Blending and the Mind's Hidden Complexities*. New York: Basic Books.

Fillmore, Charles J. 1977. "Topics in Lexical Semantics." In *Current Issues in Linguistic Theory*, edited by Roger W. Cole, 76–138. Bloomington: Indiana University Press.

Freeman, Margaret H. 2020. *The Poem as Icon: A Study in Aesthetic Cognition*. Oxford: Oxford University Press.

Freeman, Margaret H. 2023. *Emily Dickinson's Poetic Art: A Cognitive Reading*. London: Bloomsbury Academic.

Gavins, Joanna. 2007. *Text World Theory: An Introduction*. Edinburgh: Edinburgh University Press.

Gronas, Mikhail. 2011. *Cognitive Poetics and Cultural Memory: Russian Literary Mnemonics*. New York: Routledge.

Jacobs, Arthur M. 2015. "Neurocognitive Poetics: Methods and Models for Investigating the Neuronal and Cognitive-Affective Bases of Literature Reception." *Front Hum Neurosci* 9: 186.

Jeffries, Lesley. 2022. *The Language of Contemporary Poetry: A Framework for Poetic Analysis*. Cham: Palgrave Macmillan.

Kahneman, Daniel. 2011. *Thinking, Fast and Slow*. New York: Farrar, Straus and Giroux.

Lakoff, George, and Mark Turner. 1989. *More than Cool Reason: A Field Guide to Poetic Metaphor*. Chicago: University of Chicago Press.

Levin, Iurii, Dimitrii Segal, Roman Timenchik, Vladimir Toporov, and Tat'iana Tsiv'ian. 1974. "*Russkaia Semanticheskaia Poetika kak Potentsial'naia Kul'turnaia Paradigma.*" *Russian Literature* 3 (2): 47–82.

Muth, Claudia, and Claus-Christian Carbon. 2013. "The Aesthetic Aha: On the Pleasure of Having Insights into Gestalt." *Acta Psychologica* 144 (1): 25–30.

Prokopenya, Veronika, Denis Akhapkin, Ekaterina Saenko, and Alina Zhunussova. 2021. "Deixis Am Phantasma as a Background Element and Its Influence on the Processing of Poetry." *The Russian Journal of Cognitive Science* 8 (3): 46–59.

Riffaterre, Michael. 1978. *Semiotics of Poetry*. Bloomington: Indiana University Press.

Segal, Erwin M. 1995. "Narrative Comprehension and the Role of Deictic Shift Theory." In *Deixis in Narrative. A Cognitive Science Perspective*, edited by Judith F. Duchan, Gail A. Bruder, and Lynne E. Hewitt, 3–17. New York: Psychology Press.

Shakespeare, William. [1604] 2006. *Othello, The Moor of Venice*, edited by Michael Neill. Oxford: Clarendon Press; Oxford University Press.

Skulacheva, Tatyana, Natalia Slioussar, Alexander Kostyuk, Anna Lipina, Emil Latypov, and Varvara Koroleva. 2021. "The Influence of Verse on Cognitive Processes: A Psycholinguistic Experiment." In *Tackling the Toolkit: Plotting Poetry through Computational Literary Studies*, edited by Petr Plecháč, Robert Kolár, Anne-Sophie Bories, and Jakub Říha, 151–162. Florenc, Czechia: Institute of Czech Literature of the Czech Academy of Sciences.

Soshkin, Evgenii. 2015. *Gipogrammatika: Kniga o Mandel'shtame*. Moscow: Novoe literaturnoe obozrenie.

Stockwell, Peter. 2002. *Cognitive Poetics: An Introduction*. London: Routledge.

Taranovsky, Kiril. 1976. *Essays on Mandel'štam*. Cambridge, MA.: Harvard University Press.

Tsiv'ian, Tatiana. 2001. "*Nabliudeniia nad Kategoriej Opredelennosti-neopredelennosti v Poeticheskom Tekste.*" In *Tsiv'ian T. V.: Semioticheskie puteshestviia*, 169–183. Saint Petersburg.: Izd-vo I. Limbakha.

Tsur, Reuven. 2008. *Toward a Theory of Cognitive Poetics*, 2nd expanded and updated ed. Brighton: Sussex Academic Press.

Wetzsteon, R. 2012. "Allusion". In *The Princeton Encyclopedia of Poetry and Poetics*, 4th ed., edited by Roland Greene, Stephen Cushman, Clare Cavanagh, Jahan Ramazani, Paul F. Rouzer, Harris Feinsod, David Marno, and Alexandra Slessarev, 42–43. Princeton: Princeton University Press.

Zolian, Suren, and Mikhail Lotman. 2012. *Issledovaniia v Oblasti Semanticheskoi Poetiki Akmeizma*. Tallinn: Izdatel'stvo Tallinnskogo universiteta.

Index

About the Contributors

Tom Dolack graduated with a PhD in comparative literature from the University of Oregon. He has taught at the University of Chicago, the University of Pennsylvania, and Middlebury College, and is currently a senior professor of the practice of Russian at Wheaton College in Norton, MA, where he lives with his wife and two children. His research interests include translation studies, theories of imitation, poetry, and, obviously, cognitive approaches to literature. He is currently working on a book on Dostoevsky and cognitive science.

Denis Akhapkin is an independent scholar from St. Petersburg, Russia. His interests include literature, with a particular focus on poetry, poetics, and cognitive literary studies, as well as academic writing and innovative pedagogies. He is the author of two books about Russian-American poet and essayist, Nobel Prize laureate Joseph Brodsky: *Joseph Brodsky: After Russia* (2009) and *Joseph Brodsky and Anna Akhmatova: Amidst a Deaf-Mute Universe* (2021, second edition 2024) (both in Russian), and numerous papers. For two decades, he worked at Smolny College, St. Petersburg State University. He also was a visiting research fellow at Helsinki University Collegium (2007) and The Princess Dashkova Russian Centre, University of Edinburgh (2014).

David Bethea is the Vilas Research Professor (Emeritus) in Russian studies at the University of Wisconsin-Madison. He has written on major literary figures such as Alexander Pushkin, Vladimir Nabokov, and Joseph Brodsky, as well as on Russian thought and cultural mythology. His publications number six original books, seven edited volumes, and more than one hundred essays in scholarly journals and media outlets, and they have been recognized by the Guggenheim Foundation, the NEH, the ACLS, and the *New York Times*. In 2003, his professional scholarly community (AATSEEL) awarded him a lifetime achievement award for "Outstanding Contribution to Scholarship." His most recent book is *The Pushkin Project: Russia's Favorite Writer, Modern Evolutionary Thought, and Teaching Inner-City Youth* (Academic Studies Press, 2023).

Ekaterina Chelpanova received a PhD from the University of Kansas, Department of Slavic and Eurasian Languages and Literatures, in 2022, and she is now a full-time lecturer and director of the Russian program at the University at Buffalo. Her dissertation focuses on the construction of the body, illness, and disability in post-war Soviet cinema and literature. Her research on the body in culture is not limited to medical humanities. Currently, she is working on a project on the female body and embodiment in contemporary post-Soviet culture and the quest for alternative, non-Western models of feminism in the post-Soviet space. Ekaterina's other research interest is nineteenth-century Russian writers' engagement with Medieval and Renaissance grotesque.

Brett Cooke is professor of Russian at Texas A&M University. Author of *Pushkin and the Creative Process* (Florida), *Human Nature in Utopia: Zamyatin's* We (Northwestern; now augmented and translated into Russian by Academic Studies Press), and *Tolstoy's Family Prototypes in* War and Peace (Academic Studies Press); coeditor of *Sociobiology and the Arts, The Fantastic Other, Biopoetics: Evolutionary Explorations in the Arts, Critical Insights:* War and Peace, *Evolution and Popular Narrative,* and related special journal issues. He is completing a book on Europe's most popular operas. In 2013, Moscow's *Literary* Gazette recognized him as "a star of international Russian studies."

David S. Danaher is professor of Slavic studies in the department of German, Nordic, and Slavic at the University of Wisconsin-Madison. His teaching and research interests include comparative cultural linguistics and cognitive approaches to literary analysis. His most recent book is the coedited volume (with Kieran Williams) *Václav Havel's Meanings: His Key Words and Their Legacies* (2024).

Kelly Knickmeier Cummings, PhD, is a lecturer at Howard University, where she teaches Russian language and Slavic literature and culture courses. Her interests are interdisciplinary in the areas of literature, philosophy, and language pedagogy. Her work has appeared in *Slavic Review* and *The Russian Language Journal*. With the support of an NEH award, she is developing a textbook examining Black intellectuals' engagement with the cultures of the Soviet Union. Kelly helps codirect the REEES Think Tank (Russian, East European, and Eurasian Studies), an equity-minded undergraduate program serving underrepresented students in the field.

Katherina B. Kokinova (assistant professor of comparative literature, Institute for Literature, Bulgarian Academy of Sciences), PhD on Witold Gombrowicz and Vladimir Nabokov (Sofia, 2016). Working on a book on their instructive metafiction and on developing a cognitive reception theory, she is also curious about the intersection of literary research and literary translation. Having published in the peer-reviewed journals *Narrative*, *Nabokov Studies*, and elsewhere, Kokinova also compiled and edited a special journal issue on Gombrowicz (*Philological Forum* 2019); coedited and compiled a special journal issue on reception theories (*Littera et Lingua*, spring 2016); coedited and compiled a special newspaper issue on Nabokov (*Literaturen vestnik* #23/2013).

Anna A. Lazareva is an independent researcher with a PhD in philology (specializing in folklore studies). Her main research areas are the folklore of the Eastern Slavs, folklore semiotics, and the narrative grammar of stories about prophetic dreams. During 2019–2021, she worked as a university lecturer at the Center for Social Anthropology of the Russian State University for the Humanities. She developed a method of revealing and describing a system of invariants of Eastern Slavic folklore narratives about prophetic dreams. In the framework of the project "Creation of a Type and Motif Index of the Folk Tales about Dreams (East Slavonic Material of the Twentieth and Twenty-First Centuries)," supported by a university grant in 2020, she published a monograph that includes the description of this system of invariants (171 story structures) in the form of a motif index. She has written over fifty papers devoted to story schemas of folklore dream narratives, their variations, historical transformations, and the usage of narrative grammar in processes of meaning-making during dream telling and interpretation.

Julia Lerner is an anthropologist, a senior lecturer working at Ben-Gurion University of the Negev and an associated researcher at Eur'Orbem, CNRS & Lettres Sorbonne Université. Her research interests are in the fields of anthropology of knowledge, migration, and emotions. In her recent publications, she analyzes cross-culturally the role of psychological therapeutic language in public and private domains (*Russian Review* 2024 83(1), *Emotions and Society* 2021 3(1), *European Journal for Cultural Studies*, 2020 24(5), and *American Behavioral Scientist*, 2024).

Irina Meier is a senior lecturer of Russian and the director of the Russian program at the University of New Mexico. She holds a PhD in comparative literature from the University of South Carolina. Her work focuses on violence in modern society, the culture of Russian terrorism, postcolonial collective memory in Chechen culture, Russian and Chechen film, and digital humanities methods.

Sarah B. Mohler earned her doctorate in Slavic Studies from Princeton University. She is an associate professor of English at Truman State University in Kirksville, Missouri, where she directs the English master's program and chairs the child studies and cognitive science interdisciplinary minors. Her teaching and research focus on cognitive literary theory, Russian and South Asian literature and film, children's and young adult literature, literary adaptation, New Fabulism, and Fake Lit. She is the recipient of two National Endowment for the Humanities grants.

Michał Mrugalski is a *Privatdozent* at the Institute of Philosophy, University of Tübingen, where he is the Work Package Lead in the Horizon2020 project "Computational Literary Studies Infrastructure" at Humboldt University of Berlin. After obtaining his PhD in literary studies at the University of Warsaw, he received his habilitation at Tübingen University with a venia legendi in comparative and general literary studies as well as Slavic literature and culture. His research interests include narratology, computational literary studies; interrelations between literature and the arts; transcultural intellectual history of aesthetics, literary theory, and comparative literature (with a focus on Russia, Poland, Czechs, German and English-speaking countries, and France).

Anna Novikova is a professor at the School of Media, National Research University Higher School of Economics (Moscow, Russia). Her research interests include media anthropology, cultural semiotics, and transmedia studies. Her publications include "Transmedia Storytelling in Education as a Practice of Media Ecology" (2023), "Soviet Cinema and Nostalgia for the USSR in the Russian Village" (2019), and "Yuri Lotman's Cultural Semiotics as a Contribution to Media Ecology" (2015).

Angelina Rubina is a linguistics PhD candidate at the University of South Carolina (graduating in Spring 2025). She also received an MA in comparative literature in fall 2023. Her research interests in linguistics stem from her experience as a language educator and lie at the intersection between second- and heritage-language acquisition and psycholinguistics, with a focus on the acquisition of Russian grammar. Her literary research interests are related to Russian literature of the Soviet period through the lens of twentieth-century literary criticism and theory. She focuses on different psychological interpretations of Soviet literature, especially the psychology of resistance and nonresistance.

www.ingramcontent.com/pod-product-compliance
Lightning Source LLC
LaVergne TN
LVHW091525200926
848483LV00002B/311
* 9 7 8 1 6 6 6 9 4 1 6 9 2 *